DANCING AROUND THE ELEPHANT
CREATING A PROSPEROUS CANADA IN AN ERA OF
AMERICAN DOMINANCE, 1957–1973

BRUCE MUIRHEAD

Dancing around the Elephant

Creating a Prosperous Canada in an Era of
American Dominance, 1957–1973

UNIVERSITY OF TORONTO PRESS
Toronto Buffalo London

Printed in Canada

ISBN 978-0-8020-9016-4

Printed on acid-free paper

Library and Archives Canada Cataloguing in Publication

Muirhead, Bruce
    Dancing around the elephant : creating a prosperous Canada in an era of
American dominance, 1957–1973 / Bruce Muirhead.

    Includes bibliographical references and index.
    ISBN 978-0-8020-9016-4

    1. Canada – Foreign relations – United States.   2. United States –
Foreign relations – Canada.   3. Canada – Foreign relations – 1945– .
I. Title.

    FC249.M85 2007   327.71073'09'045   C2005-902189-6

University of Toronto Press acknowledges the financial assistance to its publishing
program of the Canada Council for the Arts and the Ontario Arts Council.

University of Toronto Press acknowledges the financial support for its publishing
activities of the Government of Canada through the Book Publishing Industry
Development Program (BPIDP).

This book has been published with the help of a grant from the Canadian Federation
for the Humanities and Social Sciences, through the Aid to Scholarly Publications
Programme, using funds provided by the Social Sciences and Humanities Research
Council of Canada

Contents

TABLES AND FIGURE   vii

PREFACE   ix

Introduction   3

1 The Diefenbaker Years and the United States   10

2 The Liberals Manage the American File, 1963–1968   51

3 A Difficult Relationship: Pierre Trudeau and the United States   95

4 Canada, the Wheat Economy, and North American Relations   139

5 Unrequited Expectations: Britain and Canada Move Apart   177

6 Canada, the GATT, and the European Economic Community   215

Conclusion   242

NOTES   247

ILLUSTRATION CREDITS   305

INDEX   307

Illustrations follow page 118

Tables and Figures

Tables

2.1   Exports to and Imports from the United States of
      Automotive Equipment   78

3.2   Percentage Changes from Old Parities; Required Changes for
      Payments Adjustment   128

4.1   Commercial Wheat Exports as Percentage of World Market   140

4.2   Canadian and U.S. Exports of Wheat and Wheat Flour   167

5.1   British Application under Section 37A of the Canada Customs Act   212

6.1   Canadian Exports and Imports with the EEC   227

6.2   EEC Self-sufficiency Ratio   236

Figures

3.1   Disposition of Canadian Oil, 1960–77   104

Preface

The time from 1957 to 1973 was a tumultuous one in Canada. Beginning with a Conservative government led by the populist John Diefenbaker, it ended with his antithesis as prime minister, the cerebral Pierre Elliott Trudeau. Those years encompassed, among other things, rapidly-rising prosperity in Canada and the development of its welfare state, as well as an increase in Canadian nationalism and a questioning of the country's relationship with its continental partner. Memories for those of us able to remember that far back reflect these developments: rising incomes for our parents, medicare and the Canada Pension Plan, the Vietnam War, and U.S. control of significant parts of the Canadian economy.

We also remember the contempt we felt for government, especially those Liberal ones led by Lester Pearson, as he bowed and scraped in the face of American power and was steamrolled by that juggernaut. Why wouldn't he simply stand up to the United States and not embarrass us? Certainly the popular and academic presses, largely dominated by left-nationalist adherents, wanted this to happen as did millions of high-school-age kids.

But was that the reality? This book suggests it was not. To the contrary, where the United States was not concerned about its national security, Canadian governments, even Pearson's, worked assiduously to promote their country's interests in Washington to the point of violent disagreement. The Auto Pact, for example, that cornerstone of Ontario's economy for the past forty years, reflects that, as did Canada's representations to the United States over wheat, oil, and a host of other commodities. It was all extremely difficult, time-consuming, and enervating. And oddly enough, it was the supposedly ultra-nationalist Diefenbaker government that was especially outraged when Americans put impediments in the path of further continental economic integration.

I owe a debt of gratitude to a number of people who helped me in the research and writing of this book. First, I would like to thank Len Husband, the UTP editor for this project, for his unfailing help and guidance in seeing it through the lengthy process that is academic publishing. As well, Margaret Tessman did a wonderful job of copy-editing the manuscript; I am always surprised, given my multitude of drafts, how little I really know about sentence construction and grammar. Margaret made that clear. UTP's Frances Mundy was stellar in her vetting of the manuscript. As well, thanks go to the Social Sciences and Humanities Research Council which provided research funding. Without SSHRC assistance, writing a book based on archival sources could not be easily done. Council funding also made it possible to hire two young men who were then graduate students at the University of Ottawa and are now professors at two other Canadian universities: Stephen High and Gerald Wright. I have rarely used such well-indexed and documented research notes. As well, acknowledgement is due to those unnamed archivists at various institutions who unfailingly responded to my questions about documents and sources. I would also like to thank Lakehead University for providing me with a reduced teaching load that helped me to more easily research and write. It was invaluable.

Finally, a special note of thanks to my parents, Colin and Eleanor Muirhead, for their direction and guidance as I grew up through much of the period covered by this book. My father, in particular, was (and remains) extremely well informed and interested in politics, both local and global. It was he who instilled in me my passion for history, and for Canada, despite, as he would say, its political leaders. Arguments on school buses with friends in 1968, for example, merely parroted his thoughts about Trudeau. For all of that, this book is for them.

DANCING AROUND THE ELEPHANT

Introduction

The evolution of Canada's foreign economic policy between 1957 and 1973 largely followed the general pattern laid down during the first post-war decade.[1] At that time, only Americans were able and willing to spend the billions of dollars on Canada's exports that the country required to ensure domestic prosperity. Inconvertible European currencies and a myriad of trade barriers had prevented those consumers from buying from Canada, a hard currency country with a dollar as solid as that of the United States. That situation persisted until well into the post-war period and in some cases, until the early 1960s. However, given that Canada was a country whose prosperity depended upon the sale of goods and services abroad (approximately 25 per cent of its gross national product came from exporting), this inequity was intolerable. It was only natural that Ottawa should do all in its power to cultivate markets in the United States; to have done otherwise would have been negligent. Thus, during the decade after 1945 Canada's policy was multilateral by preference, bilateral by necessity, and manifestly continental by default.[2]

Despite the unrequited expectations of that first post-war decade, multilateralism and non-discrimination remained the preferred policy option during the 1960s for a variety of Canadian governments in their foreign economic policy development. But it remained that the Europeans, and increasingly the British, were not particularly interested in developing deeper and wider commercial linkages with Canada. If the developing world was not carved up into various empires by that decade, it was also the case that large-scale trade between it and Canada was virtually impossible. Similarly, Communist China had largely cut itself off from the West, although the Canadian Wheat Board did sell increasing amounts of wheat there after 1961. Ottawa had few options other than the United States when developing its trade policies; by 1970, 73 per cent of Canada's exports and 60 per cent of imports went to and came from the United States.

In an economic sense it was undeniable that Canada benefited greatly from this arrangement. Could Canada have done better? Could it have been more aggressive and less complacent in searching out new markets? Could it have made the Europeans and Japanese take greater note of its products? The answer to these questions is probably 'yes.' Would the results have been any different? The answer to that is probably 'no,' an assertion borne out by the sad history of the Third Option after 1972 and the agreements signed with the European Economic Community (EEC) and Japan in 1975 and 1976 respectively.

And what about the volume of U.S. investment that poured like a tsunami across the country in the 1950s and had been necessary for Canadian development, but that was also the focus of so much nationalist comment during the later 1960s and 1970s? The Americans had wanted oil wells, mines and smelters, and manufacturing plants, and by 1964, 80 per cent of the US$12.9 billion invested in Canada was from U.S. sources. The portions of various sectors gobbled up by capital from south of the border were well-known: by 1963 these numbers totalled 60 per cent of manufacturing, 75 per cent of oil and gas, and 60 per cent of Canada's mines and smelters.[3] Could Ottawa have reduced those numbers? Again, probably yes, but only at a cost to Canadian economic development and employment prospects over the medium term. But it was also true that Canada was an open economy, with very little by way of government control on investment inflows. Moreover, as the U.S. secretary of state, John Dulles, told Prime Minister John Diefenbaker in July 1957, that investment was the result of the free enterprise system and not the result of some American plot to secure control: 'If Canada wished to get investments from other countries, it was, of course, entirely up to them [sic] to do so.'[4] Politics is the art of the possible, however, and Dulles's suggestion was simply not a practical one in the prevailing global context.

The extent of foreign ownership was not a serious issue in the fifteen years following 1945, as memories of depression and destitution haunted the imaginations of a generation. They craved the employment and security that American investment seemed to bring in its wake, and woe to any government that did not provide it. With prosperity and affluence seemingly secure and the 1930s an increasingly distant memory, the magnitude of American control over Canada's economy only began to disturb a significant minority of Canadians by the late 1950s, and it became an issue that gathered momentum during the next decade. The left-leaning Co-operative Commonwealth Federation/New Democratic Party made this discussion its focus, but even the more centrist, main-line political parties could not afford to ignore it, or the growth of nationalist feeling associated with it.

By the mid-1960s, foreign ownership and continental economic integration had become the *bête-noire* of Canadian politics. It signified U.S. control over

Canada's economy, to be sure, but for the critics it also implied U.S. interference in Canadian politics and society to the point where Canadian sovereignty seemed almost meaningless. While Canada might not be a banana republic (although that was debatable for many), it was not far removed from one. For example, the practice of extraterritoriality, where U.S. law applied to subsidiaries of U.S. firms based in Canada, was often cited as *the* manifestation of the loss of Canadian control of its own destiny. Blocked sales of Fords to the People's Republic of China and of bunker C oil for Canadian ships carrying wheat to communist countries, together with a vaguely expressed sentiment that acquired the status of shibboleth suggesting that *all* of Canada's international transactions were controlled/interfered with/directed from the United States, became firmly fixed in the popular imagination as 'proof' of Washington's meddling. Ottawa, with its comprador and weak governments, was merely a tool of American imperialism.

Against that backdrop the forces of Canadian nationalism gathered momentum. Students took to the streets in Canada in the later 1960s to protest an unpopular U.S. war in Vietnam, critics began to talk about the cultural penetration of the country by Hollywood and the major U.S. television networks, while some in the labour movement began to seriously talk about the day when international (read American) unions no longer exerted any influence on them. Even post-secondary education was affected, as Robin Mathews and James Steele rallied opinion against the employment of American professors in Canadian universities. Polls taken during the decade routinely demonstrated the unpopularity of the United States among Canadians and the celebration of Expo 67, during Canada's centenary, was also an occasion to revel in one's Canadian-ness. Crowds occupied Parliament Hill for the ultimate high on 1 July, while everywhere in the country homemade signs and banners proclaiming 'I'm proud to be a Canadian' could be seen.

It was *the* time for Canadian nationalism and also to subscribe to the opposite side of that coin, anti-Americanism. Al Purdy's collection entitled *The New Romans: Candid Canadian Opinions of the US* was a good example. Many of its contributors, including Margaret Atwood, Peter Newman, Farley Mowat, Mordecai Richler, Larry Zolf, Louis Dudek, Robert Fulford, and Cy Gonick, represented the elite of Canada's chattering classes. Most of them '[hit] below the belt' in their assessments of Americans.[5] For example, Atwood, in a poem entitled 'Backdrop Addresses [American] Cowboy,' wrote that 'you are innocent as a bathtub/full of bullets ... I am the space you desecrate / as you pass through.'[6] In another piece, Louis Dudek asked rhetorically 'Who owns Canada? You know who owns Canada,'[7] while the novelist Farley Mowat, wrote in 'Letter to My Son' that there could be 'no other real choice open to a Canadian except to resist the Yanks and all their works so that we, as a people and a nation, may escape being ingested into the Eagle's gut, never to emerge again except – maybe – as a patch of excrement upon the pages of world history.'[8]

Nationalism in the Writing of Canadian Economic History

Given this context, the 1960s gave birth to a new industry in Canadian criticism – decrying the extent of U.S. investment in Canada and the overwhelming proportion of Canada's trade that went south. Critics marshalled their facts and wrote polemics to change minds and practices. Most often their arguments were sound, at least when documenting the extent of American ownership of Canada's economy. Kari Levitt's *Silent Surrender* was a masterful itemization of that fact, using government-generated data from the likes of the stolid Dominion Bureau of Statistics to support her case. Theirs was the dominant paradigm for a generation in part because of their prolificness. The critics uniformly denounced 'sellout' Liberal governments (but oddly, not an equally sellout Conservative one), building on the thesis first proposed by historian Donald Creighton in the 1950s, and given form in his contribution to the centenary series, *The Forked Road*.[9] George Grant's 1963 *Lament for a Nation: The Defeat of Canadian Nationalism* had provided fodder and context by presenting the 'nationalist' Diefenbaker's defeat in April 1963 as coming at the hands of Liberal continentalists.[10] And Canadians as a group were so ready to distance themselves from the United States that, while they might not know the specifics of the arguments presented, they largely supported them.[11]

But the critics went too far in their condemnation of federal policy and the federal government. Implicit or explicit in the critics' analysis was the element of choice – that governments with more backbone or insight into Canada's problems would have designed different policy options to secure Canadian independence from the United States whether in issues of trade or those relating to the development of the branch plant economy. It was Ottawa after all, they argued, that had refused to set limits on American involvement in Canada's economic development or to search out alternatives to the U.S. market. The short-term gain had been more than offset by medium- and long-term pain. However, their analysis of federal personnel and policy was flawed and their critique does not stand up. While the very conservative and overwhelmingly continentalist private sector might have been content to throw in its lot in with that of its American counterpart, this book will argue that the public sector was not. Canadian officials and politicians spent much time attempting to negotiate multilateral trade deals through the General Agreement on Tariffs and Trade (GATT), as well as expressing concern about the developing protectionist EEC. Of course, Ottawa had to be sensitive to U.S. issues and concerns. To have been otherwise would have been irresponsible, for as Pierre Trudeau remarked during his first visit to the new Nixon administration in March 1969, 'Living next to you is in some ways like sleeping with an elephant. No matter how friendly and even-tempered the beast, one is affected by every twitch and grunt.'

As well, the nationalists complained, Canadian governments were so compromised and directed by Washington that the country did not have an independent voice. That was probably true with respect to matters of global importance to Americans or in areas dealing with their national security; Ottawa did have little room to manoeuvre. But neither did other larger allies like Britain and West Germany when those matters were at stake. In other ways, as this book will demonstrate, Canada was able to influence or oppose American policy throughout the period under investigation in ways that were important to Canadians.

Moreover, Ottawa did have insight into the issues outlined by the critics. Indeed, many in cabinet and the bureaucracy were writing critical and informed analyses of Canada's situation that anticipated the Rotsteins, the Laxers, and the Watkins of the so-called nationalist school in later years.[12] They were not part of a weak comprador system; theirs was a world of hard negotiations and tough-minded opponents. They were also well aware of the limitations placed on Canada as a middle power, yet were determined to push for the best possible deal for their country and its citizens despite the overwhelming economic power represented by the United States.

From the implicit veto given to Canada over American wheat sales to third countries, through the Auto Pact that almost single-handedly helped to solve Canada's balance of payments problems, to the various exemptions to punitive American legislation that were given over the decade, Ottawa had rolled the dice with Americans and had occasionally won, a not inconsiderable feat. In the case of the Auto Pact, even Walter Gordon, then the minister of finance and an implacable and unrelenting critic of U.S. investment in Canada, welcomed the benefits it bestowed on Canada. And while a cynic might claim that such an initiative merely enhanced continental integration to the further detriment of Canada, that agreement was not what the United States wanted. Indeed, the Canadians stuck to their policy guns and arguably out-negotiated the Americans, playing a kind of Russian roulette in the process. As Brian Tomlin and Peyton Lyon have correctly observed, not all the good cards in the hand lie with the stronger power in international affairs. In certain areas Canada was able to exert its influence to sway the United States to its point of view. As they note, 'the Canadian policy community is smaller and better able to concentrate its main attention on relations with Canada's giant neighbour.'[13] In the final analysis, these federal successes and the continuing prosperity that they brought was all that mattered, at least for the great plurality of the population, as Liberal governments (with a brief Conservative interregnum) followed one after the other.

It also seems clear that Washington had adopted a relatively benign view of Canada, at least until the election of the Nixon administration, which Canadians exploited. To claim that the United States was altruistic in many of its dealings with Canada in the 1960s might leave one open to charges of naïvety or worse, as superpowers, we are told, have interests and not friends. But the historian is left wondering why those various U.S. governments treated Canada so mildly, often in the face of provocation, such as that presented by Walter Gordon's 1963 budget. It seems clear that a special relationship existed between the two countries from 1945 until 15 August 1971, when President Nixon's New Economic Policy was announced. It is an argument of this book that until Richard Nixon, from the floor of the House of Commons in Ottawa in May 1972, encouraged Canadians to grow up and no longer demand special favours from his country, they had come to expect a degree of consideration not accorded others.[14] And that came as a shock for a country that had had it all for so long. The experiment that Canada launched itself upon at that time, the third option policy, did not turn out so well as even the most assiduous of 'diversifiers' in Ottawa could not get the Europeans, the Japanese, or pretty much anyone else to take their overtures seriously.

This brief discussion of the rather furious activity surrounding a search for Canada's identity in the roughly ten years following 1965, whether it be in literature, the economy, or politics, was important. Many Canadians were stimulated by it and repelled by the excesses of the American empire. Moreover, these entreaties fell on ready ears as the first wave of baby-boomers were hitting universities, clearly unhappy with the status quo. 'Don't trust anyone over thirty' or so the saying had it. With a growth in student population from 196,700 in 1962–63 to 513,400 by 1972, post-secondary education now opened more doors. To respond to the demand new universities were established, such as Brock, Lakehead, and Trent in Ontario, Simon Fraser in British Columbia, and the Université de Québec system. More often than not, those new minds were influenced by the writings and lectures of converts to the new orthodoxy.

This book is an attempt to tell all of the economic story and not just that of American domination of Canada's economy. It also argues that Ottawa made the best of the hand it was dealt. As Lester Pearson said in an address to the Radio Club in Ottawa in 1969 following his retirement from office, he had never realized how difficult it was to maintain his country's separate existence in North America until he became prime minister. Canada was faced with a neighbour more than ten times its size with an economy ten to fifteen times larger, and with very similar culture, history, traditions, and perhaps most importantly, language. Canadians not only carved out their own very successful niche on the continent, but did so using a federal government and civil service despised by the left-nationalists as weak and uninterested in, or incapable of, projecting a Canadian interest, especially in its relations with the United States. It was anything but, as this book will demonstrate. Rather, official Ottawa was self-assured, deliberate, and very conscious of its responsibilities.

Chapter 1

The Diefenbaker Years and the United States

The Conservatives Win

The election in June 1957 of the minority Progressive Conservative government led by John Diefenbaker seemed to signify a new beginning to Canadian-American relations, both political and economic. The Conservatives had traditionally been identified as the party of the old British Empire that had ceased to exist, except perhaps in the mind of the new prime minister and some of his cabinet. Donald Creighton, then an influential professor of Canadian history at the University of Toronto and the unofficial voice of conservatism in Canada, put the party's position clearly in a lecture he gave at Carleton College a number of months before the campaign began. His contention was that with the British Empire in decline, William Lyon Mackenzie King, Canada's Liberal prime minister from 1935 to 1948, had abandoned that sinking ship; with 'an old man's infatuated obsession with the now antiquated and meaningless cause of autonomy within the British Empire (he) chose this particular time to cut us off from necessary associations with Great Britain and to plunge us deeper and deeper into continental commitments with the United States.'[1]

For Creighton, that was a sin. The 'uneasiness' which many Canadians were then experiencing towards the United States, at least according to Creighton, was a result of rising U.S. economic, military, and political influence in their country. The second secretary at the embassy in Ottawa, Wesley Kriebel, commented that 'While it can be expected that in an election year it may be considered politically expedient for Conservative politicians to raise the bogey of American "domination," the Embassy is surprised to find this tack adopted by a man of unquestioned intelligence and integrity who is held in the highest regard in Canadian academic circles.' This criticism was a harbinger of things to come. Of course, it was the path steered by the Conservatives, who had validated the anti-American idea since Confederation.

While leader of the opposition (and in a pre-election mode), Diefenbaker had attacked U.S. domination of Canada's economy, telling potential voters that his party would 'preserve Canadian economic independence vis-à-vis the United States.'[2] Part of that campaign meant using data published in the January 1957 *Preliminary Report* of the Royal Commission on Canada's Economic Prospects – headed by a future Liberal minister of finance, Walter Gordon – which had been very critical of Canadian development policy with its reliance on U.S. investment.[3] The commission's proposals about foreign direct investment would principally affect U.S. money, a fact that the American embassy in Ottawa had deplored. It had also considered the recommendations 'discriminatory ... unrealistic and impractical.'[4] It remained disconcerting to the embassy, however, that a pretender to the throne in Ottawa would use such sentiments in his public statements.

A Meeting of Canadian and American Minds

But what was the reality? Soon after taking office, Diefenbaker, along with a few of his ministers, met in Ottawa with John Foster Dulles, the U.S. secretary of state and the architect of so much American policy in the Eisenhower administration. The new prime minister and the main protagonist in the Cold War were fundamentally in agreement on the global strategic situation, which translated into some understanding on the economy. Indeed, Diefenbaker offered to issue a statement to the press that would explicitly bring Canada's position on disarmament and any nuclear weapons inspection scheme into line with that of the United States. With respect to the recognition of the People's Republic of China, the two men were also in accord; Diefenbaker, the virulent anti-communist, 'said that his position had not changed since 1954 when he had said that he would oppose in the House a move recognizing Peking.'[5] On economic questions, differences were matters of degree rather than substance.

On a slightly different tack, Donald Fleming, the new minister of finance, spoke strongly about restrictive U.S. trade measures and how they were designed, often unfairly it seemed to him, to meet the demands of certain segments of the American population. That, of course, was not surprising; governments the world over, including Canada's, had done similar things. However, the United States did seem to be in a class by itself, largely because of its type of government. Given the system of checks and balances and the fact that Congress controlled trade policy, representatives and senators were more subject to grassroots pressure than legislators of most other countries. Arnold Heeney, Canada's ambassador in Washington in the late 1950s, surely got it right when he told a small gathering of senior officials in 1956 that 'In the last analysis, if the wishes of a substantial section of [American] voters had to be weighed against the views of the Canadian Government on a specific economic issue, the former would win out.'[6]

In raising this issue, Fleming was particularly concerned about the case of lead and zinc and the recent exclusion of Canadian hardboard from the United States. It was abhorrent to the Diefenbaker government that political considerations should keep Canadian exports out. Livingston Merchant, the U.S. ambassador in Ottawa, replied that his country was guilty as charged. However, it was also true that Canadian hands were not clean: 'One might get the impression from Canadian statements and newspaper editorials that Canada practiced nothing but complete free trade and avoided protection of any kind. Since [Merchant's] arrival ... however, he had been involved in protesting a great many arbitrary measures by the Canadian government. He referred particularly to restrictions on Florida grapefruit about which the Floridians felt very bitter. He mentioned the regulations on turkeys as the latest of this kind.'[7] Merchant referred to those cases, he said, only to demonstrate that the problems were mutual and that they could best be solved by both sides considering them jointly.

But it was clear that the United States had entered a more protectionist phase. A few years earlier the *Globe and Mail* had pronounced that the United States stood 'as the leading advocate of dog-eat-dog [trade]' and that that approach had not changed.[8] Indeed, things seemed to have gotten worse. As the 30 June 1958 date for the expiration of the Reciprocal Trade Agreements Act (RTAA) approached, Canadians were not sanguine about its chances of survival. As one document noted, 'failure to renew it would be a serious set-back.'[9] R.G.C. Smith, the commercial counsellor at Canada's embassy in Washington, thought that the forces of protectionism were in the ascendant. The counsellor placed the blame squarely on the administration and the president for their withdrawal from the fight for multilateralism and non-discrimination. The apparent deterioration in American support of organizations designed to oversee the development of global trade was a sobering reality for Ottawa. And while the RTAA was ultimately renewed with a large majority, it did not assuage Canadian concerns.

Finally, in response to a Canadian intervention over the magnitude of U.S. direct foreign investment in Canada, Dulles quite rightly pointed out that it was the result of the free enterprise system and not in any sense a deliberate policy designed to gain a slice of the Canadian economy. And given the continuing Canadian need for investment capital to develop the country, it would have to be on a grand scale.

There was no criticism or denunciation of Dulles' position by Diefenbaker or Fleming. In fact Fleming was to say a few years later that 'Canada was chronically short of capital,'[10] and Diefenbaker had told the Toronto Board of Trade in the run-up to the 1957 campaign that 'the flow of investment capital into Canada must not be discouraged.'[11] In the international context existing in the late 1950s there was no real alternative to the United States as a source of finance, nor would the Conservatives choose to impose controls on the inflow and outflow of U.S. dollars. Indeed, they could do so only at their peril. Canada suffered a large annual trade deficit with the United States that had reached CAN$1.4 billion by 1956, funded in part through the inflow of capital from that country. Indeed, the CAN$10.3 billion of foreign long-term investment in Canada that had come from the United States since 1950 was critical in that respect. Any interference with it could cause trouble, a scenario which would be realized in July 1963 with the implementation by Washington of the Interest Equalization Tax.[12]

But U.S. foreign investment in Canada did not really seem to be an issue with the new government. In July, Merchant had told Douglas Dillon, the deputy undersecretary of state for economic affairs, that Diefenbaker's attitudes toward it were not easy to discern; the prime minister 'has not yet unraveled his ideas on the general subject and that he is still thinking in terms of political expediency rather than coherent policy.'[13] However, he did not think that Diefenbaker was opposed to the general foreign investment policies of the U.S. government, nor that he was particularly concerned with the size or scope of American private investment in Canada. Indeed, a few months later when the dust from the Conservative's unexpected election victory had cleared, an internal U.S. document noted that 'Mr. Diefenbaker is not critical of general U.S. foreign investment policies and has repeatedly stated that he welcomes U.S. private investment in Canada.'[14]

The new prime minister departed from this attitude, however, when it came to the *concentration* of U.S. investment in certain Canadian extractive industries and in some sectors of Canadian manufacturing. Diefenbaker thought that too many of Canada's raw materials were exported for processing to the United States. He also objected to the fact that much of this investment was in the form of wholly owned U.S. businesses from which Canadian directors, managers, and financial and research participation was excluded. Merchant believed that this particular criticism was a legitimate one that would become more important in the future. To address Conservative complaints, however, would not be too difficult. Some combination of greater participation by Canadian capital and management in U.S. projects, a greater use of Canadian components by U.S. subsidiaries, a higher degree of processing raw materials in Canada, and a greater diversification of U.S. capital in fields other than mineral extraction and certain manufacturing activities were all that was required.

Diefenbaker's recollections of his attitudes toward foreign direct investment and Canada's trade with the United States, published in his memoirs almost twenty years after his first election victory, are disingenuous, perhaps clouded by the passage of time. As he recalled, he had 'considered ... Liberal policy [to be] selling our birthright (the ownership and control over our resources) [and it was] too high a price to pay to maintain our standard of living and our post–Second World War rate of economic growth. It was simple logic that Canada could not maintain its independence if we continued existing Liberal policies ... If we failed to diversify our trade, Canada would cease to belong to Canadians; we would have no destiny to fulfill.'[15] Over the Chief's time in office, however, American investment in all sectors of Canada's economy grew without hindrance or complaint, as did its trade, although not without some bumps along the way.

A Developing Canadian Consciousness

The opportunity for a new beginning with the Canadians must have been welcomed by the Americans whose relations with the previous Liberal government had grown more difficult. As John English has pointed out, powerful Americans came to view the Liberals, and in particular the heir apparent to Louis St Laurent, Lester Pearson, with some suspicion. Pearson, on his part, had more and more disagreed with the strident and virulent anti-communism that emanated from Washington[16] and which had been at least partly responsible for the death of his friend, Herbert Norman, in 1957.[17] The approval of a trade resolution at the 1958 leadership convention that anointed Pearson was a sign of changing Liberal policies, admittedly now from the Opposition benches, which the U.S. embassy in Ottawa quickly forwarded to the department of state. It proposed that a 'Liberal Government would give immediate and sympathetic detailed consideration to the British proposal for the gradual establishment of free trade area between UK and Canada and would take account both of new opportunities that might be opened for Canadian industry and the importance of maintaining existing industries and living standards in Canada.'[18] This was, of course, a Liberal attempt to embarrass the government that had recently turned down a British proposal for an Anglo-Canadian free trade area despite Diefenbaker's pro-British rhetoric of mere months before.[19] But it was also suggestive of much more; with some understatement, Merchant thought that 'Despite heavy political motivation underlying this resolution ... this could prove significant.' It seemed that the Liberals had veered to the left after their 1957 defeat and espoused a nationalist rhetoric to rival that of the Conservatives. This shift reflected the growing influence of Walter Gordon, a close friend of Pearson's, and his first minister of finance when the Liberals returned to office in April 1963.[20]

The Americans were acutely conscious of a developing Canadian nationalism and actively tried to deflect its more serious ramifications. As they formulated policy to deal with the first Conservative government in twenty-two years, senior members of the administration did not want unnecessary provocations to set the new relationship on edge. Dulles in particular was very conscious of this, ordering Clarence Randall, the chair of the Council on Foreign Economic Policy (CFEP), to terminate the council's study favouring a North American free trade area. In considering the recommendation days before his July trip to Ottawa, the secretary wrote that he considered it 'inappropriate for the United States to propose an economic integration of the United States and Canada. The Canadians are proud ... of their national independence and are eager to control their own destiny ... Because the United States economy at the present time is so much larger than that of Canada, there might be Canadian concern that the economic integration of both countries would in effect subject Canada to preponderant United States economic influence.'[21]

The Problem of Oil

Despite the fundamental harmony that existed in broad strokes between the Diefenbaker Conservatives and the Dwight Eisenhower Republicans, the honeymoon soon ended as specific issues raised temperatures on both sides of the border. Among the most contentious of these was commercial policy development, and deteriorating trade relations between the Diefenbaker government and the United States. Dulles, for example, commented during a press conference in Washington in mid-February 1958 that the relationship was 'at a difficult point.' There were differences of opinion with respect to U.S. wheat disposal policies (discussed in chapter 4), on the restriction of Canadian oil exports to the United States and other policies that related to trade across the border. Significantly, Dulles also mentioned the Canadian objective of diverting 15 per cent of their trade from the United States to the UK even though this had long been disowned by Ottawa. As well, there remained the perennial concern that extremely high levels of American investment might result in economic policies that were not in Canada's best interests.

Among the disputes was a very significant one over oil. The Conservatives had begun to deal with energy policy development, striking the Royal Commission on Energy Policy headed by Henry Borden in·October 1957. Its purpose was to develop recommendations that would inform government policy and especially suggest what to do about American restrictionism. The U.S. government had blocked off a large and very lucrative trade in energy for its own producers. From the vantage point of the early twenty-first century with its oil price volatility and shortages this action seems ludicrous, but Ottawa filed a number of complaints with the United States protesting oil restrictions when they were first imposed in July 1957. Beginning in January 1958, then again in June, October, and November, the Canadian government made its views officially known. As the first note to Washington pointed out, the 'action [was] taken in spite of the strongest possible representations made by the Canadian Government to the United States Administration on numerous occasions in recent weeks. The Canadian Government cannot accept the view that there is any justification for U.S. limitations on oil coming from Canada.'[22]

The Canadians wanted continued oil development and exploration in western Canada, not easily possible if the United States shut off markets in the northwestern and north-central parts of the country. As an American document noted, 'Canadians believe their oil deserves, and should have, on security grounds, a preferential position in the United States relative to other imported oil. They regard the application of the US import control system to importers from Canada as a sign that Canada will not have such a position in the U.S. market.'[23]

The Conservatives made a point a number of times for the continental market for fossil fuels in North America.[24] The Pacific Northwest, they claimed, constituted 'a natural and economic market for Canadian oil and, in the event of an international emergency, that region would unquestionably depend to a very considerable degree on Canadian supplies of oil.' If the Americans restricted Canadian exports, then it could not help 'but have a discouraging impact on the search for additional oil in Western Canada – an area of tremendous strategic importance to the United States, since it is internal to the North American continent.' Quotas could also have a deleterious effect on Canadian-U.S. relations; Douglas Harkness, the minister of agriculture, told a meeting between Canadian ministers and Dulles that U.S. policy had had a serious psychological effect in Western Canada that was slowing development.[25] The discrimination against Canadian oil exports caused strong resentment against the United States.

Given Conservative suspicion of the United States and recent nationalist rhetoric emanating from Ottawa, it is interesting that the government was so outraged by U.S. policy. In any event, the Americans did respond in the way that Canadian ministers had hoped as they pestered secretaries, that 'in the interest of national security and consistent with a healthy and dynamic domestic industry, the continued development of petroleum resources readily available to the Western Hemisphere must be encouraged.'[26] Preference would be given to imports from Canada and other U.S. neighbours like Venezuela, and on 30 April 1959 restrictions on the importation of Canadian oil were lifted by presidential edict. The Canadians were appropriately grateful and were also pleased that the Americans had acceded to their request that oil discussions be held on a close continuing basis.[27] In the House, Diefenbaker noted that 'the exemption will be of direct benefit to the export sales of Canadian crude oil and products. As important, if not more, is the benefit which will follow in terms of a normal, healthy development of the Canadian petroleum industry, which is thus restored to its appropriate place as an important and natural supplier of the North American markets.'[28]

Growing Canadian Nationalism

For the present, Dulles' musings on the state of the continental relationship were more appropriate, especially following Diefenbaker's resounding election victory on 31 March 1958, ten months after his first minority win. Wesley Kreibel interpreted the victory to mean that 'there may well be an intensified expression of Canadian nationalism which will be reflected particularly in acts of self-assertion in future relations with the United States.'[29] On the basis of the election returns Diefenbaker had every right to think that way – his party had won 208 seats out of the 265 being contested, while the Liberals held on to a mere 49 and the Co-operative Commonwealth Federation only 8. Basil Robinson, who had been assigned by the Department of External Affairs to the Prime Minister's Office, perceptively confided to his diary that the prime minister 'now feels himself in the saddle with a long clear road ahead.'[30]

Kriebel pointed to some the issues that he thought might animate Canadian-American relations. Clearly, national self-assertion was a political asset in Ottawa and Washington, given Conservative rhetoric, could probably look forward to attempts to reduce Canadian dependence on the United States together, perhaps, with some measures designed to strengthen Canada's Commonwealth ties. A recession, then beginning to bite, and intensifying pressure from certain protectionist-minded groups might reinforce that direction. As well, during the recent election campaign, Diefenbaker had propounded his vision of Canadianism and the country's national destiny, which included some distancing from the United States.

Kreibel was prescient – barely had the post-election celebrations ended before there was some criticism being voiced of the extent of U.S. ownership of Canadian industry. It was not then widespread, although it would become more so in the near future. Indeed, in his report to the department of state, the U.S. ambassador thought it was not an issue that had concerned many voters. Still, a postwar consensus that Canadian and American interests were sufficiently similar for the two countries to be in lockstep on most issues was beginning to break down by 1958. That was not yet obvious, however, and Kreibel thought that 'fundamentally Canadian need for capital should out-balance excessive concern about national control. Competition between less-developed provinces for capital should also have moderating effect on any central government tendencies toward control.'[31] Merchant also focused on the crux of the Canadian problem:

> Primary concern government over Canadian international economic position must continue be basic terms of trade. Preoccupation with imbalance of trade with United States would be lessened if Canada could diversify export markets but this prospect

limited by convertibility problems especially in period of recession. Canadian dependence upon flow United States capital to balance trade widely recognized as major element vulnerability and government effort in some fashion obtain greater economic security only natural. Thus while government now disavows 15 percent goal in diversion idea and while artificial means diversion now unlikely, government will continue uneasily trying make Canada less dependent on United States economy, although recognizing large measure dependence inevitable.

For those advocating a more made-in-Canada economic and trade policy, the country's position resembled nothing less than being stuck between a rock and a hard place, a very difficult situation to be in.

That view, however, was one that came with prosperity. Poor societies did not obsess about autonomy or self-fulfillment. That was what the Americans could not understand: Canadians were rich beyond their wildest dreams with the second highest standard of living in the world. What was there to complain about? In search of an answer, the National Security Council (NSC) convened several times following the Conservative's landslide victory to discuss U.S. relations with Canada. This attention by a very high-level group (the president also attended) was unprecedented. On 12 June the NSC circulated a memorandum among the departments of state and defense and the office of defense mobilization requesting a study and a report to the council on the need for a policy statement on U.S. relations with Canada. One month later, another memorandum transmitted a 'List of Problem Areas with Respect to Canada,' which enumerated six items for discussion, including Canadian dependence on U.S. trade and investment, U.S. import restrictions that affected Canada, and inadequate understanding by the Canadian public of U.S. policies.[32] The Americans believed that some form of public relations campaign was needed to counteract the 'misinformation' engendered by the 1958 election campaign. Some measures should be directed toward offsetting unnecessary apprehension among Canadians about, for example, Canada's unfavourable commodity trade balance with the United States. Indeed, Canada enjoyed a favourable worldwide balance on international account that was partly provided by the substantial net outflow of dollars from the United States for defence and foreign economic programs, dollars that were then spent in Canada to purchase Canadian goods.

Clearly, the Americans had little idea as to what the Canadians were complaining about, and some believed it was based purely on political expediency. Eisenhower, for one, told the meeting that he had 'doubts as to the genuineness of [the alleged inadequate understanding of US policies in Canada],' noting 'that the Conservative Party in Canada had largely based their successful political campaign on a platform of reducing Canadian dependence on the United States. The whole issue was largely politics, and the Canadian Conservatives themselves did not believe what they said.'[33] With respect to the problem of U.S. investment in Canada, Sinclair Weeks, the secretary of commerce, pointed out that the Canadian dollar traded at a premium, which suggested that international financial markets did not think that the Canadian economy was suffering. The secretary of defense, Neil McElroy, said that the premium was caused by heavy U.S. investment in Canada, 'and rightly or wrongly, this was the problem that worried the Canadians. Secretary Herter observed that this was essentially an internal Canadian problem, about which the United States could do little or nothing.'

At minimum it was decided that the two sides should continue the practice of periodic consultation which 'had very great potentialities for good.' That practice had yielded some benefit in dealing with agricultural issues that had been a real sore spot in US-Canadian relations. Now the problem had eased, largely because of continuous consultation (and the fact that Canadian stores of wheat had been greatly reduced by the summer of 1958). Eisenhower agreed, urging that such meetings become habit; the more contact between Ottawa and Washington, the better it would be.

Policy Making on the Run

Not all of that interaction was useful, however, especially as election promises came back to haunt the Conservatives: domestic pressure groups began converging on Ottawa to collect on commitments they thought had been made. Growers of fruits and vegetables, for example, urged the government to help them against U.S. imports. On 1 April 1958, A.F.W. Plumptre, the assistant deputy minister of finance, invited officials from the U.S. embassy to his office to discuss possible relief measures for those farmers against U.S. imports at distress prices. He wanted a minimum valuation procedure for fruit and vegetable imports based on a floor price that would bear some relationship to prices during the previous five- or seven-year period. Fred Rossiter, the agricultural attaché at the U.S. embassy in Ottawa, told the department of state that Canadian officials had 'been able to resist such procedures in the past but are less able to do so under the new ... Government.'[34] The U.S. participants, when discussing the Plumptre request, agreed that, to the extent that Canadian producers had a problem with respect to competition from U.S. imports, it should be possible to deal with it by means of ordinary tariff measures – extraordinary reactions, like minimum valuation procedures, were not necessary. Canadian producers suffered a disadvantage vis-à-vis their U.S. counterparts because they tended to use less efficient and more costly production methods. As well, certain agricultural areas in Canada were more vulnerable to import competition because of their geographic location. Ottawa's hidden agenda, or so the Americans believed, was to extend protection to marginal producers of fruits and vegetables. Rossiter attributed 'this latest Canadian proposal for minimum values for duty purposes on fruits and vegetables to campaign promises made to producers, to the vociferous protectionist demands of the Canadian Horticultural Council, and to the fact that Canadian fruit and vegetable producers have thus far been more aggressive in bringing pressure to bear on the government than other producer groups.' As well, there was a need for a U.S. public relations campaign to counteract common Canadian 'misconceptions' and press 'distortions' with respect to U.S.-Canadian economic relations. The committee would recommend that the United States oppose the Canadian action because it represented 'a reversal of announced [Canadian] policy ... [and] would create a damaging precedent for international trade in agricultural products, which would be tantamount to a price support program at the expense of U.S. exporters.'[35]

In short, the American participants would urge their embassy in Ottawa to acquaint the new Canadian cabinet with Canada's obligations under the GATT. If Canada went about changing duties on any product sanctioned by the General Agreement on Tariffs and Trade (GATT), it would have to apply for an upward revision of tariff concessions on fruits and vegetables under the procedures of GATT article XXVIII (Renegotiation of Schedules), and the United States would not object. The principal American complaint over the proposed minimum valuation procedure was that it would be restrictive of international trade and inconsistent with the provisions of GATT article VII, which provided that contracting parties should base the calculation of customs duties on the actual value of an imported product, which was defined as 'the price at which ... such or like merchandise is sold or offered for sale in the ordinary course of trade under fully competitive conditions.'[36] Obviously, the United States would have difficulty in agreeing to a restrictive trade measure that would represent a reversal of announced policy and create a damaging precedent for international trade in agricultural products, a sector already rife with protectionism. This move would make it very difficult for Washington to ignore pressure from its own agricultural community for similar price support measures.

Accordingly, the United States would resist the Canadian proposal, and caution Ottawa against using distorted or unrepresentative price data, as the Americans believed their neighbour had done in the past. For example, they were very aware that Canadian pressure for the withdrawal of tariff concessions on new potatoes had come from British Columbia producers, and not from Maritime farmers who actually exported to the United States. In the case of frozen peas, BC growers had also complained about unfair American competition when the reality was that eastern Canadian farmers were hurting their western counterparts.

As well, Canadian import controls on turkeys was a festering irritant that was raised by the U.S. delegation at the joint meeting of U.S. secretaries and Canadian ministers in January 1959. Ottawa had imposed controls in July 1957, one month after the first Conservative election victory. Government had reacted in part because U.S. exports to Canada had reached about 12 million pounds, 20 per cent of total Canadian production, and threatened to submerge the domestic industry in an ocean of cheap American turkey. Washington had made formal representations several times to Ottawa. It expressed concern at the lack of prior consultation before the import controls were imposed and indicated that it considered these restrictions to be in breach of Canada's trade agreement obligations under the GATT. The Americans were on the point of making a formal complaint in the GATT but had been dissuaded by Ottawa's decision to establish a quota of 300,000 pounds for imports of turkeys during the last two months of 1958. However, they were unhappy with the size of this quota and had made threatening noises that if it were not raised to at least 7 million pounds in 1959, they would make a formal application that the GATT investigate at the next session in May 1959. For good measure, they also mentioned pressure was building in the United States for the imposition of import restrictions on Canadian cattle. In the final analysis, a Canadian government paper pointed out, the United States was on relatively firm ground with its complaint. While it had access to a waiver of its GATT obligations for agricultural goods (as explained in chapter 5) it had 'used its powers to impose restrictions on agricultural products with restraint and moderation.'[37]

The American Riposte

There were also some general trade policy implications to consider. Canada was concerned to ensure that the United States in its own commercial policies would comply as closely as possible with Canada's trade agreement requirements and would take into account Canadian trade interests. Ottawa had consistently pressed Washington to provide the freest possible access for Canadian goods. Where the United States had applied restrictions, Canada had demanded the establishment of adequate quotas for Canadian goods and had reserved its rights to take compensatory measures if its interests were seriously affected. Moreover, the country was continuing to urge the removal of import restrictions in other parts of the world. It would be very difficult, if not the height of hypocrisy, to demand standards of behaviour that Canadians themselves did not meet.

Still, U.S. secretaries and officials remained unhappy with overall Conservative policy and the protectionist talk being reported by the embassy in Ottawa. From their perspective, there seemed to be far too many Commonwealth economic conferences where conversations ran freely about enhanced linkages and preferential linkages. Moreover, there had also been Diefenbaker's since discredited 15 per cent diversion proposal which had stuck in American craws. They believed that a general effort should be made to acquaint Canadian cabinet ministers with their country's obligations under GATT. That job was assigned to the U.S. secretaries attending the next meeting of the Joint Canada-U.S. Committee on Trade and Economic Affairs; they should be very firm about Canada's import restrictions and perceived GATT violations. As the Conservatives were discovering, developing trade policy and responding to legitimate complaints by GATT contracting parties was a sensitive and difficult issue. While in opposition one might point to perceived government acquiescence to American interests in trade matters – while in government, the situation was very different.

First, however, the Americans would begin their public relations campaign designed to impress the Conservatives. Their biggest gun would be used to convince the Canadian government that they had only the best intentions toward Canada. In July 1958, President Eisenhower would pay a visit to Ottawa and address a joint session of Parliament. Dulles told the president his view of the purpose of the visit: 'The improvement of our relations with Canada under its Conservative Government. We seek to establish the same mutual confidence and close working relationship with the new government that we enjoyed with the Liberal Government for 22 years.' Canadian nationalist feeling had been nourished during the recent election campaign and the United States had been made, at least according to Dulles, 'the whipping boy for many of Canada's ills.' The president should attempt to convince the Conservatives that '(a) United States policies are reasonable; (b) far from taking Canada for granted, the United States prizes its intimate relationship; and (c) the United States recognizes that problems exist in our relations and is determined to find constructive solutions on the basis of mutual give and take.'[38] In short, it was prepared to take the time and effort it thought necessary to improve relations with Ottawa.

The Canadians similarly viewed the visit as vitally important as they also had an agenda. The normally restrained Louis Rasminsky, then a deputy governor at the Bank of Canada, pointed out in a memorandum to the prime minister that 'This is a moment of great strategic importance in the relations between the United States and the rest of the Free World.' It was imperative that the United States recapture the liberalizing spirit that had animated much of its post-war trade policy development: 'What is required ... is a revitalization, in the context of the present economic situation, of those policies which form the hardcore of the traditional foreign economic policy objectives of the United States.' Canada, he thought, could be instrumental in encouraging that spirit.[39]

Good connections between the two countries were arguably much more important for Canada given the potential American ability to wreak havoc with Canadian economic growth and prosperity. The list of grievances against the United States could be almost endless. If enacted, quotas on lead and zinc, copper, and aluminum had real potential to shut down parts of Canada. As noted above, a satisfactory Canadian oil export policy depended on American goodwill, and there were rumors coming from Washington that tariff restrictions were about to be imposed on Canada's live cattle exports. When the Canadians raised this issue with the Americans, they were told that at present there were no plans for such protection, although Canadian proposals for increased protection of fruits and vegetables would have a bearing on the thinking 'of otherwise liberal minded agricultural opinion in the US.' It seemed to some, despite the American charm offensive launched by the president, that the United States was continuing along its protectionist path in its foreign economic policy.

As rumour became reality, Ottawa became increasingly concerned and absolutely convinced of the centrality of the U.S. market for Canadian exporters. In September 1958, Washington did impose quotas on imports of lead and zinc, to which 'the Canadian government attached great importance.'[40] In 1957, exports to the United States of these metals were valued at CAN$55 million, constituting 59 per cent by volume of all Canadian lead and zinc exports and 51 per cent of all Canadian production. As with oil, any U.S. action that threatened to tilt Canada's current account balance further into deficit had to be protested. The U.S. initiative, Diefenbaker told the president, would adversely affect the Canadian lead and zinc industry 'as well as the longer term prospects for the exploration and development of new resources which we regard as a major contribution to the strength of the free world.'[41] Smelters and mines would close and Canadians would be thrown out of work to support unproductive and inefficient U.S. producers.

Some Canadians took the quota announcement as an American retreat from multilateralism and non-discrimination, an indication that the administration was 'no longer prepared to resist protectionist measures.' The success of the mineral lobby could be construed 'as an acceptance of the doctrine that even the most inefficient producers must be protected for security reasons or for political reasons – the reason may not be important, the principle of protection at all costs is very nearly propounded.'[42]

The prime minister was chagrined that the U.S. announcement came while the Montreal meeting of Commonwealth countries was underway in September 1958. As discussed in chapter 5, the meetings were designed to 'foster economic expansion throughout the Commonwealth,' and the timing most unfortunate.[43] It was also perhaps a warning to the assembled delegations not to further entrench preferences or any other restrictive trade measures as had happened in

Ottawa in August 1932. The prime minister ended a letter to Eisenhower that dealt with U.S. protectionism with a request for a repeal of the quota legislation: 'It seems to me that both of our countries have a compelling interest in encouraging [multilateralism and non-discrimination] and, conversely, in doing nothing that is likely to reverse them or that will be in conflict with the objectives and undertakings to which you and we and others have all subscribed. I would very much hope, therefore, that you will review the position with respect to lead and zinc at the earliest possible opportunity and restore the traditional access which Canada ... [has] had to your market for these commodities.'[44] It was an important matter of general principle, a Canadian briefing note pointed out, 'that Canada should not be put in the position of acquiescing in limiting her exports to the United States, whether with respect to lead and zinc or other commodities, for the sake of accommodating the United States in her protectionist policies.'[45]

The lead and zinc issue was deemed so important that it was brought by a number of countries to the United Nations conference relating to the materials. The conference first met in late 1958 and again between 28 April and 1 May 1959, to be followed by the inaugural meeting of a continuing lead and zinc study group. Canada was in the forefront of the movement to convene these talks. The country's interest, cabinet was told, was 'to maintain freedom of access to all major consuming markets of the world and especially that of the United States.' Canada, as was made clear to the United States, did not consider the American restrictions justifiable and believed that they were in contravention of United States obligations under GATT: 'the difficulties faced by US marginal producers arise from the world-wide decline and the earlier governmental stimulation of US production and not because of US obligations as regards imports, including tariff reductions undertaken in the GATT.'[46] Ottawa reserved its right under the GATT to take action if a satisfactory solution was not reached.

However, lead and zinc liberalization was not going to happen in the short term and the quotas remained into the 1960s. Indeed, invoking the bugbear of congressional control of trade policy during one of the Joint Canada-U.S. Committee on Trade and Economic Affairs meetings, the American delegation said that the 'Administration was in the position of having to restrain the legislative branch from setting up further barriers to the import of these metals.'[47] Moreover, despite the potential disruption for Canada, in 1959 Washington permitted imports of Canadian lead that were at their highest level since 1954, and zinc shipments that were at their highest levels since 1956. While the situation might not be as bad as had been anticipated, it was the principle that stirred Canadians. The Conservatives were now very alive to the fact that Canada's prosperity depended mightily on the U.S. market. That said, lead and zinc and oil represented aberrations from past practice; of 16 possible trade restriction cases of interest to Canada since 1945, there had been only two where inhibitions to trade had been imposed after consideration by the Tariff Commission. Given the central importance of the United States for Western prosperity, it was, as J.H. Warren told a group of Canadian and British ministers, 'not always easy to be objective about United States trade policies.'[48] Amen. '

The Relationship Improves

These distortions in the developing relationship notwithstanding, the continental connection in the later 1950s seemed to be fairly cozy, as certain U.S. initiatives like the Eisenhower visit of July 1958 had done something to soothe Canadian sensibilities. Richard Wigglesworth, the U.S. ambassador to Canada from December 1958 until October 1960, commented favourably on Canadian attitudes following his first meeting with Canadian officials, a meeting marked by a 'friendly attitude towards the US.' As proof he referred to one of his meetings with then secretary of state for external affairs (SSEA) Sidney Smith, who had told him 'how pleased Canadians were with cabinet level defense committee meeting Paris and efforts of U.S. to meet Canadian needs in defense field.'[49] Similarly, a department of state memorandum, written in mid-1959, thought that 'the number of abrasive issues with the Canadians are remarkably few,' and that Diefenbaker 'was most appreciative of U.S. actions' on files like oil exports and wheat surplus disposal.[50] A year later, the Americans observed that 'There are no serious major issues in US-Canadian relations at this time ... In the economic field ... relations have improved over the last two years.'[51] Eisenhower's analysis was that keeping Diefenbaker onside was not difficult 'if he were kept informed in advance.'[52] Following the election of John Kennedy as president in November 1960 there was to be a 'deterioration in the cordiality and mutual confidence between the two governments, largely for reasons that originated north of the border.'[53]

As noted above, the Americans carefully managed their relationship with Canada, recognizing the latter's importance in defence and economic issues. Even the president kept a watching brief over the state of the relationship, commenting when it seemed to be coming off the rails. For example, in April 1960 Eisenhower telephoned his secretary of state, now Christian Herter, to discuss an official's analysis of a perceived deteriorating North American nexus. It was, he said, 'something that he had not been aware of; that we have done so much to keep good relations.' The solution was to invite Diefenbaker to Washington 'and while he is merely a Prime Minister, the President thought that he could give him a little more of the red carpet treatment since he is the Prime Minister of such a close neighbor.'[54] The visit took place on 3 June 1960, to the satisfaction of all involved.

Why were the Americans so concerned to keep the relationship in good repair? While some of the rationale had to do with a developing special relationship, a more important part related to continental defence, a vitally important consideration for Washington. The U.S. government had entered into agreements to build radar lines with (and in) Canada, and had also negotiated the North American Air Defence Command (NORAD) in August 1957 to patrol the continent's skies. Certainly Arnold Heeney, Canada's ambassador in the U.S. capital, was very sensitive to American paranoia in this area; during visits to Ottawa in meetings with the prime minister and the SSEA, now Howard Green, he often emphasized the importance of national security issues for the United States. Following these conversations, he records in his memoirs (with some prescience) that he 'realized that the whole area of defence cooperation was going to be a delicate and difficult one.'[55]

It was not made any easier by a new Canadian SSEA who was intensely anti-American, anti-nuclear, and pro-disarmament. Green met with Christian Herter while the two were in New York City attending the fifteenth session of the United Nations General Assembly. Herter told him that he had recently received 'very disquieting reports about serious antipathy and antagonism toward the United States in Canada. He would like to know Mr. Green's views on whether there was anything we might do and, if so, what ... It began to appear to [the Americans] that the two Canadian parties [the Liberals and Conservatives] were in fact vying in cresting anti-American sentiment.' The two thrashed out the issue for the better part of an hour with Green suggesting that it was a part of Canadian politics, always had been and always would be, and was not so serious as it seemed. Certainly there were differences of opinion over the Soviet Union and the People's Republic of China (PRC). In the realm of defence, however, Green did offer that the United States was too belligerent for most Canadians and, he thought, even for the Canadian military! Green's suggestion that 'Canadians "were not nearly so worried about the Russians" as [they] were Americans,' surely took Herter aback.[56] It was also patently false.

Foreign Direct Investment and Early Concerns over Extraterritoriality

Another area of concern was the ongoing question of control by U.S. business of Canadian subsidiaries. Even though this issue did not involve the American government directly, it was a symptom of the same illness. 'The Canadian Government,' Green suggested, 'might have to bring in legislation to control this situation. The Canadians could not have decisions about Canadian industries made by offices here in New York. There were many difficulties, sometimes involving the government, such as attempts to investigate Canadian firms under

US anti-trust laws. It was unacceptable that Canadian enterprises should be so treated.' Green also mentioned that there would probably be an election some-time in the spring of 1961, and anti-American rhetoric sold well with many vot-ers. When the Conservatives were in opposition, Green told Herter, 'his party used to accuse the Liberals of being lackeys of the Americans. Now the Liberals were using the same club to beat the Conservatives' with an attendant upward movement in the polls.[57]

Green was correct that the extent of foreign ownership and the control that U.S. firms exercised over subsidiaries was an increasingly sensitive area of concern in Canada. Even the governor of the Bank of Canada, James Coyne, was warning his countrymen of its dangers. He gave speeches throughout the country pushing a perspective that a former Bank official, George Freeman, labeled a 'fierce Cana-dian nationalism.'[58] While his position was similar to Green's, it appeared that Diefenbaker's government was irritated by the way in which he communicated his message almost as much as by his subject. As well, some Americans did not disagree with aspects of the Canadian complaint in this area. As Anderson had told an [NSC] meeting, 'Canadians do not like the practice by which a US com-pany establishes a branch in Canada and then informs Canadian citizens that the only way that they can share in the profits of the new Canadian company is to purchase stock in the US parent company. This seemed ... a readily understand-able irritation. Secretary McElroy thought so too, but pointed out that this ... was not an easy problem to solve.'[59]

Irritation, however, did not mean that Ottawa would move to restrict foreign investment, at least in the late 1950s. Indeed, the minister of finance, Donald Fleming, with Diefenbaker's blessing, went out of his way to emphasize to the American delegation at a joint U.S.-Canada committee on trade and economic affairs meeting held a number of months prior to Green's encounter with Herter that 'in spite of all the Canadians have said on the subject [of foreign invest-ment], they welcome foreign capital. In fact, the Government would continue to improve the climate for foreign investment in Canada.'[60]

However, there were specific issues that existed between the two countries because of the extent of foreign ownership in Canada. First among these was extraterritoriality, where U.S. law extended to subsidiaries of U.S. companies established in countries like Canada. As Melville Watkins has correctly pointed out, the United States believed 'that it has the unilateral right to decide the reach of its law and policy, and to use its corporations and its technology as a means to enforce its foreign policy.'[61] A review of foreign assets control (FAC) regulations and their effect on American-owned subsidiaries and other foreign firms was undertaken by the Council on Foreign Economic Policy (CFEP) in mid-1958. Clearly, it was becoming a problem as close U.S. allies like Britain, Canada, and

Japan began to question the applicability of U.S. law to their industry. Dulles had discussed the issue with Canadians in his July 1958 visit to Ottawa, and a rubric had been developed. At that time the Conservatives had agreed with his submission that the United States would be 'prepared to grant a permit to parent companies in the U.S. which would enable subsidiaries in Canada to engage in a transaction when this had an appreciable effect on the Canadian company and the Canadian economy ... US laws should not operate to the disadvantage of a Canadian company.'[62]

In Canada, there had been a number of cases involving the extension of U.S. law. With respect to pulp, an American company in Canada had received an exemption from FAC to export bleached sulphite pulp to China, but had decided against doing so. The reason, it was thought in Ottawa, was partly because Washington had put pressure on the company not to seek the business as tensions with the PRC increased over Quemoy and Matsu, two islands between Formosa and the PRC that the United States had made certain commitments to defend. Several American companies based in Canada, like Louis Dreyfus, Cargill, and Range Grain, and some flour milling companies like Robin Hood, Pillsbury, and Quaker Oats, were restrained from searching out grain sales in China in the late 1950s because of their American parents. The Canadian Wheat Board (CWB), in particular, was very concerned as those companies all had global connections and experience and were in a good position to obtain export business for Canada probably not available to smaller Canadian companies.

As well, Chrysler Canada had made application in August 1958 for an export permit covering the sale of 12,000 passenger car engines and spare parts valued at CAN$6 million. While the attitude of the U.S. Treasury was sympathetic to the Canadian request, the parent company did not file an application in support of its Canadian subsidiary and the order died on the books. Moreover, U.S. foreign assets control exercised an influence over the activities of some *Canadian* companies toward trade with China (and even Hong Kong) as well as their trade with other Canadian companies which might export to the PRC. The Aluminum Company of Canada, for example, refused to consider trade enquiries from China or willingly permit Alcan metal to be supplied to third parties for resale to that country. As a Canadian document pointed out, 'The company expresses its concern in terms of the possible impact on public relations in its important U.S. market, but the Washington representative has also drawn attention to the citizenship status of the directors of the controlling company – the president and six other directors out of fifteen are US residents.'[63] Inco was equally concerned, and had barred its British subsidiary, Mond, from trading with the Chinese and another Canadian firm from exporting manufactured nickel product.

More examples of extraterritoriality abounded as the practice continued. In the early 1960s, Canadian wheat sales to the PRC became an indirect *cause célèbre*. President Kennedy told Diefenbaker that he could see how the sales helped the communists, but did not see their advantage to the western alliance. Then Imperial Oil, a subsidiary of Standard Oil of New Jersey, was asked to supply bunker oil for the Canadian ships that would carry the country's wheat to China. When the parent had approached the treasury department for permission, it had received a very cold reception. President Kennedy had told the secretary of the treasury, Douglas Dillon, to permit the sale only if the Canadian government asked him and if there were no other Canadian companies available to supply the fuel. That, however, was 'politically inflammatory,' and would create 'great antagonism' towards the United States. After all, Imperial Oil was a Canadian company, incorporated in Canada and doing business in that country. Diefenbaker was to tell Kennedy that 'Canadians could not understand the United States Government dictating the actions of a Canadian corporation.'[64]

More generally, while the Americans were forthcoming on the issuing of permits to Canadian subsidiaries, the latter found the process to be too intrusive. Officials in Ottawa prepared memoranda for their ministers relating to FAC. While realizing that it would remain an aspect of the Cold War over which American allies would have little influence, a paper prepared for ministerial consideration suggested a number of alternatives which they could raise with their U.S. counterparts. The government should ask U.S. secretaries to agree that they would not discourage U.S. parent companies from applying for exemption from the provisions of FAC regulations in respect of proposed export and import transactions of Canadian subsidiary companies with the PRC. Where applications were made, the United States would consider these favourably where refusal might be to Canada's economic disadvantage and that the word of Canadian ministers be accepted in this regard. In this connection, the Americans would not insist as a prerequisite to the issuance of the permit that evidence be brought forward that no independent Canadian company was in a position to undertake the trade. Finally, ministers should question whether the purposes of foreign asset control should apply to U.S. citizens and residents so far as liability under these regulations might arise as a result of their being directors, executives, or shareholders in independent Canadian companies.[65]

Even given the sometimes rancorous debates that took place between the two sides on issues like FAC and Green's official attitudes toward Americans, the general tone of the relationship was friendly as the two sides came to know each other better. Indeed, Diefenbaker often expressed his tremendous respect for, and admiration of, Eisenhower. The Conservatives certainly appreciated the frank and amiable tone of American secretaries as expressed in venues such as the joint Canada-US committee on trade and economic affairs that usually met once per year. The United States also found them to be a valuable forum where issues could be anticipated and raised before they became public and problematic. A memorandum prepared prior to the 1959 meeting highlighted their objective. 'To broaden the scope of mutual agreement in the economic field, to give sympathetic airing to differences and resentments on either side, and to instill in the Canadian Ministers, who might otherwise be swayed by the emotions of economic nationalism, a more reasonable attitude in their economic relations with the United States.'[66] As Dillon later told an NSC meeting that 'we had discovered in the economic field that our problems with Canada could be solved by high-level conversations.'[67]

But not all problems could be so readily dealt with. For a jingoistic and self-obsessed country like the United States, it is odd that its officials seemed unable to understand the attraction of Canadian nationalism for Canadians. That issue was raised at the 1959 joint U.S.-Canada meeting. Earlier, the Americans had cogitated among themselves over 'the present attitude of radical nationalism' in Canada, as well as some of the activities of the Conservative government. The government had gained in experience since the last joint committee meeting in October 1957, Americans believed, but some Conservatives continued to behave 'as if they were still campaigning for public office.' Ottawa had shown itself 'increasingly responsive to domestic protectionist sentiment, particularly vis-à-vis trade with the United States, and has evinced something less than due regard for established procedures for prior consultation.' Those were quite remarkable sentiments expressed by U.S. cabinet members. And while the United States had taken no specific retaliatory measures against Canada as yet, that position could change.

Similarly, Ottawa had its own complaints about U.S. procedure. In the area of export financing, for example, Canadians were concerned about the credit facilities offered to U.S. exporters by American institutions such as the Eximbank, a semi-public Washington bank involved in helping to finance U.S. exports and imports. As well, its export guarantees had been broadened to cover commercial risks for up to five years. While Canadian exporters had urged that similar facilities be established in Canada to help them in what was becoming an increasingly competitive world, the government was unable to do so largely because of the potential cost. The stark reality was that 'Canada was short of capital [and] the Canadian government could not enter into competitive export financing.'[68]

That was a problem, especially as the United States had entered into a period of balance of payments difficulties that would plague it for more than thirty-five years. The first imbalance was sustained in 1958, and by the early 1960s, the U.S. had experienced deficits totaling US$11 billion. During the 1960s industrially developed nations around the world began to insist that Washington take steps to deal with this problem, and it ushered in a series of responses that eventually helped to destabililize the post-war monetary system. But for the present, Finance Minister Fleming asked the American secretaries at the February meeting 'whether there would be any tendency for the United States, in view of its Balance of Payments difficulties and the political pressures which might develop this year, to link its aid programmes more extensively to export promotion,' which, the minister left unsaid, would compete 'unfairly' with Canadian exports.[69]

The Americans would make every attempt to minimize the impact of export promotion on Canada, but they would not alter the policy, a very unsatisfactory response. The Eximbank provided fairly short-term credit for U.S. exports, but on occasion it did make longer-term loans that were closely tied to U.S. exports, and American calculations as to the boost these would provide was in the range of US$200 million. Anderson explicitly stated that the United States 'was making every effort to increase exports in order to reverse the trend in the balance of payments which had in 1958 for the first time since the war developed an adverse balance on goods and services. No definite proposals had yet been put forward but the matter was under active consideration.'[70]

The balance of payments problem had implications far beyond those around North American trade. The United States remained the engine of global economic growth, and its deteriorating economic condition was of great concern to Congress. When, for example, Fleming asked Douglas Dillon, the undersecretary of state for economic affairs and also a delegation member, if the U.S. administration would attempt to secure from legislators further tariff-cutting authority beyond that provided by the current extension of the Trade Agreements Act, the American said no. International conditions were not such as to warm congressional hearts toward more tariff reductions. And what they would do when the Trade Agreements Act expired in 1962 depended upon the prevailing circumstances at that time. As things stood, the political atmosphere was less favourable with respect to further trade measures. Dillon noted the recent increases in U.S. imports and the weakness on exports, which led to its balance of payments problems. Only if U.S. exports increased more rapidly than imports could he be sanguine about the possibilities for renewing the Trade Agreements Act.

Despite the rather harsh tone of the Ottawa memorandum, the meetings, led by secretary of the treasury, Robert Anderson, went well. Upon his return to Washington, he told the Eisenhower cabinet that 'they had been very cordial this year, as compared to their strain last year.' Dillon echoed those remarks, saying that he wanted 'to re-emphasize the wonderful spirit. The lesson from this: consultation works both ways. We must realize there are numbers of actions we take, as of minor import, which are viewed by the Canadians as highly important. So we all need to take much care.'[71] The upshot of it all was that the Canadians promised not to unilaterally impose restrictions on commodities as they had with turkeys while the Americans tried to impart a greater understanding of their actions with respect to lead, zinc, and oil.

It became more and more important for the Canadians to get along well with the Americans, especially as the percentage of trade between the two countries increased. From Canada's perspective, a relatively small country heavily dependent on the export of natural resources, the United States represented its largest and most secure market. Turbulent economic times characterized the later 1950s, most of it caused by a relatively serious U.S. recession that lasted into early 1961. In 1958, for example, unemployment reached the staggering (for then) figure of 7.1 per cent and remaining in that region for the better part of two years. And while there had been substantial growth in employment amounting to 5 per cent during 1958 and 1959, it was the unemployment figure that grabbed people's attention.[72]

The Second Coming: The Election of John Kennedy

The Canadians would have to deal with those problems in the context of a new president as Eisenhower left office in January 1961 and was replaced by John Kennedy, a young and dynamic figure on the world stage. Many Canadians welcomed the change in government and some, like Norman Robertson, the undersecretary of state for external affairs, thought that the new administration would be less focused on communism and defence, which would be good for Canada. Penning an analysis a few days later, Robertson suggested that the new government 'should have much less obsession with communism at home and abroad as being the synthesis or epitome of all problems in foreign affairs.'[73] Kennedy was even thought to be a little 'soft' on opening lines of communication with the PRC, and had told the prime minister during his first meeting with Diefenbaker on 20 February 1961 that he had hoped that 'tensions [between the PRC and the United States] might gradually be lessened and a tolerable relationship brought about ... Mr. Kennedy said that he himself [was] "anxious to do better" with Communist China, but the Peking government persisted in their "deep belligerency."' To the last part at least, the old anti-communist Diefenbaker could only agree, remarking upon 'the intransigence of the Chinese Communist authorities.'[74]

Initially, the two leaders seemed to get along well. Indeed, following that first meeting the new president told Livingston Merchant, his ambassador-designate to Ottawa, that 'he liked the prime minister,'[75] while A.D.P. Heeney, Canada's ambassador in Washington, recorded that Diefenbaker 'was very happy about his first contact with the President.'[76] Still, the seeds of a poor relationship later to bear fruit were sown early, at least for the prime minister, despite the results of his February meeting with Kennedy. On a Sunday morning, a day normally given to contemplation and rest for the staunchly Baptist prime minister, Diefenbaker telephoned Robinson at his home to enquire if there had been any reply from Kennedy to the congratulatory message that had been sent to the president-elect from Ottawa on 9 November. When Robinson said there had not been, 'the Prime Minister expressed a good deal of irritation that this should have been overlooked by Kennedy and his people.'[77] Indeed, a reply was sent that originated in Washington and not Miami where Kennedy was then staying only 'after prodding from our side,' which further upset Diefenbaker.

Diefenbaker and Kennedy also differed over the substantive issue of defence, which was to cause so much hardship in the relationship. Robertson had earlier thought the Americans would downplay defence, specifically the Canadian refusal to authorize either the equipping of their forces with nuclear weapons or their storage in Canada for use by Americans. Merchant was prescient when early on he told secretary of state Dean Rusk that 'the greatest single outstanding problem between US and Canada is Canadian failure to face up to question of nuclear warheads.'[78] Despite Diefenbaker's firmly held anti-communism, Ottawa held a different perception of the Soviet threat than Washington. The Conservative government, quite rightly, 'tended to believe that a nuclear war would be so disastrous that the West must operate from the premise that East-West agreements must be achieved and that the West must avoid acts which appear threatening to the Soviets lest any chance for fruitful negotiations be jeopardized.'[79]

'In general,' a briefing note written for the president prior to the February meeting noted, 'the Canadian Government has tended to attach less weight than we have to the need for ostensible military strength, has given greater credence to Communist threats, has more readily accepted as sincere Communist protestations of good faith, and has been more inclined to worry over suggestions involving risk.'[80] The United States could not comprehend that attitude when the threat to Washington was so clear. The Americans were mystified as to why the idea of neutralism appealed to some in Canada. Adelai Stevenson put it most succinctly in a speech in Toronto in late 1960: neutrality was 'a luxury for which the US may not have much indulgence.'[81]

However, any suggestion of U.S. influence or pressure exerted on the nuclear weapons dossier caused Diefenbaker to recoil from a decision. The prime minister told Merchant that cabinet had been close to resolving the matter in September 1960, but press stories emanating from the White House 'to the effect that the President had sent a personal message on this subject to the Prime Minister had made it impossible for the Canadian cabinet to appear to be acting under pressure from Washington.'[82] It seemed to be important that Canada maintain its nuclear virginity while selling as much uranium for U.S. nuclear warheads as it could to the American military, and complaining when Defence Production Sharing Agreement (DPSA) contracts were terminated or directed elsewhere. The issue continued to plague Canadian-American relations until the election of the Pearson Liberals in April 1963, when the new government accepted nuclear weapons.

There were other incidents that came to adversely affect how Diefenbaker and Kennedy viewed each other. Diefenbaker received an unauthorized copy of a memorandum written by Walter Rostow, the deputy special assistant to the president for national security affairs. Entitled 'What We Want From the Ottawa Trip,' and dated just prior to the Kennedy-Diefenbaker meetings in May 1961, the memo called for action to move Canada into adopting a more America-centric foreign policy. The delegation was urged

1 To push the Canadians towards an increased commitment to the Alliance for Progress.
2 To push them towards a decision to join the OAS.
3 To push them towards a larger contribution for the India consortium and for foreign aid generally.
4 We want their active support at Geneva and beyond for a more effective monitoring of the borders of Laos and Vietnam.[83]

That memorandum drove Diefenbaker to distraction and in a tirade directed at the outgoing U.S. ambassador on 4 May 1962, he denounced the United States and Kennedy. A federal election was then in progress, and the prime minister threatened to use the paper to expose the true United States. That, and a few other *casus belli* that he would use would 'blow [Canadian-American] relations sky high.' In a letter to George Ball, then the acting secretary of state, Merchant noted that Diefenbaker 'was excited to a degree disturbing in a leader of an important country, and closer to hysteria than I have seen him.'[84]

In his memoirs, however, Diefenbaker suggests that the straw that broke the back of cooperation was not atomic bombs but vacuators, a special piece of suction equipment used to unload up to 600 tons of grain per day from ships and made by the Dunbar-Kattle Company of Batavia, Illinois. The vacuators had been ordered by ships transporting Canadian grain to the PRC and had been delivered to the Port of Vancouver when the order came from the U.S. treasury to return them to the United States on the basis of a foreign assets control regulation order. As a result, the prime minister made 'personal representations' to the president: 'I had to tell him that unless he released the unloading equipment, I would go on national television and radio to tell the Canadian people that he was attempting to run our country, and that he would have to think again if he thought this United States action acceptable ... The grain unloaders were released, but that was the end of any friendly personal relationship between Kennedy and myself.'[85] Whatever the reason for the breakdown in the relationship, Diefenbaker had become for the Kennedy-ites 'a grandstanding, insincere, sanctimonious, platitudinous old bore.'[86] Robert Kennedy was to later tell Arthur Schlesinger that his brother 'hated' Diefenbaker and 'had contempt for him.'[87]

As far as the prime minister was concerned, Kennedy was everything that he was not: young, attractive, and very charismatic. He had also come from a different world than had the Canadian leader and had Eisenhower, with whom Diefenbaker had developed a cordial relationship. The former had been born in 1895, had spent his formative years in Saskatchewan, and became prime minister at age sixty-two; Eisenhower had been born in Texas in 1890 and lived his life in Abilene, Kansas, when not serving in the army. He had been elected president when he was sixty-two. Moreover, both claimed German heritage. In short, they had much in common. On the other hand, Kennedy at forty-three was the youngest president then ever elected. He knew nothing of waving fields of wheat or the hardship of life in western North America. Kennedy grew up in Brookline, Massachusetts near Boston and attended Harvard and the London School of Economics. The prime minister was strong in his condemnation of the president: 'He was Sir Galahad on a white horse; rich, young, a silver spoon in his mouth. Diefenbaker always had an irresistible urge to put the guy in his place.'[88] Given this unenviable situation both American and Canadian officials spent some time trying to work out how best to deal with each leader and how to keep the continental agenda on a more or less even keel.

They accomplished this task well and the deterioration of the relationship did not adversely affect either the trade nexus that had developed between the two countries or the common front the two countries generally presented to the outside commercial world. For example, the North Americans continued to press for the same things in such institutions as the GATT and the Organization for Economic Cooperation and Development (OECD), as well as in an attempt to (unsuccessfully) steer the developing EEC in a more liberalized direction. At high-level meetings such as the joint U.S.-Canada committee on trade and economic affairs held in early February 1962 that did not include the prime minister, relations were usually cordial. In this case, the Canadian delegation leader, Donald Fleming, impressed the media by referring to his American counterpart, Douglas Dillon, the secretary of the treasury, as Doug. Dillon, for his part, called the minister Don.[89] Moreover, as Basil Robinson writes, at a working level things usually went well. He recalls the atmosphere during a visit to Washington prior to taking up the position of first minister at Canada's embassy as replete with a 'sense of abundant confidence ... so radically different from the uncertainty and disarray which prevailed in Ottawa.'[90] It was also refreshing 'to feel that cooperation in important matters of mutual interest was still possible [in 1962].' As well, the two countries' own trading relationship continued to grow during the early 1960s, despite some Canadian concern about American domination. Canadian access to the U.S. market was generally good and of Canadian exports to the United States were valued at CAN$3 billion, more than 85 per cent entered at tariff rates of 10 per cent or less. The remainder, which entered at rates of between 10 and 20 per cent (and sometimes higher), were all wholly manufactured goods. And although the Canadian press had made much of the escape clauses in U.S. trade agreements that could adversely affect Canada, they had been very sparingly used.

But that troubled prime ministerial-presidential relationship lay in the future. Immediately following Kennedy's election the Canadians plotted their strategy designed to let the United States know where they stood on various issues and that Canada deserved special consideration given its unique position vis-à-vis the United States. They would have to elbow their way into the lineup, or so Heeney thought. By January 1961 there were 'abundant signs that official Washington and its huge diplomatic corps are panting to make contact with the members of the administration.'[91] The queue was a long one and growing longer. However, Diefenbaker was the first foreign head of government to visit the new president. He travelled south on 20 February to discuss issues of mutual concern, primarily defence questions and the worldwide fight against the spread of communism.

Early Meetings with the New Administration

Educating the new administration as former Eisenhower staffers cleared out their desks in favour of incoming Democrats was very important work, for despite a relatively warm reception in the new Camelot, Canadian-American problems remained. When Kennedy and Diefenbaker first met, the prime minister recognized an excellent opportunity to acquaint the new president with the issues from his side of the border. He would mention Canada's persistent and serious unemployment, exacerbated by the country's very harsh winter. He would also tell the new president that unemployment was 'tied into trade and the very severe competition from imports – imports from the United States which has a greater industrial base, imports from Europe, which has lower wages and modern industry, and imports from Japan, Hong Kong and other low-cost Asiatic countries.'[92] The sobering reality for any prime minister was Canada's dependence on exports to maintain domestic prosperity: about 25 per cent of the country's gross domestic product came from sales abroad.

The Americans, for their part, were also interested in trade matters, but would more particularly emphasize continental defence. They also seemed to be willing to begin to address Canadian trade concerns if Ottawa was more forthcoming on the defence dossier. According to the memorandum to the President in February 1961, at a minimum it was imperative to counter the evolving Canadian attitude 'of introspection and nationalism.'[93] U.S. wealth and power had engendered 'a Canadian inferiority complex,' reflected in a sensitivity to any real or fancied slight to Canadian sovereignty. In American eyes 'the essential element in problems involving Canada tends to be psychological.' While Canada wanted to be separate from the United States, the memo informed the president, 'the Canadians desire, and believe themselves entitled to, a privileged relationship with the United States.' It seemed to some Americans that their northern neighbours wanted to have their cake and eat it, too. However, the meeting went well and Diefenbaker returned home greatly heartened that the positive elements of the Canadian-American relationship would continue much as they had under Eisenhower.

A fortuitous meeting of the Canada-United States trade committee had been scheduled for March 1961 and Ottawa seized this opportunity to try to influence American policy while it was in a state of flux. Heeney advised the department of external affairs to emphasize the 'broad community of interests and objectives' between Canada and the United States with respect to international trade policy. The Canadians 'might also make more of an impact regarding our bilateral problems if we could relate these to the broader issues of general policy which are bound to be uppermost in the minds of U.S. Secretaries at this time.' What Canadian officials were focused on was the future of the U.S. Trade Agreements Act which allowed the president to enter into trade negotiations. Heeney believed that there was 'possibly no single issue [that was] of greater importance to the future of Canadian-U.S. trade relations.'[94]

From Ottawa's gray buildings the perspective remained rather sobering into the winter of 1960–1 with officials trying to forecast the end of the U.S. recession. It was thought that unemployment could reach the staggering figure of 12 per cent of the labour force, around 750,000 people.[95] And even if the United States began to recover, Canadian unemployment would remain stubbornly high. The winter of 1961–2 could also be a tough one for Canadians and many of those who were unemployed would be ineligible for unemployment benefits. In the context then prevailing, it was difficult to count on an upsurge of demand for staple Canadian exports such as had underlain the expansion of the 1950s. Clearly, Canada could not expect to achieve an expanding economy when the United States was stagnant. As a consequence unemployment could remain an issue into the next election and perhaps well into the decade.

A Canadian Recession and the Growing Problem of
Foreign Direct Investment

Various suggestions were put forth as to how to ameliorate Canada's economic woes. One of the most persistent was to devalue the Canadian dollar, which then traded at a premium vis-à-vis its American counterpart. A department of finance paper pointed out that 'our exchange rate is still too high and should be reduced substantially.'[96] Until then, 'demands for direct protection [of manufacturing and other sectors] will continue to mount and will presumably have to be accommodated in some degree.' A Bank of England report, written by R.M. Mays-Smith on the basis of a two-week long trip to Ottawa, reflected that sentiment: 'Canada's present difficulties are certainly made no easier by the high level of her exchange rate and it seems very likely that both her current account balance of payments and her internal situation would improve if the exchange rate were lower, say, at par with the US dollar.' However, the governor of the Bank of Canada, James Coyne, felt it inappropriate to advocate the devaluation of the dollar, while Canadian thinking more generally was 'far more laissez-faire than it is in [Britain] or in the United States, and there is a feeling that it is dangerous to interfere with a market rate which has been freely determined by supply and demand.'[97]

   That situation could be made much worse if the U.S. recession persisted. As a department of finance research paper pointed out, 'The United States is the key element in the situation. They are ... already in a recession at the moment and are showing no signs of recovery. If US economic activity declines, our exports will fall and there would be considerable excess capacity in our export industries with little incentive to increase that capacity.' That is exactly what happened. Canada's balance of payments deficit increased in the second quarter of 1960 as a sharp decline in exports to the United States threw economic forecasts off. Moreover, a prolonged recession could impact adversely on private investment in Canada. While critics and some in government might rail against U.S. investment in Canada's economy, it was also true that investment remained essential to Canadian prosperity. The dry prose of the finance paper belied the intense concern that underlay any slackening of investment: 'Our economy has become accustomed to a high rate of investment to GNP; even with the declines in 1960, public and private investment accounted for 22 percent of the GNP in the second quarter of this year. If the ratio and the level of investment should drop significantly there would be a further increase in unemployment and economic dislocation.'[98] For a government moving into the second half of its mandate and considering an election in the not-too-distant future, it was very important to maintain a vibrant economy.

   On the basis of a wide canvass of opinion in Ottawa, Mays-Smith suggested the consensus among officials seemed to be that while there were any number of ideas about what to do to ease the country's economic situation, 'few seem to offer any great hope of immediate recovery except in so far as they are helped by developments in the United States.' He suggested a possible remedy to the Canadian situation, but it was one that would have appealed to neither the Bank of Canada nor the government. 'In general,' he wrote, 'the Canadian authorities left too much to the market and more positive attempts to control the economy were desirable, however unpopular anything which smacks of "dirigisme" is to Canadian opinion.'[99]

That rather simple suggestion was not a possibility in the early 1960s, or so it seemed, given the rather heated atmosphere that quickly came to surround any talk of the advantages of foreign direct investment. Coyne had hinted in a speech made in Hamilton that the flow of foreign investment should be curtailed by means of direct regulation of foreign exchange and investment, an idea with which the minister of finance took exception. But the governor, with his tight money policy, was indirectly encouraging Canadians with sufficient means to seek out cheaper money in New York. And that, as professors Bothwell, Drummond, and English have pointed out, raised 'Canada's foreign indebtedness.'[100] As well, Fleming was repelled by Coyne's advice and his attack on foreign direct investment in Canada. Investors, he said in the House, came to this country because it was an ideal location to do business. Investment was 'a reflection of strong confidence in our economic prospects and brings into Canada not only capital funds, but also technical know how, and often also brings with it an assurance of export markets.' He went on:

> We have been following constructive and realistic policies in matters of trade and finance, policies appropriate to the present and foreseeable circumstances. What are the alternatives to such policies? A programme of government controls? The imposition and enforcement of import restrictions and quotas? Individual restraints upon Canadians desiring to travel abroad and on the amount of money they could take with them? The creation of a centralized capital issues committee which would dictate to provinces, municipalities and to private business as to where, when, on what terms they could borrow? ... They may be justifiable in the midst of a national crisis. In peace and prosperity, in a free society, they are not warranted. Indeed, some of them may be unconstitutional. Moreover, I believe that some of these so-called remedies would actually cause the disease that they are supposed to prevent or cure. Government controls, by interfering with freedom, cause confidence to falter, initiative to freeze and capital to take flight.[101]

Gordon Churchill, the minister of trade and commerce and a man of some influence in the Diefenbaker government, also took exception to Coyne's message, welcoming the inflow of foreign investment as vital to Canada's future prosperity. He reinforced Fleming's point, adding, 'I make no excuse whatsoever for taking an optimistic view of Canada's future during this decade of the sixties.'[102]

The issue of American domination of Canada's economy, so prominent during the 1957 and 1958 elections, had been muted by the government by 1960. Diefenbaker, perhaps disingenuously, went so far as to tell the newly elected Kennedy during their first meeting in February 1961 that 'there was no widespread [anti-Americanism] in Canada.'[103] That view, however, had not deterred Coyne from becoming increasingly vocal about U.S. domination, and he used his position as governor to warn the country of the dangers of continentalism. But the government was not keen to proceed on this basis, at least in terms of the economy. To the contrary, it was increasingly concerned that Coyne's pronouncements could help to compromise the flow of investment money into Canada upon which the country was so dependent, especially in the midst of a recession. Mays-Smith spoke to a number of officials at the Bank, and while there was little support of the Coyne position, there was definitely a sense that the current account balance of payments deficit was the key problem then confronting Canada and that American investment (and the floating exchange rate) had tended to conceal how serious that situation was. As Mays-Smith wrote, 'It is a question of judgment how far a country can allow its industry to be owned by another country and still maintain its independence, but the Bank feels that when over half of Canada's manufacturing industry and an even higher percentage of mining and oil industries are foreign owned, it is time to be considering how much longer this can go on ... As the public was largely unaware of this ... two years ago, Mr. Coyne's speeches have performed a considerable public service,'[104] or so Mays-Smith reported to his superiors.

The pro-investment rhetoric by Fleming and Churchill in support of the March 1960 budget shifted by December and the release of the so-called baby budget. By then Fleming seemed to have come around much more to the Coyne point of view. In a story headlined 'Ottawa Moves to Check Foreign Capital Inflow,' the *Globe and Mail* noted that the government had implemented 'far-reaching measures to discourage the inflow of foreign capital and promote increased investment by Canadians in their own resources.'[105] Ottawa intended to encourage foreign investment by a withholding tax of 15 per cent on virtually all interest and dividend payments going out of the country and a hefty tax on pension and savings funds that had been invested abroad. These measures, the *Globe* opined, 'endorse[d] Coyne's view.' They did not save Coyne's job, however, as the Conservatives fired him in July 1961, much to their everlasting regret.[106]

The Liberals had also shifted position and their rhetoric had adopted a more nationalist tone at their convention, held in Ottawa during February 1961. Pearson's speech contained references to the danger of U.S. economic domination, but the original draft was watered down avoiding any anti-American sentiments. In the House, the leader of the Opposition attempted to embarrass the government by throwing Coyne, and his concern over foreign investment, at them. This was an appropriate beginning to the 1960s as that decade as no other would focus attention on U.S. economic penetration in Canada.

Not surprisingly, even given the incipient Canadian debate over foreign ownership, the Americans brought 'no urgent bilateral *economic* problems requiring the President's attention' to the meeting of Diefenbaker and Kennedy in Ottawa in May 1961, and they worked to keep other problems separate from economic issues.[107] The United States pushed on the nuclear weapons question but it had not yet reached a crisis level, at least according to Washington, and the Americans were prepared to be patient. On the Canadian side there were the usual complaints, like the extent of U.S. investment in Canada, some CAN$16 billion by 1961, the CAN$1 billion annual deficit in Canada's current trade account with the United States, American restrictions on some imported Canadian goods, and the U.S. practice of extraterritoriality.

In particular, the Canadians wanted to get their trade deficit down to more manageable proportions, and would urge the president to do what he could to encourage a new Congress to reduce restrictions on dairy products, lead and zinc, and to let the quota on rye expire. As well, they would push for more defence expenditures by the American military in Canada, under the auspices of the DPSA of 1959. The Canadians knew that anything that appealed to Washington's sense of security would be a most fruitful avenue when pursuing defence contracts. The United States had liberalized its 'Buy American Act,' simplified procurement procedures, and eased security regulations to enable Canadian defence industries to bid for U.S. contracts.

The DPSA was linked with the termination of the Avro Arrow CF-105 project that had begun in 1952. The contractor, the A.V. Roe Company, had built a number of very advanced jet interceptor prototypes. As costs had escalated, the Conservatives became more and more edgy, resulting in the infamous 11 February 1959 notice that the project was cancelled, throwing thousands of high-tech employees out of work. Instead, Ottawa would cooperate with the Americans in the establishment of the SAGE-Bomarc system, a surface-to-air missile system tipped with nuclear warheads designed to shoot down incoming Soviet ICBMs over Canadian territory. The quid pro quo for the cancellation of the Arrow and the acceptance of the new missile system was Canadian access to the lucrative U.S. arms market – they could now become sub-contractors for U.S. weapons systems.

While the arrangement might create jobs and swell Canada's current account balance, it also had a significant downside. In an intelligent piece, the *Economist* editorialized that the move called into question Canada's diplomatic and political independence. 'What freedom of action,' it asked, 'remains in Canadian diplomacy?'[108] All defence business for Canadians plants, 'in any advanced technological field such as aircraft and electronics, must come – if it comes at all – from American subcontracts ... Canada's new policy on North American defence carries such sweeping implications that few people have yet grasped their scope ... This concern arises from fear that Mr. Diefenbaker, in a characteristic fit of absence of mind, may have surrendered control over the most vital of Canadian policies. Defence decisions are directly involved. The pattern of Canada's industrial future is at stake at only one remove. And only two removes away is the question whether Canadian foreign policy and Canadian diplomacy must also be paralyzed.' The new defence policy was 'a patchwork of service recommendations slung together with little realization of the profound implications for Canada's industrial future or for its freedom of economic and political decision-making.'[109]

Official Ottawa did not see it that way. The government had applauded when Canadian supplies and services had been specifically exempted from all U.S. balance of payments actions taken by the department of defense in the procurement area that might adversely affect the DPSA. This program was responsible for more than US$200 million of new business for Canadian firms in 1959 and 1960, and the Canadians continued to press for a greater U.S. effort to share the 'continental' wealth. A briefing note for President Kennedy said that Canada believed that 'the production resources of both nations should be used cooperatively to achieve the best combined results.'[110] In short, or so the Americans believed, while Canadian cooperation in continental defence 'carrie[d] a price tag,' it was not much, and in any case it was one well worth paying.[111]

Similarly, in spite of its own developing balance of payments problems, the United States continued to permit Canadians to borrow in the New York market up to CAN$1 billion to cover their current account deficit with the United States. The governor of the Bank of England, Earl Cromer, enquired while on a visit to Washington about this willingness to allow the Canadians privileges that were not extended to others and was told that 'this has been accepted by the US.'[112] Of course, Canada was a net contributor to the U.S. balance of payments, having provided more than CAN$6 billion over the ten years since 1952 to help cover U.S. deficits. That fact, and the idea that the two North American countries had a special relationship, even despite Diefenbaker, was a large part of the reason that the United States helped Canada through its financial crisis of 1962.[113]

The 1962 Exchange Crisis and Its Context

An exchange crisis resulted when government expenditures increased 7 per cent in the first nine months of 1961 over a similar period in 1960, leading to a substantial deficit. While that had been useful in 1961, given that the economy was in the doldrums, the governor of the Bank of Canada, now Louis Rasminsky, believed that a similar gap between revenue and expenditures in 1962 would cause difficulty. It did, and was made worse by the Canadian election, called for 18 June. When the dust had cleared, the Conservatives held on as a minority government, dropping from 203 seats to 116. The Liberals rose to 99, Social Credit took 30, and the New Democratic Party, 19. The future had not looked promising for the government even before the vote and it would not, or perhaps could not, take action during the campaign that would damage its chances of re-election. The most that it would attempt was to stabilize the international exchange rate of the Canadian dollar at 92.5 cents in relation to the U.S. dollar. For the next nine years, US$1 was to equal, more or less, CAN$1.08. The period of the floating rate upon which Canada had embarked in September 1950 was at an end. It was, however, too little too late and as the economy seemed ready to implode, drastic action was necessary.

A program developed by Rasminsky and the deputy minister of finance, Ken Taylor, was designed to begin the process of repairing the damage. Of most short-term significance, the governor arranged support from other lenders totaling US$1.050 billion. Of this amount, the significant figure of US$250 million came from the U.S. federal reserve and US$400 million from the Export-Import Bank. As well, the program included among a list of special measures a temporary graduated surcharge on certain classes of imports, ranging from 15 per cent for less essential imports through 10 per cent on items such as imported cars to 5 per cent on about CAN$2.5 billion worth of imports. The surcharges would allow the government to raise CAN$200 million to add to federal revenue in the crisis but could have a tremendously adverse effect on U.S. exports to Canada (about US$3.6 billion in 1961 or 17 per cent of U.S. exports). Also, the government imposed a temporary reduction in the exemptions from customs duties accorded to Canadian tourists on goods brought back to Canada. As many Canadians travelled to the United States, the added duties represented a large potential decline in goods bought there.

Washington had done more than its share to help resurrect confidence in the Canadian dollar and economy, and was concerned when it seemed as if the Diefenbaker government intended to leave the import surcharges in place for up to one year. As well, they had been imposed without the required consultation in the GATT 'and little effort was made [by Ottawa] to demonstrate that they were consistent with the letter of Canada's commitments.'[114] The surcharges smacked of protectionism, and the GATT's contracting parties were not convinced of the rightness of the Canadian position or their professed determination to get rid of them as soon as possible.

Undersecretary of state George Ball wrote to Dillon in early July 1962 complaining about the Canadian action. He began by noting that he had 'the uncomfortable feeling that the Diefenbaker Government is being less than straightforward with us, and I think we must be careful not to let the Administration be put in an indefensible position.'[115] Clearly, he believed that the United States had been sold a bill of goods over the 'temporary' import surcharges. The Americans were very suspicious about them and took every opportunity to remind the Canadians of their opposition. In a meeting with Louis Rasminsky, the U.S. treasury's Robert Roosa remarked on the surcharges, attributing 'the opposition to the Canadian import surtaxes in the US administration to concern about the passage of the US administration's trade legislation and to concern in principle that a 'leading member of GATT' had had recourse to measures of this character.'[116] Of course, as has been noted by others, 'Canadian government postwar commitment to multilateralism and non-discrimination in international trade was not absolute.'[117] As well, the Canadian Manufacturers Association continually pressed for more protection, regularly urging the government to oppose any tariff reductions on manufactured goods. It was their rather fantastical position that foreigners should have no more than 10 per cent of the Canadian market in any product![118] Indeed, Fleming was not immune to the blandishments of some protectionism, remarking in his budget speech of 20 June 1961 that he had not been 'convinced that a sweeping elimination of our tariffs in relation to any existing trade grouping can be reconciled with a healthy secondary industry or the balanced growth of the Canadian economy.'[119]

In the American analysis, Diefenbaker had gone so far as to suggest that Canada's foreign exchange problem would be solved by an increase in exports or 'by producing in Canada at competitive prices more of the commodities that we are now importing.' The prime minister's statement 'sounded like pure protectionism' to Ball, and would call for some sort of U.S. response if the Canadians went ahead. The surcharges would, Ball thought, have 'a progressively corrosive effect in Canada and on US-Canadian economic relations.'[120]

While that effect might animate American concern, Ottawa was relieved over the shift in its terms of trade brought about by the surcharges. A department of finance paper on this subject noted that 'there is little doubt that the surcharges on imports, coupled with the 92½ cent exchange rate, will result in a considerable amount of business being shifted from external suppliers to Canadian producers. The surcharges will also provide a strong incentive for Canadian buyers, both corporate and individual, to carefully explore all possible sources of supply in Canada.'[121]

The forecasts of that paper, written in late June soon after the program was implemented, were confirmed over the course of the year. The devaluation of the Canadian dollar and the effects of the import surcharges meant that imports into Canada were less that they had been at the end of the 1954–7 expansion. The surcharges no doubt exerted an important restraining influence on the volume of imports. And while the paper agreed that the surcharges were a short-term measure, the government hoped that they would result in long-term change: 'Business ... must realize the importance of improving their competitive position through better methods of operating, *the need to increase their Canadian content* ... and to investigate both domestic and export markets with vigour and imagination.'[122]

Given the success of the program, rumours circulated in Ottawa that the government would ask the GATT for a waiver to maintain the restrictions, a move that could have a very serious effect on the United States. The immediate problem for the Kennedy administration was that the Trade Agreements Act, which would authorize it to participate in what would become the Kennedy round of the GATT, was still winding its way through congressional committees and had yet to come to a vote in the Senate. While the bill was eventually approved and signed into law by the president on 11 October, the Canadian action was raising a few congressional eyebrows and there were now calls from affected American producers to do something about what looked like a deepening Canadian protectionism.

Ottawa had also irritated members of the administration with its reaction to the Trade Expansion Act, which needed international help as congressmen scrutinized it for flaws. Four members of the Kennedy cabinet met privately with six of Diefenbaker's ministers 'to make their pitch' for the measure that had been announced by the president on 11 January 1962. In the end, only a vaguely worded communiqué was forthcoming, which noted that the Canadians would 'play a constructive role in the promotion of freer world trade.' As Peter Newman points out, this approach did the Conservative government no favours. It sent the message to Washington and other capitals that Ottawa was only interested in maintaining the status quo, which largely meant leaving Commonwealth preferences intact.[123] Fleming, who attended the meeting, confirms this, but as he suggests in his memoirs, it was one of the darker moments in his career. Rather than follow his principles that favoured the U.S. program, he instead deferred to a Diefenbaker/Howard Green conspiracy, both of whom were opposed.[124] More likely, Fleming's memory was faulty when recalling the incident more than twenty-five years later. As a politician he 'possessed a limitless faculty for self-delusion ... When political circumstances changed, [the minister] would simply execute a complete turnabout in positions then vigorously defend his newly-acquired stand with exactly the same pious vigor he had previously expended on the vindication of diametrically opposed ideas.'[125]

To be fair to Diefenbaker, the *bête-noir* of the piece, the prime minister was irritated by an American investigation into Canadian softwood exports which had been brought by lumbermen from the Pacific Northwest. Washington had requested the imposition of voluntary quotas on lumber exports which had totaled some CAN$250 million in 1960. The dispute was an ongoing sore point, and given the American protectionist attitude in this case, the prime minister doubted whether the Kennedy program *could* win congressional approval, hence his scepticism when approached by the American ministers.[126] Canadian politicians could only agree, concerned as they were about the threat posed by any large-scale tariff reduction program for secondary industry.

But for the present, as events developed on the protectionist front, the crisis passed and so too did the necessity of the surcharges. The Canadians had gone out of their way to assure the International Monetary Fund (IMF) and the U.S. treasury that surcharges had been the only possible revenue measures to improve the budgetary situation, and that they would be replaced as soon as possible not by permanent tariff increases, but by longer-range tax measures. These would, or so the Canadians hoped, also 'spur the development of Canada's industry, increase competitiveness, and propel an expansion of exports.'[127] The surcharges were finally withdrawn by Ottawa on 31 March 1963.

Nevertheless, the country continued to be plagued with a formidable balance of payments problem. It consisted of a top-heavy current account deficit arising mainly from current invisible transactions like defence and aid expenditures, dividend and interest payments on U.S. investments in Canada, and Canadian payments for advisory and technical services. Indeed, the striking fact about the balance of payments problem was that it was not a merchandise trade problem but an invisibles one. In 1961, Canada had net international liabilities of CAN$18 billion made up of foreign long-term investment in the country of CAN$24 billion, reduced by CAN$6 billion of Canada's long-term investment abroad. Since 1950, the Canadian net *trade* deficit had been between 2 and 3 per cent of exports, not large numbers. If the country was to adequately address the invisibles issue, it would need to attain a stronger merchandise export balance sufficient to overcome the current invisibles deficit.

The End of John George Diefenbaker

The 2 May pegging of the (now devalued) Canadian dollar would help the balance of payments, or so theory suggested, but accomplishing that policy objective would also mean addressing a particular point of concern for Ottawa, the trade in automotive parts and cars. Of the deficit of CAN$1 billion, about one-half of it arose from the excess of imports over exports of automotive industry products. On 1 November 1963, a new Liberal government would introduce its Automobile Export Incentive Scheme, which would provide for a refund on duties paid on automobiles and parts imported into Canada to any firm that increased the export of autos and parts. That scheme, and the ensuing Auto Pact, will be discussed in chapter 2.

A number of other items stimulated officials' interest in the aftermath of the exchange crisis in the campaign to increase the country's merchandise trade surplus. Among these were the need to increase efficiency through specialization and rationalization, to examine the Combines Act to see if it needlessly prevented industry amalgamations, to examine policies and practices to ensure that Canadian industry was getting its raw materials at prices comparable to those of its competitors, and to investigate ways and means of ensuring that U.S. subsidiaries operating in Canada were given export freedom by their parents. As Glen Williams and others have pointed out, these reforms were not a part of the mandate of a branch plant and it was of little use for Ottawa to encourage and implore firms to explore export markets outside of North America. As Williams points out, the results of a 1969 survey of nearly 1,000 subsidiaries *with a declared export interest* operating in Canada were not encouraging. '58 per cent of US branch plants and 43 percent of other foreign subsidiaries were faced with import restrictions imposed by their parent companies.'[128] The government had also undertaken an export promotion drive, supervised by Gordon Churchill, which had had notable success in a number of fields. This iniative would entail increasing the number of trade fairs and sample shows, and sponsoring more trade missions.

There was also some discussion in Ottawa about making Canadian industry generally more competitive. 'Size of market and economies of scale are important factors in making certain lines of industry more competitive,' suggested one department of trade and commerce document. 'On the thesis that additional protection is not the best way to increase Canadian manufacturing efficiency, the required additional market outlets to permit volume production must be found outside Canada as well as in the domestic market.'[129] The comprehensive list of things to do to improve the country's balance of payments read like a series of imperatives. The country should be prepared to adopt whatever policy necessary at the end of the UK-EEC negotiations over the former's entry. It must participate in the Kennedy round of GATT tariff negotiations with a view to improving its access to foreign markets for manufactured goods as well as the more traditional raw materials and foodstuffs. It should play an active role in drawing up 'the rules of the game' for the next round of tariff reductions. In short, it seemed as if Canada needed help with many problems, a sentiment conveyed to Willis Armstrong by Green in mid-1962.[130] Defining those problems, however, was the issue. The Americans felt they had the answer: The biggest issue, at least from their point of view, was the question of Canada and nuclear weapons. Any forward movement on the trade file would have to depend in part on defence.

The new ambassador in Ottawa as of 11 December 1962, Walton Butterworth, was in the forefront of the move to push Washington into taking a tougher stance with Canada on the defence issue and others. A former Rhodes scholar, he was an abrasive, egotistical, hot-tempered, intelligent, 'pompous ass,' whose appointment by Kennedy seemed 'designed to infuriate' the prime minister.[131] Almost immediately, his preferred method of dealing with the Conservatives on the defence and nuclear questions was accepted in Washington: Take a tougher line with Diefenbaker, he counseled, and when he says something that is not true, call him on it. His specific issue was Canadian-American negotiations to provide nuclear weapons for Canadian forces if and when needed. Discussions had been dragging on for some months and seemed to be going nowhere, despite the Canadian acquisition of CAN\$685 million worth of defence materiel that was effective only if armed with nuclear weapons.

The prime minister put the cat among the pigeons with a statement made in the House of Commons denouncing the U.S. position. In response to a stinging attack from Pearson who said that a government led by him would accept nuclear weapons, Diefenbaker let his position be known:

Any suggestion that we have repudiated any undertaking by Canada internationally is false in substance and in fact ... Canada has cooperated and will cooperate, but she will not be a pawn nor be pushed around by other nations to do those things which ... are not in keeping with her sovereignty and her sovereign position ... We will do nothing to extend the nuclear family ... We will maintain Canadian sovereignty, regardless of the pressures, of the views, of anyone [a reference to General Lauris Norstad, NATO's retiring commander-in-chief] visiting our country or otherwise ... We never sold Canada ... My prayer is that we will be directed in this matter. I believe that the western world has been directed by God in the last few years, or there would have been no survival. I believe that will continue. My prayer is that we shall so live as to maintain not only the integrity of Canada and its high reputation for carrying out our responsibilities, but at the same time that we will be right, that the Canadian people will be able to say that, whatever decision is made, it was made with every consideration being given to all those moral and psychological things that form one's make-up. I would rather be right so that those who come after may say 'He refused to be stampeded. He refused to act on the impulse of the moment. He and his colleagues brought about a policy, in cooperation with their allies and by influence over their allies, that led to the achievement of peace.'[132]

It was, by all accounts, quite a performance and according to the Americans, full of distortion and evasion.[133] Butterworth's advice, that 'prompt action should be taken ... to clarify the record and to sweep away the confusion which Diefenbaker's statement can cause in Canadian minds,' was accepted. A state department press release soon followed that completely refuted the prime minister's version of affairs, and created a tempest which Diefenbaker found difficult to counteract. Charles Ritchie, Canada's ambassador in Washington, was recalled in protest, the only time in the history of Canadian-American relations that that has happened. Ritchie, for his part, told Diefenbaker and Green that he thought his 'absence from Washington would not be particularly shattering to the United States Government.'[134] He was permitted to return to his embassy.

The Americans were fed up with the prime minister by early 1963. Telegrams from the ambassador to state are replete with very undiplomatic language; in one of his missives Butterworth used such phrases as 'unrealistic Canadian view of external world,' 'pretentious posturing in various international arenas,' 'traditional psychopathic accusations of unwarranted US interference in domestic Canadian affairs,' and 'essentially neurotic Canadian view of world and Canadian role.' Diefenbaker was an 'undependable, unscrupulous political animal' and should be so treated. When Butterworth later thought he detected some Washington backsliding on the treatment of Canada he deplored the fact to Ball, hoping that the state department was not 'reverting to its old ways of treating Canada like a problem child for whom there was always at the ready a cheek for the turning.'[135]

While most American officials and politicians were not as hard as the ambassador, they were nevertheless relieved when the Diefenbaker Conservatives were defeated by the Liberals of Lester Pearson in the election of April 1963. Many sectors of Ottawa officialdom were happy with the result as well. For example, some at the Bank of Canada had told U.S. embassy officials while the campaign was in full swing that 'they were frankly concerned the election would have an adverse impact on the foreign exchange situation, particularly if the campaign should take on an anti-American tone.'[136] That concern became a non-issue. The Canadian ambassador in Washington heaved a sigh of relief; while he liked Green, Ritchie considered Diefenbaker's defeat 'a deliverance; there should be prayers of thanksgiving in the churches. And these sentiments do not come from a Liberal.'[137] Similar feelings infected American considerations. Kennedy cabled his congratulations to Pearson, saying that 'the establishment of close relations [is] a matter of great importance to me.'[138]

However, Pearson was to find, as had Diefenbaker, that managing the North American relationship was not always easy.[139] There were compensating factors despite the Diefenbaker-Kennedy rancor, Canada did hold a privileged place in the American constellation. Moreover, some of the greatest Canadian economic successes would come in the next half-decade, among them the Auto Pact, which helped sort out Canada's balance of payments condition while providing hundreds of thousands of new, well-paying jobs.

In the end, Diefenbaker fell not necessarily because of American pressure, but because he could not decide what he wanted to be – populist, nationalist or continentalist. As George Grant has written, populism and small town free enterprise, which the Conservative leader epitomized, 'could not come to terms with the society that had arisen since the war. Central Canada had grown into an industrialized complex. Any government to remain in office had to meet the new needs of this sector. A government set upon national revival had to do even more; it had to reverse the trend that was taking the keystone of the country and integrating it with Michigan and New York. Diefenbaker's administration did neither. He did not meet the needs of this heartland and he realized no national ends. His remarkable achievement was to alienate the support of the rulers and the ruled in both Ontario and Quebec.'[140]

Still, the Conservative government had bargained hard to ensure that the United States was well apprised of Canada's needs and that Washington not unilaterally abrogate, or subtract from, commitments made under the GATT. In areas perceived as vital to Canada's economic prosperity, Ottawa approached Washington as an equal with its own agenda, determined to win the best deal from the often-reluctant Americans. In oil, in lead and zinc, and in agricultural products, Canadians vigorously protested U.S. protectionist policy. In this regard, they were not so much different from the Pearson Liberals who followed them.

Chapter 2

The Liberals Manage the American File, 1963–1968

Given the problems and difficulties that the Americans had experienced in dealing with the Diefenbaker regime over the past several years, they most certainly welcomed the election of Lester Pearson and the Liberals as the government of Canada on 8 April 1963. Indeed, McGeorge Bundy, the special assistant to the president for national security affairs, sent a memorandum to the secretaries of state, defense, the treasury, commerce, and the interior, the attorney general, the director of the Central Intelligence Agency, the chair of the Atomic Energy Commission, and the special representative for trade negotiations, telling them that the president wanted all discussions with Canada to be coordinated under his personal direction through the department of state. As Bundy wrote, 'The advent of a new government in Canada has naturally stirred nearly all branches of the government to new hope that progress can be made in effective negotiations with this most important neighbor on all sorts of problems.'[1]

The First Meeting: Pearson and Kennedy at Hyannisport

Soon after the election, the new prime minister travelled to Hyannisport, Massachusetts, the site of the Kennedy compound, for a meeting with the American leader. This early visit fit into an evolving Canadian policy of improving relations with the United States. The idea, as Norman Robertson, the undersecretary of state for external affairs, told Canada's ambassador in Washington, Charles Ritchie, was 'to encourage the new government to approach relations with the United States in a fairly methodical manner ... The object ... is ... to put ministers in the right frame of mind about these relations.'[2]

Pearson's visit was an inspired moment for those who had craved something better in North American relations than the Diefenbaker-Kennedy conflict had provided. Ritchie recorded his impressions of that meeting in his diary, 'tinged [as it was] with euphoria ... '[3] He went on: 'The atmosphere was that of clearing skies after a storm – the clouds of suspicion covering Canada-US relations had parted, the sunshine of friendship shone ... it was mutual relief at the departure of Mr Diefenbaker from power which gave added savour to the encounter between them.' Nor was this assessment confined only to Canadians. William Tyler, the assistant secretary of state for European affairs, remembered that during the talks 'the President seemed very much at ease with Pearson. Pearson was always very articulate, very smooth, with a light touch, and the President seemed to like that and to warm to Pearson.'[4] As John English writes, 'Mike Pearson was John Kennedy's kind of person ... Much has been made of how Pearson impressed Kennedy with his baseball statistics that spring day on Cape Cod, but ... Kennedy's interest preceded his awareness that Mike knew what Walter Johnson's earned-run average was. Mike, *inter alia*, had the Nobel Prize that Kennedy coveted, was a close friend of *New York Times* columnist Scotty Reston, whose approval the administration craved, and expressed in a North American accent that British global sense he so admired.'[5] This meeting was probably the high point in the Canadian-American relationship over the next number of years as the business of governing Canada created problems with the Americans.

It was also true that the economic relationship continued to develop, despite a number of irritants. This growth contributed to the perception of the Pearson government that was to dog it while in power and for long afterward (and pushed by John Diefenbaker, now in the Opposition) that it continued the sellout of Canada to the United States that had begun under Louis St Laurent. The critics who were to set the interpretive tone in later years in support of this position, like Kari Levitt, Melville Watkins, and Abraham Rotstein, misconstrued the nature of the continental relationship. When, for example, Levitt writes critically of its 'special aspects' like the Interest Equalization Tax (IET) exemption or the Auto Pact for which, she suggests, 'there [was] a price to be paid,' she misses the point.[6] In one sense she is correct – there was a price to be paid, but it was the price that resulted from the give and take of negotiating international agreements. While Canada's behaviour was constrained by the provisions of the IET or the Auto Pact, the result was not nearly as deleterious as she implies. The case could easily be made that Canada prospered as a result. With the exemption, its economy righted itself, while the Auto Pact almost single-handedly fixed Canada's visible balance of trade deficit. As well, *American* behaviour was affected by these arrangements to the point where, for example, President Johnson was to tell Canada's ambassador in Washington, Charles Ritchie, that Canada had 'screwed' him in negotiating the latter. Policy-makers pursued the Canadian position and did not cave in to American demands whenever push came to shove. In short, the reality of these five years of Pearsonian government does not fit the popular perception, at least in the economic field. Canadians were self-possessed, confident, and sure of the rightness of their cause.

In preparing to greet the Canadians, President Kennedy himself took the lead in convening meetings to deal with potential Canada-U.S. problems. This was an important event and he 'indicated a strong need to be briefed for the Hyannisport meeting and asked into how much detail Pearson would want to go.'[7] Walton Butterworth, the U.S. ambassador in Ottawa, called to Washington for the meeting, suggested that the new prime minister 'would not be well prepared ... and would not bring up details.' The group then ran through potential issues, like defence and nuclear weapons storage in Canada. The Defence Production Sharing Agreement (DPSA) was discussed; officials informed the president that they 'wanted a better balance in the program which has been against us recently, although the Canadians would probably point out that the overall trade balance is heavily in our favor.' The assistant secretary of defense, Paul Nitze, told the president that the program would continue, but perhaps not at the level then prevailing. Similarly, the president raised issues concerning the Columbia River treaty, Canadian oil exports to the United States, the extension of the Canadian coastal zone to twelve miles, bilateral air transport relations, Canadian lumber exports to the United States, and the country's potential membership in the Organization of American States.

During the discussions, the new prime minister was frank. On trade matters, he emphasized that Canada's heavy payments imbalance with the United States of CAN$1.2 billion was crippling, a condition that could be ameliorated by American attention to some areas like permitting more of Canada's oil to be purchased in the United States. As had Diefenbaker, he noted that western Canada in particular had to develop its economy on the basis of oil exports and base metals. While the present oil agreement with the United States ran out in July 1963, the prime minister hoped that it would be renewed and would provide for an increase of Canadian exports given the country's balance of payments problems. Ottawa was particularly interested in exports to U.S. oil districts one through four, comprising most of the central and eastern sections of the country. Pearson made the obvious point that American security could be assured only if they had their supply on the same continent. He also noted that 'the United States owns over 60 percent of Canadian oil, so [it] might as well take exports from Canada.'[8]

In this area, the Canadians were up against U.S. oil producers, who were concerned about the overall level of imports. Since the inception of the U.S. National Oil Policy in February 1961, Canada's exports had increased from 113,000 barrels per day to about 250,000.[9] Canadian exporters had also been granted an overland exemption in 1959 which provided the means by which Canadian crude entered the United States free of quotas, competing only with

U.S. domestic oil rather than with cheaper offshore supplies. The overland exemption had recognized the concept that a barrel of Canadian oil was just as safe as a barrel from the United States from the point of view of national defence, on which the American Mandatory Oil Import Program had been established. U.S. producer complaints had roused the administration to amend the overland exemption category in November 1962. This decision had impaired Canadian shipments, especially worrisome given that American refiners were running short of domestic crude and wanted greater access to oil from Canada. That was where matters stood as Pearson and Kennedy met.

The prime minister again raised the issue, as had Diefenbaker, of foreign direct investment. Ottawa did not want to discourage the import of capital; those investments had been most helpful in terms of Canadian development, but the fact remained that more than one-half of Canadian industry was controlled by U.S. owners. Pearson gave the president a heads-up of sorts on what to expect from the new government: 'Canada was going to take steps which would not penalize US investments, but would encourage Canadians to buy in, so as to have a real sense of participation,'[10] a very oblique reference (the Americans would have called it opaque) to the budget that his government would bring down about one month later. That Liberal budget would cause much difficulty in the management of the North American relationship and lead the Americans to believe that they had been misled.

Further, Ottawa was also going to establish the Canada Development Corporation (CDC), essentially the creation of Walter Gordon, which was designed to provide a pool of capital for national development projects that would not pay off for some time. The CDC had a long lineage, having been first proposed in the 1950s by Gordon Ball, the president of the Bank of Montreal. He had wanted 'the creation of a corporation to invest in new Canadian ventures or existing enterprises "that cannot obtain adequate financing from other private sources."'[11] Such a corporation would, of course, alleviate some of the need to search out funding in American markets and help to ease Canada's current account deficit. Unfortunately for the minister's grand plan, the CDC remained stillborn until the mid-1970s for a variety of reasons. For the present as the two leaders sat in Adirondack chairs discussing the future, it was all harmony and happiness and it seemed as if 'the log-jam of pending issues was broken.'[12]

The 'Nationalist' Budget and Its Fallout

Cozy chats between national leaders had their limitations when it came down to developing and implementing policy as Pearson quickly discovered when his government's first budget was announced on 13 June 1963. *The Economist* called the document an example of 'astonishing inadvertence'[13] and journalist Richard Gwyn suggested that Gordon 'blew it ... the long-awaited exercise of his magical financial skills was a fiasco.'[14] Certainly the prime minister's nemesis, John Diefenbaker, had a field day savaging it, much to Pearson's dismay.[15]

The revision of the 15 per cent withholding tax on dividends paid to non-residents caused immediate difficulty. The government proposed to reduce the tax to 10 per cent on companies that were more than 25 per cent Canadian-owned, while an increased rate of 20 per cent would be applied to those outside that category. Gordon had also levied a 30 per cent take-over tax on sales of shares by Canadian residents to non-residents, and to companies controlled by non-residents in Canadian companies listed on Canadian stock exchanges. The proposed taxes were not in Canada's best financial interest, given the potential for American retaliation for what could only be interpreted by Washington as an egregiously anti-American piece of legislation. The taxes introduced the principle of discrimination based on nationality into the Canadian tax system and, or so some believed, were not in line with the spirit or substance of the recent Hyannisport conversations.[16] The prime minister had told Kennedy that he had a 'nationalist' element in his party and that some unpleasantness might result from the Liberal budget to be tabled in the next few months. A 10 May memorandum reconstructing the substance of those talks and reviewed for accuracy by Willis Armstrong, the American minister in Ottawa, and Basil Robinson, Canada's minister in Washington, had recorded what the prime minister had said. The Kennedy administration believed that the Canadian action went far beyond 'unpleasantness,' and let the Canadians know what they thought.

The Americans believed that they had been misled by Pearson and said so to A.F.W. Plumptre, the assistant deputy minister of finance, who had been sent to Washington in mid-June to make the rounds and inform American and International Monetary Fund (IMF) officials of the budget's contents and likely impact.[17] Commentary by U.S. officials was not sympathetic. McGeorge Bundy asked if the burden of Canadianization would not be too great for Canada's financial system to bear. What would be its effects on the balance of payments? Griffith Johnson, the assistant secretary of state for economic affairs, was more pointed, did those discriminatory taxes 'contravene Canada's international obligations?' He also 'regretted' the example such a discriminatory budget set for underdeveloped countries and warned that it might cause difficulties for Canadians raising capital in New York. That remark, according to Plumptre, 'seemed to imply some veiled threat of official intervention.' But as the Americans were to point out later, making it more difficult for Canadians to access U.S. money for investment via the markets in New York would surely help to push forward the Canadianization policy. As well, Johnson expressed 'doubts and questions' regarding the practicability of the 30 per cent tax on takeovers.[18] While it was designed to begin the process of 'repatriating' the Canadian economy from its largely American owners, the tax was so far removed from what was possible that it was withdrawn a mere six days later.

What drove the Americans to distraction was the budget's retroactivity. Butterworth articulated administration sentiment when he noted in a telegram to Rusk that 'Gordon apparently fails to see the difference between changing the ground rules for *new* investment and the discriminatory measures contained in his budget which removed national treatment from foreign firms which established in Canada on the basis of national treatment. Indeed, he does not view his budget as discriminatory.'[19] Gordon and the ambassador intensely disliked each other; the minister later told Peter Stursberg that Butterworth 'never should have been allowed out of the United States.'[20]

Ottawa's problems didn't end with Washington; Canadian institutions also reacted poorly. Eric Kierans, then the chief executive officer of the Montreal Stock Exchange and later a Liberal cabinet minister, launched a bitter attack on the budget, claiming that 'Gordon seemed to have no comprehension whatsoever of the impact this was bound to have on stock exchange values.'[21] It should be noted that Kierans later recanted, going so far as to dedicate his Massey Lectures 'To Walter Gordon who foresaw most of this long before the rest of us.' However, in 1963 he reportedly told his associates to sell Canadian stocks, which led to a steep decline in both the MSE and its Toronto counterpart. It did indeed seem as if, according to the first line of the 'highly intemperate' letter Kierans gave to Gordon, that 'The financial capitals of the world [had] had just about enough from Canada.'[22]

Louis Rasminsky, the influential governor of the Bank of Canada, also expressed his opposition, although more quietly.[23] He regretted the imposition of the withholding tax and the 30 per cent take-over tax and believed that the economic expansion then underway was likely to continue into the next years, following Canada's devaluation of its dollar to 92.5 cents U.S. and an increase in business investment. In the interests of lowering unemployment, he thought it necessary to avoid any action that would bring expansion to a premature end, or create unsettled economic conditions. The budget could only be interpreted as taking a hostile view toward foreign investment and it could result in a massive liquidation of non-resident-owned securities in Canada, precipitating a new exchange crisis. The country's balance of payments was in no shape to support large capital withdrawals, given Canada's current account deficit of between CAN$600 to CAN$800 million per year. It was very difficult to believe, or so Rasminsky thought, that Canada would be allowed to continue to borrow in New York, further destabilizing the country's currency. Finally, about one-third of new private business investment in Canada was made by foreign companies, a share that could easily decline with adverse effects on growth and employment.

Rasminsky had legitimate concerns about the budget's impact on the Canadian economy, especially with Canada's exposed economic position and its dependence on international investors, primarily American, to make up its current account deficit. He rightly believed that the country had limited freedom of action to pursue policies that potentially alienated the United States. If Ottawa wanted to take such initiatives, it had to put its own economic house in order; to do otherwise was to make it too vulnerable, a reality brought out starkly by the IET of July 1963. Improving the country's economic health, however, required difficult decisions which a Liberal minority government, intent upon winning a majority the next time around, could not easily contemplate.

The taxes were withdrawn on 19 June, yet there were still some repercussions. Basil Robinson was sent to call on the state department, this time alone, where he indicated to officials that he was 'speaking on instructions from people close to the centre of the current [budget] crisis in Ottawa, including the Prime Minister.'[24] Robinson pointed out that first, there was a cabinet crisis over how the problems presented by the document could be handled and second, unfounded as events transpired, that there was a very precarious parliamentary situation facing the government that could result in it being overthrown.

He suggested too that if U.S. officials made any formal representations to the government on the budget resolutions, it would make it very difficult, if not impossible, for the Liberals to contemplate further changes because of the state of Canada-U.S. relations and the heightened state of Canadian nationalist feeling. The leader of the opposition, John Diefenbaker, had already asked the government whether the Americans had made any budget enquiries, and if so, had these been made on the grounds that certain budget measures were discriminatory or anti-American. Robinson asked that the United States remain silent – how the administration felt about the budget 'was already well understood within the Cabinet, where there [was] support for the United States' views on these questions. The Prime Minister asked Mr. Robinson to say that he hoped people in the US Government would realize that the points in the Budget about which the US would be concerned are already being made forcefully both outside and inside the Government.'

The Americans followed the Canadian advice and waited a week before letting their views be known. Robinson thanked them 'for [their] understanding ... in not making immediate formal representations in view of the unusual circumstances prevailing in Ottawa.'[25] Meeting with a U.S. team led by Griffith Johnson, an implacable critic of the budget, Robinson and Maurice Schwarzmann, the economic minister at the Canadian embassy, heard the American complaints. While among themselves U.S. officials believed that Canadians needed 'a psycholanalyst's couch' when contemplating financial questions; with Robinson and Schwarzmann they used slightly more diplomatic language.[26] In short, the Americans had been very surprised at the discriminatory features of the budget. While Pearson had suggested at Hyannisport that consideration was being given to some measures regarding investment, the Americans had not been under the impression that any measures were being contemplated that would affect U.S. investment so directly. Indeed, Butterworth later told Bundy that 'what Pearson said [at Hyannisport] and what Gordon did were not consistent.'[27]

In particular, Johnson expressed his concern over the Liberal's apparent disregard for the principle of national treatment. American status was 'highly important to us and we presumed that Canada would think it also important, particularly in the context of United States-Canadian relations. However, features of the Budget clearly discriminate against the United States.' There was also the question of the practical effect of those discriminatory features. What, for example, would be their effect on U.S. companies in Canada wanting to sell a 25 per cent stake to Canadians, but not finding any buyers? Would it then be fair to penalize the firm? Johnson also noted the magnitude of Canadian purchases that would be required over a relatively short period of time, equity capital amounting to perhaps US$2 billion. Where would that money come from, given that Canada was perennially short of exchange? Of course, what the Canadians wanted was to discriminate in favour of investment by debt capital from the United States; Canadians would borrow on the New York market for investment in Canada, as opposed to the investment of equity capital by U.S. investors. And that, Johnson told Robinson, 'would have an adverse effect on our balance of payments.' He also noted that there was already some concern over the use of the New York market by Ottawa and the provinces and by private business.[28] For example, in early 1963 Canadians had been very large borrowers in New York. This trend had been capped by a US$300 million loan to Quebec to finance a portion of the US$800 million cost of nationalizing the province's electric power companies. The Americans thought the loan was too onerous, and had asked the Canadian government to do what it could to slow down the rate of Canadian borrowing. However, as the secretary of the treasury, Douglas Dillon, wrote to Kennedy, 'Though Canadian issues constituted a large part of the total foreign flotations ... it should be noted that the significance of such borrowing by Canada is different from that of other countries in several respects. In the first place, a large volume of such Canadian issues has long been a normal and traditional element in our capital market and in our balance of payments. Secondly, in the Canadian case, this flow of US portfolio investment has in the past served, in effect, to finance large US exports to Canada. Finally, even when the dollar proceeds of such borrowing move into Canadian official reserves, these dollars are not likely to become a claim on our gold as would be the case in many other countries.'[29] The imprecise perception of many important Americans was that much of the net drain on the U.S. balance of payments went to Canada. Washington was reluctant to interfere with the capital market, but it was one of the areas that had to be watched and if Canada made things worse, then the issue would become more important for the administration and for Congress. Johnson found it 'extremely unfortunate, particularly as a matter of principle, to erect new barriers between Canada and the United States in an area where none [had] previously been extant ...' We are very unhappy about the proposals in the Budget and we would hope that in the course of their detailed debate, the Canadian Government will take into account the points we have made in considering the question of approval. While we recognize Canadian anxiety over foreign investment, we hope there will be full recognition of the advantages to Canada of such investment and the consideration of other, less objectionable, ways of accomplishing the general goal.' At least Robinson could not claim the Americans were unclear in their critique of the budget. His boss agreed, 'The Americans,' Ritchie noted in his diary, 'are intensely irritated by our new Budget.'[30]

What could the Canadians say in response? Nothing was likely to easily soothe American outrage. To claim, as Schwarzmann did, that the budget was a domestic policy judgment in an attempt to encourage partnership was clearly not enough. Nor was it enough to point out that no political party in Canada could ignore the political difficulties associated with foreign investment because of its ubiquity, and the rise of Canadian nationalism. Clearly the United States had taken aim at what it considered to be the worst aspects of the budget and wanted action taken to minimize their effect on investment.

The Pearson government survived a vote a confidence in early July which left the Americans with the problem of how they should continue to respond. On 8 July the department of state registered an oral protest with the Canadian embassy to keep the matter open, but was uncertain as to how to proceed from there. The United States had already achieved some success with the withdrawal of the takeover tax and the proposal requiring 25 per cent Canadian ownership was eventually modified to require 25 per cent ownership by persons other than the parent company as a basis for exemption. Ultimately, that revised budget was passed by parliament on 14 November 1963.

The IET and the Canadian Reaction

For the present, the Americans turned their attention to addressing their own serious balance of payments problem, forecast to total US$6 billion during

1963–4.[31] The principal causes of the deficit had been the net outflow of private capital of around US$4 billion during the early 1960s (which was to reach a staggering US$6.4 billion in 1964) and government program spending, which had offset a substantial surplus on current account of US$6.7 billion in 1964, and US$5 billion for 1965. These deficits had led to a net decrease in U.S. gold stocks of approximately US$650 million per year between 1950 and 1964, and a further US$1.6 billion in 1965.

In early 1963 the Americans had circulated memoranda to suggest solutions to the problem, and the cabinet committee had considered options in April. Dillon, for example, had urged cabinet to consider reductions in military expenditures abroad, especially in Europe, of about US$350 million in 1963–4 at no real cost to military preparedness. These cuts could easily be sold to the Europeans 'in view of the fact that Europeans generally believe that our military effort overseas is carried on in a highly luxurious fashion.'[32] As well, aid, agricultural programs, export promotion, and tourism were proposed as possible avenues of either saving money or encouraging foreigners to help balance the U.S. deficit.

Another part of the attack on the deficit was formulated slowly over the weeks following this critical cabinet meeting and the submission of the treasury plan. It entailed implementing the IET designed to increase the cost of foreign borrowing in U.S. markets and thereby slow the outflow of both equity and portfolio investment, despite the fact that the United States was then the world's largest creditor nation with net international assets of more than US$40 billion.[33] The country was also running an annual current account surplus to 1963 of between US$2 and US$3 billion, after factoring in large and extraordinary payments for international assistance of all kinds. Despite its current account surplus, however, the United States had been experiencing deficits in its overall balance of payments. Its large foreign loans and investments had been exceeding the surplus earned on current account transactions. This had resulted in losses of gold and increases in short-term liabilities. The IET's effect on Canada was immediate; as Louis Rasminsky recalled when the IET was introduced, 'all hell had broken loose on the Canadian market.'[34]

The extreme reaction resulted from the fact that Canada was, in all likelihood, the world's largest debtor, with net international liabilities of about CAN$20 billion, most originating in the United States. Indeed, in bilateral transactions with the United States, Canada's current account deficit exceeded $1 billion per year, which was met partly by raising capital in the United States, partly from paying Americans the net proceeds from Canada's overseas transactions, and partly from the country's newly mined gold. Stock prices plunged as Ottawa fiddled, and it was left to the governor of the Bank of Canada to set things right. The Americans could be forgiven for proposing the IET; as Livingston Merchant later stated,

'Canada's interests [i.e. the Canadianization budget] had been taken into account [by Washington] and ... the Canadians shouldn't object to this since it merely served to implement announced Canadian policy.'[35] The American plan would help Ottawa to staunch the flow of equity and portfolio investment pouring into the country, against which Walter Gordon had set his budget's sights.

That was not the kind of help Canada wanted, and the government turned its attention to securing an exemption from the IET. First, the department of external affairs sent ambassador Charles Ritchie to the state department to register Canadian horror. The fallout had scattered debris over a wide area – he told Secretary Dillon on 19 July that as a result of the tax, 'Canadian markets [had] plunge[d].'[36] Ottawa also pointed out that Canada was not part of the U.S. balance of payments problem as it had contributed more than CAN$6 billion net to U.S. coffers from 1952 to 1962; over that decade, Canada's current account deficits with the United States totaled CAN$14.2 billion, of which only about $8.5 billion had been covered by borrowing in the United States. American officials were certainly aware that Canada was a source of support to the United States in this area, and that if the country did not have access to U.S. capital, then it would have to reduce its current account deficit with the United States and the latter's balance of payments would not be improved at all. Indeed, in April Dillon had told the U.S. cabinet that 'Long term borrowings by Canada in our market have averaged some $350 million a year for many years. These borrowings are closely related to Canada's balance of payments deficit with the US ... Any action on our part to shut off Canadian access to our capital markets would force Canada to undertake reprisals against our trade. Two other points are important. First, Canada has always been a willing holder of dollars, and increases in Canadian reserves do not lead to gold sales. And second, the recent large volume of Canadian sales of bonds in New York include two large, unusual and one time issues totaling $550 million. There is no reason to expect the rate of the past six months to be continued.'[37]

The Liberals had their own political agenda in mind in arguing for an exemption. They were concerned about charges being made by the Conservatives 'together with the conclusions being drawn by some of the public and press in Canada that the measures were retaliation for the recent Canadian budget measures.' The Americans weakly denied the charge. The undersecretary of the treasury, Robert Roosa, had also held a press conference to dismiss that interpretation. The purpose of the IET was simple: 'to slow down utilization of the U.S. money markets but not to stop such use.' However, as the Canadians had raised the retaliation flag Roosa made sure to point out that the United States 'had shown much restraint in reacting to the Canadian budget measures ... In addition, United States assistance to the Canadian Government during the 1962 balance of payments crisis was mentioned.'

Ultimately, the Canadians received a partial exemption from the IET, which allowed the stock markets to stabilize, and the economy to right itself. The exemption decision came directly from the president. Dillon, in Washington negotiating with the Canadian delegation over the possibility of an exemption, had telephoned Kennedy at Hyannisport. James Reed, the assistant secretary of the treasury, was present when the call came. As he remembered, 'It was interesting to see his reaction. He was entirely familiar with the bill. He was entirely familiar with what the prospects were going to be to our balance of payments if this bill was passed. He was entirely familiar with our relationship with Canada – how it was ... He had confidence in Secretary Dillon, so when the Secretary put the question to him, he said, "Mr. Secretary ... if you think that's what is best under all the circumstances, that's alright with me."'[38]

In return, the Canadians promised to keep their reserves to within a range prescribed by the negotiations between the two countries. This provision was to raise issues between Washington and Ottawa in the near future, but for the present, the partial exemption helped to stabilize Canada's markets. The budget and the IET were both object (or abject) lessons to Ottawa. However much it might want to 'repatriate' ownership of the economy, it had to set its own house in order before it could do so. Rasminsky put it down in black and white for the prime minister: 'If we are to be free of the risk of recurrent and unpredictable shocks in the conduct of our economic affairs originating from the varying fortunes and attitudes of the United States, we must eliminate the remaining deficit in our current account balance of payments and our remaining dependence on net imports of capital from abroad. The first goal of our economic policy should be to become self-supporting internationally, for it is only by so doing that we shall be able to achieve a reasonable degree of independence.'[39]

The U.S. tax was also the main subject of conversation during the eighth meeting of the joint U.S.-Canada committee on trade and economic affairs, held on 20–1 September, where the Canadians again made their case against it as well as for a full exemption. Walter Gordon had taken the same approach six weeks earlier during a visit to Washington where he met with George Ball. Ball had been very disturbed by evidence of Canadian nationalism, and had pointed out that the United States had exercised restraint in not publicly protesting the Gordon budget. 'That sort of thing,' he told the finance minister, 'can lead to friction and difficulty between two countries.'[40] It was not a propitious moment to ask for a full exemption of the IET; however, Gordon, the minister who was so worried about U.S. influence in Canada, did so. The exemption was not granted, but the general tone of the discussions led Ball to remark that 'Canada-US bilateral relations, far from being the most easy in the world, were in fact amongst the most difficult; each "made life difficult" for the other.' The partial exemption remained.

The exemption issue had been a difficult one for the Pearson Liberals, and a number of lessons had been learned. Some months later the prime minister went out of his way to cultivate Butterworth. During the course of a luncheon to discuss North American problems, the ambassador asked about Walter Gordon's recent statement in the House of Commons that the budget tax provisions with respect to foreign-owned Canadian subsidiaries was only the first step in a long road of mitigating the effects the American investment. Pearson was at pains to point out that the minister of finance had also said that the situation was under review and that, 'speaking in strict confidence, PM said, in his determination, emphasis should be placed on statement that situation under review.'[41] The prime minister also added that Gordon had begun work on the 1964 budget, 'and he would have to take into account the views of other members of cabinet or else he would have to go. He volunteered that not a mistake but a blunder had been committed; that caught up as he was in slipstream of "sixty days of decision" he had neglected to give consideration to implications of budget.' Butterworth noted that he had discussed this topic at considerable length on a number of occasions in the past with the prime minister and that this was the first time that he had spoken in such categoric terms. That might have been so, but it was also historical revision of the worst kind – Pearson was minimizing his role in the debacle.

However, Gordon had learned a salutary political lesson. With his 1964 budget under construction, he travelled to Washington to get the sense of the thinking there. He was not going to be blindsided as he had been the previous year. Butterworth told both Rusk and Dillon the importance of this meeting would be 'hard to overestimate.'[42] The Americans saw it as an opportunity to modify the 1963 budget and to 'revise draft 1964 budget.' They could only believe that the latter would be as noxious to them as had been the former, despite what Pearson had said, and they agreed with the ambassador's characterization of Gordon: 'Although he is an attractive person with considerable worldly experience, Gordon approaches the subject of reducing US ownership and control of Canadian industry and resources with an inflexible crusading spirit. He feels certain that he was right in enacting discriminatory tax legislation against foreign investment ... He has continued to take this position in spite of growing criticism of discriminatory tax measure and accumulating evidence that such measures are neither urgent nor essential.'

The Americans did, however, have two aces that could be played against the finance minister. First, Gordon was very anxious that Washington renegotiate its double taxation treaty so that its withholding tax on Canadian investments in the United States would not rise automatically to 30 per cent when Canada's increased to 20 from 15, effective 1 January 1965. The Canadian law legislating the rise had been passed by parliament on 5 December 1963. Apparently, one of Gordon's senior officials had told Butterworth that the United States 'could finish [Gordon] off' by stalling on that. However, it might not want to do that; although the state department was anxious to protect American investment in Canada from what it perceived to be the discrimination inherent in the recent changes in Canadian tax law, 'State [was] reluctant to have the US Government blamed for Gordon's ouster.'[43] The Americans were also hopeful that Canadians would do that all by themselves; Gordon had received a large volume of mail from businessmen expressing their concern over the possibility of an increase in the U.S. withholding tax.

The second ace, discussed more fully below, related to the use of the countervail against a scheme designed to increase the export of Canadian automobile parts and cars. It was Butterworth's considered opinion, with which Rusk and Dillon agreed, that 'We should not hesitate to make known to the Canadians that the present very benevolent attitude of USG in this particular area could change if discriminatory treatment of US investors is not significantly modified.'[44]

For the present, what could the U.S. government do, now that the budget debate had run its course? Butterworth counseled that U.S. corporations with plants in Canada should involve themselves in the next round of budget discussions. 'While [Gordon's] mind appears closed on the subject of US investment,' he wrote, 'it could nonetheless be constructive for US business and financial interests with present or potential holdings in Canada to take this opportunity to present their case to Gordon and more important to other cabinet members.'[45] It was vital for American interests to stress their relevance for Canadian economic development. They could also 'tactfully' note the problems for potential investors faced with the inconsistency between provincial governments encouraging U.S. direct investment and the federal government's action in discouraging it. The problem for the federal government was that the provinces were the major borrowers in New York, something over which Ottawa had little influence.

Rasminsky was succinct in assessing the federal-provincial issue: 'The broad political situation in Canada was such that [restricting provincial borrowing in the United States] was [an] impossible position for the federal government to be put in.'[46] Examples of this muddled message were everywhere. Quebec, in the midst of its Quiet Revolution, was nationalizing those sectors of its economy that it thought important, like hydro generation and distribution. As a result, Jacques Parizeau, then the province's deputy minister of finance, met with Robert Bryce, the federal deputy minister of finance, to inform him of the importance to Quebec of having reliable access to the New York market subject only to that market's own judgment on the provincial credit and how much it was prepared to lend.[47]

As the state of the Canadian federation became more tangled, so too did relations with the United States. It was safe to assume, as Charles Ritchie did, that by August, 'the Hyannisport honeymoon [was] already over.'[48]

By late 1964 the Americans were in an agitated state over the upward trend of Canada's reserves, which they thought had been fixed with the IET negotiations. As well, Canadian governments and corporations were borrowing heavily in the New York market, well beyond the roughly US$350 million per year rate that Americans had thought reasonable. In 1964, the figure was approaching US$800 million, which was horrifying to Washington. Dillon and Rasminsky met to discuss it in December 1964 and the conversation was unsatisfactory, at least from the latter's point of view. When told by the treasury secretary that Congress was involved and that it was 'capable of irrational action,' Rasminsky reminded Dillon 'that Congress was not the only body that was capable of irrational action, and if they did act irrationally as regards Canadian access to the US capital market it was inevitable that this would provoke reactions in Canada which would be injurious to US as well as Canadian interests.'[49] And he meant that. Given his approach and the determination of the government, it was not the case, as Kari Levitt has written, 'that the Canadian government voluntarily negotiated away the vestiges of its control over monetary policy.'[50] However, the fact remained that Canada was running a substantial deficit on current account of roughly CAN$500 million in 1964, CAN$1.5 billion in 1965, and about CAN$1 billion a year later. Those were very large numbers that government and Bank of Canada policy would have to take into consideration.

The Merchant-Heeney Report

Where did all this acrimony and bitterness take the two countries? Not to any place they wanted to go, and the Americans, it appeared, were more concerned about the disquieting noise of the relationship than were the Canadians. As early as July 1963, the state department had approached Canada's embassy in Washington with a view to 'concluding a bilateral agreement that would take account of the special trade and investment relations' between the two countries.[51] By September, George Ball, the undersecretary of state, had prepared a paper on the subject and regarded it as 'a personal initiative.' The assistant secretary, Griffith Johnson, told embassy officials that he thought 'discussion on this topic would provide an opportunity to devise a philosophical framework which might make it possible to deal with specific issues in Cdn USA relations in a somewhat different manner from that which applies to relations with other countries.' The North Americans had a 'unique relationship' which created 'special opportunities as well as special problems and seemed to warrant mutual understanding as to the principles which should underlie [Canada-US] relations.'[52] By January 1964, the prime minister and the president had appointed A.D.P. Heeney and Livingston Merchant respectively, to conduct a formal study of the relationship between the two countries.

The Canadians thrashed out their strategy during a meeting on 12 February. It included some discussion of the notion that 'a more onerous obligation on the United States to consult Canada than vice versa would follow logically from a true recognition of the relative influence of each country on the other but [this] would be difficult to express in terms acceptable to the United States.'[53] In the final analysis, however, the interdepartmental committee which considered the Canadian side concluded that any report would not be worth much – principles may well turn out to be a search for improved consultative procedures instead. Nor did some Ottawa mandarins take it too seriously. Louis Rasminsky, for example, needed several proddings from Heeney before he submitted his brief, which related to the IET and the Canadian budget. For a busy official, this exercise rated far down the list of priorities.

When the report was published as *Canada and the United States: Principles for Partnership* in June 1965, it was met with a hail of criticism, although the department of external affairs thought it a very sensible document.[54] Its central premise, that differences 'should be expressed and if possible resolved in private through diplomatic channels,' was denigrated. That did not suit the Canada of the mid-1960s, which was becoming more nationalistic and anti-American as the decade passed. As John English has pointed out, even 'Charles Lynch, no radical, said the report was a bureaucrat's dream: "Keep it quiet boys, work it out, we will all keep out of trouble and things will go smoothly."'[55] That sort of relationship, as much as External might want it, clearly belonged to a bygone era.

FDI Again

The Merchant-Heeney report did not add measurably to the discourse in North American relations. In February 1965, with the U.S. balance of payments problems seemingly spiraling out of control with the growing foreign exchange costs of U.S. military expenditures arising out of Vietnam and large-scale U.S. corporate investment in the EEC, Dillon wrote to Johnson that Canada had also become a 'special problem for the United States balance of payments position.'[56] On 10 February, just before the president was to announce his voluntary guidelines for the patriation of more profits on the part of U.S. multinationals, his treasury secretary told him that 1964 sales of new Canadian issues in the U.S. market exempt from the IET had totaled US$687 million. The Americans wanted some assurance that this number would not get larger. They also warned Ottawa that the exemption could be withdrawn if it did.

The Johnson guidelines extended the IET to 31 December 1967, reduced the duty free exemption of U.S. tourists returning home, and increased incentives for foreigners to invest in American corporate securities. The most interesting part of the program, however, was to publish guidelines, advice, and suggestions to encourage U.S. investors and companies to voluntarily reduce foreign lending and investment. For American firms operating abroad, the president hoped that they would respond with:

1   Repatriation of capital sent abroad on a short-term basis and the reduction or postponement of direct investment where it [would] not result in early expansion of exports or investment income;
2   Acceleration of the repatriation of income earned in developed countries and the use of foreign capital markets for the raising of equity capital required for expansion abroad.[57]

Several months later, John Connor, the secretary of commerce, delivered a speech that focused on the U.S. balance of payments program and the Canadian economy. He observed that exports to Canada should be expanded as much as possible and that companies should accelerate repatriation of income earned in Canada. As well, he thought that U.S. companies should offer some of their shares for sale to Canadians, in that way assisting the balance of payments through sharing ownership with citizens of the host country. The first two points caused much consternation in Canada.

Further measures were announced by Washington on 6 December 1965. Their significance for Canada lay in the fact that non-bank financial institutions were asked to limit the increase in their holdings of long-term foreign investments to a ceiling of 105 per cent of the amount held in September 1965. That measure could have had serious adverse effects for Canada, but it obtained an exemption from that particular guideline on the same grounds as the IET. In return, Gordon had told Henry Fowler, the secretary of the treasury after 1 April 1965, that Canada would maintain fluctuations in the level of the country's foreign exchange reserves that was a little lower than the mid-1963 figure of about CAN$2.6 billion. The minister also indicated that Canada would be prepared to buy outstanding Canadian securities held in the United States to offset any excess inflow of U.S. capital.

As well, the ceiling guidelines for non-financial corporations were extended from 500 to 900 companies, and included subsidiaries in Canada as well as other countries. Fowler described the basic strategy of the program: It called 'for each chief executive to maximize his company's contribution to the balance of payments through measures such as export expansion, repatriation of income from abroad, repatriation of short-term financial assets, and the maximum use of funds obtained abroad for investment purposes.'[58] In addition, industry was given a separate target for direct investment abroad, to limit it in 1965–6 to 90 per cent of the amount during the three-year period following 1962.

A Canadian analysis of the program noted that it was not unusual for a national government to call upon the trading community to expand exports, but this particular approach contained certain twists. Of most importance to Canada was its exploitation of 'the large element of control which individual American companies hold over Canadian industry for purposes which could be detrimental to individual Canadian business and the Canadian economy.'[59] The paper went on to point out that

> In being asked to submit individual reports on the extent of the overall contribution to the national balance of payments position, American parents might see in this request an implicit obligation to show a positive contribution ... Some of these companies might find that the easiest way, or perhaps the only way, to make a contribution to the national objective would be through expanding production or service operations of the parent at the expense of foreign subsidiaries ... Some indication of Canada's vulnerability to this type of influence is given by the fact that Canadian affiliates of the United States companies account for 46 percent of all Canadian purchases from the United States, most of this being bought directly from parent companies.

Kari Levitt, writing in *Silent Surrender*, could not have put this any better.[60] Nor could she have offered any better solution than the one proposed by the paper – it encouraged the government to resist American policy by whatever means possible, and that included seeking an exemption.

The fact that the United States emphasized export expansion and rejected the notion of import restraint was not as helpful to Canada as might have been expected. Within the context of international company trade, exports from Canada to the United States consisted largely of raw materials in which the latter was deficient and which Washington would not want to limit. However, the fact that imports were to be reported meant that individual companies would be subject to persuasion in the event of any substantial increase considered by American authorities to be contrary to the national interest. Conversely, imports from the United States within the sphere of international companies consisted largely of American-made manufactured goods and parts, the expansion of which could well detract in a major way from the economic development of Canadian secondary industry. The ultimate effect, of course, was unknowable, which also caused Ottawa some concern – investment demanded stability and predictability.

The issue was raised at the Canada-U.S. ministerial meeting in early March 1966, where the Canadians let their worries be known. Martin and Sharp reported to cabinet that the discussions had been very helpful. Rusk had emphasized to the Canadians that U.S. subsidiaries 'were to act as good citizens of Canada.'[61] Ministers had asked that Canada be given an exemption from the guidelines, or that there be a clarification by the United States to the effect that branch plants were not expected to act in ways detrimental to the interests of the host country. The Americans had agreed, and Fowler had gone on to note that the 1966 program had been intended to prevent subsidiaries from acting *abnormally*. The U.S. government was quite willing to issue a statement that branch plants 'were perfectly free to conduct their affairs in a normal manner.' That was almost more than the Canadians could have hoped for.

The campaign for access to U.S. money markets as well as equity investment continued. Clearly, it was recognized that large capital imports had added substantially to the levels of investment in the country and had enabled the economy to grow at a high rate while simultaneously allowing Canadians to maintain a high level of consumption. However, that fight was under increasing scrutiny later in the decade. Walter Gordon's 1963 budget had attempted to repatriate some control of the Canadian economy from its largely American owners, but his obstinacy and the U.S. reaction had obscured that point. With foreign control and ownership of Canadian industry approaching 35 per cent, it was also time to apprise American secretaries of its distorting effects on economic development. The prime minister did let Canadians know, although not in the hard-hitting way that Gordon would have appreciated. On 1 February 1967, he appeared CBC television, noting that: 'It is our objective that Canadians should own and control as much of our industry as is possible; should have the maximum possible control of the resources and economic development of our country, through maximum Canadian investment in Canada. We will achieve this objective, however, not by action which is unfair to foreign interests, but by positive action which will marshall and encourage Canadian capital to invest increasingly in Canadian enterprises. In this way we will be able to reduce our dependence on foreign capital in the years ahead.'[62]

And so it went. The partial exemption was maintained into the mid-1970s and while it did continue to cause difficulties between the two over that period, Canadian access to U.S. capital was not restricted. As the IET rolled across the political and financial landscape, another scheme was taking shape in Canada which would also cause quite serious difficulties between the two neighbours.

The Evolution of the Auto Pact

During the autumn of 1963, the United States was confronted with the Canadian announcement of a new policy designed to ease the country's balance of payments problems, the automobile export incentive scheme, introduced by the government on 25 October 1963 and implemented on 1 November. The scheme was a logical progression for Canadian policy and followed upon two connected issues. The first was the 1961 *Report* of the Royal Commission on the Automotive Industry, conducted by the University of Toronto's dean of arts, Vincent Bladen. The Bladen commission had focused on the change in the Canadian auto industry during the late 1950s. In 1955, Canadians had bought 22,000 British and foreign cars; by 1959 the number had reached 114,000. By the beginning of the next decade, about 32 per cent of total car sales in Canada consisted of compact models from Europe. This increase paralleled a rather startling decrease in domestic passenger car production in Canadian plants, down about 20 per cent between 1955 and 1959, from 375,000 units to 300,000. Employment in the industry had also dropped, from 67,000 to 56,000.[63]

These statistics were certainly worrisome for a government beginning to look toward the next election in the critical southern Ontario region where most auto jobs were held, but there were other affected sectors. The automobile industry was the country's leading manufacturing sector and the second largest manufacturing employer. Approximately 60 per cent of the total production of Canadian rubber firms, which employed 20,000 people, went into cars. As well, the output of Canada's mines, iron and steel, glass, and chemical plants all contributed to car manufacturing. In short, it was in the eyes of government a very special industry.[64]

Faced with this situation, the United Auto Workers had lobbied Diefenbaker on 5 July 1960, who had then responded with Bladen. As an interim measure while it awaited the Royal Commission report, the government announced a change in the valuation on imported cars for duty purposes which would add between CAN$100 and CAN$300 to each vehicle sold in Canada. Bladen 'recommended various inducements that might produce a more extended integration of the North American car industry' and thereby increase employment in the Canadian industry.[65] While the recommendations of the report largely gathered dust, there was some movement in this area. The Conservatives had introduced a program in 1962 that covered automatic transmissions and a stated number of stripped engines. It provided for a refund on duties paid on automobiles and parts imported into Canada by any firm that by itself or through independent parts manufacturers increased the export of cars and parts. One dollar of exported Canadian content would earn the remission of duties on one dollar of dutiable imports. The objective was to increase Canada's share in the production and trade of automobiles, particularly vis-à-vis the United States. In so doing, it would help to ameliorate Canada's current account deficit with its southern neighbour which was running at CAN$1.116 billion in 1962 and CAN$1.158 billon the following year. Autos accounted for about CAN$500 million of that amount. The Kennedy administration had opposed the Canadian program, but it had not worked to stop it. For finance minister Gordon, reducing the deficit was an absolute necessity if the U.S. capital inflow that caused him so many headaches was to be made smaller. It was also quietly questioned, but not opposed, by the United States; Griffith Johnson later told A.F.W. Plumptre that it broke 'all accepted commercial practices.'[66]

The Canadians had also raised the current account deficit issue at the IMF and the Organization for Economic Cooperation and Development (OECD). Following their normal procedures, papers on Canada had been prepared and discussed during early 1964. Both the IMF and the OECD had accepted the validity of Ottawa's position, namely that 'A point of major emphasis in Canadian economic policy is elimination of the deficit on current international account. The expectation of Canadian officials for 1964 ... is that this deficit will show a further decline but that there will not be much, if any, improvement apart from the effects of the special wheat sales.' Plumptre, the assistant deputy minister of finance attending the meetings, told ministers that 'In reviewing my notes I find that the Executive Directors representing Germany, the Netherlands, the United States and the United Kingdom, all give explicit approval to this particular Canadian objective.'

In the auto sector, the numbers were simply appalling for the finance minister; by 1963, Canada was exporting only 16,000 vehicles, down from 52,000 a decade previous. That situation did not seem likely to improve on its own and members of cabinet knew the figures well. Canada made up 9 per cent of the total U.S./Canada population during the 1960–4 period, yet accounted for the production of less than 7 per cent of North American consumption of passenger cars, less than 7.5 per cent of the consumption of trucks and buses, and less than 6.5 per cent of the use of original equipment motor vehicle parts made in Canada or the United States.

The incentive scheme was also designed to improve the efficiency of a major Canadian industry that had to export in order to achieve lower costs. That objective had not been possible to date because of restrictive corporate decisions made by parent firms in the United States. The major problem in this regard was Canada's limited domestic market that allowed Canadian producers only short production runs resulting in higher costs than those of volume producers in other countries. Nor had Canadian auto manufacturers been able to adopt the latest technological advances in production techniques, a problem made worse by the multiplicity of models demanded by consumers. These shortcomings adversely affected the competitive position of the Canadian automotive industry in both home and export markets. The Canadian measures were designed in large part to overcome these institutional barriers to trade in order to help the vehicle and parts industries to compete more effectively in both markets through the economies of specialization and longer production runs. The government was clear – the industry's competitive position had to be improved through access to wider markets. That could only happen if 'barriers to trade and procurement [were] relaxed so that Canadian vehicle and parts makers [had] access to world markets and automotive manufacturers in other countries [were] willing to go beyond their domestic sources of supply.'[68] The measure would not involve the payment of a subsidy. Rather, the plan called for conditional free entry of vehicles and those parts on which there would otherwise be a duty.

Improved efficiency in the Canadian automotive industry would displace vehicles imported from countries other than the United States and the net result would be a larger market in Canada for auto parts from the United States. A Canadian document demonstrated that this trend had been discernable in 1963, when American manufacturers had exported an additional US$113 million of parts to Canada for a total of US$545 million.[69] The measures announced also did not take a bilateral approach. 'There were already firm indications,' or so the government believed, 'that a sizable portion of the exports resulting from the plan will go to third countries.' Much of this new trade was in finished cars, which created additional demand in Canada for U.S. production parts.

The scheme was discussed in both governments, and President Kennedy took a personal interest. Indeed, in October he had that instructed all reports and negotiations with Canada were to flow to him through William Brubeck, the White House staff officer for Canadian affairs. A memorandum from McGeorge Bundy had emphasized this point, noting that 'All aspects of Canadian-American relations are of intense interest and concern to the President ... The President desires that the White House be fully informed of all significant negotiations or plans for negotiation with the Government of Canada.'[70]

Washington was not entirely unhappy with the announcement of the incentives in late October, but it faced some legislative hurdles that could result in legislation that would penalize the Canadians. A senior American delegation met with Canadians to draw their attention to a U.S. law dating back to 1897, updated in the Tariff Act of 1930, which provided for the mandatory imposition of countervailing duties on imports that enjoyed a grant or bounty from the government of the exporting country. In mid-November, the treasury noted that it had received complaints about the Canadian plan that requested the imposition of countervailing duties, and it was now investigating whether it constituted a grant or bounty within the meaning of U.S. law. There was every indication that if Ottawa did not satisfy U.S. concerns, the aggrieved parties would take their case to the U.S. judicial system where their case would be upheld, or so Secretary of State Dean Rusk believed. He telegraphed George Ball, then in London, noting that if the scheme unfolded as state thought it would, then 'USG faced with possibility of having to impose duties whether this desirable or not as matter of policy.'[71]

Despite Rusk's conviction, that was not entirely the case. From the White House, Bundy confirmed an understanding that he thought had been reached, namely that when initially discussing their responses to the Canadian action, the Americans should not 'take the line that the law leaves us no choice whatever, but will rather indicate that several manufacturers have asked the Treasury to impose countervailing duties and that the first reports of the lawyers indicate that the problem may be a very sticky one.'[72] It seemed to him important that American negotiators on the file maintain as much freedom of action as they could.

The delegation from Canada, which included Simon Reisman from finance and B.G. Barrow from industry, was told by Rusk that the United States was 'sympathetic' to Canada's stated objectives of freer trade and the rationalization of production. However, the United States faced a real problem when Ottawa took measures to achieve these objectives that reduced actual or potential business for U.S. manufacturers. As a result, Ottawa faced a real political problem from determined U.S. businessmen pushing for executive action. Reisman suggested that the Americans had it all wrong, that the scheme was really a method of defending a liberal trade philosophy. He also pointed out that the U.S. countervailing duty legislation from 1955 had not been applied in any instance to date, despite the fact that it was broadly worded. The secretary of state suggested that the treasury had simply not received any requests for action from U.S. industry. The case was different with the Canadian scheme; it had already resulted in several demands that something be done, demands that 'could be expected to increase' over time, especially if incentive were extended to other sectors of industry, such as office machines.[73] Rusk did emphasize that the administration wanted to avoid action 'which would cause difficulties in our relations, but reiterated that the matter was not entirely in [its] hands.'

Butterworth in Ottawa was not nearly as generous as Rusk had been. He met with Pearson for lunch and asked if the prime minister had been briefed on the delegation's talks. He had not and the ambassador's subsequent briefing must not have pleased Pearson. Butterworth denounced Reisman's 'liberal trade philosophy' remark and urged the prime minister not to go ahead with the program. Instead, the Canadians should focus on their economic upturn and an unemployment rate less than the Americans. In addition Canadian wheat sales 'had removed any justification for hasty emergency measures.'[74] The conversation went on:

> It is interesting and I think significant that Pearson at one point in our conversation asked me why we had not reacted when the Diefenbaker government applied this scheme to transmissions. I said I thought that this was a significant illustration of one aspect of how Canadian-American relations are conducted and should not be conducted; that if the Canadian action regarding transmissions had been taken by a friendly European country, we would have immediately reacted adversely, but since we were instinctively predisposed to treat Canada in a very special category, we did not. By the same token Canada, having taken an inch and not having been called, then was prepared to take a mile ... As I interpret the situation, the present trend of Canadian policy cannot be checked unless we cease temporizing with their undesirable actions. If we had applied countervailing duties when they adopted the tariff remission subsidy scheme for automatic transmissions and motors in 1962, we would not be faced with the current problems.

The first part of Butterworth's accusation might have been true; that Canadians grabbed the mile definitely was. In this first meeting following the policy's announcement, the Canadians rejected the idea that Washington must respond to American businessmens' concerns. Indeed, they pushed that point – 'discretion of interpretation [was] possible,' and the administration need not observe the law as they had indicated. As well, the delegation categorically rejected any suggestion that Ottawa would attempt to expand the scheme to other sectors. Barrow emphasized that any press comment on business machines was 'entirely unfounded,' and that while the government wanted to help strengthen all parts of Canada's economy, it would do so using other methods. Rusk instructed his ambassador in Ottawa to check on the accuracy of this intention with Pearson in a later meeting that was scheduled between the two; such a confirmation 'would be most helpful in allaying concern created by [press] reports.' He also told Butterworth that the Canadians believed it was unthinkable that the United States would apply countervailing duties in this case.[75]

Pearson confirmed the Canadian position but that did little to soothe American concerns. In a memorandum to the president that referred to the Pearson conversation, William Brubeck noted that Butterworth thought 'the Canadian assurances largely irrelevant, since he believes the Canadians will ... simply seek other means to the same end of redressing their trade balances with the US.'[76] At bottom, Kennedy was sympathetic to Canada's aspirations in this case, but it would fall to another to see the dispute through. Kennedy was assassinated in

Dallas on 22 November, and Lyndon Johnson became the thirty-sixth president of the United States. Prime Minister Pearson lost a kind of soulmate that day; as John Kenneth Galbraith has commented, 'Pearson and Kennedy – now they were compatible, were very much alike.'[77] Pearson and Johnson, it appears, were not. Canada's ambassador to the United States, Charles Ritchie, noted in his diaries that 'The adventure is over, "brightness falls from the air", that probing mind, that restlessness of spirit, are snapped off as if by a camera shutter. We shall no more see that style of his, varying from gay to grim and then to eloquent, but always with a cutting edge. Now for the anticlimax – to L.B. Johnson. We have come from the hills to the plains.'[78] Clearly, the Canadians did not think much of the new president's abilities.

The change of president in midstream might necessitate a re-evaluation of Canadian policy and approach, or so some thought as Pearson travelled south to attend Kennedy's funeral on 25 November, and also to meet with Johnson. A good sign from the prime minister's point of view was that almost the first words out of the president's mouth were 'that he wished to maintain close and harmonious relations with Canada.'[79] That remark could only be reassuring to a Canadian prime minister dealing with a new president from Texas, although as John English points out in his biography of Pearson, the prime minister and the president 'never found the easy familiarity that Kennedy and Pearson had.'[80] For his part, Pearson suggested that some problems remained to be addressed and launched into a recitation of them; indeed, his approach was quite extraordinary, made more so when he told Johnson that 'there were more bilateral problems than was generally supposed. Likewise ... Canadian sensitivities were not always understood.' It was important to make sure the new president comprehended the nature and the extent of the relationship. Pearson ended by noting that the United States could count on Canada's support 'on the big issues.'

The meeting also gave the Americans an opportunity to step back and reassess their connections with Ottawa.[81] In December, Dean Rusk briefed Johnson on the state of North American affairs, and he was rather pessimistic when it came to Canada: 'Our relations,' he began, 'have grown increasingly sticky.'[82] Rusk thought that Canada had manoeuvred itself into 'an impossible dilemma.' The country's economic prosperity depended upon the continual inflow of U.S. capital, which brought in its wake U.S. control of certain sectors of the Canadian economy. Regardless of the political party in power, every government felt compelled to try to reduce the economic control that accompanied reliance on U.S. capital. While the Pearson government was, 'in spirit, friendly to us and, in principle, much more sympathetic [than Diefenbaker] with US objectives ... it, too, has felt compelled to take a series of measures that have kept our relations on the edge of tension.' With that rather terse comment, the consideration of the automobile incentive scheme would continue to wind its way through the bureaucracies on both sides of the border.

The Auto Pact Plot Deepens

Pearson and Johnson met for the second time on 21 and 22 January 1964, a gathering that little stirred the interest of the White House, at least according to Canada's ambassador in Washington; it was 'treated as of marginal importance.'[83] The prime minister did spend more than an hour with Johnson, a part of it walking in the White House garden and exchanging views on various topics. Earlier, the Americans had discussed the intransigence of the Canadian automotive position and had suggested that Johnson obtain Pearson's agreement to strike 'an intergovernmental committee to explore continental rationalization of the auto industry.'[84] While an agreement would not be possible at these discussions, it would come up again later in the year. For the present, the president referred several times to Studebaker's decision to transfer their plant to Canada, a subject that was obviously of concern to him. There were lost American jobs to think about, but also a possible flood of cheap cars from Canada.[85]

Pearson vigorously denied that the Studebaker move had anything to do with the rebate scheme, 'but from the fact that, in view of the particular administrative circumstances of the firm, operation was more economical in Canada.'[86] Paul Martin, the secretary of state for external affairs, emphasized to a high-level American delegation that the move 'gave them some opportunity to stay in business' in view of their crippling financial difficulties.[87] The Americans remained skeptical, and Ball noted that he was having difficulty dissuading American firms from taking court action to force the application of countervailing duties. An easier way around this issue had already been raised – would the Canadians be interested, Ball asked, 'in establishing a joint group to examine the auto industry on a continental basis, to see what might be done of a broad and general nature.' In the meantime, the White House intended to advise the Big Three that it expected them to 'go slowly in taking advantage of the Canadian scheme because of the possibility that countervailing duties may have to be imposed.'[88]

When Prime Minister Pearson joined the Martin meeting following his own with Johnson, Ball put the same question to him. The Canadian response was the same. The rebate scheme had already been announced and that was the policy. Ball, however, wanted to make two points to the prime minister: First, that Congress was 'getting disturbed' which would lead to speeches and excitement, and second, that some firm might apply for the application of countervailing duties 'and this might release a chain of events that we cannot control.' While the Canadians insisted that there was no subsidy involved in the Studebaker decision, there was a real possibility that U.S. courts would find the opposite. That was where the matter stood as the meeting adjourned.

In a rather patronizing report that followed the meeting to cabinet, Paul Martin talked of the differences between Kennedy and the new president:

> The approach of President Johnson was very different from that of President Kennedy. He did not seem to like to discuss problems at length or in great detail. While he was undoubtedly an astute politician, he appeared to be paying little attention to the responsibility of government and matters of state. For example, the President had, the previous day, received some fourteen different delegations which had nothing to do with current government business. This was a luxury which a President of the United States could ill afford. However, the President had only acceded to his new position recently; this was an election year, and his attitude might become a more reassuring one in the longer term.[89]

Pearson and Martin obviously had some profound reservations about Johnson's leadership, and he, clearly 'was not Mike's [and Martin's] idea of what a president should be.'[90]

The automobile scheme was up for consideration later in the year at the joint U.S.-Canada committee on trade and economic affairs where ministers from each side met to discuss problems and issues. The Canadians were aware that the U.S. administration was coming under increased pressure from independent parts manufacturers with respect to the Canadian plan, and that in early April an official application had been made to the U.S. commissioner of customs for the use of countervailing duties against the import of Canadian-made radiators. The investigation had begun partly as a result of the perception among certain 'US domestic industries ... that Treasury is not pursuing dumping duties with sufficient vigor ... it should be noted that there is now considerable support for a number of bills to amend the antidumping law in a manner which would make it more protectionist.'[91] Opposition to the scheme was increasing in the departments of commerce and state, and Luther Hodges, the secretary of commerce, was undertaking new initiatives to have the measures set aside. At the April meeting it was understood that Hodges would ask that the Canadian scheme be abandoned and that Ball's earlier recommendation of a joint study of the rational integration of the North American automobile industry, what would become the Auto Pact, be instituted in its stead.

As Ball had predicted, Congress was beginning to turn its attention to the provisions of the program, and it was not pleased. Senator Vance Hartke of Indiana had recently written to Johnson, linking the Canadian plan to the layoff of 700 employees by the parts manufacturer Borg-Warner. The Canadians had denied

TABLE 2.1
Exports to and Imports from the United States of Automotive Equipment
(CAN$millions)

	Export to US		Import from US		
	Exported amount	Change from previous year	Imported amount	Change from previous year	Balance
1961	9	–	325	–	316
1962	10	1	432	107	422
1963	32	22	545	113	513

Source: LAC, DFR, vol. 3943, file 8522-U-585 (64), Joint United States–Canadian Committee on Trade and Economic Affairs, Trade Policies and Problems, April 1964.

this, suggesting that the layoff was the result of a number of factors resulting from a decline of production on the part of U.S. users of Borg-Warner transmissions and an increase in competition by other manufacturers. Hartke remained unconvinced. The Canadian rebuttal ran to three pages, including table 2.1, which suggested the U.S. manufacturers were actually increasing their share of the Canadian market.

Another problem concerned the Whittaker Cable Corporation of North Kansas, Missouri. That company had written to the president and its letter was tabled in the congressional record by the senior senator from Missouri, Stewart Symington. This corporation was in competition with the Essex Wire company, an American firm which had a subsidiary in Canada manufacturing wiring harness. Whittaker claimed that it was having difficulty in competing with the Canadian subsidiary on low volume wiring harness because of lower Canadian material and labour costs. For good measure, the Missouri company also asserted that Studebaker's move to Canada was most certainly the result of the new automotive program.

The Canadian response suggested that the best defence was a good offence. The paper outlining Ottawa's position noted that 'the ... measures are of far too fundamental importance to consider either being set aside or frustrated by United States Government action. They are an important cornerstone of the Government's policy to strengthen and make Canadian manufacturing industries more efficient and competitive.'[92] If the program was frustrated by Washington, such action would have 'the most serious implications for Canadian – United States relations.' As well, Ottawa could point out that the program had the support of the Big Three manufacturers, Chrysler, Ford, and General Motors. The Canadians were leery of entering into a joint discussion of the possibilities of integrating the North American automobile industry, but would have little option if it was put on the table.[93] Their caution lay in the fact that should this course be pursued, it would result in an extremely close economic relationship between an important sector in Canada and its U.S. counterpart.

In their attack against American economic arguments why the scheme should be repealed, the Canadians carried the day. However, they found no answer to the legal arguments the United States put forward regarding the necessity of initiating action under its countervailing duty procedures. As Douglas Dillon, the author of the summary memorandum to the president, wrote, 'They showed no give whatsoever on the substance and originally refused to even consider joint working level talks looking to a possible solution. However, when they realized that a public [countervailing] proceeding would soon begin in the US, they agreed privately that joint technical studies should be undertaken immediately by a working party. Publicly they maintained their position of no give.'[94] The Canadians had manned their guns and dug in for a long battle.

As Dillon had emphasized, Ottawa only agreed to a joint working party because of the implicit threat to the industry posed by the countervail procedure. In fact, the government largely dismissed countervails. The finance minister held that Canadians 'weren't interested in having no tariffs; all they were interested in was business for Canada.'[95] However, another minister, Charles Drury, 'said Gordon was not the majority of the Canadian Government; that when they go into this they really need to try to do something.' Dillon thought that the key person on this file was Drury, not Gordon, and that he was 'a top fellow, sensible and really trying to do what he can to work it out.' Naturally Gordon's rather stark remark about jobs brought Dillon's rejoinder that that was indeed 'the key to the whole business.'

Despite the potential for conflict over auto policy, the next joint U.S.-Canada committee on trade and economic affairs meeting, held in May 1964, went well. The American side was moved to record in their final report for the president, written by Dillon, that it 'was characterized by a far greater spirit of cooperation and understanding than had characterized our first meeting with the present Canadian Government in September [1963].'[96] Dillon also noted that both publicly and privately, the Canadians made a big point of improved relations with the United States. The secretary thought that interesting; 'While the present government retains the traditional Canadian sensitivity on matters of national pride, they now apparently consider it good politics in Canada to play up their success in improving relations with the US.'

A U.S. Countervail

Ottawa would need some American goodwill in the near future as the countervail process in the United States moved ahead. Dillon had determined that an investigation was warranted on the basis of a complaint filed on 15 April by the Modine Manufacturing Company of Racine, Wisconsin, a producer of automobile radiators. The petitioner charged that the Canadian export incentive scheme constituted a bounty or grant on the export of car parts to the United States and requested that a countervailing duty of 22 per cent be levied. Philip Trezise had then told colleagues that 'unless the [Canadian] scheme could be modified in some way ... it would cause headaches and heartaches in the United States and lead to a very disagreeable situation for Canada.'[97] The treasury had then published, on 3 June, a notice of investigation of the suspected bounty or grant, giving an opportunity to both sides to present their views on the questions involved. By 3 August fifty-five submissions had been received, with thirty-four in favour of the imposition of countervailing duties and twenty-one opposed. Ironically, the most oppositional submissions came from the Big Three American automobile manufacturers, who strongly supported the Canadian automotive incentives plan. As G. d'Andelot Belin wrote to Rusk, 'The American manufacturers, whose subsidiaries for all practical purposes are the Canadian automobile manufacturers, feel the Canadian scheme's duty rebate will be to their economic advantage and fear that if the scheme is frustrated the Canadian Government will take other measures ... which will be expensive and objectionable to them.'[98]

The administration was now playing hardball. Their actions brought a flurry of telephone calls from Ottawa to Washington as Martin and Gordon sought out their U.S. counterparts. Both were upset with the contents of a press release issued by state about the case; as Ball recorded, the two ministers had thought that the treasury would propose the application of a countervailing duty only on products, in this case car radiators, made by the Modine Manufacturing Company and not demand the much broader hearing that had been decided upon and which had been pointed out in the release. The Canadians wanted the press release pulled, an impossibility given that it had gone to congress and that all senators had copies. Ball 'didn't see that much could be done about it.'[99] Martin was not finished, however. The release 'would create quite a sensation' in Ottawa, and would be 'a bombshell;' as well, 'it could not come at a worse time, not only for them personally but because of other situations i.e. the debate this coming week on Columbia.'[100] Gordon asked Ball if he could telephone the Big Three car companies 'and reassure them a bit because they are the ones that really count and they are all in favor of the program; what they don't want is Chrysler or General Motors stopping what the are doing pending a decision by the Bureau of

Customs.' The press statement was eventually fixed to the satisfaction of Canadians, although Gordon later complained to Dillon that the Big Three were slow-timing their response, awaiting the countervail ruling.

The Canadians were deadly serious about the possibility of countervail and they reminded the Americans periodically about that fact. As a memorandum prepared for Rusk pointed out, 'Several of the Ministers [among them Martin and Gordon] have taken the occasion more than once to point out forcefully that the Pearson Government attaches the greatest importance to this plan, that it is heavily committed politically to its success, and that it could not withdraw the scheme without the most serious results.'[101] One result could well be the defeat of the Liberal government, or so it had been suggested. For the Americans, there was another sobering possibility to contemplate, quite apart from 'a violent [Canadian] reaction'; given Pearson's 'damaged' standing, the countervail would 'help Diefenbaker.'[102] The whole case was complicated by the fact that the Canadians had not really believed that the United States would impose the duty.

What might Canada do? Gordon told Dillon that he had initiated a study in late May to determine the feasibility of producing a car made entirely in Canada that could be sold competitively. Such a move would necessitate the overhaul of the whole Canadian auto industry, a step he did not like to contemplate, but which might be necessary. Or, he observed to the secretary, he could impose his own countervailing duty on U.S. manufactured cotton goods 'on the ground that the US was subsidizing the raw material for its cotton manufacturers.'[103] While Canadian law permitted him to do this, 'he was extremely reluctant to initiate this sort of action ... he realized that Canada was a small country and would undoubtedly be the one to get hurt most if this kind of retaliation started. Gordon stated that it would also be a sad way to start the Kennedy Round [of the GATT],' a not unimportant consideration. Dillon agreed and had an issue of his own to deal with: the United States did not want U.S. parts manufacturers to lose their lucrative US$800 million parts market in Canada. Therefore, he was prepared to seek alternative solutions to the problem.

Given U.S. intransigence, Ottawa decided in June, following a report submitted by an ad hoc committee of officials chaired by Simon Reisman, to enter into the negotiations that the United States had been pressing for, designed to lead to a continental North American automobile market. Even Gordon, a strong economic nationalist who opposed continentalism in principle, ultimately supported the new approach.[104] Mitchell Sharp remarked in response that '[we] were surprised that [Gordon], who would have opposed integration of industry in this way, actually proposed it. It was worked out by his officials with American officials and proposed by him.'[105]

Negotiations were fitful for months as the two sides pondered their next moves. American officials travelled to Ottawa on 6 July and again on 17 August in the hopes of moving ahead. Momentum, such as it was, had stopped by then when the Canadians had demanded a commitment from the United States that would assure them a specific (and increased) percentage of the North American market. At that point such a commitment was not possible, and the discussions were at such a complete impasse that Luther Hodges wrote to Rusk indicating his belief that there was no reasonable grounds to hope for an equitable solution. For the Americans, negotiations had stalled because the Canadians had demanded too many guarantees that they could not give. As James Keeley has pointed out, 'The American negotiators found the Canadian position "too concrete to be saleable" and observed that [the] more definitive the Canadian aims had become, the more difficult it had become to accept them.' For their part, the Canadians remarked 'that "the Americans were not in the same league" and made some pointed observations about the choices facing Canada.'[106] One Canadian position was that the defeat of the automobile arrangement would seriously prejudice the Kennedy round on which the United States had pinned its hopes for further trade liberalization.

Ambassador Butterworth, for once sensitive to Canadian issues, counselled against breaking off negotiations: 'I do not think Canadian proposal should be rejected out of hand. Canadians may or may not need such guarantees, but they do have special problem. There are some institutional factors – even if less serious than Canadians profess to believe – which could work against expansion of automotive industry in Canada.'[107] The day was saved by Butterworth's intervention, and by a letter sent to President Johnson by Henry Ford, outlining his views on the situation, helped along in part by conversations with Canadian officials.[108] Ford noted:

> We must recognize that the Canadian Government has the right to try to alleviate its serious accounts deficit, which over the past ten years averaged $1 billion annually ... Other governments faced with this same problem have frequently resorted to mandatory requirements increasing the percentage of local components which must be utilized in automobiles sold in those countries ... it is important to keep in mind that the United States is now exporting about $500 million more automotive parts to Canada each year than we are importing. It is my considered judgment that the imposition of countervailing duties would not only fail to alleviate economic hardship in this country, but could seriously undermine America's hope for achieving success at the forthcoming GATT negotiations.

The letter, and the fact that Ottawa was prepared to try one more time to reach a successful conclusion, propelled the talks forward.

In the meantime, an affirmative decision was handed down in the Modine case. Punitive duties against Canadian exports merely awaited Douglas Dillon's concurrence before being implemented, and he believed that by law he was obligated to impose a countervail no later than 1 October, to take effect on 1 November. He was only held in check by other concerned cabinet members and officials and by the debate that raged within the administration, which included the president himself. As events transpired, the Americans would wait until after the November 1964 elections to announce the decision to avoid any appearance that it was motivated by electoral considerations. Dillon would, however, have to implement the countervail by 1 January 1965 or, as he told McGeorge Bundy, 'face jail.'[109] In that case, 'all hell [would] break out,' so it was best expedient to find a solution.[110]

In the final analysis, the administration was little interested in applying countervailing duties, as a memorandum prepared for the president noting the advantages and disadvantages of reaching agreement with the Canadians on a continent-wide program suggested: 'If we are required to put on countervailing duties, the result certainly will be to cause the Canadians to retaliate. We could easily find ourselves in a major trade fracas, which would have the most serious consequences for our commercial and political relations with Canada,' given that the auto parts scheme was a key policy of Pearson's government.[111] Ball agreed; unless an agreement were reached, 'we will be hit by something harmful to the economic interests of this country ... A free trade arrangement between the US and Canada in this area would be important over the political "long-pull." This could be a break-through toward free trade between the two ... It would be a major element in our relations with Canada.'[112] There was some sense that the Americans 'owed' Canada following Pearson's use of Canadian troops to separate two NATO allies, Greece and Turkey, in Cyprus in 1964. As John Holmes perceptively noted, 'A highly political animal like L.B. Johnson was ready to offer help on the auto pact when Canada had been helpful over Cyprus.'[113]

On the other hand, the advantages of the pact more than compensated for any plant closures in the United States contemplated under the new scheme. The countervailing duty case would be dropped, and 'it would allow our industry, which operates on both sides of the border, to rationalize production on a continental basis.' As well, it would increase the Canadian market for U.S. cars and it would be 'a major step toward closer commercial ties with Canada after several years during which we have had a considerable amount of bickering and ill-feeling on both sides.' Finally, it had the enthusiastic support of Chrysler and Ford and the grudging concurrence of General Motors. It was decided that the administration would do its best to secure approval. A memorandum suggested how the president might accomplish that. It would be necessary to begin a foray into the congressional realm of trade policy and he should speak with the chairman of the ways and means committee, Wilbur Mills, as well as other key House and Senate leaders to encourage them to pass the necessary legislation. In particular, the White House had to obtain Mills' agreement to push the necessary implementing legislation as the president did not have the authority to reduce U.S. tariffs to zero on goods from a particular country. The congressman agreed.

By mid-November, a memo for the president explained that 'common sense [had] now prevailed' and a possible bargain was shaping up. It entailed that

- both Canada and the United States would eliminate tariffs on automobiles and most automobile parts originating in the other country.
- the Canadian Government would make a side deal with the major automobile producers who operate on both sides of the border; the producers would commit themselves to increase somewhat the fraction of their output originating in Canada. The shift is to take place over four years and would be made easy by the rising market for automobiles both here and there; it should cause us very little trouble.[114]

The Agreement was contrary to neither countries' obligations under the GATT. During November, the Americans also asked for and received a waiver under article XXV section 5 of the GATT of its Most Favoured Nation (MFN) obligations. The Canadians, on the other hand, did not need to; their part of the agreement entailed the extension of free entry on an MFN basis to motor vehicles and original equipment parts from all sources by or on behalf of a qualified Canadian manufacturer. The Canadian provisions were therefore fully consistent with the GATT.[115]

The Canadians considered the situation during a cabinet meeting on 21 December. Despite their initial misgivings about entering into this kind of comprehensive, continental agreement, comments were now very positive. They estimated that by 1968, Canadian firms' production should increase by one-third. Gordon spoke of its 'very great importance ... [and how] the achievement of this new program would represent a major success in economic and commercial policy.'[116] Mitchell Sharp, the minister of trade and commerce and the ideological opposite of Gordon, fully supported his colleague's intervention, as did Charles Drury, the minister of industry. Indeed, Sharp wondered why Congress would approve the agreement given that it seemed so heavily weighted in Canada's favour, with its side agreements that guaranteed a certain minimum percentage of Canadian production. He raised this in cabinet, noting that there was 'not full reciprocity from the United States point of view, i.e., the United States would grant unlimited free entry whereas Canada granted entry only to vehicle manufacturers as defined.'[117] Obviously, the political and strategic implications of no agreement, which was the alternative, were too costly for the United States to contemplate. Cabinet also agreed to rescind the current tariff rebate scheme in return for solid guarantees that would commit the United States to go to Congress for the necessary legislation during the winter.

All the ducks were lined up on the American side. Francis Bator, the deputy special assistant for national security affairs, told the president that the Big Three and American Motors were on side as were Walter Reuther and the United Auto Workers; the plan included an adjustment assistance deal to address the needs of any workers made redundant by the Auto Pact. The government was in line, except for the Tariff Commission, but its concerns were minimized. Similarly, opposition from U.S. parts manufacturers, especially the smaller ones, could be ignored. Indeed, when the Automotive Service Industry Association filed suit against the secretary of the treasury on 12 January 1965 asking that a writ be issued to compel the secretary to levy the countervailing duties requested, the administration could not have been less interested or intimidated. Moreover, the president was motivated to tackle approval with Congress, and as Canadian officials knew, 'Mr. Johnson has a well-deserved reputation for being quite an effective arm-twisting persuader.'[118] 'Taken as a whole,' Bator observed, 'this package is a reasonable solution to a very tough problem.'[119]

The agreement was signed by the president and the prime minister on 16 January 1965, and was brought into effect by Canada on 18 January. Ottawa amended the order in council to provide that duty remissions would not be paid as a result of any exportation after 17 January. The treasury then terminated its investigation on 18 January, and the District Court action filed by the Automotive Service Industry Association was dismissed on 18 May. The approval process was slightly slower in the United States, even though a Canadian document noted how 'pleased' the government was 'that the President and Congress gave this legislation such a high priority.'[120] It was finally approved in October and made retroactive to 18 January.

The Canadians were delighted with the agreement, believing that they had out-negotiated the Americans, despite their initial reluctance over integrating Canada's automobile industry with that of the United States. As Pearson remembered (perhaps with a touch of justification) he did not think that 'the trade agreement ran counter to our anxiety about increasing American control of Canadian economic development, because we gained considerably in an economic sense. The automobile agreement did not in any way exacerbate the problem of US intervention in our industrial affairs. This was an industry that was already 99 percent American-controlled; there was no Canadian-owned automobile industry. The Auto Pact's real economic advantage to Canada was confirmed from the first by the way in which the Senate of the United States reacted to it. They wanted to scrap it or have it amended.'[121]

As they celebrated its first birthday, a briefing memorandum for consideration by ministers noted that the Auto Pact was 'one of the most important and imaginative arrangements ever made between our two countries.'[122] The manufacture of cars required constant technological upgrading, many thousands of workers, and large volumes of industrial materials and services, all of which would be beneficial for Canadian development. In short, the 'growth and efficiency of the motor vehicle and automotive parts industries have a very great influence on the economies of both countries.'

Problems remained to be dealt with, and the Canadians knew that addressing them would be 'a hard, slow process,' but there were opportunities as well. It would be 'unrealistic to expect that they could all be overcome in so short a period of time.' However, some were more pressing than others, and Roderick Markley, a Ford vice-president, brought one of these to the attention of Joseph Barr, the undersecretary of the treasury. Given the required annual review of the agreement, Markley thought that there would be 'a strong push by the production executives in the automobile companies to exceed the minimum requirements spelled out in the agreement. In other words, there [would] be a strong temptation to move more plants and jobs to Canada than is absolutely necessary to meet the minimum terms established.'[123] Markley thought it a good idea for Dillon and John Connor to speak to the car manufacturers to keep them on side and to urge 'that they implement the agreement with great discretion,' given Congressional suspicion.

The scenario as outlined by Markley was precisely how the agreement unfolded. The early indications of exports and imports between the two countries suggested that while the import of cars and parts into Canada had gone up by CAN$148 million between the model years 1964 and 1965 to CAN$952.2 million in 1965, Canadian exports had also risen, to CAN$265 million. Ottawa hoped that the increases were the beginning of a trend. As it transpired, they were.

The following year, an assessment by government suggested that those early problems with the pact still remained. Transitional safeguards for Canadian industry had been a part of the agreement, as had been a clause stating that a review of resulting developments must be held not later than 1 January 1968. That clause had been necessary to secure Congressional approval, as certain members had expressed fears that the agreement might damage U.S. automotive producers. As a result, Congress had insisted that a review be made after an initial period of operation. A report was submitted to the president in March 1967, which pointed out that the results were encouraging. In 1965 and 1966 there were record levels of production in both countries, and a very significant expansion of trade. The report, prepared by the committee on finance of the U.S. Senate and favourable in tone, noted that automotive-related employment had increased by 128,000 jobs between 1964 and 1966, and that the U.S. export surplus in automotive trade with Canada had expanded to US$692 million in 1965.

Canada was prospering, too, despite some Canadian concerns. By centennial year, autos and parts formed the largest single item in North American trade. During the two years following 1964, U.S. exports in the sector, the bulk of which went to Canada, had risen from US$660 million to US$1.3 billion. Canada's exports, mainly to the United States, had soared from US$75 million to US$900 million. Other numbers were equally encouraging. Canadian vehicle production was up by 35 per cent and employment by 27 per cent.[124] So successful had the agreement become from Canada's point of view that in late 1966, and despite the initial review of developments by the Senate, President Johnson told Canada's ambassador in Washington that 'You screwed us on the Autopact.' The Bank of Canada's 1969 *Annual Report* reflects a similar sentiment. 'The trade balance with the United States, which had strengthened by about $800 million in 1968, improved by a further $140 million in 1969. The change in 1969 was more than accounted for by a reduction in Canada's trade deficit on automotive products.'[125] That same sentiment was expressed in the *Ninth Annual Report of the President to the Congress on the Operation of the Automotive Products Trade Act of 1965*, submitted to the Senate finance committee in January 1976. It was manifest, the report noted, 'that the only true concessions granted in the agreement are those granted by the Government of the United States according duty free treatment to imports of automotive products manufactured in Canada.'[126] The agreement contained no substantive concessions, or so the report pointed out, on the part of Ottawa except those subject to the commitments and obligations to the government of Canada in the letters of undertaking.

In part, 'screwing' the Americans contributed to a worsening U.S. balance of payments situation. Against a background of global upheaval in currency relationships caused by the November 1967 British devaluation and the huge capital movements that it precipitated, the U.S. dollar came under attack by speculators. An adverse balance of payments for the fourth quarter of 1967 was sure to be announced, and could result in a wave of speculation that would shake confidence in the world's monetary system. A preventive strike was necessary, or so the U.S. administration thought, to deal with this situation. On 1 January 1968, it announced yet another balance of payments program designed to help redress a deficit of US$3.4 billion. It came as 'a severe jolt to Canada,' given the country's dependence on the U.S. market for both exports and finance.

The situation was made worse by Washington's consideration of an import tax that would apply to about CAN$2 billion worth of Canada's exports. A Canadian document noted that 'Apart from the obvious implications for our balance of payments, new barriers on our export trade are bound to have serious effects in terms of the production, investment and marketing plans of Canadian industry, particularly at a time when many producers were gearing up to take advantage of Kennedy Round opportunities.'[127] A hasty instruction from cabinet to officials resulted in a letter on 22 January that deplored unilateral U.S. action, despite the country's very significant economic problems. Pearson told Johnson that it would be preferable to submit the U.S. program for international consideration and 'that some re-examination of the international rules would be timely and would avoid the danger of misunderstanding leading to competitive action ... I believe that in this way we can avoid a cumulative process of action and counter-action whose consequences would be very damaging not only to the gains achieved through the Kennedy Round, but also to the whole system of international trade and payments created under United States leadership since the war.'[128] A trade war at this juncture was not what was needed.

The Americans came through with an exemption for Canada in this case as they had with every other program implemented during the 1960s, although not before the country experienced yet another exchange crisis. On 5 March, the secretary of the treasury granted Canada a complete exemption from the provisions of the 1 January program, and the situation was saved. The Americans could adopt such a policy with respect to Canada because 'most capital flows to Canada come back to us in one form or another.'[129]

As Johnson had suggested in his remark to Ritchie, the Auto Pact seemed to work quite effectively in favour of Canada's balance of payments, and against that of the United States. While American producers had a surplus in the automotive related current annual balance of payments with Canada from 1965 to 1967 of US$485.6 million on average, from 1968 until 1973 the balance was to be in deficit by an annual average of US$294 million. Of some concern to Ottawa was a new administration as of 20 January 1969 and its renewed fight against a growing balance of payments deficit. The new president, Richard Nixon, and his officials made public statements about the sharp decline in 1968 of the U.S. trade surplus with Canada. Specific reference was made to Canadian performance under the Auto Pact as a major contributing factor. The Americans were correct; in that year the United States had an overall trade deficit with Canada for the first time in the twentieth century.[130] On 12 and 13 November 1969, Bud Drury had met with U.S. officials over the Auto Pact, and the Americans held to the position that 'the time had now come to move to a rather freer trade position than had been the case up to the present.'[131] They wanted some movement on the agreement's safeguard provisions, which the Canadians would not give. Ottawa was happy that car and truck production had increased by more than 18 per cent between 1968 and 1969, from about 1.1 million vehicles to more than 1.3 million. Criticism of Canada was relatively muted in Congress as the United States experienced its second overall balance of payments surplus in a row – it now stood at US$2.7 billion. However, that surplus was to go horribly wrong in short order, reaching a deficit of more than US$3 billion in 1970.

Muted criticism did not mean no criticism, and some in Congress complained about the agreement because of past administration assurances that the U.S. trade surplus in the automotive sector would not decline below US$500 million. To the contrary, Canadian automotive production had expanded by substantially more than would have been necessary simply to meet the conditions as laid down in the agreement. The Canadians recognized that Nixon's Republican administration would not be nearly so forgiving to them as the Kennedy and Johnson Democrats. They were, however, determined to make the United States view the automobile agreement 'in the general context of its balance of payments perspective as a whole' and to ensure that it was aware 'of the importance Canada attach[ed] to having a viable Canadian automobile industry.'[132] As Chrysler's Bryan O'Keefe told the U.S. Senate's committee on finance on 19 July 1968, to Canadians, 'the subject of more extensive Canadian manufacturing is not a theoretical concept, it is a matter of national pride.'[133]

In particular, Ottawa wanted to make the Americans see the benefits, at least from the Canadian side, of maintaining the safeguards with respect to the latter's production. Indeed, this issue became the focus of meetings between the two sides. The safeguards were put in place to help offset the differences between Canada and the U.S. in 'the size and financial strength of the respective industries, the patterns of ownership and control, the differences in labour productivity, the deeply imbedded habits and customs prevailing in the industry, and the many other institutional impediments to trade.' Canada had no satisfactory means, short of the safeguards, to insulate the Canadian industry from undue U.S. corporate influence. Of some importance in this regard, institutional barriers still remained: 'industry purchasing [had] been centralized in the United States since the agreement was implemented; Canadian wages [were] moving toward parity, while labour productivity, although improved, is still substantially below that of the United States. Fluctuations in the North American market could have disproportionate adverse effects on Canadian production, in the absence of effective safeguards.'[134] As well, the thinking went in Ottawa, Canada was not in a position to remove the restriction which limited duty free imports of vehicles to vehicle manufacturers. That move would give rise to unrestricted competition in the Canadian market from third countries. By mid-1967, the United States was determined to press for the elimination of the transitional safeguards for the Canadian industry. In that rather dangerous climate, a briefing paper suggested that the delegation should emphasize the difficulties that remained and the need for a continuation of the special transitional feature.

The Canadians wanted further concessions from a strapped United States, some which they claimed had been negotiated in the agreement. At various meetings, delegations from Ottawa pressed those from the United States to bring under the Auto Pact a number of Canadian products which, in their view, 'were clearly intended to be covered by the Agreement, but which were inadvertently overlooked. These included pressure sensitive labels and panels, certain glass items, parts and accessories of reinforced or laminated plastics and trim panels.' Long-standing Canadian requests for the necessary tariff accommodation had been denied on the grounds that the relevant U.S. officials were unable to recommend that the president take action on them at this time, so they remained under review. A Canadian paper noted that 'This stand clearly does not accord with United States obligations under the Agreement and Canadian industries [were] being denied intended benefits ... while facing competition from duty free imports from the United States.'[135] The Canadians were very tough-minded and unyielding in making their demands of Americans.

Jean-Luc Pepin, the minister of industry, trade and commerce in the first government of Pierre Elliott Trudeau following the election win in June 1968, continued to press this case with the U.S. over the summer. He also ensured that the Big Three stuck to the commitments they had undertaken with respect to levels of production. Pepin told Butterworth, for example, that it remained impossible 'to move from initial commitments to no commitments.'[136] He also stressed that the government must make certain that the companies 'would not become mere errand boys of their head offices in the United States.' However, the Americans had their problems too, one of which entailed congressional scrutiny of the agreement. In thát regard, the new minister told the ambassador that 'he would take a reasonable position [on that issue] and would do nothing to create political problems for [the United States].'

Nationalism and Other Issues

The rebate scheme and the Auto Pact negotiations were lengthy and time-consuming issues between 1963 and 1965, and arguably the most important economic negotiations to take place between Canada and the United States in decades. At the same time there were other serious trade and financial problems that provoked discussions between the North Americans, however slight they might seem by comparison. For example, the question of softwood lumber exports was raised by the United States, in particular the question of the stumpage advantage enjoyed by British Columbia producers, and Canadian export controls on softwood logs. The softwood issue reflected the sentiments of a recent meeting between American lumber producers and officials from the department of commerce. It was suggested that the timber pricing policies of the BC forest service constituted an unfair subsidy to the province's log consumers.[137]

As well, oil, copper and zinc, and some agricultural products continued to cause mild upset in the relationship, although during the Diefenbaker and Pearson years there had been a growing interdependence with the United States. Virtual free trade had been achieved in industrial raw materials, fossil fuels, forest products, fish, some agricultural commodities, farm machinery, and automotive products. As the U.S. ambassador, Walton Butterworth, took his leave of the country where he had served for six years, he penned a lengthy memorandum of his thoughts about the past and what the future might bring. He welcomed this continentalization in the use of resources and some industry. He also welcomed the election of Pierre Trudeau as Liberal leader and prime minister in April 1968. The new government 'gives some initial promise of being more pragmatic than was Pearson's; at the very least we can hope to continue our economic cooperation without the emotional, irrational braying and caterwauling of Walter Gordon.'[138] With Mitchell Sharp as the new secretary of state for external affairs, relations should be better; he had told Butterworth twice that he thought Canada would be an easier neighbour to live with now that Pearson and Martin were gone.

However, other issues were becoming hotter than the movement of goods across the border. Foreign asset control, Canada's relations with Cuba, and extraterritoriality had raised their ugly heads often enough to raise Canadian ire. Asset control was not a new problem, having plagued Diefenbaker's relationship with the United States as well, but in the period after Canada's centennial and the celebrations at Expo 67, nationalism was more a factor than ever before. Canadians did not appreciate the application of U.S. law to their country, and the issue grew in importance for both sides, with Dean Rusk, the secretary of state, at one point phoning Ed Ritchie, the undersecretary of state for external affairs, to discuss the 'general drift of Canada-US relations,' talking 'harshly about "a wave of anti-Americanism" that was abroad in Canada.'[139]

The Economic Development Review Committee's report for 1967 suggested the tack that Ottawa would take in the future, or it at least reflected what officials believed. In its first ten paragraphs it went to some lengths to explain that the Canadian economy was so closely tied to that of the United that the government had 'little latitude to guide the economy.'[140] This could be a useful position, especially in demanding special treatment from the United States. The Americans rejected that view; the 'Canadian tendency to blame economic problems on close relationship with US must constantly be resisted.' The latest example, according to Butterworth, was Ottawa blaming the United States and its balance of payments program for the weakening of the Canadian dollar. The drop in the dollar allegedly caused American subsidiaries in Canada to transfer abnormally large amounts of profit to their head offices. The United States was the 'scapegoat.' What about Canada's own fiscal and monetary policy, which the ambassador called 'failings'; what was the role of the 'loose talk [in Ottawa] about the devaluation of the Canadian dollar,' as well as the continued yearning in and out of government for a return to a floating exchange rate, which Canada had fixed in May 1962? Finally, there was a highly speculative international atmosphere where currency traders were hypercritical of any perceived governmental inconsistencies. So the list of Canadian grievances went on, with Butterworth rejecting each one.

The next few years were shaping up to be difficult ones for the continental relationship. The Americans were increasingly hard pressed by their own considerable balance of payments problems and by the escalating war in Vietnam. Adversely affected by their falling productivity levels and a virtual tsunami of Japanese exports rolling across the Pacific, as well as by a combative and unhelpful EEC, Washington was in no mood to cater to what it perceived to be Canada's self-absorbed neuroses.

The dissolution of the government in May 1968 as Lester Pearson retired and the advent of the Trudeau regime was a welcome event for most Americans connected to the Canada dossier, no more so than Ambassador Butterworth. He left Ottawa in 1968 but before he did, he penned a scathing indictment of Pearson and his bumblings as seen from the U.S. side:

Five years of spastic performance by Liberal Party government of Canada under Prime Minister Lester B. Pearson ended on April 20 with the succession of a new Liberal Party leader and Prime Minister, Pierre Elliott Trudeau ... Pearson had announced in December of 1967 his intention to retire this spring but, in quite characteristic fashion, his schedule almost aborted when the Opposition defeated a money bill before Parliament on February 19, 'Black Monday,' and Pearson managed to keep his Government in being and avoid a general election only by obtaining last-minute support from the tiny Creditiste Party. To its close, the Pearson administration of two minority governments sputtered and bungled, variously timorous and strident, striking vainglorious poses but failing to meet satisfactorily Canada's national and international problems. It left the electorate dissatisfied with the political leadership of rancorous old men, weary of political ineptitude, deeply troubled over internal tensions arising from federal-provincial and French-English disputes, worried about growing economic strains and disparities, and confused over national security and foreign policies. The Pearson (and Diefenbaker) years were failures, and Canadians for once were prepared to forsake the traditional 'politics of complacency' and go for a change.

With respect to domestic affairs, Butterworth commented that the Pearson government 'Continued to fulfill nearly all expectations that it would mismanage affairs if it possibly could. Pearson defied the most elementary rules of Cabinet reorganization and Government administration with the same blithe regard which Icarus had for natural law. His Ministers argued publicly at cross purposes, Trade and Commerce Minister Robert Winters even stating to a public, which could no longer be surprised or disappointed, that he intended to resign his portfolio because he could not support the Government's program of fiscal irresponsibility. There were no Cabinet secrets and in fact no clear and consistent policies, whether political or economic.'[141]

Butterworth hoped that Trudeau would concentrate his attentions and resources on Canada's domestic political and economic problems and not 'crusade abroad' so much in the 'ludicrous' style of his predecessor. Butterworth wrote that 'Throughout its last four months, the Pearson Government continued its feckless way in foreign affairs, the flower child dreaming the world's rocky fields were Elysian, hoping to become involved in international disputes and seeking only to do good among the deserving poor and to give wise counsel to the wicked super-states.' If past is prologue, Butterworth's successor sixteen years later could not have written a more fitting epitaph for Trudeau. In tones reminiscent of Pearson's defeat of Diefenbaker, the ambassador was generous to Trudeau: 'In all his statements,' Butterworth wrote, '[Trudeau] has recognized the key importance to Canada of good relations with the US, whose interests in Canada he has discussed most circumspectly.' Not so far in the future a new president, Richard Nixon, would let it be known that he thought the Canadian prime minister to be 'an asshole.'

Butterworth would also have been encouraged with Mitchell Sharp's appointment as secretary of state for external affairs. He had a lengthy interview with Sharp soon after Sharp's appointment, which he reported to Washington. The ambassador noted that Sharp thought that 'Canada would behave as an easier neighbor in the days to come. He felt that there had been a rise in Canadian self-confidence, well-being and patriotism, stimulated by the flag, Expo, etc., and, on the other hand, the US had been experiencing all too evident difficulties which led Canadians to be less envious, that the combination of these two factors would, he hoped, make Canada an easier partner with whom to deal. To which I said Amen, figuratively but not literally.'[142]

Butterworth's departure, notwithstanding the fact that he was viewed in Washington as an excellent and informed ambassador, was as fitting as had been Pearson's. He had become an implacable critic of what he perceived as Canadian failings which sometimes obscured reality. A few years prior to his departure from the foreign service, a memorandum prepared for President Johnson suggested that he was 'a grand old warhorse' and an 'excellent political analyst. His mind is acute. He quickly finds the heart of an issue. – Able advocate and negotiator. He is a diplomatic virtuoso – a one-man band. – Many of his oral and written communications are masterpieces of precision. – He is forceful, forthright and persuasive ... He has boundless self-confidence.'[143] When he had been appointed, his predecessor in Ottawa and long-time friend, Livingston Merchant, had also observed that 'He's the s.o.b. the Canadians deserve.' It was perhaps the latter characterization that animated Ottawa, not the former. Butterworth's style was not appreciated by 1968.

The next years in Canada-United States relations would be troubled ones, which the election of a new prime minister did little to make better. Many of same North American irritants that had plagued Pearson's handling of affairs would remain with Trudeau. Indeed, things between the two countries got worse as the U.S. economy proved unable to sustain the par value system, established in 1944 at Bretton Woods, the collapse of which destabilized Western economies. Americans also found themselves being out-produced by the Europeans and the Japanese and their current account deficit grew to what many believed were unmanageable proportions. The war in Vietnam continued at a tremendous cost of American (and Vietnamese) life and coin. As Washington cast an increasingly critical eye around the world, Canada was caught in its gaze with results that were not beneficial to the country. The *coup de grâce* for any close and meaningful relationship between Ottawa and Washington came with the election of the Richard Nixon Republicans in November 1968. The Liberals could only batten down their hatches.

Chapter 3

A Difficult Relationship:
Pierre Trudeau and the United States

A Buoyant Economic Climate

As Pierre Elliott Trudeau took on the onerous burden of responsibility, Canada's economy was in recovery mode. A period of subdued growth that had lasted from the spring of 1966 until the final months of 1967 had given way to a sharply accelerated economic expansion in 1968, led by a very strong demand for Canadian exports, the primary source of which was the United States. Real output was up, unemployment was down despite a large increase in the labour force, and the deficit on current account was the smallest it had been for a number of years.[1] As well, the global economy seemed to be on a much more stable footing by mid-1968. The U.S. balance of payments program, announced on 1 January 1968 and designed to help address a 1967 deficit of US$3.4 billion, had 'come as a severe jolt to Canada.'[2] Before its exemption from the program, Canada had been included in a group for which direct investment from the United States was to be restricted to 60 per cent of the 1966 figure. That decision had led to near-disaster, but by the time Trudeau took over the government, the crisis had passed and receded into the national unconscious.

Developments were almost as promising in the United States, Canada's largest and most important market. Gross national product (GNP) increased by 9.5 per cent in value and 5.5 per cent in volume, well above the 5.5 and 2.25 per cent respectively achieved during the previous year. Unemployment averaged around 3.5 per cent and inflation was 4.7 per cent, as compared to 3.1 per cent in 1967. Most importantly for Canada, that strong economic growth had generated an exceptionally large increase in U.S. imports.

Comparisons between the two countries also favoured Canada, as its economic growth was more solidly based. Manufacturing output per employee increased more in Canada than in the United States, while income per employee rose less rapidly. As a result, unit labour costs in Canadian manufacturing increased by only 2 per cent over 1968 while they were up by more than 4 per cent south of the border. Profits were up, but price increases for Canadians were no larger than those in the United States for the first time in several years. It was as good a time as any over the past decade to become prime minister, or so the economic indicators seemed to suggest.

The only serious cloud in an otherwise blue sky was inflation, which was causing some anxiety at the Bank of Canada and was ultimately to prove a most intractable problem. The price index of all goods and services as measured in the GNP was to rise by 4 per cent during 1968, and by larger numbers in the very near future. Because of inflationary pressures, interest rates, overseen by the Bank, rose from 6 per cent in September 1968 to 8 per cent the following July, the highest rate of the post-war period to date. Much of this inflation had carried over from Lester Pearson's last year in office, and Walton Butterworth, the U.S. ambassador in Ottawa, was correct when he had reported to the department of state that only belatedly had the prime minister and the minister of finance, Mitchell Sharp, recognized 'that they [had] maneuvered themselves through both action and inaction behind the eightball with respect to the present inflationary situation, for which they must take much of the onus.'[3] An anti-inflationary budget, passed in November 1967, simply proved to be ineffective following very large wage increases to Seaway workers to ensure labour peace and the price increases paid to ensure that Expo 67 was finished on time. To be fair to the Pearson government, inflation was also a North American phenomenon, as the Bank of Canada's *Annual Report* suggested:

> A major factor that made it more difficult for Canada to achieve good price performance in 1968 than in the immediately preceding years was the marked intensification of demand pressures from beyond our borders, particularly from the United States. By the end of the year, unemployment in that country had fallen to its lowest level in fifteen years; the rate of price increase in 1968 was the highest since the Korean War. In the course of the year the US consumer price index rose by 4.7 percent compared to a rise of 4.1 percent in Canada. This meant that international competition imposed less restraint on price increases in Canada than had been the case in earlier years.[4]

Addressing inflation would take some pain domestically; that was what Louis Rasminsky, the governor of the Bank of Canada, told Trudeau during his first meeting with him in May 1968. In a wide-ranging discussion, he elaborated upon the same advice he had given Diefenbaker and Pearson in their day: the government should address the current account deficit. Only by so doing would

Canada cease to be dependent on an inflow of capital from the United States that had, in the recent past, produced distortions in the country's economic and financial development. He put the case clearly in response to Trudeau's question about the effect and political cost of dealing with this issue. Would it, the prime minister asked, result in a lower standard of living for Canadians? Rasminsky thought not: 'On a purely arithmetic basis what was involved was that consumption would increase a bit less rapidly than it could if we were large net importers of goods and services. The problem was ... one of organization on how to bring about the desired result.' The prime minister also wondered whether it was a nationalistic objective to seek to eliminate the current account deficit: 'I said that I did not think so provided it was done by trying to become more efficient and competitive and not through import restrictions.'[5] Trudeau appeared to accept this advice, as Rasminsky later recalled, but the government's policies did not reflect it. To the governor Trudeau remained an enigma, and on economic affairs, about which Trudeau knew very little and cared even less, the adviser offering the last piece of advice was often the most successful.

Sage counsel like Rasminsky's was what the reinvigorated Liberals needed to keep the economy on the proper track. By the autumn of 1968 inflation had become a greater worry and it was not easily responding to the traditional cures. And what could be done about rates of productivity and economic growth? Rasminsky knew that adequately addressing those problems would be very difficult. One reason was Canada's location – it was 'a small country [in economic terms] living side by side with the United States, the greatest economic power in the world.'[6] That proximity caused distortions, some real and some fancied. Canadians had always been fascinated by the never-ending spectacle of the United States, with its zest for life and its seeming invincibility. They also wanted the same standard of living as this economic giant – everything their American neighbours had along with very costly government services, like Medicare and a national pension plan.

George Ball, the former undersecretary of state and soon-to-be U.S. representative to the United Nations, had commented on the seeming incompatibility of some Canadian objectives in his 1968 book, *The Discipline of Power*.[7] To the outrage of most Canadians, he wrote that he believed Canada was destined to be tied ever so closely to the United States:

> Living next to our nation, with a population ten times as large as theirs and a gross national product fourteen times as great, the Canadians recognize their need for US capital; but at the same time they are determined to maintain their economic and political independence. Their position is understandable and the desire to maintain their national integrity is a worthy objective. But the Canadians pay heavily for it

and, over the years, I do not believe they will succeed in reconciling the intrinsic contradictions of their position. I wonder, for example, if the Canadian people will be prepared indefinitely to accept, for the psychic satisfaction of maintaining a separate national and political identity, a per capita income less than three-fourths of ours. The struggle is bound to be ... a losing one.

That very real struggle was on Trudeau's mind as he set about establishing a government and winning a federal election called for June. He was very conscious of the overwhelming power and influence of the United States on Canadian affairs, and wanted to change that. In Kitchener, Ontario, for one of many campaign stops, he spoke to the city's chamber of commerce about the economic issues facing Canada. Because the country did not have the range and breadth of the United States it should, he told his audience, 'concentrate on those areas in which it has a competitive strength such as nuclear energy, electronics, satellite communications and solids pipelines.'[8] He disputed Ball's contention that Canada would suffer eventual absorption into the United States because of its growing interdependence with a much larger economy. Later, in an interview with the *Globe and Mail*'s George Bain, he mentioned that he would have more influence on the government's economic policy than many people then believed and that he would work to make Canada's economy less dependent on that of the United States: 'When we begin to ... perhaps ... develop the CDC (Canada Development Corporation) to expand the Canadian economy, people on the other side will be saying ... that we are too much left wing.'[9] That was where he would take the government following his electoral win of 25 June – his Liberals won almost 46 per cent of the popular vote and 155 seats, crushing the Conservatives with their 72 and the New Democrats, who took 22. Still, it is a truism that foreign policy and foreign economic policy do not win elections. In 1968 the main topics for debate were taxes, housing costs, unemployment, and Canadian unity.

The U.S. perception of the new government was important. While relations between Canada and the United States would soon sour at a governmental level, in the beginning there were aspects of Trudeau's behaviour which appealed to the Americans. For example, despite some of the campaign rhetoric they thought him to be 'not an ardent economic nationalist and unlikely to raise [the] subject of US investment.'[10] Washington could be forgiven its misplaced characterization of the early Trudeau months because Canadian views on U.S. investment and ownership in Canada were generally much less critical than when Walter Gordon '[had] influenced [the] previous Liberal government.' Moreover, Trudeau was not a nationalist and had made that clear in his writing and speeches. It was easy to project from that to the notion that he would not implement nationalist economic policies. Generally, that issue seemed to have cooled considerably in the minds of Canadians. Even the Task Force on the Structure of Canadian Industry, struck in March 1967, championed in cabinet by Gordon, and headed by the left-wing University of Toronto economist Melville Watkins (one of the 'new' nationalists) reflected a moderate mood. When it reported on 15 February 1968 after a year's investigation of the effects of foreign ownership on Canada's economy, it '[was] surprisingly mild in both tone and recommendations.'[11] Watkins hmself acknowledged that the report was not radical: 'It simply said the multinational corporation is here to stay ... They're subject to a good deal of pressure from Washington, and therefore the Canadian government should have a policy which is essentially a kind of regulatory policy.' The report 'stimulated very little response from the public or in the business community' and was buried following Walter Gordon's second resignation from cabinet on 11 March.[12]

This relative unconcern was manifest early in the new mandate by the minister of finance, Edgar Benson, who reflected the continentalist position in the Liberal party; one of his first foreign trips had been to Washington where he had extolled the benefits of foreign direct investment. In the presence of the Tax Executives Institute, the minister said that 'We have been doing this for a long time and as Canadians we are well aware of the important role foreign capital has played in the development of the country.' The Canadian Press, obviously with Walter Gordon in mind, wrote that Benson 'did not mention fears expressed by previous finance ministers about the weight of U.S. ownership and control of Canadian resources that accompanies foreign control.'[13]

The difference between the Pearson and Trudeau Liberals approach to economic nationalism might be called semi-substance, despite Benson's beliefs. Where the former had been content to draw almost exclusively on U.S. money markets for investment, the latter intended to diversify that effort slightly, encouraging foreign investment from other sources like Western Europe. An indication of this approach was the new prime minister's recitation of loans arranged by Canadian businesses, in particular one for CAN$62 million from a German bank: 'In a month or two we will see other Canadian borrowing in other European markets.' He did not dispute that Canada needed foreign investment for development, only that any investment should be conducive to the country's political and social goals. If American money accomplished that end, then it would be as welcome as it had been in the past. There would also be no attempt to buy back foreign-controlled industry since 'Canada should concentrate on buying [the] future, not [the] past.'[14]

While Trudeau and his government might not have been overly sensitive to nationalists' concerns about U.S. investment, some Canadians were and more would be infected with an anti-American virus before the decade was out. An indication of that was advice the prime minister received prior to his first visit in March 1969 with the recently elected Richard Nixon. The Liberal *Toronto Star* encouraged him 'to put Canadian-American relations on a new footing by behaving like a leader who means to push Canada's independence to the limits of practicality and wisdom.' Stephen Clarkson, then a young assistant professor at the University of Toronto, also counselled Trudeau in the *Star* 'Pierre baby, you've got to sock it to [Nixon]. Drop the passive "I'm here to learn" pose and come on talking. You've got two days to penetrate those Republican gray cells with a single, simple message: "Canada thinks differently, therefore Canada is different."'[15] Trudeau ignored the counsel, and despite the later rancour of their relationship, the two leaders got along well. Indeed, Trudeau was on record as saying that he liked the president and that he had established a good personal relationship with him.

The growing disenchantment with Canada's superpower neighbour was spread in part by the prosperity that U.S. interdependence had brought to Canada and by its antics in different parts of the world. It could be overbearing, aggressive, nasty, and vindictive, such as in Vietnam, where it was fighting a very unpopular war. In Canada, this change in attitude among a certain segment of the chattering classes was influenced by the likes of Clarkson, Rotstein, and Watkins as they published op-ed pieces and generally spread the faith.[16]

As a new decade began, the Liberals could not ignore a rising backlash against U.S. influence in Canada and a sharp increase in Canadian nationalism. A Gallup poll caught that mood in late 1970. In response to the question 'Is it your impression that Canada and the US have been drawing closer together recently, or getting farther apart?' the results were as follows:

	Closer together	Further apart	The same or can't say
1966	33%	8%	59%
Today [1970]	38	26	36

Among English-speaking Canadians the widespread belief was held that the two countries were growing further apart, with 36 per cent agreeing as compared with 11 per cent among French Canadians. With respect to foreign investment, the poll provided a snapshot of attitudes over time:

	Enough Now	Like More	Undecided
1964	46%	33%	21%
1967	60	24	16
Nov 1970	62	25	13

Those numbers were worse, at least from the politically important perspective of Ontario with its many parliamentary seats, as the following regional breakdown demonstrates:

	Enough Now	Like More	Undecided
Maritimes	53%	38%	9%
Quebec	48	33	19
Ontario	70	18	12
The West	67	22	11

Source: USNA, RG 59, Box 729, file E-CAN-U.S., 1/1/70, American Embassy Ottawa to Department of State, 11 December 1970.

Continuing Problem in the Oil Industry

The U.S. ambassador in Canada, Harold Linder, suggested that the attention paid to U.S. investment reflected the large degree of economic interdependence between the two countries. 'The US inevitably loom[ed] large.'[17] It was also accentuated by the significant role that foreign trade played in the domestic economy. With exports then accounting for about 20 per cent of GNP and many of those sales being made in the United States, prices and employment could be influenced directly by trade fluctuations. As a result, Ottawa was extremely sensitive to American trade policy development. While cheered by the Nixon administration's public commitment to liberal trade policies, the Canadians were greatly exercised over the extension of import restraint agreements to, among other sectors, steel and textiles. As well, they wanted to sell more oil to the United States than was specified in the 1967 oil agreement between the two countries, and to encourage Washington to think of oil as a continental resource, as the Diefenbaker and Pearson governments had attempted to do. Trudeau made that pitch to Nixon when the two met for the second time in June 1969, a meeting that, from the U.S. point of view, would permit the president to 'establish a personal relationship [with Trudeau] and provide a widened and deepened basis for continuing discussion between the two governments.'[18]

The Canadians had U.S. dollars dancing in front of their eyes in the form of export earnings when they requested lightened oil-sales restrictions. However, over the next few years, both countries' considerations evolved. The Canadians became less willing to support, although on balance still in favour of, an increase in oil exports to the United States, while the Americans became much more interested in Canadian oil exports. The path of continental oil negotiations was rather tortuous. Following the Nixon-Trudeau meeting of June 1969, there was some informal discussion among officials of working out a continental oil arrangement that would include such elements as unlimited U.S. access to Canada's oil, joint security programs against interruption of supply, and the development of Arctic reserves. In March 1970, however, Washington unilaterally imposed quotas on Canadian oil. Even though they 'were short-lived, they signaled a decisive turning away from cooperation on energy matters between the two countries.'[19] That suited the developing Canadian agenda, since by the early 1970s, 'a much more nationalistic attitude was emerging in Canada ... that made any kind of "continental harmonization" politically unacceptable.' The assessment on the U.S. side by 1971 was that 'the Canadian Government is ambivalent in its desire for free access to the U.S. market, desiring the export earnings while at the same time not wishing to continue unlimited export of its natural resources.'[20] Indeed, a few months later when the Americans, who had again changed their policy, proposed a comprehensive energy agreement that would guarantee that a certain proportion of Canadian production would go to the United States, Ottawa declined. Canada's needs would be met first as Donald Macdonald, the minister of energy, mines and resources told the House: if the Americans were 'suggesting in reference to a continental energy policy that we should enter into an arrangement whereby there would be not only a pooling of the assets of the continent, but a pooling of the shortages   as well ... this is a policy which this government would not intend to follow.'[21] Limited export controls were imposed by the National Energy Board in March, and more were to follow in the coming months. In September, the government placed a forty cent per barrel export tax on oil, much to the chagrin of the U.S. government. The revenues raised by the tax were to help equalize oil prices across Canada.

Developing Canadian policy was fleshed out for some American officials by Jack Austin, Macdonald's deputy minister. When Peter Flanigan, an official in Nixon's White House, pressed for a time frame for the determination of an agreement between the North Americans on oil from Canada, Austin pointed out that Ottawa 'was reviewing its thinking with regard to the export of its natural resources. The problems with which they were struggling included the direction in which their economy should go, the degree of dependence on the US, the effect of exports on Canadian security, and the like.'[22] In the meantime the increased negotiating and organizational strength of the Organization of Petroleum Exporting Countries and diminishing U.S. reserves had led Washington to become more interested in imports from Canada, and it removed quotas from Canadian oil flowing to the United States. As a result, 1.2 million barrels a day of Alberta crude were exported to the United States. However, Ottawa had just received its own shock – that Canadian reserves were a fraction of what had previously been thought, which would cause the government to reassess those

exports. This disconnect between the projections and the reality led Judith Maxwell, the director of economic policy analysis at the C.D. Howe Institute, to later
write that it was a mystery to her as to 'how a country could get into this situation.'[23] It also led to the establishment of Petro-Canada, the state-owned oil company. The majors could not be trusted and government believed it needed a
window into the industry that its own company would provide.

By 1973 and the first oil shock that saw prices increase rapidly, the United
States was very interested in secure supplies of oil from Canada. But the more the
Americans pushed, the greater the Canadian reaction. A major problem for both
governments was the disillusionment of voters with the Trudeau government.
The October 1972 election reduced it to minority status, making the Liberals
dependent on David Lewis and his slightly left-of-centre New Democratic Party
for survival. Consequently, 'the atmosphere in Ottawa [was] very strained [and]
the minority government cannot do anything without weighing the domestic
political repercussions exceedingly carefully.'[24] In any event, as the United States
lifted its quotas on Canadian oil in March 1973, 'Weighing the domestic political repercussions carefully' meant that any continental oil policy was out; the best
the Canadians could offer in terms of language was 'best endeavour' – they would
make every effort to supply the United States in the event of a global shortage.
That promise, however, was inadequate to American needs. Flanigan told A.E.
Ritchie, the undersecretary of state for external affairs, that 'unless [the United
States] could get a commitment as expressed in our "will maintain the level of
exports" language, the game was not worth the gamble.'[25] So be it, Ritchie
informed him, because Canada could not undertake commitments of that kind.

Canadian policy development had changed and with it came two ironies. The
first was that since the Diefenbaker era, Canadians had been hammering at the
United States for free trade in oil. When free-trade could finally happen in 1973,
Ottawa chose not to take advantage of the opportunity and went so far as to
impose quotas of its own on the export of oil in March. In November 1974 the
government announced that it would phase out exports to the United States
entirely by the early 1980s because of the National Energy Board's considered
forecast that Canada would be a net importer of oil by that time. The country's
oil would be necessary for its own needs, especially since it became government
policy to supply the region to the east of the Ottawa River with western oil. The
second irony lay with the United States. Following years of discouraging Canadian oil imports, Washington was irritated that its requirements would not be
met by Canada.

With respect to steel, the United States had announced that iron and steel producers in the European Economic Community (EEC) and Japan had voluntarily
agreed to limit their exports of steel products to the United States until 1972.

Figure 3.1 Disposition of Canadian Oil, 1960–77 (million barrels per day)

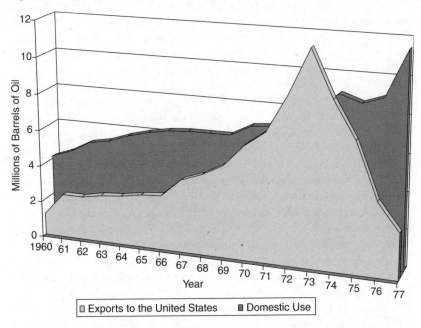

Source: Carl E. Beigie and Alfred O. Hero, eds., *Natural Resources in US-Canadian Relations*, vol. 1, *The Evolution of Policies and Issues* (Boulder, CO: Westview Press 1980), 309.

Although Canada was not strictly part of the agreement, the feeling in Ottawa was that the country was included by implication.[26] Total U.S. steel imports were less than had been allowed in 1968 and were limited to 14 million tons in 1969, 14.7 million tons in 1970, and 15.4 million tons in 1971. The number three supplier to the U.S. market was Canada, and its steel producers had already gone on record as being opposed to any suggestion that they should limit their exports to the United States.

If U.S. programs interfered with the freer flow of goods south, the Trudeau government in consultation with Canada's steel manufacturers would impose restraints on those products coming from the United States. In addition to these direct economic effects, there was another aspect to this problem: the restraint program 'remove[d] trade policy from multilateral, legal procedures and put it in bilateral, political negotiations where the Canadian voice [was] weaker.' In response, Canada loudly espoused its commitment to the General Agreement on

Tariffs and Trade (GATT) and to the Organization for Economic Cooperation and Development (OECD), and stressed their strongly internationalist consultative and mediatory functions.

Growing Bilateral Problems

Ottawa would do what it could on its own to push its multilateral and non-discriminatory approach. The government unilaterally accelerated to early 1969 the implementation of the Kennedy round tariff reductions, scheduled to come into effect in 1972, and which represented an average tariff reduction of about 3 percentage points on imports worth about CAN$2 billion per year, 80 per cent of which came from the United States.[27] The Canadian ambassador in Washington was instructed to tell senior U.S. officials that the move was made because of considerations bearing on the North American economic relationship and international trade policy more generally. More specifically, Canadian authorities were conscious of the desirability of offering a positive example at this juncture, when there was not only a lack of forward momentum towards freer trade, but also an increase in protectionist pressures in the United States and elsewhere. They also took into consideration the level of concern among U.S. officials with the border tax adjustment issue. Ottawa attached great importance to U.S. officials recognizing the significance of border tax action, action that would place the Canadian government in a very tough position in light of its unilateral decision on the acceleration of the Kennedy round results.[28]

Moreover, Canada changed the allowances for tourists returning from the United States with the stated goal of simplifying administration; of much greater consequence was the wish to respond to U.S. views. Ottawa had never subscribed to the American notion of reciprocity in this area, but by 1969 it had recognized that the existing arrangements incorporated an element of discrimination. The new measures explicitly dealt with that disparity and, as a telegram to the embassy in Washington pointed out, provided 'for treatment that is fully as generous as can be envisaged without specifically encouraging shopping expeditions.'[29] None of these changes was easy and Canada was faced with an expected revenue loss of about CAN$50 million in the 1969 fiscal year.

The June 1969 joint Canada-U.S. ministerial committee on trade and economic affairs provided a forum to discuss these evolving issues as well as American investment in Canada. Canadian ministers were very conscious of the fact that this Republican administration, the first in eight years, had not had much exposure to Canadian issues and bilateral problems. Ottawa's delegation wanted to explain the rationale behind the Task Force on the Structure of Canadian Industry. It was not merely an exercise in U.S.-baiting: ministers wanted to make sure that the secretaries were aware of the nature of past problems in this area and the sensitivity of Canadian public opinion to the increasing amount of foreign ownership and control of Canadian industry. Foreign ownership now totaled about 60 per cent of Canada's manufacturing and mining industries, and approximately 75 per cent of the petroleum and natural gas sector. The total book value of non-resident owned direct investment in Canada at the end of 1965 had been US$17.2 billion, of which almost US$14.5 billion was American.

Some of the most troublesome issues affecting Canada-U.S. intergovernmental relations in recent years had occurred over the differing perceptions among Canadians of the usefulness of foreign direct investment. On the one hand were U.S. charges of discrimination against their investment in Canada in the few sectors in which there were restrictions, like financial institutions and magazines.[30] On the other, Canadian complaints to the Nixon administration related to the extraterritorial application of U.S. law to Canadian subsidiaries of American corporations and over the dominance of U.S. owned or controlled firms in important sectors of the economy. To 1969, the North Americans had had to cope with these problems bilaterally; now increasing attention was being devoted in industrialized countries generally to the role of, and problems created by, the emergence of the multinational corporation. Discussions were then underway in such forums as the OECD that might result in multinational guidelines to resolve problems of the multinational firm and related foreign investment problems. Despite the bright hopes, nothing substantive was to result, in large part because the Americans were not willing to participate fully.

Another area of potential trouble was the adverse U.S. balance of payments situation and Canada's contribution to it. A more assertive (or defensive) Washington could take action that would hurt its neighbour's economy. Ottawa had fought those battles with two administrations during the 1960s but had never won the war. The country had been exempted from the restrictions imposed on others by the Interest Equalization Tax (IET) and the two Johnson programs. The Canadians would urge that the new Nixon government take up the challenge of securing Congressional approval for further tariff reductions, despite pressing balance of payments problems. A briefing paper prepared for the delegation suggested that they 'may wish to have as their central objective the encouragement of the new Administration to formulate its policies on international and bilateral trade and other economic matters from a larger perspective: the United States should be urged to resume as soon as possible its role of initiator of liberal trade and financial policies throughout the industrialized world.'[31] It was important to point out how shortsighted it would be if the U.S. government were to contemplate restrictionist policies in its trade and economic relations with Canada for balance of payments reasons. Canada had already done its part for the

United States, or so Ottawa believed, by implementing the results of the Kennedy round ahead of schedule.

It was a simple matter to raise these issues in briefing papers; it was much harder to convince Americans. The Canadians had a particularly difficult problem – the Auto Pact. Trade in automotive products was a significant element in the U.S. current account balance with Canada, and therefore relevant to the idea that the balance of payments problem should be corrected through action on trade. The Auto Pact was a large target, given the huge reversal of an American surplus in automotive products in the mid-1960s to a deficit by 1970. The Canadian-American Committee, a private sector group of chief executive officers, offered an interesting evaluation that would inform the discussions but not necessarily U.S. decision-making: 'Both Canadians and Americans are inclined to focus not on the overall gains, but almost exclusively on the issue of the distribution of production ... Worse yet, each country has measured this relationship by a yardstick which presents the situation in the most unfavorable light for itself. The seeming preoccupation with shifts in the shares of total production and sales make it appear that one country's gain is the other's loss – whereas in fact such changes *can* occur while both nations are improving their net position. Americans have come to judge the Agreement largely in terms of the deterioration of the U.S. automotive trade balance with Canada since 1964.'[32] The United States would surely refer to that gap in terms of its overall trade position, a fact that would not be good for Canada especially since the country's output and assembly of passenger cars had gone up dramatically following 1964. In that year, Canadians had built 560,000 cars; by 1969 that number had risen to 1.033 million. The Americans would also likely suggest that the special safeguards that had protected Canada's producers since 1965 were not now required to help offset differences between the industry in Canada and the United States. Indeed, the Auto Pact's old foe in the Senate, Vance Hartke of Indiana, had been joined by Albert Gore from Tennessee, who had introduced a bill in the Senate in early 1967 that would repeal the enabling legislation that had permitted the agreement. Gore was on record as believing the Auto Pact to be 'unwise.'[33]

If the Canadians were to discourage these attitudes and the American inclination to see the declining U.S. balance in its trade with Canada in automobiles as a specifically bilateral issue in that particular sector, the ministers would need to situate the Auto Pact in the general context of the balance of payments and to ensure that the Republican secretaries recognized the importance that Canada attached to a viable automotive industry. Moreover, they must stress the mutual benefits of it; since its inception in 1965, two-way trade had increased from CAN$800 million to CAN$5.4 billion. Even so, the Canadian position might prove to be a tough sell.

And it was. President Nixon himself took the lead on this file by directing that a committee be established to review U.S. trade policy in the late 1960s, and to offer suggestions as to what it should be in the 1970s. Overseen by the National Security Council (NSC), the committee was to initiate a thorough study to explore the range of problems that had to be faced in the near future. Included within its parameters were tariffs, non-tariff barriers, agriculture, and foreign production by U.S. corporations.[34] It was generally assumed that the Republicans would take a much harder line against liberal trading policies than had the Democrats.

Surging Anti-Americanism in Canada

Would U.S. trade policy really matter in the developing Canadian context of the turn of the decade? Surely there were alternatives to the United States and the government would commit itself to developing other trade options. Western Europe and Japan were certainly possibilities that would better mesh with Canadian sensibilities. The United States was increasingly isolated in the world as many believed it deserved to be. Race riots in Detroit provoked the Canadian singer Gordon Lightfoot to record 'Black Day in July,' whose lyrics were suggestive of how his countrymen had come to perceive the United States. 'And the streets of gutted buildings / Strike terror to the heart / And you wonder how it happened / And you wonder how did it start?' Washington had also lost whatever moral capital it had possessed through its vicious pursuit of an imperialist war in Vietnam. More Americans were to lose their lives there than in any other conflict in U.S. history. As well, more than two million Vietnamese were killed and their countryside devastated. The weakened American resolve contributed mightily to the inflation that increasingly wracked their lives.

Under those circumstances it was not surprising that Canadians were rejecting much of what the United States stood for. In a poll taken in 1970, 81 per cent of respondents replied when asked how they would feel if Canada joined the United States 'with a variety of rejections ranging from the formal negative to the unprintable.'[35] As well, 72 per cent believed that union at some time in the future was not a foregone conclusion. It was easy for the economic nationalists to gain a hearing, especially as they wrote about the possible absorption of Canada into the United States given the extent of American control over the Canadian economy. This 'sellout' was laid directly at the feet of continentalist Liberal governments who had either ignored or encouraged U.S. investment in Canada, what Abraham Rotstein called 'a no-policy policy towards multinational corporations.'[36]

The American government could deal with those sentiments expressed by Canadian citizens and not be overly concerned; in a democracy protest was a part of the political fabric. When anti-Americanism began to emanate from government, however, the U.S. embassy in Ottawa became alarmed. For example, it reported extensively on a speech that Jean-Pierre Goyer, then the parliamentary secretary to Mitchell Sharp and later the minister of supply and services, gave in Toronto entitled 'Canada's Relations with Europe – Will They Change?' The Americans were flabbergasted by Goyer's interpretation of the NATO treaty and that he seemed to suggest that Canada faced a military threat from an aggressive United States. The embassy grilled external affairs officials about the genesis of the speech; the assistant under secretary, Ralph Collins, and the head of the department's NATO/NORAD division, Charles Marshall, disclaimed any responsibility on the part of their department. Indeed, the latter said that he 'had experienced the wonderment of disbelief' over the speech. Still, the Americans remained unconvinced, especially as they believed that Goyer's speech might reflect the new prime minister's views.[37] Moreover, as Peyton Lyon was to point out following a number of Canada-U.S. crises, 'United States officials [complain] that middle level Canadian officials ... now seem to delight in being difficult.'[38]

The general tenor of the relationship seemed to reflect a revitalized and much more sensitive Canada, personified by Pierre Elliot Trudeau and reflected in the foreign policy review he commissioned. The prime minister was determined to change the way in which a stodgy department of external affairs conceived of itself and its mission in the world. As J.L. Granatstein has written, in the beginning it was an exciting and long-overdue exercise: 'Trudeau, the man who turned Canadian politics on its ear in 1968, did much the same to Canada's external and defence policies. This was the year of street corner policy-making, of university teach-in diplomacy, and of startling, frank comments on a host of issues. It was fun, it was refreshing, and it seemed just a little dangerous after the more soporific style of Lester Pearson and Paul Martin.'[39]

The review was to examine the main trends in Canadian foreign policy between 1948 and 1968 including: 'support for the UN, NATO, and NORAD in the quest for collective security; the internationalistic approach based on the premise that peace and security must be the foremost goal of any country's foreign policy; "quiet diplomacy" in dealings with allies; and, a belief that the United States and the countries of Western Europe were Canada's best and most natural friends.'[40] It also rejected the past, (Pearson was not even consulted by Trudeau) and defined Canada's national interest as the key component of policy. Granatstein soon soured on the process and the documents produced by 1970; rather than the excitement promised two years earlier, what had resulted was the rather sublunary premise that 'the purpose of Canadian foreign policy now ... was to serve the interests of Canadian investors and businessmen abroad.'[41] External affairs officers were to become little better than sales agents abroad for Canadian products.

The review reflected Trudeau's ideas of what was important and the eventual result, *Foreign Policy for Canadians*, did not even contain a booklet on Canada-U.S. relations, although the United States remained by far Ottawa's biggest and most pressing interest. This omission spoke volumes in terms of defining the evolving nature of the continental relationship from the Canadian point of view. Five other booklets focused on Latin America, Europe, the United Nations, the Pacific, and International Development. The six themes identified as the principal ingredients of Canadian foreign policy were: fostering economic growth; safeguarding sovereignty and independence; working for peace and security; promoting social justice; enhancing the quality of life; and ensuring a harmonious natural environment.[42]

In very briefly addressing the American economic impact on Canada, the review simply noted that 'Canadians must choose very carefully if they are to resolve satisfactorily the conflicts which do arise between maintaining their high standard of living and preserving their political independence. They can have both.'[43] Not a ringing endorsement of the continental tie. The absence of any sustained analysis of the Canada-U.S. nexus meant that the entire process was viewed as dubious at best by critics. It was, in short, a flawed document but had aroused a Washington that was normally relatively unconcerned with Canadian practices.[44]

Another increasingly important issue, at least in the medium term, was Quebec. After Quebec separatists blew up mailboxes in Westmount during the 1960s, the Front de Libération du Québec (FLQ) crisis erupted in October 1970 prompting the government to impose the War Measures Act for only the third time in the country's history. Soldiers in armoured personnel carriers patrolled Ottawa's streets and the threat to Canadian unity and the continued viability of the Canadian state seemed to be in question. Potentially, the FLQ crisis was disastrous, a fact communicated by a worried American secretary of state, William Rogers, to Nixon. Following the November 1970 meeting of the joint U.S.-Canada committee on trade and economic affairs, he sent a memorandum to the president: 'Canadian ministers and officials spoke freely in private conversations about the possibility of a break-up of the country, even speculating about what choices might then be made by the different regions and provinces. In the formal discussions, the dominating Canadian theme was the search for national unity. And as is to be expected, attitudes toward the United States are colored by this constant concern for holding Canada together. To some extent ... the US serves as a convenient whipping boy for Canadian politicians.'[45]

The Canadian file was closely followed by the U.S. ambassador in Ottawa, Adolph Schmidt. He was also keen that Canadian and American delegations get along at the joint committee meeting. While the North Americans had met often since the Republican election victory in November 1968, Schmidt believed it worth calling the attention of the American secretaries 'to continuing growth in sensitivities of [the] Canadian public about US economic and cultural "domination."'[46] These sensitivities could put Ottawa in a tough spot if it was perceived to be cozying up to the United States: 'Strains of ... nationalist mood may well cause a certain testiness among your [Canadian] counterparts.' The Americans were advised by the ambassador to ignore such sentiments.

To adopt the position advocated by Schmidt, to ignore eruptions of Canadian nationalism or the adoption of policies that the U.S. found undesirable was easier said than done. Canada had implemented strategies that greatly irritated Washington, such as the move to allow its dollar to float in the spring of 1970. This decision was contrary to the rules of the International Monetary Fund (IMF) and had been made unilaterally and without any consultation. Even the fact that the Canadian dollar had appreciated by 8 per cent against the U.S. dollar (a very desirable result) made little impression. Indeed, the float had driven the normally even-tempered Arthur Burns, the chair of the Federal Reserve Board, to tell William Lawson, a deputy governor at the Bank of Canada 'that the absence of consultation ... made a mockery out of consultative procedures such as the Balance of Payments Committee that [Lawson] was attending. He wanted me to know that U.S. foreign economic policy was determined by the financial people in Washington, and that they were not satisfied with bland exchanges of views or polite social gatherings.'[47] Burns went on to point out that 'he was surprised that the Government of Canada could be so naïve as to suppose that it could make exchange rate decisions on a unilateral basis. Canada was lucky ... that cool heads had prevailed in Washington that week-end or we would have had reason to worry about our currency being too weak on the exchange market rather than too strong.'

Why was that, Lawson asked? The Canadian decision to float had taken place against a backdrop that involved an appreciation of its value vis-à-vis the U.S. dollar and that, generally speaking, was not viewed as contrary to the interests of other countries, especially the United States with its serious balance of payments difficulties. The Canadians had been told by other American officials of the importance that Washington attached to an improvement in that balance and they supposed that Burns and his crowd would welcome the move. It was helpful rather than harmful and Lawson found it difficult to understand why the chairman had found the Canadian float to be prejudicial to the interests of the United States. Burns had not, pointing out that 'the United States could look after itself,' but it was prejudicial to the interests of the international financial community. It was a scene replete with irony as a senior U.S. official held up the merits and indispensability of the multilateral approach, and a Canadian suggested unilateralism. Try as he might, Lawson was unable to turn the American's thinking around.

What the Burns interjection and the various unsatisfactory meetings with respect to access to Canadian oil suggested from the U.S. point of view was a country in the midst of finding its way in different sort of world than it was used to. Since 1945 the United States had been committed to the idea that it was a global leader economically, militarily, and politically. By the early 1970s, that notion was coming under fire from abroad and certain U.S. officials began to speculate internally on the country's changed position. The war in Vietnam had sapped the moral fibre of the country and taken its gold to pay for bombing runs in the north and troops in the south. American technology seemed to be second-rate in comparison with Japan's, as did U.S. business organization. Decision-makers were forced to confront on various levels the reality that their nation was less powerful and less essential to global prosperity than it had been in the past. Their declining position made Americans more defensive and less willing to adopt a policy of noblesse oblige when considering requests made by smaller suit-ors like Canada. American attitudes reflected 'a certain self-doubt ... a rather per-vasive pessimism.'[48] The fact that the U.S. current account balance had gone from a small surplus in 1970 to a deficit of US$3 billion in 1971 did not help at all. Nor did the numbers. In 1970, for example, total output in Canada grew by some 3 per cent in contrast to the U.S., where there was no growth. The North American commercial relationship was about to enter a new phase.

The End of the Special Relationship: The Nixon Program

One of the first attempts to raise the sensitive topic of a United States in eco-nomic decline, as well as to suggest some policy prescriptions, was made by Peter Peterson, the assistant to the president for international economic affairs. In a thought-provoking and insightful essay, he laid out for Nixon his anxiety over the future of the United States: 'Recently, I have been discussing with you my view that we should think through whether the rapidly changing economic, tech-nological and social world we are living in doesn't require more systematic approaches to projecting the future development of our economy in order to understand more clearly the long-term choices for public policy. We are making these choices today, if only by inaction, but in some ways we are making the choices in the dark.'[49]

That realization was stimulated by the knowledge that the United States was living in a much more competitive world than at any time since 1945, trying to outdo a number of countries, like Japan and West Germany, that devoted a great deal of time and effort to shaping their futures. It seemed that the traditional U.S.

method of planning that relied on the private sector and market mechanisms to suggest a road to the future was limited in its effectiveness. The role of government in the planning process had always been degraded in Washington, but recently it had played a major role in financing or stimulating new products and new technology like nuclear power, aircraft, and satellite communications. Peterson's memorandum to the president, remarkable in its analysis of the strengths and weaknesses of the American economy and for its suggestions as to how to get out of the economic morass in which the United States seemed to be mired, marked out a different path to the future.

Another reason for hardening U.S. attitudes was the change in key personnel over the past years. Nixon had appointed John Connally, a man with experience in neither international finance nor diplomacy, as his second secretary of the treasury in late 1970. Connally's appointment had stunned foreign financial capitals and impaired the American relationship with a number of countries in part because of his beliefs.[50] Along with Henry Kissinger, the president's assistant for national security affairs, Connally thought that the devaluation of the U.S. dollar would not be catastrophic, a view not shared by the previous Democratic regime and especially its secretary of the treasury, or by other countries. Also, the new treasury secretary felt that foreigners were becoming more, not less, protectionist. As one adviser later recalled, 'Connally was "vociferous about how the United States was getting the short end of the stick in trade matters," delivering "an unbelievable diatribe" against the European Community and Japan in one Cabinet-level meeting with the President.'[51] He was convinced that in order to effect a major international realignment, it was necessary to shock American allies into a major belief change. He wanted, he said, to use 'a baseball bat to get the mule's attention.' Connally's reaction was largely caused by the fact that the United States had its first balance of trade deficit since 1893.[52]

The sharp turn of the path epitomized by Nixon's New Economic Policy announced on 15 August 1971 took American trading partners and allies by surprise. It also shocked some American officials who had not been told of this most significant policy change. Peter Towe, the Canadian minister at the embassy in Washington, told Mitchell Sharp, the secretary of state for external affairs, that the 'content of the package put together at Camp David seems to have come as a surprise even to senior USA officials left in Washington.'[53] Most of these officials, and especially those from the state department, would have been opposed to the Nixon plan. The president had earlier pointed out as a rationale for excluding State, 'that agency [only] represented the interests of foreign governments.'[54] At Camp David, the solitary voice of Arthur Burns put the opposing case, objecting that the type of program suggested 'would squander the valuable good will of foreign governments,' and he warned of retaliation. Connally responded: 'We'll go broke getting their good will ... So other countries don't like it. So what? ... Why do we have to be "reasonable"? Canada wasn't [when it imposed import quotas] ... Let 'em [retaliate]. What can they do?'[55]

Trudeau was out of the country when the Canadians were told of the Nixon program, and Mitchell Sharp as acting prime minister received the news, later saying that he 'thought it was part of a dream.'[56] The New Economic Policy was the construct mainly of Connally, who had outlined all of its major points in a meeting with the president on 2 August. It was launched to great effect by Nixon and driven along by Connally who was determined 'to head off what the Administration believe to be the most important non-military threat to US national security: economic competition from Japan and Western Europe.'[57] It was meant to address a declining balance of payments situation that pressed in upon U.S. policy makers and that no previous policies had been successful in improving. These failures resulted in a much more thorough program this time around.[58]

Among its more worrisome provisions from a Canadian trade point of view were a 10 per cent surcharge on imports, the introduction of a 10 per cent tax credit for investment in new, American-produced machinery and equipment, renewed proposals for the implementation of the Domestic International Sales Corporation (DISC) export incentives, and a job development investment tax credit (JDITC). It was all legal under article XII of the GATT, as long as the United States did not discriminate in favour of any country and a new, tough United States meant to see it through. The policy was draconian and, as Peter Dobell has pointed out, 'It [was] no exaggeration to suggest that the effect in Canada of these short-term measures and of the negotiations that followed their introduction produced a national catharsis.'[59]

The element that most exercised Canadians was the 10 per cent import surcharge, described by one senior banker in Toronto as 'a nuclear warfare type of tax' that threatened Canadian prosperity and employment by hindering the flow of goods to the United States.[60] It was estimated that it would affect about 25 per cent of Canada's sales to the United States and the dollar figures were stark – out of a total export bill to the United States of CAN$10.6 billion, it would affect something on the order of CAN$2.5 billion and was forecast to cost 90,000 jobs if it remained in force for one year. The only redeeming feature from the Canadian point of view was that it would not apply to imports that were then entering the United States duty free or under a mandatory import quota program, like oil and autos. The intent of the surcharge was, as Connally spelled out in a press conference, 'to provide a means and a time where American industry and American workmen can regain their competitive spirit and their competitive capabilities.'[61] The administration also suggested that as a condition for the removal of the surcharge there should 'be substantial progress toward the dismantling of specific trade barriers' to be named later by American officials.[62]

Similarly, the JDITC, which provided for a deduction from U.S. tax liability of up to 7 per cent of the cost of depreciable business property acquired after 15 August, had a potential effect on trade. The credit could not be claimed in respect of foreign-produced property acquired while the import surcharge was in place or ordered before it was terminated for delivery following. Foreign-produced property was defined as that whose manufacture was completed outside of the United States, or if completed in the United States, was comprised of more than 50 per cent imported materials. It potentially affected about CAN$1 billion worth of Canada's exports to the United States, nearly one-third of which were also subject to the import surcharge. Affected industries included metal fabricating, agricultural machinery, trucks, electrical equipment, and industrial machinery. U.S. firms, anticipating the enactment of the credit, began adjusting their purchasing plans almost immediately in favour of U.S.-made machinery and equipment.

It was clear to Ottawa that Canadian manufacturers of industrial machinery and electrical equipment, faced with an additional price disadvantage in the U.S. market of more than 20 per cent because of the surcharge and the credit, would receive very few U.S. orders before the surcharge was terminated. It might even cause some Canadian companies to relocate to the United States. Massey-Harris, the farm implements manufacturer and a company with a long lineage in Canada, was thought to be a likely candidate. Most of its market was in the United States and if head office decided that the credit would discriminate against imports for a long time, it would pack up and leave. The situation was similar with the country's truck producers. By December they had experienced a sharp decrease in their order books and would have to cut back production if the credit made business too difficult.

The DISC was equally problematic. It was developed by the U.S. treasury in response to what it considered to be a bias in the U.S. tax system which encouraged American firms to serve foreign markets by investing in production facilities abroad rather than by exporting from the United States. Its effect was to enable U.S. exporters to defer almost indefinitely payment of American corporation taxes on at least one-half of the profits arising from the production and sale of exported goods. It was estimated that the DISC would increase U.S. exports by US$1.5 billion per year.

Enactment of the DISC scheme would have three effects on Canada. First, almost all categories of U.S. exports to Canada would be eligible for an export subsidy equal to as much as 5 per cent of the selling price of these goods. Second, U.S. exports to third countries would be more competitive with Canadian exports. Finally, investment in production facilities in Canada by U.S. and Canadian firms would be much less attractive because of the incentive given by DISC to serve the Canadian and overseas markets from American factories. The tangible disadvantages affected industries like those in the automotive sector; Ottawa feared that it might encourage the Big Three to undertake future expansions of production in the United States rather than in Canada.

A Canadian Exemption?

The Nixon program vaulted the United States back into the centre of Canadian calculations, from whence it had strayed following the publication of *Foreign Policy for Canadians*. Ottawa's denunciations of the surcharge began almost immediately. Sharp had only been apprised of it at 2 a.m. as he had just crossed the Atlantic.[63] He suggested to the Ottawa press corps that even President Nixon could not believe that the import tax should apply to Canada. In a wonderful example of twisted logic that missed the entire point of the program he said:

> The President [has] made clear that the purpose of this import surcharge ... was to bring about a correction of unfair exchange rates and bring about modifications in discriminatory tariff and non-tariff barriers against the United States. Now, we have had a floating dollar since May of 1970; the Canadian dollar itself has appreciated substantially in value since that time, we do not restrict imports from the United States. In the President's own terms, and I would quote from his speech yesterday, he said: 'This import tax is a temporary action, not directed against any other country, but an action to make certain that American products will not be at a disadvantage because of unfair exchange rates. When the unfair treatment is ended, the import tax will end as well.' In the President's own terms, the import surcharge should not apply to Canada; and this will be the burden of representations that will be made by the Canadian government to the United States administration in the next few days.

As Trudeau was to later say, he 'certainly wanted to make sure that President Nixon [was] aware of the dilemma for Canada in terms of our future orientation in this North American continent' that he was creating with his program.[64] He endorsed negotiations that were underway by 19 August. Edgar Benson, the minister of finance, and Jean-Luc Pepin, the minister of industry, trade, and commerce, headed the Canadian delegation that went to Washington to seek American favour. They were completely unsuccessful, although Canadian officials put up a good fight.

The world's reaction to this program was similar to Canada's and most of it centred on the import surcharge. In Japan, stock markets fell and there was upward pressure on the yen. The Nixon administration gloated, 'pleased at the shock effect the new program had produced on the Japanese.'[65] Julius Katz, the acting assistant secretary of state for economic affairs, had told Peter Towe that he viewed the Japanese as the key to the reordering of international trading and financial arrangements. There was also a punitive element to this; what Tokyo did to keep U.S. imports out was 'unconscionable,' according to Connally.[66]

The Japanese were not, it seemed, the primary target, at least in the very early days. On 16 August, Connally had laid out his views about Canada on NBC's *Today* show:

[The Canadians are] going to come down and complain and ask that they be exempt from the imposition of the surcharge. We're going to be cooperative ... but I'm going to point out that when they imposed a surcharge in 1962, we went up there to ask for relief for American products, they said no. I'm going to point out to them that in 1965 when they had real economic problems, we entered into an automotive agreement with them. At that time, we had a surplus trade balance with Canada of US$650 million per year. Last year, we had a deficit, a negative trade balance of US$1.6 billion, so we had a net change of US$2.3 billion in our trade with Canada in the last five years. I must say that I don't think that their bargaining position is as strong as it might be.[67]

While it might be true that the country's balance on merchandise trade with the United States remained in surplus, its overall current account balance remained in deficit to the tune of CAN$845 million in 1969, CAN$165 million in 1970, and CAN$282 million in 1971. The numbers reflected a U.S. *surplus* in non-merchandise trade from 1969 to 1971 of CAN$1.317 billion, CAN$1.286 billion, and CAN$1.491 billion respectively. The United States actually benefited from its Canadian connection and that advantage was only possible so long as Canada ran a merchandise trade surplus. Still, no amount of Canadian argumentation, logic, bluster, or fury could penetrate American minds in this case.

As Katz told Towe, the United States could not practice discrimination in the application of the import surcharges even if it had wanted to for legal reasons, but Washington would, he thought, 'be more disposed to consider the special problems created for "cooperative trading partners."'[68] One way for Canada to cooperate was to make quick progress on modifying those elements of the Auto Pact, signed in 1965 by President Johnson and Prime Minister Pearson, that remained a sore point with the Nixon administration and Congress. Indeed, Connally had made the general point earlier that the surcharge and the job development tax credit would be removed more quickly it there was 'substantial progress toward the dismantling of specific trade barriers,' which was how he viewed the Auto Pact provisions.[69]

The United States wanted action on the Auto Pact. At first it demanded its abrogation, but the administration was convinced to reconsider. In the end, the White House wanted Canada to agree to the removal of the transitional safeguards and to Ottawa's limitation on duty-free entry to bona fide car manufacturers.[70] It also wanted some changes to the Defence Production Sharing Agreement of 1959, having been alarmed over a cumulative surplus in trade account on defence purchases of more than US$500 million in Canada's favour. As well, the newly established Michelin Tire plant in Nova Scotia drew some fire from U.S. officials who focused on the government assistance provided to the French company that had resulted in its location in the Maritimes. Michelin had received a CAN$5 million grant from the province and a Department of Regional Economic Expansion grant approaching CAN$10 million, plus a commitment that the company be allowed to import into Canada duty-free steel cord radial tires of a class not yet produced in Nova Scotia. Approximately 60 per cent of the tires produced at the plant were expected to be exported to the United States. Finally, Washington wanted reciprocity in tourist allowances.

Ottawa rejected the secretary's position when Canadian ministers and officials met with him. Canada, they said, did not 'maintain unfair trade barriers against the United States,' and the country 'could hardly be expected to pay for the removal of U.S. restrictions which in our view should not have been applied to Canada in the first place.' Despite that hardline position, Ottawa did recognize the necessity of negotiating with Washington. At bottom, 'it [made] sense to see what could be done in the short term to deal with these issues and thereby facilitate prompt removal of the US surcharge.'[71]

Given the failure of the ministers' meetings, an official delegation, led by the deputy minister of finance, Simon Reisman, demanded an exemption from the United States and let the Americans know precisely what they thought. Following a brief lesson for the benefit of the U.S. delegation on Canadian economic development since 1867, Reisman said that the type of relatively open economy that Canada then had 'was not consistent with sharp, arbitrary changes in the world trading framework.'[72] Unless the United States saw the error of its ways and either provided Canada with an exemption from the import surcharge or repealed the measure altogether, 'a profound adjustment in Canada-USA relations was at stake.' The Canadians were moving beyond producing primarily raw materials and agricultural products, a direction in which the population wanted the country to shift. Reisman emphasized that 'There was no doubt that reorientation of basic Canadian economic and social policies could have a vital impact on Canada-USA relations.'

Even though Diefenbaker and Pearson could not really stand the sight of each other, they were also good politicians, sharing a joke for the camera. Also present for this official state dinner was Mrs Diefenbaker.

Happy days. Eisenhower and Diefenbaker. The two leaders, similar in so many ways, got along remarkably well.

Where the real power lay. Opening ceremony in the Diplomatic Reception Room, Department of State, for the fifth meeting of the Joint United States–Canadian Committee on Trade and Economic Affairs. Seated, left to right: Minister of Agriculture Douglas S. Harkness, Christian A. Herter, Minister of Finance Donald Fleming, and Minister of Trade and Commerce Gordon Churchill. Standing, left to right: Ambassador A.D.P. Heeney, Under Secretary of State for External Affairs Norman Robertson, C. Douglas Dillon, Frederick H. Mueller, Robert A. Anderson, Fred E. Seaton, Ezra T. Benson, and Richard B. Wigglesworth. 16–17 February 1960.

A powerful scene: Jackie, the President, and Dief on the steps of the Parliament Buildings. This photo was taken following JFK's address to Parliament, 1961.

Smiles hide the truth. Kennedy, Governor General Georges Vanier, and Diefenbaker out-side Rideau Hall. Kennedy badly hurt his (already ailing) back while planting a tree on the grounds. Even so, his dislike for the Canadian prime minister was already intense.

A quiet moment following JFK's funeral in November 1963. While Canadians (including Pearson) did not generally like Johnson, it was important to establish a good relationship.

Reminiscent of an earlier era, but still emotionally significant for many Canadians, Queen Elizabeth II holds court with her Canadian ministers. Note the three future prime ministers in the crowd – Pierre Trudeau, back row extreme left, and John Turner and Jean Chretien, back row extreme right.

Pearson attending a Commonwealth meeting in London. From Canada's point of view, not much was accomplished at these conferences by the mid-1960s, but they were still a joy to attend.

Deep in the heart of Texas. Signing of the Canada–United States auto trade agreement at the LBJ ranch: Mr McGeorge Bundy (standing), Hon. Paul Martin, Rt. Hon. Lester Pearson, President Lyndon Johnson, Mr Dean Rusk.

Pearson with British Prime Minister Harold Wilson. The two had known each other for many years and were friends although, when this photo was taken, Wilson was intent upon getting into the European Economic Community and Pearson was overwhelmingly conscious of his country's relationship with the United States.

A light moment among future rivals. Trudeau, Turner, and Chretien were all in cabinet by 4 April 1967 when this photo was taken. Altogether, the three were also to occupy the prime ministerial seat for twenty-six years.

Trudeau and Nixon in the Parliament Buildings following the president's address to Parliament in May 1972. The two leaders found each other's company distasteful. Nixon had referred to the prime minister, although not to his face, as a son-of-a-bitch.

Was it Washington's intention to, in Reisman's words, 'manhandle' Canada in an abrupt and arbitrary way? What was the philosophy behind the U.S. surcharge and the DISC proposal? Did the Americans want Canada to adjust to their measures, or was it an attempt to convince Canadians to change their entire way of doing business? Moreover, Reisman pushed the point that Canada's external position was getting worse, the result of a more natural adjustment process than that foisted on the world by the Nixon administration. For example, the country's current account surplus in 1971 would only be 50 per cent of that in 1970. Long term capital inflows to Canada had fallen in 1970 and would reflect a similar trend in 1971. Canadian cost and price trends were not favourable and the 8 per cent appreciation of the Canadian dollar had not yet been fully reflected in Canada's external accounts.

Paul Volcker, the U.S. undersecretary of the treasury for monetary affairs, replied, addressing Canadian trade complaints. His country was, he suggested, 'at the end of the line' and 'on the short end of the stick' in a number of trading arrangements around the world. Such innovations as the DISC proposal reflected its effort to emulate programs in other countries that practiced trade discrimination. In terms of foreign commercial policies, the EEC's preferential system and its common agricultural policy, as well as Japanese trade barriers were very important issues. Canada's Auto Pact fitted in here as well, and if the protectionist pressures that were building in the United States were to be defeated, Ottawa would have to help Washington in its efforts to redress the imbalance, particularly in trade in autos and parts. The United States did not appreciate Ottawa's efforts to stimulate industrialization based on specialization if it meant '[more] export[s] to the U.S.A.' Washington would prefer a Canadian economy based on more 'normal market forces.' Given this rather hostile response, Reisman offered that Ottawa would have 'to look to its defenses and what Canada might have to do would not please the USA.'[73]

The Canadians continued to be perplexed as to why they did not fit into a special category as they had in the past, especially as their condition vis-à-vis the United States had not changed since the 1960s. Moreover, to lump Canada in with the EEC and Japan was, in their view, ludicrous. Certainly they figured that they had done their bit; a memorandum prepared for Trudeau suggested that the country had met the test of good neighbour and trading partner. The Canadian dollar had been allowed to float and it had appreciated in value against the American. Canada did not maintain any discriminatory or unfair trade restrictions against U.S. imports, and it had unilaterally accelerated the Kennedy round tariff reductions which had helped American exports to the country. The take-no-prisoners American approach suggested that the so-called special relationship between Canada and the United States was over. Indeed, Ottawa was very surprised to learn that it was among the primary targets of the new economic policy – an almost unthinkable position for Canada. The Americans really believed that 'The strong Canadian external position was a major counterpart of the weak USA external position.'[74]

For its part, Canada also had issues it wanted to raise. The U.S. Atomic Energy Commission had restricted the use of domestic enrichment facilities for imported uranium and effectively created an embargo against uranium imported for enrichment to be used in electrical generating stations. Since 1964 that embargo had resulted in estimated Canadian sales losses of CAN$250 million, which would rise to a projected CAN$1 billion by 1980. Ottawa had been pressing for some time for access for Canadian uranium since Canadian production was built up almost solely to meet U.S. demand and the American prohibition ran counter to their trade agreement obligations.

As well, the Canadians criticized the failure of the United States to live up to the provisions of the internationally agreed anti-dumping code negotiated at the end of the Kennedy round in 1968. The U.S. Tariff Commission refused to regard itself as bound by the code. Similarly, there were complaints about the American tariff on agricultural machinery and parts, and aircraft and parts. Canada had duty-free entry for these products. On balance, Ottawa had at least as many examples of unfair and discriminatory American trading practices as Washington believed it had with Canada. In the face of this U.S. onslaught, Canada did what it could to protect its own manufacturers and announced an aid program to help see them through the worst of the crisis.

The U.S. Offensive: A Realignment of Currencies

As Peter Dobell has pointed out, the crisis phase of the Nixon trade restrictions lasted for about six months and by the summer of 1972 concern had passed from the scene altogether.[75] That process was helped along by meetings of the G-10, a group comprised of Canada and the United States, the largest European economies, and Japan. The meetings provided a forum for participants to compare experiences, purge emotions, and let the Americans know precisely what they thought of the Nixon program. The G-10 met first in London on 15–16 September, in Washington on 26 September, and in Rome in late November.

At the London meeting, discussions were heated as the various participants went around the table with their issues and problems with the United States. Connally was a major reason the talks became acrimonious. He remained very keen to put pressure on Europe to do something to help out the United States with its balance of payments problems. In response to a point raised by the head of the British delegation, that Connally state the specific conditions necessary for

the removal of the import surcharge and that the United States make a contribution in currency realignment through a devaluation of the dollar in terms of gold,
the secretary exploded:

> I thought I covered that. I find it passing strange that it should be constantly sug-
> gested that the US acted heinously in imposing its surcharge ... The people most
> critical of it have the most experience with surcharges ... I have been asked time and
> time again for clarification. Well, I thought I said that the surcharge was temporary,
> unlike many actions by others to impose import and border taxes and subsidies. But
> I said that the US has no disposition to remove the surcharge until it has some
> answers from others. I could put it another way, perhaps more negatively: If we take
> the surcharge off today, what are you prepared to do? What are you prepared to
> do?[76]

The United States would not talk in terms only of a realignment, Connally continued. First it wanted a productive discussion on defence burden sharing which
could be done collectively or bilaterally. In response to the suggestion that it
would take a great deal of time to settle unfair restrictions in trade practices Connally replied, 'It's not that tough if governments are really prepared to settle.' And
if other delegations believed that the solution now rested with the United States,
it did not: 'We don't have a plan – we've acted. If people want to see the US
engage in self-flagellation, we've done that. For 25 years we have tried to 'contribute something.' We have already made the strongest political moves. We have
taken unprecedented monetary, economic and political risks at home. We have
humbled ourselves at home and abroad by saying we're broke ... we've done our
penance.'

With respect to gold, he said that he had not been authorized by the president
to alter the U.S. position in the slightest degree. As well, the surcharge was less
onerous than restrictions imposed by nations whose representatives he was then
negotiating with. The United States had come to London to ask for help and
to establish a cooperative context in which its problems could be addressed,
although that cooperation was difficult to perceive. Canada's finance minister,
Edgar Benson, the chair of the meeting, was desperate to end it, and was put off
by this demonstration of American 'arrogance' and 'ignorance'. A compromise in
the communiqué allowed him to adjourn with a minimum of delay. It had been a
very trying day for international cooperation.

Benson had also had discussions with Connally earlier in the day in which the
secretary had complained that 'Other countries are using the US as the whipping
boy, and we are entitled to better treatment than that.'[77] The minister demurred,
suggesting that other countries were prepared to do a great deal to help; indeed,

even the French were 'softening [their] stand on a change in the franc.' He did not, however, know how quickly progress could be made on the trade front as others were not nearly so concerned about the surcharge as Canada and the Japanese 'did not even know what DISC is.' Canada, Benson pointed out, did not like the surcharge and the DISC proposal would be even worse. He was also concerned about the danger of nationalist reactions if progress on dismantling the American program was not made quickly. 'Barriers to trade and payments will build up and we will lose what we have gained in the past 30 years.' The secretary's response was that he wanted progress too but not at the cost of submission, and he noted that 'The Common Agricultural Policy [was] an unconscionable evil [and] Japan does unbelievable things to keep our goods out.' Indeed, the Europeans greatly irritated Connally. The United States had asked them to make a gesture on 'day to day agricultural decisions,' but the EEC, taking the hardline French position as its own, had declined. Indeed, the EEC reaction was strongly coloured by 'resentment and suspicion of US intentions.' There seemed to be little reason to rush into any sort of negotiation as both the EEC and Japan were adjusting well to the imposition of the surcharge, thereby diminishing, according to Kiyoaki Kimura, Tokyo's G-10 representative, 'US bargaining power.'[78]

Benson also raised the issue of a possible U.S. countervail of the Canadian assistance program overseen by the department of regional economic expansion to help Canadian exporters through the crisis. The program constituted a subsidy of exports, at least from the U.S. point of view, and Canadian protestations that its purpose was to maintain employment by helping firms increase their sales in the domestic market fell on deaf ears. Connally understood that 'the assistance [was] only available to firms which export to the US. It seems to me that there is an export subsidy as long as they continue sending any of their production to the US'[79] Benson hoped that Washington would not take action; Connally's matter-of-fact response was 'We probably will.' The Canadians would then be left with few options. One that was raised by Benson was a reduction of oil and gas exports to the United States. That suggestion also seemed to make no impression on the secretary. Indeed, it seemed as if he relished the chance of a fight: 'We gave careful thought to the possibility that our action would lead to a trade war. We hope that it will not happen but we have to find a remedy for our own problem. You in Canada have, of course, special relationships with the United Kingdom; perhaps we are going to have to think about new forms of relationship between Canada and the US and also Mexico in the trade and economic fields.'[80] Connally's response was harsh, and even given the recent New Economic Policy imbroglio, the Canadians were stunned.

The American position led Ottawa to undertake a reassessment of its overall economic policy with respect to the United States, in many ways a logical complement to steps already undertaken by the Trudeau government. The Trudeau Liberals had wanted to stake out a more independent posture for Canada on various political issues without the 'nationalist' spirit of the Diefenbaker government. Until 1971 it had been constrained in respect to changes in economic relations both by the advantages of current policies and by the resistance of many regional interests in Canada to the pursuit of stronger national policies. Until the shock of 15 August and the gradual realization that Canada would not be exempted from the import surcharge, the prevailing view was that the country could get 'the best of both worlds' in its relations with the United States, combining the effects its economic advantages, proximity, open markets, and the 'special relationship' with the enjoyment of complete political autonomy.

The failure of the Trudeau government to obtain the surcharge exemption, however, and concern about the DISC program and the Buy American provisions of U.S. investment credits in face of rising unemployment in Canada (7.1 per cent by October, the highest rate in a decade) focused public attention on U.S.-Canada relations. As the *Globe and Mail* noted in an editorial, 'We have lately learned, and are still learning, that Canada's economic and political dependence on the United States is not as easy, secure, or undemanding as Canadian complacency has tended to assume in the past.'[81] The editorial advocated the government investigate the development of closer ties with the rest of the world and while the newspaper could not claim total credit, it was not without influence in terms of encouraging a change of policy. Certainly the Liberals were keen on alternatives to the United States, and the prime minister had suggested the possibility of a 'fundamental policy reassessment' (*Foreign Policy for Canadians* aside) if Washington permanently raised barriers to Canadian manufacturers thereby relegating Canada to the role of a supplier of raw materials. Sharp later confirmed that as a prudent step in the face of uncertainty a reassessment was underway.

Part of that re-evaluation involved rhetoric suggesting a closer relationship with the Soviet Union. The corollary of Trudeau's statement in the press with respect to the Nixon program, 'We thought we were friends,' was an eight-day visit to Canada by Soviet premier Alexi Kosygin in October 1971. Kosygin's visit followed on the heels of a trip made by Trudeau to the Union of Soviet Socialist Republics in May where he had drawn attention to the overwhelming influence of the United States on Canada after which, at least according to Mitchell Sharp, 'he could have bitten his tongue off.'[82] The Kosygin visit was the first ever to Canada by a Soviet head of government. The prime minister told the Russian to the amazement of the United States that 'In its geographical position, Canada would like to have relations as friendly with the Soviet Union as they have been for many years with the US.'[83] The gift of a new Canadian telephone from Bell Canada to the premier was eagerly accepted. The Soviets were very interested in Canada's technology and manufacturing capability as well as its goodwill. They succeeded in that goal to the extent that the *Winnipeg Free Press* complained in an editorial that 'There [was] at least an implicit neutralism in [the Canadian reaction] to Kosygin's visit.'[84] For their part, the Russians were keen to show their flag in Canada because it would be 'useful in strengthening the Soviet position in the light of Sino/American rapprochement.'[85]

While the prime minister flirted with his opposite number from the USSR, officials from various departments continued their meetings with Americans on the immediate fallout from the Nixon trade restrictions. Most of these meetings became constructive and friendly as time went on. A group led by Reisman arrived for talks in Washington in late October, while C.D. Hodgins from finance and Bernard Drabble from the Bank of Canada met in Paris with U.S. members of their OECD delegation to talk about the new economic policy and its continuing impact on Canada. These Paris discussions were also cordial and helpful, although the two Canadians were very gloomy about Canada's prospects; the 15 August measures had caused considerable speculation on the country's ability to achieve its growth and employment targets in 1972.[86]

A series of meetings began in Ottawa between U.S. and Canadian officials to discuss the implications and ramifications of the continental relationship after the events of 15 August. The first was held in A.E. Ritchie's office in early November; both sides admitted that they had no formal instructions relating to the negotiations and could only 'report to principals about talks.'[87] The American objective was for something 'more substantive and formal so progress could be made on package that would help to create situation where surcharge no longer necessary.' The assistant secretary of state, Phillip Trezise, laid out a possible agenda that his side would like to address during future meetings that included:

A Autopact, where US desires removal of residual safeguards;
B Canadian embargo on used cars;
C Canadian embargo on used aircraft;
D Duty free allowances for returning tourists;
E Defense production sharing;
F Michelin, and
G 'Artificial Stimulation' of business operations in Canada by US firms.

The Auto Pact was the real crux of the matter and had been gone over 'ad nauseum' as the U.S. delegation pointed out. Still, the safeguards that Canada continued to apply remained a major preoccupation on the U.S. side, in particular with respect to relations between the administration and Congress. The Americans believed that changes were required in all three safeguards – the 'floors' under Canadian value added, the production-sales ratio as set out in letters to car companies, and the manufacturers' privilege as set out in the agreement proper. The International Trade Commission was later to go on record as noting that Canada had not complied with the letter and the spirit of the agreement in not having phased out the transitional provisions.[88]

The second of these meetings on bilateral trade irritants took place in mid-November. This time the group made progress in identifying matters to which priority should be given, but it adjourned without setting a date for the next set. The U.S. side, led again by Trezise, had no clear idea on when action necessary for the removal of the surcharge would take place in Europe and Japan, but felt they should 'move quickly on the US-Canada aspects of the matter.'[89] The Auto Pact and Canadian (in)action was discussed yet again. Indeed, it was pretty much all that was raised. Following this meeting, and unable to get firm instructions from their political masters on how to proceed, the committee lapsed.

The Americans themselves had undertaken a comprehensive study of the U.S.-Canada relationship under the auspices of the Council on International Economic Policy to examine the trade and investment issues involved in continental economic relations and to make recommendations for U.S. policy. The study, to be completed by the end of December, was intended for use only within the U.S. government and, a memorandum noted, 'Canadian officials should not be given the impression that any unusual study along these lines is underway.'[90] The embassy in Ottawa made suggestions of its own to help the research along. In terms of overall policy, the objective was quite simple. 'The continuation of Canada as a national political entity not hostile to our interests.'[91] There were a number of other motherhood resolutions, such as the continuation of Canada as a free world ally, the continued responsible participation by Canada in world affairs generally, and the continuation, in a form which at least met minimum requirements, of Canadian cooperation in continental defence. Why was Canada important to the United States, and what should the United States government use as a guide in its relations? Embassy officials laid out five indicators: it was strategically important; it was 'an immense storehouse of natural resources for which our need will inevitably grow'; Canada was their biggest customer; American private investment was greater than in all of Europe and more than one-third of total U.S. world investment outside the United States; and 'Canadians are not Americans and don't want to be.'

Taken altogether, these meetings helped to familiarize each side more intimately with the problems and issues of the other. It was better, as some wag had once noted, to jaw-jaw than to war-war, even if it was only over trade. Nor were all Americans as eager as Connally to somehow penalize Canada. The U.S. ambassador in Ottawa, Adolphe Schmidt, for example, told the state department that a meeting he chaired between the two sides was excellent. 'Canadian readiness – eagerness – to get down to business was manifest. In embassy judgment, meeting was excellent start at sorting out bilateral irritants and getting them on way to resolution, and it is important that momentum that has been gained not be allowed to slacken.'[92]

Canada had a special interest in the further development of these talks. It was mindful of the deleterious effects that a current account deficit of about CAN$1 billion had on Canadian economic development. If the United States wanted to try to push the country back to that condition, then Ottawa could only fight. There was at least one bright spot on the horizon: the growing shortage of cheap, easily available energy in the form of oil and gas. Canada was a secure source of energy for the United States, but it was not possible, so finance officials thought, 'to assess realistically the impact of this ... on our current account balance of payments.'[93]

The log-jam that had become Canadian-American relations began to respond to treatment with a visit by Trudeau to the Nixon White House, although it would take Connally's retirement from public life in May 1972 before discussions became truly civil. Given the context, it came as quite a surprise that things went so well, with the president demonstrating a sensitivity and empathy for Canadian interests that was very unexpected. Indeed, in the prime minister's briefing book one of his primary tasks was 'To dissipate any impression in the President's mind that the present Canadian government is anti-American or pro-Soviet (pro-Communist),' which was perhaps understandable given Trudeau's recent meetings with the Russians.[94] The need even to mention that point demonstrated how far the relationship had deteriorated, and how anti-Canadian the White House might be. Instead, the Canadians were pleasantly surprised. J.L. Granatstein quotes Richard Nixon's remark that '"as regards Canada, we don't want to gobble you up." Quite the contrary: the United States did not intend to use its trade relations with Canada to accumulate a surplus with which to buy up what remained of the country.'[95]

The Smithsonian Agreement

Despite some tough bargaining and tougher words, progress was made on an altered exchange rate regime with a gathering of the G-10 at the Smithsonian Institution in Washington on 17 December 1971. Connally had convened the meeting to discuss exchange rates and what precisely other G-10 members were prepared to do to help the United States. According the Louis Rasminsky, the governor of the Bank of Canada and a member of the Canadian delegation, Connally ran the show like an auction, trying to push up the bids as he moved around the table. Rasminsky, a seasoned official, had never seen anything like it. It also fell to him to make the main Canadian presentation as the finance minister, the nominal head, had been recalled to Ottawa on government business. He rejected the treasury secretary's demands; Canada had done pretty much all it could, and that had not been insubstantial in the big picture.

Canada's currency appreciation against the U.S. dollar since May 1970 made its exports 8 per cent more expensive and imports from the United States 8 per cent cheaper. Moreover, this action was taken when it did not fit the needs of the Canadian economy, then characterized by high unemployment. While Canada's merchandise trade balance with the United States had improved remarkably, much of that improvement was due to temporary factors such as the steel strike in the United States. By later in 1971 with the economic recovery of Canada, its imports were up and the current account surplus had been falling continuously since the fourth quarter of 1970. If Canada responded favourably to the American demand that its currency appreciate a further 5 per cent, it would create havoc in its international accounts. Rasminsky would have none of that: 'There is nothing that the Canadian Government or its advisors can see in neither the domestic position nor international payments position to justify this proposal.'[96] And given the revaluation that had occurred among a number of currencies including Canada's, there really was no need for the draconian U.S. demand.

Some Americans had also begun to see the treasury secretary's interventions as counterproductive, although that sentiment would take some months before it was focused. By November 1971 the initiative to correct the American imbalance in international receipts and trade, supervised initially by Connally alone, was broadened to include Henry Kissinger, the president's assistant for national security affairs. His intervention in the conversations reflected Washington's turf wars – he felt that Connally was monopolizing the president's time and that his advice was not being heard.[97] Historian Robert Bothwell has pointed out that the secretary's antics were also spilling over into other areas, 'interfering with progress on disarmament, on détente, on China.'[98] Just as importantly, by early 1972 Connally's program was meeting with opposition from labour leaders and others who now voiced criticism of the new economic policy, especially the attempt to control wages. Those sentiments were very worrying for an administration bent on re-election and facing a date with the people in November 1972.

A Reassessment of Canadian Attitudes

Meanwhile, in Ottawa the whole monetary issue brought out another perspective on Canadian economic development, one which would move to the forefront in

TABLE 3.1
Percentage Changes from Old Parities

	IMF*	OECD	Actual Change as of 29 October
Canada	8.6	–	7.5
Japan	14.6	14.3	9.4
Germany	11.3	9.7	9.7
United Kingdom	6.2	6.6	3.8
France	8.7	9.4	.4
Italy	7.5	10.2	2.1
Belgium	10.4	8.3	7.4
Netherlands	9.5	7.5	8.1
Sweden	6.9	–	3.0
Switzerland	11.9	–	9.5
Average	9.5	9.3	6.9

* Required changes for payments adjustment
Note: This table demonstrates what actually happened (third column), as well as opinions as to what should have happened as offered by the International Monetary fund and the Organization for Economic Cooperation and Development (first and second columns).
Source: BCA, Rasminsky Papers, LR76-301, G-10 Ministerial Meeting, 'Discussion Paper,' 8 November 1971.

the years immediately ahead. For the first time in a serious and coordinated way, the government began thinking of a commercial world in which the United States did not loom so large. A briefing document prepared for Trudeau prior to his visit to Washington on 6 December laid out two possibilities: the first was 'to move closer [to the United States] with an increasing economic relationship' while the second was 'to move further away and to decrease proportionately the percentage of its dependence on the United States economy.'[99] These choices were the precursors to the government's Third Option policy, laid down by Mitchell Sharp in the autumn of 1972. By mid-1971, the minister was encouraging public debate on this issue to prepare for 'any necessary changes in direction.'[100]

This policy shift was made possible by the healthy state of the Canadian economy. The Bank of Canada's dry prose suggested just how well it was doing: 'In real terms, the Gross National Product has been rising at an average rate of 6 per cent a year since the third quarter of 1970 – a rate in excess of the long-term growth path of the Canadian economy. This is a considerable achievement.'[101] Ottawa was also in the process of increasing its efforts to diversify markets, to find new sources other than the United States for technology and capital, to increase value added to raw materials by Canadian workers, and generally to broaden Canada's industrial base. Given the American program, Pepin told the Canadian Exporter's Association on 18 October that they 'would have to try even harder at industrial and trade diversification in an attempt to decrease the degree of vulnerability of the economy.' For the present, the skies cleared when the United States lifted the application of the import surcharge against Canada on 21 December. It was quite a Christmas present. Happily, Trudeau had also received assurances from Nixon that the United States did not want Canada to be in a continual debtor position. As the U.S. embassy noted, 'the mood in business [in Canada was] buoyant.'[102]

Still, with Connally in control at treasury and continuing to have Canada in his sights, relations between the two countries could not be normal. While they again focused on discussing more mundane matters like the tariff status of agricultural machinery and used aircraft, the duty on new aircraft, defence production sharing, and the ubiquitous question of uranium, the United States had other demands of Ottawa, as it had of the EEC and Japan. It wanted its largest trading partners to take unilateral action by agreeing to a package deal with a view toward helping the U.S. correct its balance of payments deficit. Those negotiations had begun early in the new year and were carried on for the better part of two months. The Europeans and the Japanese settled quickly with the Americans but Canada did not. Washington had some specific requests: increase tourist exemptions from CAN$25 to CAN$100; do away with the 10 per cent preference in favour of domestic suppliers for military equipment built under the Defence Production Sharing Agreement; and abrogate the safeguards under the Auto Pact, especially the restriction on the duty-free import of U.S.-made cars. Other disquieting demands were floated in a leak to the *Chicago Tribune*, a newspaper with close ties to the Nixon White House, and published on 11 October 1971.[103]

The Canadians were not thrilled with the U.S. list, but did enter into negotiations. With respect to defence production, they told a U.S. delegation that 'in the right atmosphere' Ottawa would be prepared to eliminate its 10 per cent preference for domestic suppliers. James Grandy had also noted, however, that 'set-asides and exclusions on the U.S. side [had] diminished the value of defense production sharing arrangement for Canada.'[104] Some action on that front, he thought, would be necessary before steps could be taken to ease U.S. trade concerns with Canada. Ottawa also raised the issue of uranium but the United States was not interested. There had been an Ottawa-Washington exchange of notes in 1970 concerning the importation of Canadian uranium into the United States 'which had gone nowhere.' At that time the U.S. Atomic Energy Commission had 'intimated' that it would gradually remove its embargo on uranium imports but that suggestion had been replaced by a statement that no action could be expected before the end of the decade. At the same time, U.S. surplus disposal was damaging Canadian marketing possibilities. The industry was working at about 25 per cent of the 1959 level and Ottawa had had to stockpile ore at a cost to taxpayers of about CAN$100 million.

The American reply to the Canadian's 'right conditions' statement was blunt; market demand was slack and the U.S. delegation 'could hold out no hope for [a] general import relaxation soon.' When Grandy noted that the U.S. embargo was unjustified under the GATT, Philip Trezise replied that it 'would be unfortunate to take the matter to GATT because the US would be obliged to argue for a national security exception, and this would involve domestic US procedures which could "lock in" the embargo permanently.' That was a threat, he implied, that Canadians should take seriously. Only the United States, it seemed, was permitted to have a list of demands, and negotiations were helpful only insofar as they met those requirements.

Ottawa was flummoxed by this approach. Since the end of the Second World War, the two countries had talked out their differences and had always managed to come to some sort of resolution. By February 1972 the relationship had deteriorated to the point where one of the most continentalist ministers in government, Mitchell Sharp, went to New York City to complain in a speech to the American Management Association about US policy, suggesting that 'narrow and self-destructive economic nationalism [was] not restricted to countries outside the United States, but [could] be found within the U.S. as well.'[105]

Paul Volcker, the under secretary of state for monetary affairs, spoke for the administration in dismissing Sharp and Canadian concerns. In a condescending and patronizing speech at the Johns Hopkins University School of Advanced Studies (the governor of the Bank of Canada called it 'a very ill-tempered and tendentious piece') he said, '[I am] confused and irritated ... when I see some reports from Canada that the whole program of ours launched on August 15 seems to be aimed at stealing jobs from Canada. This was not exactly in the forefront of our minds, I assure you. The idea of the United States stealing a few jobs from Canada hadn't quite occurred to me, but is seems to have added to the emotional tone of the argument.'[106]

Volcker's comments on some of the issues on his 'repair' list are also telling. In Volcker's view the Defence Production Sharing Agreement (DPSA) 'quite specifically [said] the United States will import all it can from Canada and Canada should not import much from the United States' while 'in a period of Canadian difficulty they screwed down the tourist allowance pretty hard, and when they got into a strong position the screws have not been relaxed.'

The tone of Canada's position was indeed emotional and it was caused largely by the American demands. It seemed clear to them that Canada, running a substantial balance of payments surplus similar to that of the EEC and Japan, should be subject to the same scrutiny. That parity, Volcker noted, did not sit well in an Ottawa that thought that 'there [should] be special treatment in some sense for Canada.' To Volcker, this was simply wrong: 'When we look at those arrangements, not only did we say to ourselves not only was there no excuse for a special position to Canada in this case, but hadn't the time come to repair some of the special provisions made in the past?' Volcker only held out the vision of 'a more mature special relationship' which would not be, he believed, so one-sided in favour of Canada.

American concerns were formalized in a document distributed around the White House by Peter Flanigan. The problem remained that the U.S. negotiation with Canada for the purpose of developing a package of trade measures similar to those arrived at with the EEC and Japan by February 1972 had not yielded results in large part 'because the Canadians had objected vigorously to the unilateral positions and pressure tactics of the United States, and behind this posture of objection Canada refused to participate in meaningful talks.'[107] That obstinacy had greatly surprised Connally who had believed that the Canadians would eventually cave in.

The situation deteriorated to the point where Helmut Sonnenfeldt and Robert Hormats, NSC staffers with some responsibility for Canada, sent a memorandum to Kissinger in early February 1972 entitled 'A Tough Treasury Position on Canada – A Pointless Crisis,' alerting him to the stark deterioration in Ottawa-Washington relations. It also urged him 'to moderate Connally before an unnecessary foreign policy crisis with adverse domestic implications arises.'[108] A few days later, Sonnenfeldt again wrote to Kissinger about the deadlock in negotiations between Canada and the Treasury, placing the blame squarely on that department's secretary. He called it 'a crashlanding now in prospect.'[109] The assistant secretary of commerce, Harold Scott, was also scathing in telling Kissinger how he perceived U.S. negotiations with Canada since 15 August. For starters, under the secretary's guidance 'the US never had an agreed-upon position or objective' and instead looked for unilateral Canadian concessions.[110] Moreover, despite ample provocation, the Canadians were 'conciliatory and courteous [with a] desire to be helpful without abandoning their traditionally tough negotiating stance and their awareness of their domestic political climate.'

Be that as it may, Connally was seeking a masssive shift of some US$9 billion in the U.S. trade balance and Canada's share of that was US$1.7 billion, to be paid for via concessions on trade and payments policy that Ottawa had strongly resisted.[111] Canada was perceived by some influential Americans in Congress to be an 'obstinate loner that refused to play the game of "restoring world order"' as well a 'free rider.' The rhetoric came to be synonymous in Ottawa with a new and more difficult United States.

Much of what the Americans criticized had to do with the Auto Pact and the elimination of the transitional measures spelled out therein. Ottawa was under an obligation to remove these, or so the Americans believed, and the growing Congressional interest in this issue was problematic. Trade under the agreement had shifted since 1964 in favour of Canada by US$800 million, while the two countries' bilateral trade had shifted in favour of Canada by US$2.5 billion. That left three options: take no further action; take unilateral action to improve the U.S. balance of payments position; or continue negotiations.[112] Opinion was canvassed with respect to the options.

With respect to the first suggestion, it was emphasized that problems should be dealt with and 'events should be controlled and not [be] allowed to drift.' Unilateral action also posed some difficulties. In what areas, for example, would it be applied? Obvious trouble spots in the relationship from Washington's point of view have been outlined above and action on any of these was problematic. For example, the departments of state and commerce believed that the termination of the agreement would actually worsen the U.S. trade and payments balance, while the treasury (and John Connally) thought that debatable. All three agreed, however, that it would have 'a strongly adverse impact on overall US – Canada relationships.' In terms of defence production sharing, there was also a split in the advice offered the president; state thought that to end it would worsen the U.S. position while the treasury believed the opposite. On tourist allowances, any U.S. reduction in the amount allowed duty free by returning Americans would have to be applied to all countries if the United States was to observe its international obligations under the GATT. Finally, the withdrawal of the IET exemption, first awarded in July 1963, was also contemplated. While such an action would slow the development of North American resources that were important to the United States the affected provinces would bring pressure to bear on Ottawa, so the Americans believed, to yield to U.S. demands. Still, there was no certainty in the case. And again, the downside to applying the IET to Canada was the serious effect it would have on North American relations.

There was one major issue on which Canada refused to budge. Ottawa carved a line in granite: it would not scrap the third safeguard of the Auto Pact, which restricted the duty-free import of U.S.-made cars. It did, however, agree to do away with the first two, the guarantee of a minimum Canadian production in both cars and auto parts. The Canadian government also insisted that the major car companies in the United States be precluded from making use of DISC, which granted qualifyed firms tax deferral privileges on the additional export earnings generated by expanded manufacturing operations within the United States. Finally, Canada refused the American demand that the 15 per cent duty on new cars imported by individual Canadians from the United States be rescinded and it would not permit used car imports into Canada.

Under these circumstances agreement was impossible and Ottawa began an evaluation of where that would leave Canada. Certainly the ramifications were very serious; as the *Globe and Mail's* Ross Munro wrote, 'The breakdown of the talks between the United States and Canada may have set the stage for the worst period of relations between the two countries in a decade.'[113] He reported a key U.S. official as saying that he thought they were 'in a situation that borders on catastrophe ... These damn things [trade issues] have been discussed *ad nauseum*. There are going to be people on both sides who're going to say "it's a waste of time."' Connally himself believed that the negotiations were over. Jean-Luc Pepin, when pressed as to what the secretary might be thinking told a press conference that: 'Connally ... was asked to do a job. He had a number of postulates in his mind. One of the postulates is simply that Canada has now a big trade surplus with the United States ... On what grounds? On what right? Mr. Connally asks himself. He looks at that and says the United States is ten times bigger than Canada. So you multiply $1.1 billion by ten and that is the surplus he wants.'

In short, the Canadian government felt that it could not move much more than it already had. Both sides agreed that the issues were far more political than they were economic. Munro was surely correct when he noted: 'The consensus is that the Liberal Government of Pierre Trudeau sees itself hemmed in by the forces of economic nationalism ... The Trudeau government feels that it will be attacked and badly hurt by the opposition parties for making any significant trade concessions to the United States.' The Liberals had earlier been shaken by the reaction to leaked documents containing possible negotiating positions on the Auto Pact, defence production sharing, and tourist allowances. The nation-wide response was extremely harsh and very hostile, led in large part by the new premier of Ontario, William Davis, who perhaps saw in his mind many of those automobile jobs in Windsor, St Catharines, and Oshawa disappearing. The premier of Quebec, Robert Bourassa, had also voiced his intense displeasure. For his part, Connally had told anyone who would listen that Canada had to knuckle under or else. The Liberals were seemingly caught between a rock and a hard place with both the administration and Congress poised to do damage to Canada if the government did not bow to their wishes.[114]

That was where matters lay when Richard Nixon travelled to Ottawa at the invitation of the Trudeau government to sign the Great Lakes Water Quality Agreement and to lay out his vision of the new sort of North American relationship that had developed since August 1971 in an address to a joint session of Parliament. Trudeau was fulsome in his welcome to the president: 'Our relationship with [the United States] is too complex to be described, too involved to be understood fully, too deeply entrenched to be disregarded. We are no more capable of living in isolation from you than we are desirous of doing so ... The basic friendship of Canada in the past several decades has been taken for granted by the United States, as we have accepted yours. I assure you that the friendship will continue for it is a permanent feature of our relationship with you. It will adjust to circumstance and be made more articulate in the process, but it is not regarded by us as negotiable.'[115]

Nixon came directly to his point, suggesting that the two countries must negotiate a new future:

> for Canadians and Americans to move beyond the sentimental rhetoric of the past. It is time for us to recognize that we have very separate identities; that we have significant differences; and that nobody's interests are furthered when these realities are obscured ... Our policy toward Canada reflects [a] new approach we are taking in all of our foreign relations, an approach that has been called the Nixon Doctrine. That doctrine rests on the premise that mature partners must have autonomous independent policies; each nation must define the nature of its own interests; each nation must decide the requirements of its own security; each nation must determine the path of its own progress ... Our economies have become highly interdependent. But the fact of our mutual interdependence and our mutual desire for independence need not be inconsistent traits. No self-respecting nation can or should accept the proposition that it should always be economically dependent upon any other nation. Let us recognize once and for all that the only basis for a sound and healthy relationship between our two proud peoples is to find a pattern of economic interaction which is beneficial to both our countries and which respects Canada's right to chart its own economic course.

Canadians took Nixon at his word. The president also conveyed sentiments that were probably long overdue, or so some observers of Canada's foreign affairs dossiers believed. John Holmes, a long-time observer of the Canadian-American relationship, called it 'one of the best speeches an American political leader has ever made about Canada.'[116] In calling for 'a more mature relationship,' the president was responding 'to the feckless nationalism that flourished in Canada at the time.' Nixon, however, was anything but mature following his return home. He instructed his chief of staff, H.R. Haldeman, to plant a negative story with the Washington press about Canadians to 'put it to these people for kicking the US around after what we did for that lousy son of a bitch [Trudeau]. Wasting three days up there. That trip we needed like a hole in the head.'[117]

During the spring and summer, Jean-Luc Pepin met with a new secretary of the treasury, George Schultz, to talk over the meaning of what this new relationship entailed. By July, Pepin was at great pains to let him know what was on Canadian minds and what he hoped to realize from these meetings. First and foremost, the minister suggested that they both emphasize to the media how 'normal' these conversations were. He hoped to 'de-electoralize' the trade conflict; as he told Schultz, 'The government in Canada would not like to have this as an issue in the next election in either country, if possible.'[118] Pepin obviously had in mind the outraged public reaction to the leak which had hinted of compromise with the Americans over the package. As well, he hearkened back to the dark days of August 1971, telling the secretary how shocked Ottawa was with the news that Canada was to be treated like any other country. This North American relationship was 'unique' and should have been treated as such.

The two then ran through a few other issues including Schultz's thoughts on whether or not a free trade agreement would strengthen or weaken Canadian independence (the former, he believed) and the perspective of each with respect to world trade. Pepin lamented the fact that both Canada and the United States appeared to be more advanced on consultations with the EEC and Japan than they were between themselves on the coming world trade negotiations which would become known as the Tokyo round of the GATT.

On Canada-U.S. trade disagreements Schultz took over, running through the usual themes of the advantage accrued to Canada by the agreements it had reached with the United States. He spoke of the 'extraordinary advantages' provided by the Auto Pact and the DPSA. The secretary noted that Canadians had profited 'from their soft negotiations.' Pepin noted in his report to cabinet the time consumed by discussing the Auto Pact, with Schultz repeating the old American arguments about its imbalance. In the end, the Canadian noted how Schultz had 'made an interesting move: he agreed that the free market might not bring about the right balance of advantages [in the Auto Pact] and that 'an overlay of government concern,' which I understood as meaning government guidelines, might very well be needed.'

As the meeting wound up, Pepin suggested that the two countries should go back to their old way of solving problems – 'take issues one by one and solve them as circumstances permitted.' Forget this 'package' approach that had so bedeviled the North American relationship in the recent past and return to the hallowed halls of quiet diplomacy. Pepin believed that the two countries should discuss the coming international trade round, but also 'a few binational [issues]' like pulp and paper, anti-dumping, and tourist allowances. As they pushed their chairs away from the table, Pepin felt that much had been accomplished:

1 The contact at the ministerial level in *trade* matters is re-established and I will do my best to maintain it;
2 two meetings will be held *en principe* early in September;
3 a hole has been dug in the package;
4 Schultz is hoping that Canada will take unilateral action on tourism and defence sharing;

5 We could move on one and suggest three or four other technical meetings, half of
them leading to conclusions favourable to us;

6 With a view to resume also on the autopact! In the meantime, we should work on
the possible new guidelines ... and recommend to Schultz, a little later, that he
might do the same.

Later, the minister was to once again emphasize to the U.S. ambassador in
Ottawa that the Nixon program should never have been applied to Canada.
Almost 25 per cent of total American exports were purchased by Canadians,
more than the three next best customers, Japan, West Germany, and the UK,
combined. The United States also supplied more than 70 per cent of Canada's
total imports. Moreover, the country was 'big ... with small population, rough
climate, wide disparities and heavy dependence on international trade (22 per
cent of GNP vs 4 percent for US). This led to [Pepin's] main point that it had
been incorrect, unfair and inconsistent with special relationship for US to have
lumped Canada with Japan in post-August 1971 striving for package settlement.'[119]

As a show of good faith, Pepin felt that it might be possible for a unilateral
government of Canada move on tourist allowances and defence production.
Most of his conversation with Ambassador Schmidt was taken up with the
former and their increase from CAN$25 to CAN$50; Schmidt supported that
move, and added that it 'would be popular action in Canada, would be welcome
by U.S., and would cost Canada little.' When asked what he envisaged as the
proper U.S. response to such a unilateral move, Pepin said that he hoped Washington would welcome them and 'express appreciation, but not too warmly or in
any other way heighten the electorate's fears or fuel opposition parties' campaign
charges that 'other shoe (auto pact concessions) would be dropped' by GOC after
elections.' He did not want to give any ammunition to political enemies while on
the hustings.

The salient fact that confronted many Canadian policy makers and others was
that Canada's hard stand against the United States had not resulted in the smiting
of the Canadian economy. For a variety of reasons, that crisis passed, although not
without implications for both sides. Why did Ottawa come through relatively
unscathed? Peyton Lyon and Brian Tomlin offer an interesting perspective: 'The
fact that Ottawa stood firm with impunity ... suggests the difficulties encountered
by either government whenever it departs from the problem-solving approach
characteristic of Canadian-American negotiations. One government might decide
to adopt a closely coordinated approach to the other, but, given the extent and
complexity of the relationship and the diversity of objectives within each government, success is improbable; this is more true of Washington than of Ottawa, since

the Canadian policy community is smaller and better able to concentrate its main attention on relations with Canada's giant neighbour.'[120] Generally, the two political scientists note, Canada 'holds its own to a remarkable degree.' That had certainly been the case during the year following the Nixon shock.

And Ottawa continued to more than hold its own for the remainder of the year. No new negotiations were entered into, despite increasing American impatience with Canada's intransigence. When asked 'Why the deadlock?' Roderick Byers noted that 'At the most general level officials agreed that Canada's international economic position had improved considerably since the mid-1960s, while the American position had experienced a sharp decline. Nevertheless, there was no agreement on the extent to which bilateral economic relations aggravated the economic difficulties of the United States, nor on the permanency of existing economic trends ... perceptions by American officials contrasted sharply with those held by Canadians.'[121]

In September, perhaps reflecting the government's newfound confidence and having been pushed forcibly out of the continental nest, Mitchell Sharp articulated a new vision, the Third Option, whose objective was to diversify Canada's foreign linkages abroad, away from the United States. It was almost as if key cabinet members had re-read Claude Julien's 1965 book *Canada: Europe's Last Chance*. As Julien wrote, 'the key question for the European is ... will Canada allow itself to be colonized by the United States or will it strengthen its ties with Europe and help to balance the power of the United States?'[122] The third option had been opposed in the cabinet committee on external affairs and national defence by representatives from finance and industry, trade, and commerce, who had basically favoured the status quo.[123] They had considered the third option 'a sop to nationalistic sentiment and impractical to operationalize.'[124] Any other choice, however, was just not possible, given the Nixon doctrine and the president's speech to Parliament the previous May. Still, it was not fully endorsed by Canadians, as polling data showed. When asked what the best option for Canada was, 42 per cent chose the first option (the status quo), 18 per cent the second (move closer to the United States), and only 30 per cent chose the third.[125] Still, in the short term, the government remained committed to its new program.

As has been documented elsewhere, the entire third option strategy failed miserably for a number of reasons, chief among them Canadian political challenges (the election of the sovereignist Parti Québécois in 1976 and continuing federal-provincial discord), a waning prime ministerial interest, and a stark disinterest in exploring the possibilities of the European market on the part of Canadian business.[126] It was declared officially dead in 1982 by the minister of international trade, Gerald Regan. However ill-fated it might have been, the third option did reflect the Canadian search for a counterbalance to the American colossus.

That search became more important following the near-disaster of the 1972 federal election, held on 30 October. If there was a lesson in it, it seemed to be that Canadians disapproved of the government's position on economic issues, that it was 'almost apologetically moderate.'[127] The final tally was Liberals 109, Progressive Conservatives 107, the New Democratic Party 31, Social Credit 15, and Independents 2. Until the next vote, the Liberals would be dependent on the NDP to support their program, and that party articulated a certain anti-Americanism. Significantly, the government had commissioned a report championed in cabinet by Herb Gray, the minister of national revenue, which had been presented in late 1971 and dealt with the costs and benefits of foreign investment. It was leaked to the press, embarrassing Trudeau and his cabinet because of its very timid recommendations.[128] This had been a lesson of sorts and in 1974, cabinet had moved to set up the Foreign Investment Review Agency designed to screen foreign investment to ensure that it benefited Canada, although the minister of finance, John Turner, took pains to assure a New York audience that it was 'not a dam, it [was] a filter.'[129] As well, the Canada Development Corporation, first mooted in the early Pearson years and designed to 'buy Canada back,' was established in 1972. Its mandate was to mobilize Canadian investment capital. Finally, the state-owned oil company, Petro-Canada, was announced in Parliament in December 1973.[130] In short, as the global economy reeled under the shocks created by the Nixon Doctrine and the oil price increases of 1973, Canada was set to regulate the daily tasks of business.

The government was responding to what the polls told them now obsessed Canadians: economic nationalism. Certainly the pages of the *Canadian Annual Review* reflected that trend – its editor, John Saywell, devoted eight pages to the subject in 1970. A significant minority (and a majority in some provinces) wanted the tidal wave of foreign investment that had poured across the country in the past twenty years slowed. By the beginning of the decade, foreign-controlled non-financial corporations held assets in Canada of CAN$48.8 billion, representing almost 36 per cent of the assets of all non-financial corporations.

The economic world was becoming more turbulent in the early-to-mid 1970s. The Bank of Canada's *Annual Report* caught the sense of that in 1973; unemployment was rising, monetary policy did not seem to be working as expected, oil price increases were taking a toll on industrialized economies, and the slowing pace of economic activity was troubling. The report noted that 'It is clear ... in 1974 the Canadian economy faces major uncertainties that lie beyond our borders and beyond our power to influence significantly.'[131] In a very real sense it was not a propitious time to be exploring untested options.

Chapter 4

Canada, the Wheat Economy, and North American Relations

The Importance of Wheat to Canada's Economy

Wheat and wheat flour exports were very important to Canada's economic health in the twenty-five years following the end of the Second World War. Although historians generally mark 1939 as the end of the first National Policy, implemented in 1879, that sought to make Prairie development and the wheat economy the mainstay of Canadian economic development, that is not precisely true. In 1956, for example, wheat and wheat flour exports accounted for more than 12 per cent of Canada's total merchandise exports, admittedly a significant decrease from the 27 per cent they constituted in the late 1920s, but still a large proportion given that Canadian prosperity depended on the sale of goods and services to others. Certainly governments in the 1950s and 60s, whether Liberal or Conservative, perceived wheat sales abroad as vitally important. Table 4.1 demonstrates Canada's large share of the global market.

The problem, from the Canadian point of view, was the excessive cultivation of agricultural products because of a wide-ranging system of subsidies: 'Instead of a hidden hand, as defined by Adam Smith, there is an open hand offering a fistful of dollars, francs, pounds or Deutschmarks as export subsidies. Competitive protectionism is the dominant characteristic of the grain market.'[1] For a small country like Canada, competing in that subsidy game was very difficult, yet essential if markets were to be found for Canadian wheat. The country's competition with the United States in the search for customers was a preoccupation in Ottawa. As well, the government worked assiduously to demonstrate to Washington the distorting effects of its subsidy programs.

There was an attempt at rationalization of the market with a series of International Wheat Arrangements signed periodically (1949, 1953, 1956, 1959, 1961, 1965, and 1967) by the major exporting and importing countries, but these did

TABLE 4.1
Commercial Wheat Exports as Percentage of World Market, Selected Countries
and Years

	1949–53	1959–62	1963–4	1965–6	1968–9
Argentina	12	9	7	18	8
Australia	7	20	19	13	15
Canada	32	36	37	33	23
United States	39	21	22	18	19

Source: Food and Agriculture Organization, *The Stabilization of International Trade in
Grains*, FAO Commodity Policy Studies no. 20, in Jon McLin, 'Surrogate International
Organization and the Case of World Food Security, 1949–1969,' *International Organiza-
tion* 33 (1979): 52.

not adequately address all issues, such as what to do with surplus grain. They did
have some influence in terms of ironing out the peaks and troughs of the price of
wheat, and over the period from the 1949–50 crop year to 1968–9, the average
export price of number one Manitoba wheat stayed within the range of US$1.68
to US$2.32.[2] Representatives from Canada and the United States began meeting
quarterly in 1959 to discuss wheat and its marketing and hear the concerns of the
other. That did not necessarily make the situation better as U.S. domestic politics
often intruded into the process. As Donald Paarlberg, a former assistant secretary
of agriculture and the coordinator of Food for Peace, has so cogently noted with
respect to American wheat disposals practice during the course of the Eisenhower
administration, 'We sold what we could for cash. What we couldn't sell for cash
we sold for credit. What we couldn't sell for dollars we sold for foreign currency.
What we couldn't get money for we bartered. What we couldn't get anything for
we gave away. What we couldn't export by any means we stored. And still the
stocks increased.'[3]

PL 480 and American Subsidies

Much of that activity was overseen by the Agricultural Trade Development and
Assistance Act, better known as PL 480. 'An ingenious mixture of altruism, anti-
communism and a well-organised commercial lobby,'[4] the act was passed in 1954
for the primary purpose of aiding in the disposal of large accumulated surpluses
of agricultural commodities and was renewed periodically. It was divided into
three parts with a fourth added in 1959. Title I provided for the sale of surplus
agricultural products for foreign currency to be used for, among other things, the
payment of U.S. obligations, economic development loans, market development,

loans to private business and foreign governments, and common defence projects. In negotiating under Title I, the president was instructed to 'take reasonable precautions to safeguard usual marketings of the US and to assure that sales under this Act will not unduly disrupt world prices of agricultural commodities or normal patterns of commercial trade with friendly countries.'[5]

Title II enabled the president to provide emergency assistance to American allies to meet famine or other urgent relief requirements, although the president was cautioned by the legislation against interfering with cash sales. Title III provided help for Americans who were in need through non-profit school lunch programs and aid for destitute persons and charitable institutions like hospitals. It also authorized donations to non-profit voluntary relief agencies and to intergovernmental organizations, such as the Red Cross and UNICEF, for destinations outside the United States. Finally, Title IV authorized the long-term supply contracts of agricultural commodities in surplus on credit terms to assist the economic development of friendly countries. These contracts could be entered into for up to ten years.

The United States was a much larger country than Canada, with much larger acreage under cultivation, and with a large and very influential agricultural constituency. Congress bent often to their will, voting price support programs and providing subsidies to U.S. farmers against which Ottawa could not hope to compete. American advantages made Canada much more dependent on exporting wheat at satisfactory prices. The United States was also a very powerful nation that could disregard its international obligations with relative impunity if it so wanted. Such had been the case in 1955 when the contracting parties (CPs) to the General Agreement on Tariffs and Trade (GATT) had voted the United States a waiver from its agricultural undertakings negotiated in the agreement.[6] Washington had wanted the agreement to conform to its domestic legislation under section 22 of the Agricultural Adjustment Act, which permitted the U.S. government to restrict imports that interfered with price support programs on agricultural products. By the late 1950s the Americans maintained quantitative restrictions or prohibitive import fees on a number of commodities of interest to Canada, including wheat and wheat flour, cheddar cheese and dried milk products, flaxseed, and linseed oil.

At the same time that the GATT allowed the United States its waiver, almost a quid pro quo, it offered its own resolution with respect to the disposal of agricultural surpluses which was adopted by the contracting parties. The CPs recognized that surpluses might arise from time to time, and that the disposal of these stocks could disrupt normal commercial sales. They also believed that the disturbing effects of such disposals could be mitigated if interested CPs parties would consult with respect to the disposal of their surpluses. The action part of the resolution read that 'the contracting parties hereby express their intention to liquidate any agricultural surpluses they may hold in such a way as to avoid unduly provoking disturbances on the world market that would adversely influence other contracting parties.'[7]

Canada and the United States had maintained a special relationship during the 1950s and for most of the following decade, even despite the U.S. subsidy programs. The United States consulted extensively with Ottawa on its disposals policy and at one point seemed to give Canada a veto over its subsidized sales to third countries. By the late 1960s that relationship came under increasing strain as the European Economic Community (EEC), established in 1957, became a ferocious competitor with North American wheat. As the global trade in wheat became more cutthroat, the United States stepped up its trade in subsidized wheat to meet the challenge to the dismay of the Canadian government, the Canadian Wheat Board (CWB), and Canadian farmers.

The New Conservative Government as Champion of Prairie Farmers

Less than a month after its election win in June 1957, the new Diefenbaker Conservative government told its ambassador in Washington, Norman Robertson, to indicate to the United States the depth of Canada's concern over American wheat disposals policy. Diefenbaker had campaigned heavily on the Prairies for the farm vote raising hopes for cash advances for farmers, enhanced grain storage facilities, and 'the need for greater [wheat] exports.'[8] He had told cheering crowds at meetings that it was his intention to secure 'a fair share of the national income for farmers.' Robertson told secretary of state John Foster Dulles that 'the question of surplus agricultural disposal was the most important item which causes Canada concern.'[9] Canada's share of the global wheat market was down considerably from the numbers it enjoyed in the 1920–39 period, largely the result of 'a great increase [in U.S. disposals] under PL 480.'[10] Indeed, in 1955 the U.S. embassy in Ottawa had presciently warned the department of state 'that Canadian resentment over U.S. agricultural surplus disposal policy is outstanding issue today between two countries and one which easily could be inflated to unmanageable proportions.'[11] Canada was entering the 1957 crop year with 700 million bushels of wheat stocks in storage, historically a very high level. Dulles was sanguine that agreements could be arranged with Canadians and a series of meetings was held to put in place cooperative arrangements between Canada and the United States over the issue of wheat disposal. However, the secretary also told Robertson that his government used PL 480 for foreign policy purposes in addition to using it as a means of disposing of surpluses. It was a potent weapon in the global fight against Soviet communism and U.S. agricultural trade had to be seen partly in that light.[12]

Following Robertson's intervention, the new minister of finance, Donald Fleming, took up the issue with Dulles when he visited Ottawa in July 1957. Fleming was frank in his denunciation of American disposals practice; from July 1954 to May 1957, the programming of agricultural commodities under the three titles of the act had totalled US$7.584 billion, a huge sum of money. For Title I shipments, this represented 804 million bushels of wheat and 194 million bushels of feed grains. Many of these markets were also partly Canadian, which was the problem. As the economist, G.E Britnell, had told the Royal Society in 1955, 'It is the volume of our commercial sales in a number of smaller or fringe markets which largely determines whether Canada has a good export year in wheat or an average or mediocre one. Today, many of these markets have been captured or disrupted by American give-away programmes.'[13] The prime minister also spoke aggressively in support of Fleming against American disposals practice which contributed to the poor impression Dulles and the prime minster had of each other. Diefenbaker, Basil Robinson relates, 'did not altogether "trust" Dulles.'[14] The prime minister, who represented the riding of Prince Albert, Saskatchewan, knew first hand the difficulties experienced by wheat farmers even to harvest a crop. If they also had to contend with unfair practices undertaken by competitors like the United States in third countries, they could lose their livelihoods.

Dulles both understood the Canadian concern and was alert to the challenge it could pose to U.S. foreign policy. While pointing out that the U.S. practice of liquidating surpluses under PL 480 would be reduced during 1958, and 'probably by that time no longer used,'[15] he also wanted Canadian ministers to know that the United States followed·such a practice for good reasons. For example, it was employed to help countries like India and Pakistan, 'which were in desperate need and which would be in a very serious situation if they did not receive such assistance.' Perhaps, Dulles asked, the Canadians might wish to join with the United States in providing supplies to less advantaged parts of the world? They did not, and ended with a restatement of their position: the United States ought not to be giving wheat away.[16]

Ottawa did not altogether reject the notion that the United States should provide food assistance to some countries. As the Canadian delegate at the 12 November 1957 meeting of the GATT said:

[His delegation] ... did not object to genuine United States aid programmes and the extension of help to needy countries; indeed, within the limits of its capabilities, Canada had also extended aid of this kind ... The main objection was that, by a variety of techniques such as export subsidization, sales for local currencies, barter deals and tied-sales, the United States was promoting exports of wheat and flour with such determination and in such volume that it caused great damage to Canada's normal commercial marketing of these products. This was evidenced in export statistics from the United States and Canada in 1955–56 and 1956–57; while the United States exports rose from 347 million to 547 million bushels, in the same period Canada's exports fell from 309 to 261 million bushels.[17]

The Canadian attitude on wheat sales was an important reason the state department took a more critical look at Canadian-American relations. A special staff note suggested, inaccurately as events turned out, that the Conservative government 'probably will mean some weakening of Canada's strong trade and investment ties with the US'[18] as the Canadians 'resent[ed] our trade policies on wheat and certain other commodities.' As a result of this perceived hostility, the Americans went out of their way to calm Canadians' fears over their disposals policy at the October 1957 meeting of the Canada-U.S. Committee on Trade and Economic Affairs, a high-level gathering of ministers from both sides of the border. The U.S. delegation had affirmed Washington's intention 'in all surplus disposal activities to avoid, in so far as possible, interfering with normal commercial marketings.'[19] The Americans could not give the Canadians what they wanted most – concrete evidence of this intention – and the October meetings ended unsatisfactorily as the Conservatives sought to put their imprint on government after 22 years in the political wilderness.

Canadian-American relations had been uneven on a number of fronts for some time before the Diefenbaker government took office. Despite the general perception that the Liberals and the Eisenhower administration were as one on most issues, that was not entirely true. For example, in late April 1957 Thorsten Kalijarvi from the department of state told Clarence Randall, the chair of the Council on Foreign Economic Policy, that it was well known that 'U.S.-Canadian relations were strained at the present time. He mentioned ... the problem of the disposal of surplus agricultural commodities.'[20] Apart from the case of agriculture, Douglas Dillon, the undersecretary of state for economic affairs, told Gordon Gray, the director of the office of defense mobilization, that Washington had many difficult issues in its relationship with Ottawa extending back some years, 'the majority of [them] ... in the economic field.'[21]

The Americans had investigated the impact U.S. agricultural policies on Canadian wheat exports and were certainly aware of a resurgence of criticism by officials, politicians, and the press. Washington's policies, so these critics claimed, were damaging to Canadian exports. Particularly iniquitous was the U.S. practice of tied sales, where a third country would receive some advantage from American exporters. The Export-Import Bank, which helped to finance exports and other programs designed to assist potential customers purchase U.S. goods, was also a target. In 1956 Ottawa had delivered a stiff protest to the chair of the board of the Bank; his reply, 'Well, what do you expect us to do?' was hardly comforting.[22]

As Canadian agricultural exporters had discovered, their government was unable to compete with a much wealthier United States by establishing its own export promotion programs. A possible, perhaps unrealistic, alternative mooted by some Conservatives in the heady days following their election in June 1957 was that unless Washington seriously re-examined the way it did business abroad, a Canadian retreat from the liberal trade policies they had pursued since the war was inevitable. That was a dire, last-case scenario and, at bottom, improbable. The rhetoric was needed to ensure that the folks on the prairies knew their government was working for them. More likely reactions were already being felt by the United States: Canadians cut their purchases of U.S. made farm machinery and other products, discussed the matter in the GATT and in the Food and Agriculture Organization of the United Nations (FAO), and in a more general way let their hypercritical views be known. The Americans could handle that; they were more concerned about a much less cooperative Canadian approach that could compromise other U.S. economic as well as military and political relations.

Ottawa political affiliations were immaterial when considering U.S. wheat disposal policies. For example, C.D. Howe, the most powerful minister in the last government of Louis St Laurent, an American by birth, and the personification of the continentalizing forces in Canada, spoke against them. He told the House of Commons on 9 August 1956 that U.S. policy in this area had been 'very harmful.'[23] Two months later he complained to Milwaukee's Association of Commerce that the United States was attempting to capture markets with its tied agreements: 'There is, in the Canadian view, nothing to be gained by one country attempting to dump its surplus problems on the other. This can only have the effect of making the whole problem worse. I believe that we in Canada have practiced what we preach. Our wheat has all been sold for Canadian currency which ... is as hard as the U.S. dollar, at steady prices and there has been no subsidization of production or export sales.'[24]

Howe went on to tell his audience that sometimes Canadians resented the fact that the United States did not pay sufficient attention to the effects of its economic policies on its northern neighbour. Americans, he said, take for granted 'that Canada will continue to buy every year a billion dollars more from the United States than the United States buys from Canada. Americans apparently take it for granted that they will continue to be able to bring raw materials from Canada while placing high tariffs against imports of Canadian manufactures and threatening still further restrictions.'

On 4 September 1956, following Howe's speech, Norman Robertson had delivered a note to the state department that had highlighted Canadian displeasure with the United States. He was, he told the Americans,

> under instruction to express, as had been done on several previous occasions, the serious concern of the Canadian government about the effects of the surplus disposal activities of the United States upon the commercial market for wheat, and particularly upon markets which under ordinary competitive conditions would be supplied by Canada. Notwithstanding these representations, the United States has increased the pace of its wheat disposal activities with the effects upon commercial markets that the Canadian Government had forecast ... The evidence suggests to the Canadian Government that the main result of the various surplus disposal programmes has been to reduce ordinary commercial markets and to cause serious damage to the interests of friendly countries ... which, unlike the United States, depend so largely upon the export of wheat.[25]

In discussing the tied-sales feature of an agreement with Brazil recently completed by the United States, the note referred to 'discriminatory practices, so clearly at variance with the professed objective of the United States Government in matters of trade.'

At a plenary meeting of the eleventh session of the Contracting Parties of the GATT held at Geneva during late 1956, Claude Isbister, the director of the international trade relations branch of the department of trade and commerce and chair of the Canadian delegation, raised the surplus disposal problem with special reference to the United States. Ottawa had made clear to Washington, Isbister began, 'its concern about the increasing number of countries whose markets were being affected by surplus disposals. With respect to wheat, his Government had noted with regret that its representations were having less effect upon the actual transactions in this field.' Isbister was particularly incensed over the use by the United States of tied aid, where a country purchasing a surplus on concessional terms had to commit to purchase an additional quantity for dollars. This was a discriminatory practice that prevented other exporters from competing.[26]

Thomas Hockin, a member of Canada's delegation, followed up by commenting very critically on the agricultural waiver that had been granted by the contracting parties to the United States in 1955. Canada had been one of five countries to vote against the waiver, but it had been awarded by the CPs on condition that the Americans remove or relax the restrictions as soon as circumstances permitted. Canadians, Hockin pointed out, had always viewed the waiver very seriously, especially given its potential impact on Canadian exports. Over the next several years, the United States restricted the import of a number of agricultural products of interest to Canada, like wheat and wheat flour, rye, cheddar cheese, and butter and dried milk products. The waiver had also impaired the value of many tariff concessions that had been negotiated in the GATT. It had, and would continue to have, damaging effects on the agreement and on international agricultural trade.

Unfavourable press comment in Canada during 1956 on Canada-U.S. agriculture relations became the norm and generally included both Conservative and Liberal newspapers.[27] The *Victoria Daily Times* of 10 November 1956 noted that the U.S. policy 'threatens Canadian agriculture with serious repercussions.' Toronto's *Financial Post* wrote that they made 'nonsense of the various international resolutions adopted in such bodies as GATT and FAO.' The Liberal *Winnipeg Free Press* told its readers that American 'give-aways [were] being deliberately used as a lever to restrict trade competition and limit the markets open to Canadian farmers.' On a number of occasions, the *Regina Leader-Post* editorialized on the theme that the U.S. insistence that its wheat disposal programs were not hurting the marketing programs of friendly countries like Canada had 'long since been exposed as unadulterated fiction.' The *Montreal Gazette* complained that 'the United States insisted on 'escape clauses' ... for farm produce, rendering her commitments [under that GATT] so loose as to be undependable.' The newspaper went on to offer a sustained critique of American policy:

> Such deals [as the tied sale of wheat] would be serious enough in themselves. But they are only a new extension of what have become common United States trading practices. A great part of these practices concern the loans extended by the United States Export-Import Bank. If a deal can be worked out between a foreign customer and an American producer of manufactured goods, the Export-Import Bank will extend credit to that customer for purchasing these United States goods. Such credit is far beyond anything that might be granted in the ordinary course of trade. It may even extend to 20 years, and have other unusual advantages. This means ... that not only does Canada find difficulty in getting over the high tariff wall to sell her goods in the United States market; she is finding the markets in other countries being closed off by these extraordinary methods of United States Government trading.

During the second half of 1956 the Liberals were obviously assessing Canada's unreflective commitment to multilateralism and non-discrimination, and especially the country's commercial relationship with the United States although, as the Conservatives were also to find, there were no real alternatives. As Thorsten Kalijarvi had suggested, it was a time of strained relations that would get worse before they got better, a result in part of the June 1957 election of the Progressive Conservatives. In office barely one month, the new prime minister charged that the United States was violating the GATT by 'gobbling up future markets' through tied sales clauses in agreements for the disposal of 'fire-sale' wheat. He also told the press that Canada intended to extend her markets for wheat in the Far East, but this would not involve giving it away or subsidizing its purchase since Canada could not afford such an option. The U.S. embassy reported fully to Washington.[28] Diefenbaker's remarks provided a good indication of the new government's mindset, and one of the first items on its agenda was to ask the Interdepartmental Committee on External Trade Policy (ICETP), a very senior group of officials, to provide a paper for cabinet with respect to achieving a greater degree of protection for agriculture, short of subsidies.[29]

Canadian Policy and Practice

The ICETP concluded that it was certainly possible to accomplish the government's intent: most of the measures contemplated by Diefenbaker could be realized using existing legislation. The committee was much less sanguine about the results of such an initiative. The ICETP suggested that growth in protectionism would have an adverse effect on Canada's international trade relations, especially 'in strengthening the protective forces in Europe and the United States.' It could also result in serious losses in the country's exports to the United States to the extent that the Americans adopted retaliatory measures. The possibility of retaliation extended far beyond agriculture to the Canadian fisheries, which were 'almost entirely dependent on the U.S. market,' and to the trade in fur and in certain industrial products.[30]

Moreover, Canada's effectiveness in pressing for outward-looking arrangements in Europe could be impaired with possible serious effects on the overseas market for grain and flour, fish and industrial products, aluminum, wood pulp, and synthetic rubber. Those commodities accounted for about half of the value of Canadian exports to Europe, which had totaled about CAN$538 million in 1956. As well, the development of the EEC, beginning in 1955 with the Messina Declaration and comprising the Benelux bloc, France, Italy, and West Germany, potentially posed a challenge to Canada's export trade. It was in the Canadian interest to keep trade policy as non-discriminatory as possible, an outcome more difficult to achieve if Canada embarked upon a series of seemingly arbitrary support measures.

The committee's recommendation to cabinet was that import controls should be applied only as a safeguard to price support policies and not as a substitute for them. In addition, assurances should be given to other countries as to reasonable access to the Canadian market while controls were in place. That piece of the recommendation might be palatable since such methods of operation were not without precedent as far as others were concerned. Similarly, other measures including tariff changes could be used to good effect while staying within the bounds of recognized international practice.

Finally, the ICETP told cabinet that 'The [proposed] regime poses a serious problem in regard to the attitude the Canadian delegation should take at the forthcoming GATT meeting. Having in mind that we ourselves may wish in the future to obtain broad waivers from our GATT obligations with respect to the proposed measures in agriculture, we will not be in a position within the GATT forum to press for effective safeguards in the Common Market Treaty.' The Conservatives were finding out quickly that campaign promises might be very difficult to keep in light of international relations, and that the world was a much tougher and foreboding place than they might have imagined. To its disadvantage, Canada was not a large player on the international scene.

What were the implications of the program being contemplated by the Conservatives? At a minimum, it pointed to a major change in Canadian trade policy. To implement this sort of pseudo-protectionist program was to turn away from years of trade negotiation with others. Changes made by Canada which materially affected the balance of concessions made by each side under the various agreements were bound to lead to action by the others, probably on a large scale, as they adjusted their concessions with Canada's new regime. And as a country that depended on exports for its domestic prosperity to a greater extent than almost any other developed nation, that was not a road that a government could contemplate with any equanimity.

In any event, the government was under an obligation to satisfy its western voters, farmers who had helped to throw the Liberals out of office in 1957. It responded with the Agricultural Stabilization Act, passed on 31 January 1958, and designed to be the cornerstone of its agricultural policy in the upcoming election, called for March. The most important feature of the legislation made it possible to provide a guaranteed yearly price for any agricultural product for which support was necessary. This price was set based on the estimated average cost of production and other factors to ensure a fair return for the farmers' labour and investment, and to maintain a fair relationship between the price received by the farmers and the cost to them of goods and services. As the government pointed out, the legislation assured stability of income by protecting farmers against a sudden and drastic decline in prices.[31]

The domestic agricultural support program got the government neatly around the necessity of subtracting from its international commitments and by late 1959 Canada had taken a leading role in the GATT to encourage possible partners to expand their Canadian trade. In the year since the major powers in Western Europe had introduced external convertibility there had been a sea change in their financial situation. Their economies all were quite healthy, and the United

States in particular had made high-level representations to all Western European capitals and Tokyo to encourage them to reduce remaining trade discrimination and quota restrictions. The Americans also enlisted the assistance of the Canadians at the fifteenth session of the GATT held in Japan in October 1959 to make the case for freer trade. Indeed, the Canadians were already prepared to do so; the instructions to the delegation made that point clearly. It would 'join with like-minded countries to press strongly for the speedy elimination of discrimination and the further reduction of quantitative restrictions ... Many of the issues being considered at the GATT Session, such as the question of German import restrictions, the balance of payments consultations, trade in agricultural products and the implementation of the Rome Treaty, involve the question of discrimination. In all these deliberations the Delegation should oppose discrimination, particularly, of course, against Canadian goods.'[32] Obviously, Ottawa had rediscovered the value of promoting multilateral and non-discriminatory interest in trade matters.

After a very brief flirtation with alternatives to the U.S. market, relations with the Americans became somewhat better. A good part of that improvement could be laid at the feet of the president. Eisenhower flattered Diefenbaker and the prime minister was very receptive to this kind of personal diplomacy. The Americans also tried to convince Ottawa of their sincerity in considering Canadian views on surplus disposal. For example, in March 1958, the U.S. secretary of agriculture, Ezra Benson, sent 'a very stiff letter' to Senator Allen Ellender of Louisiana, the chairman of the Senate Committee on Agriculture and Forestry, dissociating his department from the committee's proposed amendments to the barter section of PL 480.[33] These amendments would have expanded barter practices to the detriment of Canada's wheat exports. Also some importance to the prime ministerial-presidential relationship was a visit to Ottawa by Dwight Eisenhower in July 1958. Diefenbaker could afford to be in a good mood having won the largest electoral victory to date in Canadian history a few months earlier. As J.L. Granatstein has explained, 'The Chief [Diefenbaker] was in power and obviously in charge, the leader of an impregnable party and government.'[34]

Continental Wheat Relations

Given Diefenbaker's commanding position in the Canadian political landscape and his interest in the wheat dossier, the Americans quickly began considering how to address it. With respect to the problem of wheat disposal programs under PL 480, John Foster Dulles urged that the president 'should avoid being drawn out further than the statements contained in your speech ... The valid objections of the Canadians to our wheat disposal effort centred on the operation of our barter programs. This program was drastically revised and curtailed over a year ago and since then Canadian experts admit that our wheat disposal program is no obstacle to Canada.'[35] They most certainly did no such thing and Dulles' comments must have been wilful blindness. Indeed, a few months later, the Canadian government sent an official letter to Washington asking for clarification of the new PL 480 barter rules that it believed would disrupt Canadian exports.

As a result the Canadians would be invited to Washington to discuss wheat disposal and the U.S. barter program 'in order that Canada may be kept fully informed of developments in the barter program and that due weight may be given to its interests and desires.'[36] Included among the topics for discussion was one which readily appealed to Ottawa: the United States suggested that the system of quarterly wheat meetings between the two countries that had been allowed to lapse should be reinstituted. 'In this way,' an American *aide-mémoire* to External Affairs noted, 'it would be possible to review and attempt to solve periodically any problems involving wheat, including those arising from the barter program.'

The minister of agriculture, Douglas Harkness, inquired of Dulles whether the Americans had given any consideration to the establishment of a World Food Bank and to NATO stockpiling. The United States had, but the prohibitive cost had been off-putting. The Americans automatically assumed that such stocks would be given as aid to others and not as a part of the commercial market. 'In general,' Dulles told the Canadians, 'the United States was hesitant about any substantial efforts to sustain [wheat] prices through government buying, because this got things too far removed from the law of supply and demand ... primary producers who must make their own way in international marketing [were] likely to have a healthier understanding of foreign trade than producers who simply sell to their own government.'[37] That was quite a statement given U.S. subsidy programs and it was also a knock at the efforts of the CWB, established in the 1920s to market wheat and barley in foreign markets on behalf of Canadian farmers. Moreover, the American government had bought huge stocks from U.S. farmers that it had given away in the name of neutralizing Soviet propaganda.

The American position ran counter to what Diefenbaker regarded as most important: the protection and improvement of his country's wheat export position. He had already strongly attacked U.S. wheat disposal policies under PL 480 as negative for Canada and believed that they ran contrary to GATT principles over which the Americans had so recently thought the Canadians lax. The Americans thought that Canada was considering 'abandoning traditional wheat export practices and searching for means to compete more strongly with the US in foreign markets.'[38] While Washington was quickly disabused of that notion, some Americans continued to believe that Ottawa would develop a program similar to

PL 480, but on a smaller scale. In any case, it would strongly push to modify U.S. wheat policies and better coordinate the marketing practices of the two countries, especially as the developing EEC had told the fifteenth session of the GATT in Tokyo that it completely rejected any attempts by wheat exporting countries to negotiate to weaken their subsidies and quantitative restrictions in place against agricultural products.

These irritants aside, the Eisenhower visit had an effect which the United States desired and relations with Canada gradually improved over the medium term. While in Ottawa, though, the president had been unusually forthright in his support of some of the issues that had divided the two countries. For example, in a CBC-TV interview, Diefenbaker had said that he wanted to get some U.S. action on surplus disposal and the restriction of oil imports into the United States. Eisenhower, in his address to a joint session of parliament, defended his government's actions, which 'came as a sharp surprise [in Ottawa] ... It had a bluntness unusual to the orations of chiefs of state visiting foreign countries.'[39] The United States intended to continue to supply PL 480 wheat to certain foreign markets, the president noted, because of famine in various parts of the world, because it needed certain strategic materials which could be bartered for wheat, and because some nations could not afford to purchase U.S. wheat.[40] The best he could do was to undertake not to damage normal commercial markets.

With respect to the U.S.-Canada trade imbalance, Eisenhower also defended the American position. The two countries were, he said, not state traders and all U.S. articles that were purchased in Canada came there through the operation of the market. It would be untenable for any country to attempt an artificial balancing of its trade file. Multilateralism, where a Canadian deficit with the United States could be offset by a Canadian surplus with, say, Europe, was the best for the development of global trade. As well, U.S. investment in Canada was good for both countries, a fact that was empirically demonstrated by the premium of Canada's floating dollar over that of the United States. Certainly the world believed Canada to be a good place to invest. Eisenhower ended his address by noting that 'The hallmark of freedom is the right to differ as well as the right to agree ... It is the desire – and the intention – of the US to keep the doors of consultation open to Canada at all times. There must never be a final word between friends.' With the bluntness came enough stroking to allow the Canadians to feel pleased that the meeting had gone so well.

Those sentiments carried over into 1959 as suggested by the American summary of the January 1959 meeting of the Canada-U.S. Joint Committee on Trade and Economic Affairs. At a cabinet meeting in Washington on 16 January, the secretary of the treasury, Robert Anderson, reported that the discussions had been 'very cordial this year as compared to their strain last year.'[41] On all the major issues, agriculture, lead and zinc, and the reduction by the United States of oil imports from Canada, Anderson reported that understanding characterized each side. Douglas Dillon, the undersecretary of state for economic affairs and also a delegation member, emphasized the 'wonderful spirit,' and took as the lesson from this that consultation works both ways: 'We must realize there are numbers of actions we take, as of minor import, which are viewed by Canadians as highly important. So we all need to take much care.' The only real trouble was in writing the communiqué – the Americans did theirs in fifteen minutes and the Canadians in thirty. It then took, Dillon said, four hours to bring the two together.

The Continuing Problem of Surplus Disposal

The admonition to consult more widely was certainly appreciated by the Canadians especially as Washington undertook to talk more often and openly on surplus disposal, responding positively to Ottawa's concern that the practice should not be permitted to cut into normal commercial markets. As well, they were prepared to discuss tied-in sales and the barter transaction conducted under their surplus disposal programs. With respect to tied sales, the Canadians had pointed out many times that these ran contrary to the principles of acceptable trade and certainly contravened Dulles' view regarding the discipline of the open market. Further, while arbitrarily reserving for itself a portion of a commercial market through its local currency sales, the United States was excluding other possible suppliers from competing for a substantial part of the remaining commercial demand. The Canadians had argued repeatedly that sales of wheat for local currency should provide for commercial purchases on a competitive basis by means of global quotas open to all.

The revisions in PL 480 made a number of months earlier on 6 September 1958 had appeared to take account of Canadian concerns. The provisions regarding sales for local currency now contained the additional stipulation that such sales 'will not unduly disrupt ... normal patterns of trade with friendly countries.' The Canadian thought those changes to be encouraging, but also wanted tied sales to be completely eliminated. Ottawa wanted firm assurances from U.S. secretaries on the tied sales issue because despite the new regulations, an agreement had recently been reached between the United States and Indonesia in which there was a tied commercial quota of 25,000 tons out of a total commercial quota of 150,000 tons. Ottawa made representation to the U.S. government as a matter of principle just before Christmas 1958.

The surplus disposals front continued to be an unsettled and shifting one. Even as the PL 480 revisions were being written, the United States was changing

its rules. On 14 November 1958 the department of agriculture altered barter regulations that would make it easier for wheat to be bartered for strategic and other
materials produced in foreign countries.[42] The changes signalled to the Canadians an expansion of the American wheat disposals program. Ottawa indicated its
displeasure in a note sent on 24 November. 'While the Canadian government,' it
began, 'favours the constructive use of agricultural surpluses in the form of aid to
needy less-developed countries, barter arrangements which interfere with normal
trade are a matter for serious concern.'[43] The changes were significant. Prior to
the rule change, a selected list of countries the Americans called Group A
required a certificate of additionality from the importing country prior to the
approval of the barter transaction. This requirement was now replaced by the rule
that the department of agriculture must reasonably satisfy itself that usual U.S.
sales would be safeguarded and that undue disruption of world market prices and
replacement of cash sales would be prevented. The new regulation applied to
countries representing Canada's major commercial markets for wheat. Ottawa
was concerned that adequate safeguards would not be observed to prevent the
disruption of world prices and normal patterns of commercial trade in wheat.

In addition to Group A, two other lists, Groups B and C, required nothing
more under the proposed agreements than the naming of countries and commodities. These countries, including Austria, Ireland, Israel, the Philippines, and
some South American nations represented a substantial commercial market for
Canadian wheat, as well as for Canadian dairy products, which could also be seriously damaged. Finally, Ottawa noted that no reference was made in the U.S.
department of agriculture announcement to the obligation laid on the secretary
of agriculture under section 303 of PL 480 to 'endeavour to co-operate with
other exporting countries in preserving normal patterns of commercial trade with
respect to commodities covered by formal multilateral international marketing
arrangements to which the United States is a party.'[44] As both Canada and the
United States were members of the International Wheat Arrangement, Ottawa
expected that this obligation would not be overlooked.

However, the Canadians also noted that 'the extent of the injury to export
trade arising from U.S. surplus disposals has been appreciably reduced' because of
more effective consultation procedures, and the Americans were largely behind
this initiative. For example, they offered to keep Canada 'fully informed' of developments in the barter program and also to give 'due weight ... to its interests and
desires with respect thereto.'[45]

The administration made a number of specific proposals for the Canadian
government's consideration. To begin with, it suggested that at the wheat meetings to be held a few weeks into January 1959, an exhaustive examination of the
operations of the barter program be undertaken. However, since the problem was

so complex, the department of state suggested that a satisfactory solution could not be arrived at such short notice; in preliminary talks it suggested that the series of quarterly meetings dealing with the wheat issue that had been allowed to lapse be reinstated. The communiqué of the January 1959 U.S.-Canada meeting also made reference to this: 'It was agreed that, in addition to other consultations, quarterly meetings of wheat experts from the two countries should be held in an attempt to solve periodically any problems involving wheat and flour, including those arising from United States disposal operations.' Given all this consultative activity, state hoped that 'by giving the problems prompt attention, areas of disagreement between the two governments could be held to a minimum.'[46]

However, the Americans also had a parallel agenda. In the spring of 1959, the United States invited all wheat exporting countries, including Argentina, Australia, Canada, and France to Washington to participate in a conference on the 'Food for Peace' proposal which had been made by President Eisenhower. Following its consideration of the invitation, the ICETP told the Canadian cabinet that while the president's suggestion was couched in terms of great humanitarian appeal, 'there seems little doubt that the main interest of the United States is surplus disposal.'[47] Why was the committee so certain of U.S. intentions? In large part it was obvious from the situation in the United States. Between the 1949–50 and 1953–4 crop years, the Americans had held about 50 per cent of the average wheat carryover of 1 billion bushels stored by the six major exporting countries and by 1959–60, they would hold more than 66 per cent of an expanded carryover of approximately 2 billion bushels. Obviously, this created pressures and problems for the United States, and came despite 'very large surplus disposal programs which have been a continuing threat to Canada's commercial marketings.' If Washington could convince the other wheat exporting countries that wheat should be used as a weapon to counter the Soviet economic offensive, it could get rid of its wheat through surplus disposal without drawing further criticism from its wheat competitors but allies in the Cold War against Soviet imperialism.

The ICETP pointed out to cabinet that Canada's primary focus should be to protect its commercial markets. Moreover, the problems created for the United States by surplus wheat were of its own making; Canada did not subsidize its producers while the Americans did. It was this artificial stimulation that created the problems of over-production. Therefore, Canadian participation in a multilateral Food for Peace program should, the committee thought, 'depend on the extent to which commercial markets are protected from continual erosion by give-away programs under any guise.' Accordingly, the ICETP recommended to cabinet that Canada should be represented at the meetings, and indicate its support for U.S. humanitarian proposals. However, it should also press for protection of normal commercial markets against surplus disposal, and other industrial countries should be invited to participate in the program as appropriate. In that way it was hoped the Americans could be reined in. There was an additional concern with respect to global over-production of wheat as well, of which the Canadians were aware; the developing EEC was in the process of ramping up agricultural production. The Canadians believed that U.S. policy was a very bad example for the Europeans.[48]

There were, in theory, some safeguards available for Canada and other aggrieved countries in the event that they lost markets to American surplus disposal. Following the initial anxiety caused by caused by the implementation of PL 480 programs in 1954, a modus vivendi based on bilateral consultations had been reached between Canada and the United States. It had been agreed that it was essential to ensure that such shipments should be *additional* to normal cash marketings. In addition to bilateral consultations, intergovernmental machinery was established under the FAO where surplus disposal problems could be periodically reviewed, and exporting countries whose markets had been adversely affected by PL 480 shipments could air their grievances. Indeed, earlier in the decade the FAO had developed the document *Principles of Surplus Disposal*, which had laid out the ground rules. As a result, the FAO was the forum which discussed the so-called Canadian proposal, first put forward in 1959 and dealt with in mid-1961. Here, the Canadians suggested that there was a 'need for further arrangements to improve the international machinery for clearing information on stocks and disposal programs.'[49]

Surplus disposal issues also came under the purview of the GATT and the International Wheat Council under an agreement signed in 1959. As well, the Wheat Utilization Committee had also been established in 1959 by the world's major exporters to promote the consumption of surplus wheat 'and to ensure that non-commercial wheat exports were compatible with commercial objectives.'[50] In the final analysis, the existence of such bilateral and intergovernmental machinery had not removed the threat of U.S. surplus disposal programs seriously affecting the markets of competing exporting countries; it only provided opportunity for complaints after the deed was done without any assurance that action would not be renewed. The Canadians considered it debatable whether coordinated surplus distribution programs under Food for Peace would leave Canada and other exporting countries in a relatively better position to ensure that their commercial markets were safeguarded.

Widening Protectionism

That proved to be so, although the EEC, dominated by France, proved assiduous all on its own in implementing a protectionist scheme, the Common Agricultural

Policy (CAP) with the acquiescence of its five partners. As well, GATT Committee II consultations dealing with agricultural protectionism were underway in Geneva during 1959. However, the Canadians were certain that some of those countries taking part in the consultations were 'not doing so wholeheartedly.'[51] J.H. Warren, a member of Canada's GATT delegation, told the Americans that his government hoped that there would be no backsliding. Excess discussion could lead to that; whereas the United States wanted to hear all sides and consider all the documentation submitted on the subject, the Canadians wanted 'the job done as quickly as it can be done well.' Moreover, the United States was in a position to provide leadership and might suggest, for example, that agricultural price supports should not be more than a specified percentage above world prices, or that support measures would be reduced at stated intervals. Similarly, if the United States would announce during the consultation that it no longer required its agricultural waiver, then an 'excellent atmosphere' could be created that would signal a changed U.S. attitude toward agricultural protectionism.

A change in the U.S. position was unlikely, however, and the pessimism surrounding these Committee II consultations led Eric Wyndham White, the executive secretary of the GATT, to tell some Americans that he was not hopeful of reducing restrictions on agricultural trade. Indeed, he thought that GATT rules covering agriculture might have to be rewritten to take account of blatant cheating; a report 'saying that there is no indication of a universal intention to accept the application of GATT rules on this subject might be helpful.'[52] Nor did the Americans change their own disposals policies, despite their professed desire not to impinge upon Canadian markets. When the United States introduced its Title IV considerations in 1959, Warren told the 17 September 1959 quarterly meeting of American and Canadian officials relating to wheat issues 'that any expansion of trade under this new Title would tend to displace commercial marketings and ... would cause considerable concern in Ottawa.'[53] So much for the goodwill generated by Washington to reinstate these discussions.

That concern became real in early 1960 when the United States entered into a disposals sale to India and also began a sales promotion drive in Latin America and Africa on the basis of more favourable credit terms than would be available to private U.S. wheat traders. Prime Minister Diefenbaker was encouraged to bring up this matter during a 3 June 1960 meeting in Washington with Eisenhower. Indeed, the prime minister 'should seek termination of United States credit practices which threaten the Canadian sales position in normal commercial markets.'[54] He did, speaking 'frankly about the concern that Canadians [felt] over recent United States wheat surplus disposal policies,' and citing the arrangement with India in particular.[55] While Canada was not a major supplier to the subcontinent, Australia was, and if American wheat muscled out Australian, the latter would attempt to find markets in other areas which could only serve to compete with Canada. Moreover, the prime minister dressed some of this up in anti-communist clothing which he hoped would appeal to the Americans: He 'drew attention to the importance of preventing differences in economic interests from weakening the solidarity of the western nations.'

Unfortunately, that cut little ice with Eisenhower. There were, he opined, 'a great many hungry people in the world who cannot afford to buy food, yet we in North America have tremendous surpluses.'[56] Countries around the world were wondering 'where we stood as a group of civilized Christian countries on this humanitarian problem.' The president also discounted Diefenbaker's suggestion that Canada and the United States could work out some sort of a plan to which each side could contribute some of its surpluses. That might be possible, Eisenhower suggested, 'if he had the kind of majority in Congress that the Prime Minister had in Parliament.'

Still, the president was not insensitive to Canadian concern, suggesting that officials from the two countries attempt once again to work out a common plan on surplus disposal. Over the next months, that was done and some Americans believed that it gave Canada an implicit veto over American surplus disposal.[57] Diefenbaker could applaud Eisenhower's initiative which met Canadian objections to U.S. disposal almost entirely. It was a striking gesture, but it also had something to do with internal American power struggles. The U.S. department of agriculture and the state department were often at odds with each other over certain disposals programs, and both hindered the Congressional intent to get rid of wheat surpluses. Indeed, 'State Department officials were more sensitive to demands of friendly competitors such as Canada,' leading one congressman to note that the department was 'afraid of offending some foreign countries and therefore has not permitted the Department of Agriculture to freely carry out the intent of the Congress to dispose of [the wheat] surplus.'[58]

The Canadians appreciated that position. During the mid-February 1960 meetings of the Joint Canada-United States Committee on Trade and Economic Affairs, the minister of trade and commerce, Gordon Churchill, had commended the United States delegation on Washington's 'sensitivity' to Canadian interests arising from surplus disposal policy: 'He was pleased with the way in which United States authorities had been cooperative in dealing with disposal problems ... Canada could have no serious complaints about the disposal of United States wheat surpluses if her commercial interests were not interfered with.'[59]

The U.S. delegation told its Canadian counterpart at the joint Canada-U.S. committee meeting in February 1960 that the administration had recommended to Congress some legislative changes that would place wheat production on 'a more realistic basis.' Benson had suggested that acreage allotments and marketing quotas on wheat be eliminated. At the same time, he had proposed to retire substantial areas from production by placing it in the conservation reserve for periods of up to ten years. The administration was also proposing that the support price for wheat be related to actual market prices. Finally, the Americans had taken remedial measures on barter – they had declared a number of their commercial markets to be ineligible.

As well, the United States and Canada were cooperating with other exporting countries in the work of the Wheat Utilization Committee which grew out of the Food for Peace conference held in 1959. Canadians subscribed to the general objectives spelled out by the committee: to raise nutritional standards; to use wheat to aid economic development on the basis which would permit most effective use of national currency funds accruing from the role of surplus food; and to promote market development work which eventually would increase commercial outlets for wheat.

The wheat discussions had gone so well, and the state of the relationship more generally was in such good repair that the minister of trade and commerce, Gordon Churchill, was to later tell cabinet that 'Canada and the United States had now reached the stage where serious or abrupt disruption of trade was less likely than in the past. It was essential to safeguard against sudden or sharp changes in trade policies and arrangements.'[60] Certainly, he was under no illusion as to whom would be more adversely affected by any sharp changes; the percentage of Canada's total trade with the United States was about 65 per cent while the total U.S. trade with its northern neighbour was approximately 1 per cent. Any serious or abrupt disruption of trade alluded to by Churchill would have a much more devastating impact on the former than on the latter.

As the minister had suggested, that was most unlikely. At the June 1960 meeting between Eisenhower and Diefenbaker, the prime minister told the president that 'it was his impression that Canadian-American relations in the past couple of years had been very good and indeed had been unequalled in the past.'[61] He later told the House of Commons that he had been struck by 'the unusual warmth of the welcome and the expressions not only of friendship, but of a desire to cooperate in every way so as not to cause harm one to the other.'[62] For his part, Eisenhower said that he wanted some reference in the communiqué to the fact that the two 'had reviewed the history of the past several years, were pleased that so many of their problems had yielded to the consultative process and they looked forward to the same processes helping further in securing the welfare of the two nations.' It was the beginning, it seemed, of quite a love-in.

The Wheat Policies of a New Administration

In the U.S. presidential elections of November 1960, a young John Kennedy defeated Eisenhower's vice president, Richard Nixon. Although relatively unknown in Ottawa, he did promise a change of emphasis which might not always be to Canada's liking, or so policy-makers believed. On the issue of wheat, it was thought that there could well be 'a strong tendency for the United States to adopt an even more aggressive surplus disposal programme.' An assessment of the new president written by the seasoned diplomat and high-ranking official, Norman Robertson, described him as 'aggressive, shrewd and tough-minded.'[63]

The Canadians decided that one problem they would immediately raise with the new administration was agricultural protectionism. They wanted to know what the Americans intended to do and also put their particular point to them, that '[t]he maintenance of the US agricultural waiver in the GATT ... has unfortunate implications for progress in the reduction of agricultural restrictions in Europe and elsewhere. The relinquishing by the US of its GATT waiver would make a significant contribution internationally and would at the same time facilitate the removal of US restrictions against Canadian goods.'[64] That was the crux of the matter as far as Ottawa was concerned. Its self-interest in this area could be cloaked in the respectability of its international commitment to multilateralism and non-discrimination when, it suited Canadian objectives.

The new administration did appear to be sensitive to criticism of surplus disposal, despite the fact that 'Farm pressures being what they are in the US, there is, at the moment, less chance ... of relaxation of the restrictions on [agricultural products].'[65] Heeney told Robertson that 'The [new] administration has given encouraging indications of wishing to maintain and strengthen consultations with Canada ... In addition USA authorities have offered to discuss with Canadian officials their plans for the future as embodied in the Food for Peace report being submitted to the President.'[66] It appeared that the Kennedy administration was committed to an expansion of Food for Peace activities, not necessarily good news in Ottawa as such a policy could conceivably impact unfavourably upon Canada's exports of agricultural goods. As a result, the government should 'emphasize the key importance of commercial trade in wheat to the Canadian economy and the need to ensure that this trade is fully safeguarded.' Agricultural protectionism with its inconsistencies, inequities, and inefficiencies, was proving to be as difficult a problem for the new administration as it had been for the old, leading Kennedy to comment to his principal agricultural policy adviser that 'I don't want to hear about agriculture from anyone but you ... Come to think of it, I don't want to hear about it from you either.'[67]

Whatever U.S. disposals policy was developed, Canadian farmers' salvation were sales to the People's Republic of China (PRC) and the Soviet Union. The first sale to China was almost 187 million bushels of wheat and 47 million bushels of barley. These deals continued as the Chinese were affected by drought and other adverse conditions, and the Conservatives 'cleared out most of the 733 million bushel carryover that had accumulated when they came into office.'[68] That was great politics on the Prairies and the minister of agriculture, Alvin Hamilton, acquired the status of demi-god among that constituency. As he told them during the 1962 election campaign, 'Go out and grow all the wheat you can because I'm going to need it to meet my commitments.' Partly as a result of Hamilton's efforts, the gross income per Canadian farm rose from CAN$5,241 to CAN$7,575 between 1957 and 1962.[69] As could be expected, these sales raised the ire of certain Americans. For example, following the PRC's invasion of northeastern India in October 1962, the U.S. secretary of state, Dean Rusk, told the British foreign secretary, the Earl of Home, that while the United States would be willing to assist the Indians in the dispute by supplying military supplies, 'It would be resented in the US if, while America was giving massive help to India ... Canada was sending food to China.'[70]

While the Conservatives were defeated in the April 1963 election, their agricultural record probably helped to deny the Liberals and Lester Pearson a majority government; the three prairie provinces voted almost solidly for them. In Manitoba, they took 10 out of 14 seats, in Saskatchewan they won all 17, and in Alberta the Conservatives were successful in 14 out of 17. On a personal level, Diefenbaker surely had some satisfaction in knowing that he had won his own seat by more than 14,000 votes over the Liberal candidate, far exceeding the 4,000 vote plurality that Pearson had over his Conservative opponent.

A Wheat War Heats Up

Defeat spared the Conservatives the necessity of explaining these grain sales to communist countries to an increasingly suspicious United States. Washington had intimated that they might create a new and detrimental dynamic in the North American relationship if continued to the same extent; indeed, there was even some talk of Canada's exemption from the Interest Equalization Tax (IET) being in jeopardy – wheat sales to the PRC and the USSR 'creat[ed] new difficulties, if not a new situation, as far as [the United States] was concerned.'[71] For their part, the Canadians emphasized that they needed those shipments in order to help address their current account deficit; Chinese and Soviet gold was needed to meet payment obligations in the United States. That was all the more important as the Americans, despite all the consultation undertaken and goodwill demonstrated, were beginning to seriously cut in on what Canadians had traditionally considered to be their markets in a number of countries, such as Japan.

The wheat situation in general, and the Japanese case in particular, were discussed by Pearson and Kennedy during the prime minister's visit to Hyannisport,

Massachusetts, the president's home on Cape Cod, in May 1963. Pricing arrangements concluded between Washington and Tokyo would result in increased sales of American bread wheats to Japan at Canada's expense. An American briefing paper for Kennedy written by the secretary of agriculture, Orville Freeman, noted that 'It is our purpose to increase our exports of hard wheat to Japan ... However, it is not our intention to drive the Canadians out of that market, but rather to regain as much of the historical share we enjoyed in the Japanese market.'[72] The Americans took credit for developing the bread market in Japan; since 1954, the president was told, the United States had 'contributed a great deal of effort and money to market development programs which have been principally responsible for expanding the Japanese bread wheat market. The net result has been to expand the market for Canadian Manitobas, which are available for West Coast export, at the expense of United States exports of White Wheat to the shrinking Japanese noodle market.' If the United States was to maintain its share of the Japanese market for wheat imports, it was essential that U.S. hard wheat exports to Japan be increased. And if that meant unfairly competing against Canadian wheat, so be it. Perhaps most tellingly, Freeman's letter noted that the impact of additional wheat sales to Japan on the United States balance of payments was an important consideration. In a time when legislation like the IET was being implemented to right that imbalance, it was important to leave no stone unturned.

Indeed, in Freeman's view, his department's responsibilities to the national interest and to U.S. producers left no doubt as to its obligations to continue its efforts to increase the export of hard wheat to Japan. The Canadian howls of outrage that it was done in such an unfair way 'only attests to a very modest degree of success in these efforts.' Freeman believed that these protests were without merit, especially in view of the predominant position that the Canadians enjoyed in the Japanese market and in recognition of the declining U.S. share of that market. 'Our alternative,' he ended his note to Kennedy, 'is to concede to Canada a growing share of an expanding dollar market. We believe such a position to be indefensible.'

That was the sticking point; Canada could, indirectly at least, dictate the terms of U.S. wheat sales agreements to third countries. In June 1960, in an exchange of notes with Ottawa, the United States had agreed to give the former a sort of veto over wheat sales on credit. A note sent by Douglas Dillon to the president with respect to wheat sales suggested that 'it appears that some additional wheat could have been sold if we had not been operating under what in effect is a ... limitation on credit for commercial sales.'[73] While credit sales should not displace cash sales, they were not to be discounted just because of opposition from Canada, especially as the Canadians were cooking up their own deals with potential

U.S. customers. Dillon explicitly remarked that 'interpretation of our understandings with Canada which results in an almost automatic veto of any credit sales no longer seems warranted, especially in view of their recent actions.'

The Japanese figured in again as the CWB negotiated a special price to Japan for Canadian wheat, a move which had tended to lower the world price. The deal had been arrived at without any consultation with the United States, counter to the promise made in the June 1960 exchange of notes between the two countries. Over that omission, as John Bullitt of the department of agriculture told Dean Rusk, 'Agriculture [was] ... very disturbed.'[74] Following Bullitt's memorandum, Dillon sent one of his own to the president outlining what state and agriculture proposed. His recommendations included that 'The June 1960 exchange of notes should not be abruptly changed by unilateral action on the part of the US. Consultation under these understandings, however, should not automatically mean a Canadian veto, as it has in the past; in cases which are obviously in the US interest, and in our judgement not unreasonable in their effect on Canada, the US should proceed to complete the sale after consultation with the Canadians, and; the question regarding credit for longer than six months on commercial sales should not be excluded from US thinking when considering export grain sales.'[75] Moreover, representatives from the two countries had met recently to discuss ways of maintaining the world grains price, and the Canadians had turned around and slashed their price in order to win sales in Japan. It seemed that there was no honour among thieves. Bullitt suggested that 'although we don't want to get into an all-out fight with Canada on grain competition, we no longer should automatically refrain from sales they object to.'

As well, Canada had sold wheat on credit to the People's Republic of China in December 1960 even though the CWB's charter permitted sales for cash only. In this first attempt, the Chinese had CAN$60 million available for purchases, which bought them 28 million bushels of wheat and 12 million bushels of barley. However, they wanted more and Alvin Hamilton had then convinced cabinet that Canada should respond to Beijing's request for 190 million bushels of wheat and 47 million bushels of barley.[76] The only hitch in the sale was the PRC's demand for 'flexibility in payment arrangements.' The Canadian government would have to guarantee any bank loans made to the CWB in order to finance the sales. Through negotiations in Cabinet as difficult as any with the Chinese, Hamilton eventually prevailed and the deal went through in early 1961 with Beijing paying 25 per cent down and the balance payable over the next nine months. That was only the beginning. In April 1961, the minister returned from a visit to Hong Kong with a deal for CAN$362 million worth of wheat sales.

These sales to communist countries were not necessarily antagonistic to the United States, despite the rhetoric surrounding Canada's partial exemption from the IET; as Hamilton later told his biographer, Patrick Kyba, he kept Washington, and particularly his opposite number, Orville Freeman, informed every step of the way. Wheat and barley sales to markets of which the United States disapproved was more often raised by the Americans as a negotiating tool in their relations with Canadians. However, Washington did object to Canadian criticism of its credit sales when Canada was disposing large volumes of grain in China in the same way.

The Americans wanted to make revisions to past trade agreements in retaliation for Canadian transgressions. They convened a high-level meeting on 7 October to complain about fixed price Canadian sales to Japan and the United Kingdom. In short, Canada's embassy in Washington reported home, 'the Americans were determined that their views would be registered so as to penetrate beyond the meeting into Canadian government channels. It was time for the Canadians to listen.'[77] U.S. officials made it perfectly clear that they 'took the strongest exception to the unilateral action of Canadian Wheat Board (without prior consultation) in undertaking fixed price and quantity agreements covering the crop year 1963-64 successively with USSR, Japan, and UK. In USA view, this Canadian action not only makes a mockery of C[anada]-USA consultation understanding that was presumed to exist, but demonstrated disregard by Cda of USA commercial interests in the international wheat trade.' The Americans ended with a threat: if it came down to a subsidy war, their treasury could stand up longer than Canada's. Cabinet decided that Pearson would register his government's displeasure when he met with the new president, Lyndon Johnson, shortly after Kennedy's assassination in November 1963.[78]

This conflict over the course of wheat sales and Canadian behaviour eventually made it to the front pages of the *New York Times* and the *Washington Post* via stories leaked by David Leonard, the assistant to the secretary of agriculture, Hans Jaenke, the associate administrator of the agricultural stabilization and conservation service, and Raymond Ioanes, the deputy administrator, agriculture, of the foreign agricultural service. The latter's comment, under the headline 'Canadian Cutback of Wheat Prices Assailed by USA,' suggested that 'USA/Canadian relations took a further turn for the worse ... with Administration accusations that Ottawa has seriously undermined this nation's position in the world wheat market. Agriculture Department spokesmen openly charged that the Canadian Government has committed future deliveries of wheat to China, Russia, Japan and the UK at fixed and cut-rate prices in contravention of free market policies.'[79] The result was that, or so the American claimed, Ottawa had ignored the supply and demand relationship, had pre-empted future sales of wheat on the open market, had prejudiced American freedom of action on wheat exports, and had disrupted the normal consultative apparatus between the two countries by resorting to secrecy. The *Times*, quoting administration officials, asserted that the secret deals 'imperilled trade ties [between Canada and the United States] and undermined the free market.' As well, they constituted 'aid and comfort to our Soviet enemies and our Red Chinese enemies.'[80]

The crux of the dispute lay, as the newspapers had pointed out, in Canada's long-range wheat deals with various countries at a fixed price. Canada had offered Japan 800,000 tons of wheat and the United Kingdom up to one million tons at a flat price of CAN$1.86 per bushel for the next eight months. This forward pricing came at time when increases of as much as 10 cents a bushel might be expected in world markets in late 1963 as a result of crop shortage in the Soviet bloc and Western Europe. In American eyes, the pricing deal amounted to 'a fire-sale of wheat.' The complaint also brought to a head U.S. suspicion of Canada in matters relating to wheat; as the newspaper reported, 'the Administration's action is the first public evidence of a long-suppressed displeasure at what USA officials regard as capricious price-setting by Canada's wheat control board. 'No matter what they say publicly,' complained one U.S. official, 'the Canadians always undercut us one or two cents a bushel in world markets anyway.'"[81]

Why was American reaction so hostile? The Canadians thought they knew; it had much to do with the state of the U.S. balance of payments. The unanticipated windfall of sudden Soviet demand would lead to increased international prices that fitted in perfectly with the administration's preoccupation to reduce the balance of payments deficit via all possible avenues including export earnings, in which wheat was an important factor. As well, the president and Congress were very conscious that 1964 was an election year and it was imperative to improve farm incomes. As the Canadians knew, 'higher domestic prices resulting from higher international prices could have a salutary effect upon the voting disposition of Western USA farmers.'[82]

This U.S. reaction could have made things very difficult for Canada. It came at precisely the time that Ottawa was attempting to find ways to reduce the more than CAN$400 million annual purchase of auto parts in the United States that accounted for a large part of the trade deficit. The Americans were strenuously opposed to the Canadian auto trade plan, and relations reached a low point in October, when both nations were confronted with a myriad of disagreements.

The Adversaries Dig In

The bilateral meetings were not the only way Canadian and American officials let each other know what was happening in wheat marketing. A few multilateral arenas also existed where that could be done. For example, the Canadians believed that the FAO's consultative sub-committee on surplus disposal worked very well. It provided a forum for the regular review of surplus operations of thirty-one members, including disposal programs under PL 480. In early 1964, for example, it undertook several studies on the nature of concessional transactions and their effects on commercial trade. The organization had also drawn up *Principles of Surplus Disposal and Guiding Lines* to be consulted by countries when entering into surplus disposal transactions. The document had formally been accepted by forty-eight members.

As well, the International Wheat Council annually reviewed the performance of member countries on the basis of a full record of commercial and concessional transactions and the impact of government assisted sales on commercial trade. Similarly, the United Nations/FAO World Food Program established an international framework for the distribution of food to meet emergencies and to experiment with food aid as a means of economic development. In this case, as a Canadian document noted, 'The application of stringent criteria ensure that such food aid does not move in commercial channels.'[83] Finally, there was the GATT Group on Cereals in which the Canadians participated and which had developed the International Grains Arrangement (IGA) that fixed maximum and minimum prices for wheat and other grains. As the instructions to the Canadian delegation to the GATT Group noted in June 1963, Canada should 'support a new grains agreement which would provide stability of prices and orderly marketing, assured access to import markets on a basis of comparative advantage, and higher prices but not at levels which would encourage uneconomic producers.'[84]

The GATT provided a forum in which the CPs could question each other as to special arrangements that might have been made in the past. For example, each year the United States submitted a report on the status of its 1955 agricultural waiver. A difficult meeting was held in April 1966 as the GATT's Kennedy round agricultural negotiations laboured on, and where the U.S. representative defended his government's maintenance of restrictions on agricultural imports. The working group, of which Canada was a member, was critical: 'It was also recalled,' the minutes noted, 'that the United States Government had subscribed to the Kennedy Round ministerial resolution on improving condition of world trade for agricultural products ... [but] the [present U.S.] report [justifying the agricultural waiver of 1955] was so negative on any improvement in the quotas that there seemed to be a contradiction with the objectives of the Kennedy Round.'[85]

In particular, the Canadian representative was exercised over U.S. wheat disposals policy. He had the support of others in the working group who thought that they detected a change in American thinking on surpluses. If they were correct, then non-commercial sales, by means of tied sales provisions and by

TABLE 4.2
Canadian and U.S. Exports of Wheat and Wheat Flour (thousands of metric tons)

Exports to	1964 C	1964 US	1965 C	1965 US	1966 C	1966 US	1967 C	1967 US	1968 C	1968 US
Costa Rica	24	26	28	18	24	37	–	46	–	71
Guatemala	13	53	6	61	1	72	–	59	1	59
Honduras	3	25	3	30	2	30	–	27	–	39
Nicaragua	14	16	14	18	7	28	–	22	–	35
Ecuador	32	25	32	37	11	55	8	58	14	63

Source: Theodore Cohn with Inge Bailey, 'Canadian-American Relations and Agricultural Trade Surpluses: The Case of Barter,' in Irene Sage Knell and John English, eds., *Canadian Agriculture in a Global Context: Opportunities and Obligations* (Waterloo, ON: University of Waterloo Press, 1986)

increased use of local currency for market development, might tend to unduly stimulate U.S. commercial exports to the detriment of other exporting countries while upsetting traditional trade patterns. The Argentine on the working group told the U.S. delegate that in this connection, his country had been affected by sales on concessional terms to its traditional markets. As an example, he pointed out that since 1954–5, shipments under PL 480 to Latin American Free Trade Area partners had increased more than fourteen-fold, while in the same period commercial sales from the United States to those countries only doubled. That had adversely affected Canadian markets as well (see table 4.2).

The arrangements noted above helped to ensure the acceptance of the principle of additionality – that concessional transactions should be additional to, and not displace, usual commercial marketings. The observance of proper critieria led to a much larger absorption of food surpluses. In addition to improved consultative procedures, other factors rendered the problem of agricultural surpluses less acute. Most importantly, the principal producing countries, particularly the United States and Canada, proved able to hold their surplus stocks, stocks not as burdensome as they had been during the previous decade. By the end of the 1961–2 season, carryover stocks of grain had declined for the first time since the beginning of the surplus accumulation in the early 1950s.

Canada had also attempted its own multilateral initiative at the twentieth session of the GATT. Naturally, the problem of surplus disposal derived from the accumulation of large surpluses, oftentimes built up through government's financial encouragement to farmers. The Canadian position was that the high levels of agricultural support and related protective measures prevailing in industrialized countries be moderated or eliminated. This, however, was a non-starter with both the Europeans and their newly minted CAP and the Americans. Both insisted that they had a right to produce agricultural surpluses, demonstrated by the CAP and PL 480, which was adopted as an integral and quasi-permanent element in U.S. bilateral aid programs.

The Canadians opposed this development, for what it was worth. Jake Warren, the Canadian delegate at the twentieth session had drawn attention to the problem of surpluses: 'There was perhaps a danger that the accumulation of surpluses and their disposal was, or should be, a normal and accepted feature of the patterns of world production and trade. Any such assumption that was unqualified would be dangerous because the basic way to deal with these problems was to assure a better balance between supply and economic demand ... It was important to these [food] exporting countries that commercial markets should be maintained and that they should reap some advantages from any increases in demand for these commodities.'[86] There was no reason, the Canadians believed, to depart from that position. While the 1955 resolution had been effective in ensuring consultative procedures, attention should now be directed to the root cause of surplus accumulation.

That cut no ice with either the Americans or the Europeans. Indeed, the latter continued to develop and expand their common agricultural policy, which encouraged uneconomic production throughout the six nations comprising the EEC. As for the former, their influential farm community would brook no reduction in the amount of agricultural support programs. As well, the U.S. government had other issues on its plate. The balance of payments deficit, for example, was more than US$3 billion in 1964, a sum which greatly concerned other Western countries. The U.S. point, made often in the run-up to the Kennedy round to its various GATT partners, was that the EEC must reduce the level of subsidy paid under the CAP and generally reduce barriers to trade in agricultural products. More access to the markets of the Six would help to ease U.S. balance of payments problems.

European Subsidies Are Added to the Mix

The subsidy war that the U.S. and the EEC had entered into would last into the twenty-first century, and while certain farmers of those commodities covered by support programs would prosper, they also cost national treasuries a large amount of money. The battle lines were drawn during the GATT's Kennedy round negotiations that lasted from 1964 to 1967. While it was primarily a U.S.-EEC confrontation, Canada was very much affected by the result. EEC policy was largely the creation of France and its nationalist president, Charles de Gaulle and the implementation of the CAP in the early 1960s had upset the Canadians greatly.

For example, in the case of wheat, producer prices had been increased, leading to greater output at the same time that wheat consumption among EEC countries had dropped. This naturally created a surplus that had to be disposed of somehow. As well, the French were intent on getting their own way, almost regardless of the damage that might be done to the EEC as a whole. The infamous French 'empty chair' incident, where France had boycotted the European Economic Commission for six months from late June 1965 until January of the following year and brought the EEC's decision-making machinery to its knees, was one example.

French policy also had implications for the Kennedy round, especially in the agricultural field where Canada, in particular, wanted a satisfactory conclusion to the negotiations. Not until September 1966 was the EEC ready to seriously negotiate. As the tariff round must end by 30 June 1967 because of the expiry of the American Trade Expansion Act, the legislation that had allowed the United States to enter into the negotiations in the first place, not much time was left for work on such a contentious area.

While the Kennedy round negotiations were largely between the EEC and the United States, with each denouncing the other's subsidy programs, Canada was much more than just an interested bystander. For example, the EEC's insistence on a self-sufficiency ratio (SSR), which would provide an agreed percentage of its wheat requirements from its own needs and leave the rest to by supplied by others, set the Canadians on edge. The EEC offered as its initial position an SSR that was above its actual degree of self-sufficiency at that time. The Canadians could see their markets in EEC countries like Italy and West Germany disappearing, to say nothing of markets in third countries. As well, the problem of the United States matching the EEC's subsidization schemes would make the problem of oversupply worse. Finally, the United Kingdom, with its balance of payments difficulties, was not interested in paying more for foreign wheat.

The British delegation was 'taking a particularly negative attitude in the Kennedy Round cereals negotiation. They [were] resisting any but the most minimal increase in the price range [and]; they are pressing to be permitted to further increase their own domestic grain production and thus to further cut back access to their market.'[87] If, the British argued, price increases to producers were awarded, then they wanted to be free to produce a higher proportion of their own grain requirements. This demand irritated the Canadians because of past unrequited expectations.

In the previous bilateral agreement on cereals that had been concluded with the United Kingdom in 1964 Canada had consented to a departure from its historic contractual right to free entry for wheat in the British market so as to enable the United Kingdom to establish import levies on wheat designed to maintain its domestic levels of minimum support prices. In return, London undertook to maintain total imports of grains at their existing levels to permit exporters to share in the growth of the British market and to take corrective measures in its domestic policy in order to restrain excessive production. The British also undertook to join with Canada in working for a broader international agreement on grains in the Kennedy round. None of those commitments had been met, at least according to Canadian analyses. British grains production had increased, imports had fallen, and London's corrective measures had been ineffective. In the end, the United Kingdom had indicated that it was unable to meet the obligations set forth in the bilateral agreements.

The Canadians complained, but to little effect. However, they did realize that the key issue for them would be the United Kingdom's position in the Kennedy round cereals negotiations, particularly on the question of price. Ottawa had decided that it should make clear to the British that unless there was a major move on the part of the United Kingdom to meet Canada's price objectives there could be no prospect of concluding a cereals agreement. That, it was hoped, would entail serious risks for the United Kingdom, not only in terms of its traditional interest in stability in wheat marketing, but also in terms of the overall results of the Kennedy round and, more generally, of Canada's trade relations with the United Kingdom.

Those concerns, and others, animated Canadian negotiators during the Kennedy round where they could claim some success. A Canadian briefing paper written in mid-June 1967 shortly before the end of the round optimistically claimed that 'Agreement has been reached on the basic elements of a new international grains agreement including a significant increase in the minimum and maximum prices for specified qualities of wheat and substantially strengthened arrangements for co-operation to maintain market stability.'[88]

The Canadian Position

The document outlining Canadian strategy for the late Kennedy round negotiations, as well as a pending meeting of the U.S.-Canada committee on trade and economic affairs scheduled to take place in late June 1967, highlighted those areas which Canada thought important. First and foremost, the country's delegation would be seeking agreement on definitions of commercial transactions as well as guidelines for non-commercial transactions so as to provide 'acceptable safeguards for marketings.'[89] It would also pursue agreed limitations on the use of export subsidies, which Canada could not afford on the scale necessary to compete against the EEC and the United States.

The Canadians thought that the successful functioning of the new grains agreement would necessitate a greater degree of consultation than under previous agreements. Accordingly, there were formal consultative procedures set out with a view to facilitating the observance of what had become a complex schedule of minimum and maximum prices. The onus would be on the major exporting countries to ensure that those procedures were effective. The Canadians also believed that it would be necessary to supplement those meetings with less formal ones with Argentina, Australia, and the United States, the other major exporting countries.

Ottawa also laid out an ambitious schedule for doing away with non-tariff barriers, which it believed constituted a major hindrance to international trade: 'The widespread adoption of national policies designed to ensure adequate incomes in agriculture combined with a tendency towards self-sufficiency result in support policies, levy systems, subsidized exports and a variety of regulations which either by design or inadvertence create barriers to trade.'[90] An attack on those barriers in any future trade negotiation must involve international agreement on national agricultural policies in developed countries. Attention would also have to be paid to the need for further liberalization of trade in the agricultural products of less developed countries. The Canadians believed that by providing export markets for the produce of those countries as well as continuing assistance to their economic development, growing commercial markets for temperate agricultural produce would result.

That position harkened back to *Trends in International Trade*, written by a committee led by the economist Gottfried Haberler and published by the GATT in 1958. Its mandate had been to analyse trends in agricultural trade and to pay particular attention to the impact of protectionism on primary products. The committee had focused on the system of agricultural support schemes as the principal culprit and recommended that countries refrain from using trade policy to achieve domestic agricultural stabilization. The report's recommendations had been shelved as governments refused to alienate their agricultural populations by making them more responsive to market forces.

In terms of Canada-U.S. agricultural trade, there remained considerable scope for trade liberalization, yet this was being held back by restrictive policies in either country. For example, section 22 of the U.S. Agricultural Adjustment Act provided for the application of quantitative restrictions on a wide range of products of export interest to Canada. Conversely, Canada applied restrictive import policies on commodities such as some dairy products. The major area for possible consideration, or so the Canadians believed, was the trade in coarse grains and wheat.

Deepening Global Protectionism

Indeed, the opposite took place as the sphere of wheat exporting became more and more competitive. The relatively benign wheat world of mid-1967 had turned vicious by July 1968 as the IGA collapsed in the face of worldwide over-production. A growing European surplus, stimulated by the CAP, now competed vigorously with North American wheat in world markets. The result was a down-ward spiral as prices were slashed below the minimum US$1.73. Canada's share of world wheat markets in 1968 continued to decline, resulting in mounting sur-pluses and increasingly desperate calls for action by prairie farmers. The United States told Canada that its intention was to pursue a more aggressive price policy aimed at meeting competition from other exporters, particularly Australia and France, and at exporting additional quantities of wheat. Efforts by the Canadians to maintain the same price levels under the IGA that the United States had sup-ported in years past were fruitless in face of an American determination to begin to address in growing balance of payments deficit and to clear out some of its stocks. In short, the Canadian-American 'duopoly' of the 1950s and 1960s as a '"surrogate system" of world food security' broke down.[91]

A series of meetings among exporters had attempted to maintain the negoti-ated minimum price per bushel of US$1.73 but the price had fallen through the floor. The United States had supported those efforts, but at the same time 'sought to obtain what it considers to be an acceptable share of the world wheat market.'[92] When Canada attempted to achieve price stability on its own by adhering to the IGA, Canadian sales declined precipitously. When Jean-Luc Pepin, the minister of industry, trade and commerce (ITC), informed the House of Commons of the suspension of the IGA pricing arrangements, he said that it was perhaps the only way to *save* the agreement: 'We may have lost a number of sales ... [but] it was worth the effort.'[93] As a result, the CWB price was dis-counted by between 2 and 7 cents per bushel on most grades of wheat, below the minimum set price. U.S. prices were cut by up to 12 cents per bushel.[94]

This drove the Canadians to distraction and the government sent a message to that effect to Washington just prior to a visit by Prime Minister Pierre Trudeau. Trudeau's first meetings with President Nixon were slated to take place on 24–5 March 1969, and wheat sales discussions would be a big part of them. The note, which Maurice Schwarzmann, the deputy minister of ITC, told American embassy officials 'was about as tough as a country could deliver to a friendly nation,' emphasized Canada's deep concern over the price race to the bottom.[95]

However, the Americans would not provide any assurances to the Canadians that they would abide by the rules in the future. Their intention was to win what they considered to be a reasonable share of the world wheat market.

As well as adversely affecting Canada's farmers, declining wheat prices also affected Canada's bottom line. By mid-1969, the government could contemplate a federal surplus, but that surplus could be jeopardized by the need to do something about the plight of western farmers. In an interview with an official from the U.S. embassy in Ottawa, the deputy minister of finance, R.B. Bryce, noted 'that the Treasury already stands to lose from the wheat situation since sales prices for wheat stored by the Wheat Board will [now] be lower than costs – a difference that the government must make up.'[96] It was also clear to the deputy minister that wheat production had to be slashed given the hostile climate of global pricing. The prime minister had raised that possibility in a meeting with western farmers in July 1969: 'It is a mistake to think that we can sell all the wheat that we can produce. We must address our production.'[97] A federal task force on agriculture struck in that year and the Lower Inventories for Tomorrow (LIFT) program were both designed to achieve just that result by paying farmers a set amount not to plant wheat.[98] Ottawa viewed the current situation as constituting a grain marketing crisis.

At an April 1969 meeting among exporters designed to specifically address the IGA price structure, it was agreed that adjustments should be made to safeguard the agreement and to strengthen world wheat prices. The meeting was followed by a degree of price stability, although France continued to offer wheat at prices as much as thirty cents below the minimum. Australia, too, maintained a very aggressive wheat export regime, while the United States made it clear that it was very dissatisfied with its export performance. In particular, Washington was disturbed by French sales of wheat to Taiwan in early 1969 at highly subsidized prices that threatened to displace American wheat and grains. The United States raised this issue with the EEC Commission's vice president, Sicco Mansholt, but with little success. It was increasingly clear to American interests that the country could not compete with the EEC given the latter's subsidy policy. As a result, Washington met the challenge head-on in Taiwan and announced a general reduction in prices in order to meet competition.

This was a challenge to Canada as well, and much as had been the case in the late 1950s, the country could simply not afford to match American subsidies. It was decided that Canada would protest at the meeting of the Canada-U.S. committee on trade and economic affairs to be held in Washington in late June 1969: 'The Canadian Government is most concerned that the United States is contemplating widespread and significant price reductions ... it has to be borne in mind that Canada has announced its intention to remain competitive. It can be anticipated that other exporters will reduce prices to match any reductions by the United States. Thus, aggressive price competition would be costly to all exporters and would not result in any significant increase in wheat sales.'[99] The Americans must know, a Canadian briefing paper suggested, that Canada could not support any U.S. initiative to recommend the suspension of the minimum price provisions of the IGA. Such a course of action would be highly contentious for Canada given the importance of the IGA to the Canadian economy and the support which it commanded in the country's agricultural sector. The most that Ottawa could do was support the convening of a special meeting of exporting countries under the aegis of the Prices Review Committee to discuss the IGA's price structure. Canada wanted to minimize any damage to the IGA as an effective instrument on international cooperation and minimize disruptive price competition.

The Collapse of International Cooperation

Canadian decision makers were forced to deal with the stark fact of a more widespread resort to national policies that gave rise to quantitative restrictions and to export subsidization. The issue was being taken up in the GATT, especially following the end of the Kennedy round. The GATT's agricultural committee had moved through the stage of assembling documentation in the attempt to quantify and assess the impact of a number of restrictive measures affecting trade in agricultural products. Canada was very active in committee deliberations, and had tabled a proposal in early 1969 to address the specific problem of export subsidies. The proposal aimed at setting up machinery in the GATT to elaborate rules of conduct relating to export subsidization in an attempt to convince transgressors to eliminate subsidy programs. As well, Ottawa had been active in the Organization for Economic Cooperation and Development (OECD) attempting with limited success to convince others to undertake reviews of their production policies. Canada was on record as supporting any action that might be taken to rationalize uneconomic support programs and liberalize international trade in these commodities. Certainly the underlying need, for the Canadians, was international discipline in production policies. As Canadian producers stated on numerous occasions, they were in competition not only with their counterparts say, in the United States, but also with the American treasury through subsidy payments, credit programs, long term loan arrangements, and other programs. In Ottawa's view, the global problems related to free agricultural trade encompassed not only high support and restrictive import policies, but also excessive government involvement in export programs.

The whole problem of increased wheat competition was made worse from the Canadian point of view by a number of factors that had affected the international market in the recent past. The trade in wheat had been declining since 1967 as a result of the reduced requirements of the Soviet Union and the lower aid needs of the Indian subcontinent following the success of the green revolution. Moreover, the Americans were to move into Soviet wheat markets by 1972, leaving Canadians behind. The situation had been aggravated by increasing production in traditional importing countries. For example, by 1970, the EEC had increased production of wheat to the extent that it was now a net exporter. As well, the United Kingdom's level of self-sufficiency in wheat had increased from 35 to 50 per cent over the 1960s. France and the United Kingdom were also the world's largest exporters of barley, a commodity covered by the activities of the CWB, and French barley, heavily subsidized, had displaced the Canadian product in the Japanese market. It was obvious that the ability of traditional importing countries to increase agricultural production flowed from the high level of support that producers received from direct government subsidies or high domestic prices. For the Canadians, it was evident that the key objective of any further negotiations to improve access for Canadian products in Europe would be to reduce those levels of European support. While the United States agreed in principle, it was not willing to see its market share further eroded by aggressive EEC pricing and could afford to prolong the wheat war with Europe. Canada was, more or less, alone in this fight.

As well, the United States was retreating from its position as the leader in the international wheat trading system, which left the EEC virtually alone to do as it wanted. The traditional followers, Canada and Australia, were forced to become more proactive, both in projecting their view of how the international wheat economy should develop and in encouraging the United States to resume those international responsibilities that it had sloughed off. As Andrew Cooper notes, 'this period [the early 1970s] ... has been a period of transition from an old order to a new one which has not yet emerged ... United States leadership and effort as the main prop of this ... system has gone, but it has not yet been replaced, or at least not replaced by any coherent system, or one of global effect.'[100] What Canada wanted in this area, as in the wider trading world, was the establishment and maintenance of a set of common and transparent rules.

Multilateral regulation would be very difficult, if not impossible, to achieve, and Ottawa set about putting its own wheat house in order. By 1970, with absolutely no indication of any revival of the IGA, Otto Lang, the minister in charge of the CWB, told the House of Commons that international representatives had 'noted the urgent need to bring production into a better relationship with demand. They agreed that governments would have to keep production policies under continuing review so that timely and appropriate measures could be taken in the interest of achieving a healthy international market for wheat.'[101] For its part, Ottawa had taken steps through LIFT to reduce the country's 950 million bushel carryover.

The LIFT program was not entirely successful, and the government initiated programs designed to get it out of the business of agricultural subsidies. When LIFT ended in 1971, wheat began to pile up once again in storehouses across the country. Indeed, in that year prairie wheat acreage increased by about 50 per cent, as did the size of the resultant crop. The 1970s, however, was also the decade in which the sale of wheat abroad became much less important for the Canadian economy as a whole; the continuity that had existed since the establishment of the wheat economy in the late 1800s had been broken. The new attitude was summed up by Pierre Trudeau, who asked Western farmers, 'Why should I sell your wheat?' a question that admittedly came back to haunt him. Ottawa still decried wheat subsidies, but not with the same force as earlier. Other, more pressing, problems took up its time during the 70s – oil shocks, third option policies, and the election of a Parti Québécois government in 1976 dedicated to the independence of that province. Farmers' demands of their government to negotiate a system of more fair international treatment were drowned out by louder, more insistent problems.

Chapter 5

Unrequited Expectations: Britain and Canada Move Apart

During the 1960s the Anglo-Canadian economic relationship continued the inexorable decline that had characterized it since the war. Indeed, Britain seemed to largely disappear from the Canadian radar screen as Ottawa out of necessity tuned in the United States more and more. By the end of the decade, imports from and exports to the United Kingdom accounted for 5 and 9 per cent respectively of the country's trade, and the percentages were to decline further in the 1970s.[1] By the beginning of that decade, the two had grown apart to the extent that when London was successful in its bid for European Economic Community (EEC) membership as of 1 January 1973, it raised nary an eyebrow in Ottawa, a sharp contrast to the reaction to Britain's application to join the Community a decade earlier. In short, expanding trade with Britain no longer preoccupied Canadian decision makers, as the import and export percentages suggest.

What could account for the change in Britain's status vis-à-vis Canada? The United Kingdom had acquired the reputation of being the 'sick man of Europe' with growth rates that lagged far behind those of its competitors[2] and a debilitating political malaise that surely altered Canadian perceptions of the country. Most importantly, the United States was now the guarantor of Canadian prosperity. If there were nationalist concerns expressed every once in a while over Canada's dependent relationship with its southern neighbour, they surely were a reflection of the good times that the North American economic relationship had brought.[3] Britain could not compete with that. It also emerged, as the 1970s began, that the United Kingdom was not as interested as it had been in competing in the Canadian market. Clearly, it was becoming more 'European' in the sense that London realized its future trade ties would be with the EEC.

Fifteen Per Cent and Other Ideas

The equivalent of a small earthquake shook the Canadian political scene on 11 June 1957. The Liberals, under the calm and steady premiership of Louis St Laurent, unexpectedly lost to John Diefenbaker's Progressive Conservatives in the federal election. For the first time in almost a generation, it was thought, a new philosophy would animate decision making in Canada. Nowhere would that be more true than in the area of foreign economic policy formation. The Conservatives had been concerned for years that the Liberals had actively promoted economic continentalism at the expense of the British tie.

Historian and Conservative Donald Creighton had articulated that anxiety in a public lecture given at Ottawa's Carleton College on 17 February 1957. There, in the words of Wesley Kriebel, second secretary of the U.S. embassy, Creighton had 'adopted a markedly unfriendly attitude toward the United States.'[4] He had suggested that 'The dangers of continentalism, economic, political and military, [are] now ... pressing in upon us steadily from every side.' Those dangers were the result of the Liberal's renunciation of Canada's birthright through 'a series of discreet, informal bargains with the United States which, since 1940, has been one of the most distinctive features of Canadian foreign policy.' In the area of trade flows, Creighton and the Conservatives seemed to have a point; by 1957 approximately 65 per cent of Canada's imports and exports came from or went to the United States. The new Conservative government, so many believed, would begin the process of reversing that tide.

Clearly, it did not. An old aphorism has it that the road to hell is paved with good intentions; Conservative policy in this area aptly fit that description. Indeed, Diefenbaker's government soon came to the realization that the development of Canadian foreign economic policy was an extremely difficult process. Canada under the Liberals had worked to improve and enhance the machinery governing the flow of international trade through such organizations as the General Agreement on Tariffs and Trade (GATT), but the accrued benefits were not commensurate with the effort. In a direct way, the United States had been the only country able and willing to absorb the billions of dollars worth of Canadian exports on which the country's prosperity depended. It has been argued that Liberal governments of the post–Second World War period had simply made the best of a bad situation, that 'continentalism' was, in a sense, unavoidable given the openness of the Canadian market and the country's economic and political heritage.[5] The Conservatives soon learned to live with that reality as well.

Diefenbaker had not been prime minister long when, without consulting any of his advisers, he made a startling pronouncement on the tarmac at Ottawa's Uplands Airport. On his return from a London Commonwealth conference, he declared it to be the policy of his government to divert 15 per cent of Canada's trade away from the United States and toward Britain. He had almost certainly been carried away by notions of imperial solidarity and a vision of the Empire/Commonwealth that had faded for most years ago. Diefenbaker's pronouncement reflected his 'almost religious devotion to the Crown and to the relationship with the United Kingdom.'[6]

If the prime minister had been aware of the judgement of the Royal Commission on Canada's Economic Prospects on that subject, perhaps he would have been more cautious. It was impossible to significantly increase exports to the United Kingdom, the commission's final report had offered, because that country experienced 'recurring shortages of United States and Canadian dollars.' While Canadian importers could buy more from Britain, 'there [were] definite limits to the amount of purchasing which [could] be diverted to British sources. By and large, Canada is not only established on the North American model, but of equal importance, we are accustomed to North American standards of service, deliveries and salesmanship ... It follows that a switch of even a small fraction of our imports from the United States to the United Kingdom would not be easy of accomplishment.'[7]

By September 1957, officials had produced the numbers needed to demonstrate the point made by the Royal Commission and quickly the firm 15 per cent diversion evolved into 'a very general target towards what the Canadian and United Kingdom governments could work over a long period of time,' at least according to Donald Fleming, Canada's new minister of finance.[8] To reach that elusive number, the government would do what it could, including shifting wherever possible its purchases in the United States to the United Kingdom.[9]

The British did not disagree with the Canadian analysis concerning the difficulty with the 15 per cent figure. In commenting on Diefenbaker's proposal, the British minister of agriculture, Lord Amory, told Fleming that 'no normal adjustment could bring about a diversion of 15 per cent or anything like it.'[10] The British were keen on a more spectacular way to change the Canada-United Kingdom economic relationship. In September, approximately coincident with the Commonwealth economic conference held at Mont Tremblant in Quebec, the *Financial Times* carried a leaked story about a British proposal for an Anglo-Canadian free trade area (FTA), complete with an arrangement under which Canada might hold a part of its external reserves in sterling. While the FTA had been secretly explored in early September between the two, the reserves issue had not been raised at all and came as a complete surprise to the Canadians.

Ottawa had no intention of accepting the British offer, with or without reserves; it simply did not meet Canada's economic reality. Even the anglophile Conservatives recognized that there were too many other considerations to bear in mind, including the reaction of the United States.[11] The prime minister was scared off; as he noted years later in his memoirs, 'As to the free-trade proposal, or more properly, the free-trade suggestion, that received so much publicity at the time of the Mont Tremblant conference, this was something that could only be taken seriously, if at all, in the long term.'[12]

Another strain of Canadian thinking was elucidated by J.H. Warren of Canada's department of trade and commerce to Sir David Eccles, the president of the board of trade, at a January dinner party. The British offer was turned down 'because [Canadians] enjoyed nearly all its advantages in the United Kingdom market already, and were therefore not willing to give something for nothing.'[13] There was some speculation among Whitehall officials that it was Fleming who led the opposition to any negotiations and that he said one thing in public and another in private. As a result, relations between the two countries soon deteriorated to the point where an internal British document called Fleming a liar. It also noted that 'Mr. Fleming is unalterably hostile to the Free Trade Area proposal and has only been restrained by the Prime Minister and other colleagues from turning it down publicly.'[14] Still, how could the government reject the offer without alienating some voters or appearing to be ungracious, especially given the prime minister's recent call for the 15 per cent diversion? Paul Martin, the member of Parliament for Windsor, later led a ferocious Liberal attack in the House of Commons over its handling of the offer, castigating and embarrassing the government over the affair: 'It is the duty of a government that speaks so feverishly of its support for the Commonwealth ... to see that that proposal ... is certainly [one] that would have been accepted by Sir John A. Macdonald ... It is a proposal put forward by a friendly government, and it should have received the kind of treatment which it deserved.'[15] In retrospect, it probably did.

A meeting between Diefenbaker, Fleming, and two senior United Kingdom ministers, Peter Thorneycroft, the chancellor of the exchequer, and Sir David Eccles, who, it was speculated, was the source of the leak to the *Financial Times*, would sort things out. The British found this exercise 'so remarkable – and so revealing.' In their patronizing account of what transpired, Thorneycroft and Eccles believed the Canadians were 'very jaded, dispirited and worried.' Following a few hour's discussion and much hand-wringing, it was decided that the official communiqué would indicate that, while the issue of a free trade area had been raised, the United Kingdom had not asked the Canadians to express any definitive view. That detail would allow the Conservatives to deflect any questions as to whether or not they had accepted or rejected the proposal. The British recorded that 'Mr. Diefenbaker chewed over this for some time, perhaps anxious to make sure that he was exposing no surface unconsciously. But he could see no snag and said so. A new light then seemed to dawn on the haggard Canadian

Ministers; they had toiled in vain for so long that they were almost ready to give up the struggle. Now, as if by magic, a formula had appeared which at once made clear that they had given nothing away and had not exposed themselves but at the same time preserved friendly relations with Britain. The [Canadian] Conservative Party could still continue to stand for the Empire and for Protection!'[16] Clearly, the Conservatives were discovering only once in office the economic and commercial reality that had been developing in North America for the past century. It was much easier to talk about changing patterns than to move toward them.

The British found the Canadian approach 'depressing'; they emphasized that their proposal should not be looked at so much from the point of view of immediate advantage or disadvantage, but as a far-reaching step that should usher in a new and significant Anglo-Canadian relationship. However, 'no recognition of this came from the Canadian side and it is impossible to avoid the impression that the Canadians have been doing their best to forget Diefenbaker's statement or to believe that somehow or other the switch can be achieved painlessly and without any new and striking initiative on the part of the Canadian Government.'[17] In a very real sense, the Conservatives had been hoist with their own petard.

However, while free trade and 15 per cent might be too difficult to achieve, a smaller number might still be feasible. Certainly it remained Conservative policy to increase two-way trade with the United Kingdom and especially Canadian exports to Britain. A memorandum produced in the department of finance on the order of Cabinet suggested a Commonwealth finance ministers' meeting be held in the near future to discuss 'a number of questions relating to trade and economic relations' among members.[18] It went on: 'Canada believes that there are opportunities for the expansion of Commonwealth trade in the next few years, to take advantage of increased productive power and resources and to meet demands in expanding markets in countries of the Commonwealth.'

Of course, what the Canadians had in mind was to add to their current account surplus with the United Kingdom and the Rest of the Sterling Area (RSA), comprising the Commonwealth/Empire minus Canada. On that count there was some room for unease. By 1957, Canada's current account balance with the United Kingdom was a mere CAN$148 million, down from CAN$388 million five years earlier, and CAN$633 million in 1947.[19] This decline was the result of a less favourable merchandise trade balance, with a fall in exports predominating. Indeed, although Canadian exports to all countries rose by 2 per cent in 1957, they had fallen to the United Kingdom by 9 per cent. Even given the downturn in Canadian business activity in 1957, imports from countries other than Britain were up by 8 per cent, while those from the United States and all other countries fell. That trend continued into 1960, and British exports to

Canada showed substantial increases, despite a number of factors like strong competition from Canadian manufacturers, an increase in the range of goods being produced in Canada, a Canadian recession in the later 1950s that bit into economic activity, and a point of view made clear by Ottawa, that increased imports from the United Kingdom were not now desired at the expense of Canadian industry.

The British had every reason to be pleased with their export performance. During the decade following 1948, British exports to Canada increased from CAN$300 million to over CAN$525 million. Even allowing for inflation, this represented an increase of 75 per cent in the value of their exports to Canada. As Louis Rasminsky, a deputy governor at the Bank of Canada, pointed out, that was 'a noteworthy achievement which has played an important part in helping Britain close the dollar gap which so bedeviled economic policy in the first postwar years.'[20] However, average Canadian exports to the United Kingdom over that period were up by only 12.5 per cent, CAN$90 million higher in 1958 than they had been in 1948. That number did not recommend itself to Canadian policy makers, but it represented the operation of British import restrictions against dollar goods as well as an inconvertible currency.

The RSA showed similar trends. By 1957, Canada's current account balance was a mere CAN$10 million, down from CAN$50 million the year previous, CAN$114 million in 1952, and CAN$242 million in 1947. Between 1956 and 1957, Canada's exports fell by 4 per cent, the result of intensified import restrictions imposed by RSA countries, tightened credit in Australia and New Zealand, and some substitution of domestic for imported products whenever possible, the result of government exhortation. On the other side, Canada's imports from the RSA were up by 9 per cent by 1957.

Reflecting their poor export performance to sterling area markets, Canadians constantly put their case for greater access to the British market in such forums as the Commonwealth committee on trade policy or the United Kingdom-Canada Continuing Committee (UKCCC), established in 1949 to allow high-level exchanges between officials of the two countries. Claude Isbister of trade and commerce commented at a UKCCC meeting that Canadian manufacturers were 'complaining with increasing frequency of the unfairness of a situation in which British goods could enter the Canadian market freely while Canadian goods were denied such access to the United Kingdom market.'[21] The case of chemicals was 'frustrating and even infuriating to Canadians who were not allowed to compete with Germans in the United Kingdom market.' He also stressed the importance to Canadian producers of a market in Britain for honey, apples, blueberries, and other fruits, all of which were subject to British import restrictions that had been imposed after the Second World War.

By 1957, with a new government in office, those pressures had become challenges to be met and conquered. Part of the battle would be waged at the September Mont Tremblant meeting of Commonwealth finance ministers. The Conservatives were interested in projecting a certain image, despite the fiasco surrounding the 15 per cent diversion announcement and their response to the British FTA proposal. They would focus on a closer Commonwealth as an antidote to American economic and political influence in Canada. At pre-conference meetings to determine strategy and illuminate issues, officials produced a number of memoranda to that end, such as 'Canadian Commonwealth Investments Outside the United Kingdom,' 'Canadian Investment in the UK,' and 'UK Investment in Canada.'

The Commonwealth and Empire Come to Canada: Mont Tremblant and Montreal

In opening the conference, Fleming raised the bogeyman of Canada's relationship with the United States. He noted that 'We Canadian Conservatives are proud that it was our first prime minister, Sir John A. Macdonald, who laboured so long and with so many disappointments, but in the end with such crowning success, to find a way in which this land of ours could become free, independent and united yet still closely associated with our mother country overseas.'[22] The minister declaimed more directly on the evils of continentalism; the danger existed 'of having too many eggs in one basket. Seventy-three per cent of our imports come from the United States and 60 percent of our exports were directed to that country. Two-thirds of all our external trade were with this one nation. Such concentration in this non-Commonwealth channel was of concern to the Canadian Government.'

For the present, the United Kingdom chose to emphasize the serious economic difficulties that it was experiencing. Short of an Anglo-Canadian free trade agreement, it appeared that the time was not propitious for an enhanced economic relationship between the two countries. The British were still working their way through the Suez disaster of late 1956, which had resulted in the loss of almost US$280 million in November, 15 per cent of their total gold and dollar reserves. Suez had also claimed the premiership of Anthony Eden as a prominent casualty, which had contributed to the overall sense of British unease.

In his reply to Fleming, Thorneycroft held out slight promise that conditions would change, largely because of economic and financial uncertainty in Britain. There was downward pressure on sterling, caused in part by the devaluation of the French franc which 'had started a crop of rumours in Europe as to whether all European currencies would not have to realign their parities with the dollar and with the mark.'[23] In addition, foreign investors were skeptical that the United Kingdom would tackle its internal problem of inflation, and there were doubts about the ability of the sterling area as a whole to pay its way.

The Mont Tremblant conference turned out to be little more than a dress rehearsal for a much more ambitious and important meeting of Commonwealth finance ministers on trade and economic affairs scheduled for September 1958 in Montreal. Between times, the Conservatives scored a major election win on 31 March 1958, securing a stunning 208 seats to the Liberal's 48 and the Co-operative Commonwealth Federation's 8. Fleming's meeting proposal was eerily reminiscent of August 1932 Conservative invitation to the Empire/Commonwealth to come to Canada. Prime Minister R.B. Bennett had gathered fellow prime ministers and others in Canada's capital to discuss trade, a meeting which had resulted in the Ottawa Agreements but little of substance by way of enhanced Commonwealth trade. Bennett had then approached the Americans in 1933, prepared to negotiate a deal with them. Diefenbaker and Fleming hoped to improve upon the results of that conference. This government recognized the importance of keeping Washington informed of its initiative, and went to great lengths to convince the Americans that the upcoming conference 'was not directed against anyone and that no exclusive associations against other countries were foreshadowed.'[24] Continuing United States cooperation was, it was generally realized, essential.

Agenda and other preparatory discussions were held by officials over the course of the next year. Directed by ministers to suggest methods to 'foster economic expansion throughout the Commonwealth,' they held a series of important meetings in London in February and again from 2–21 June 1958. Participants considered more than 50 papers on topics ranging from the role of creditor countries, to the function of the price of gold in international trade, to problems relating to agricultural products.[25] Despite the effort, however, the delegates anticipated some disappointment. Fleming remarked to Thorneycroft that 'it appear[ed] ... that while the economic side of the agenda will be quite full and promising, the prospects for development of the trade theme and actual expansion of Commonwealth trade are not nearly so promising.'[26] As for the British, the conference 'offered little scope for major innovations in Commonwealth economic relations. [Its] value would therefore be mainly political and psychological and the United Kingdom delegation would endeavour to ensure that the final communiqué emphasized the importance of continuing cooperation between the members of the Commonwealth in fostering economic expansion.'[27] Given the Canadian government's pre-election propaganda and its apparent commitment to strengthen trade relations with the United Kingdom, this was a sobering analysis.

The Montreal Commonwealth meeting was opened with much fanfare by

Fleming. If interested bystanders expected that delegations would put aside their national agendas in favour of the betterment of the whole, they would have been disappointed and rightly so. Much as had happened in August and September of 1932, each delegation talked about the benefits of Commonwealth membership and the 'brotherhood' that it entailed, then wondered how that would translate into increased exports for their country. Certainly the Canadians were no different. Their agenda included the developing trade arrangements in Europe between the European Free Trade Area (EFTA), which comprised 'the Seven,' Austria, Britain, Denmark, Norway, Portugal, Sweden, and Switzerland and was focused on the liberalization of industrial goods, and the EEC, made up of the Benelux group, France, Italy, and West Germany. As a brief prepared for the conference noted, the Canadian government regarded 'the trading arrangements of the [EEC] and the proposed European Free Trade Area [to be] of fundamental importance to Canada as a major trading nation whose economic well-being so heavily depends on a healthy and expanding multilateral trading system.'[28]

The Montreal Commonwealth meeting raised other issues for Canada. Fleming spent some time, as had every finance minister since J.L. Ilsley, speaking on the evils of trade discrimination and inconvertibility, especially as practised by the United Kingdom and the RSA. He offered that 'an absolutely perfect time for such a step might never arise in this imperfect world. But certain factors have led Canadians ... to hope that decisive progress might come sooner rather than later ... Discrimination was divisive within the Commonwealth and between the Commonwealth and their best outside friends.'[29] From the Canadian perspective, it was time for Britain to take the leap to non-resident convertibility.

This policy was finally introduced in the United Kingdom in December 1958, with Diefenbaker erroneously giving some of the credit for the decision to the Montreal meeting. In theory, non-resident convertibility meant that the case for restricting imports from the dollar area had vanished, but by 1959, despite steps taken by the United Kingdom to remove discriminatory restrictions, a considerable number of items of interest to Canada were still subject to control. Among those of special concern were meats, processed milk, fresh and frozen fish, synthetic rubber, textiles, automobiles, and larger types of aircraft. Most disturbing for potential Canadian exporters was that all the goods in question could be imported freely from the RSA. The majority had also been liberalized from Western Europe and about one-half of them from Japan. With barely concealed irritation, a Canadian memorandum noted that 'One item under control from dollar countries – fresh and frozen salmon – may be imported without license from [Communist] Poland.'[30]

What were the tangible results of the Montreal conference on trade and economic affairs? In development assistance terms, it could be construed a success.

Three major initiatives resulted, although the dollars committed to the programs were not large. First, Ottawa agreed to increase its annual contribution from CAN$35 million to CAN$50 million to the Colombo Plan, inaugurated in 1950 to assist less-developed Commonwealth nations. Canada provided CAN$500,000 in technical assistance to Commonwealth territories in Africa, and would provide help to the West Indies to the tune of CAN$10 million over five years. In addition, along with the United Kingdom, Canada launched a scheme of Commonwealth scholarships and fellowships.

However, not much progress occurred on the real central concern of the conference, increased trade. As R.B. Bennett had learned in the years following 1932 and the Ottawa Agreements, Canadian economic salvation lay in the United States. Unlike 1932, when the Empire had extended imperial preferences to its various members, by 1958 Fleming 'could detect no desire for an extension of Commonwealth preference.'[31] The world had changed enormously in the intervening twenty-six years, and following a brief upward blip in Anglo-Canadian trade, the numbers receded. The British had been mulling over the usefulness of the UKCCC, which had been an important mainstay of the Anglo-Canadian relationship since 1949. Its passing would truly mark a sea change in British policy. In the end, it remained in place until the late 1960s, but was greatly reduced in significance (the continuing committee did not even meet between July 1960 and October 1963). Even so, the Canadian government was loath to renounce what it saw through rose-coloured glasses as the country's proud imperial past, even if that picture more and more played itself out only in the minds of some members of the Diefenbaker cabinet.

Still, for the time being, the United Kingdom arguably remained the most important diplomatic posting that the Canadian foreign service could offer. The Canadian high commission in London was still Canada's largest overseas mission, with a salary budget, even by 1964, of CAN$521,969. That figure compared with CAN$419,177 for Washington and CAN$363,098 for Paris, which paid for staffs of 48 Canadians serving in London, 37 in Washington, and 21 in Paris.[32] Moreover, Lester Pearson's first trip abroad as prime minister in May 1963 was to the United Kingdom, even before his visit to Hyannisport to meet with John Kennedy.

At least for the Canadians, the UKCCC remained a reassuring symbol of Anglo-Canadian economic relations. As it gathered in June 1960 much as it had for the past eleven years, many of the names remained the same. For the Canadians, Louis Rasminsky, then a deputy governor at the Bank of Canada, Ken Taylor from finance, and James Grandy from the department of external affairs all had long lineages with the committee. On the British side, Kenneth McGregor and Sir Robert Hall were among the longest-serving members. The agenda, aside from a point concerning the developing EEC and a possible EFTA link with it, was reminiscent of the late 1940s and 1950s: the GATT, the Canadian interest in the British market, and overseas investment and aid were all up for discussion. Even though some of the officials attending the meeting might have been comforted by the familiarity of the agenda and the discussion, the Anglo-Canadian economic relationship was changing. By the mid-1960s the British market was fading in importance for Canada, and no longer were hands wrung at emergency meetings convened in Ottawa and policy papers prepared in anticipation of a further decline.

Britain and the EEC

The British were also in the process of investigating new economic angles and allegiances that did not necessarily include Canada. Ottawa was concerned that Europe's developing regional trade arrangements would expand along restrictive lines and while it had given conditional support to the EFTA based on British assurances that Canadian raw materials and agricultural exports to the United Kingdom would not be jeopardized, it had opposed the formation of the EEC from the beginning because of its restrictionist thrust. The Liberal government of Louis St Laurent had sent an *aide-mémoire* to the EEC capitals in February 1957 that had pointed out its concerns over some of the provisions of the proposed treaty.[33] Among these were the establishment of a protected agricultural system, higher tariffs, import restrictions, and long-term preferential marketing arrangements. These measures would translate, so the note suggested, into high-cost and inefficient economies, much like that of the United Kingdom. More to the point, EEC policy would raise serious problems for Canadian exports of agricultural products as under the new regime Italy, West Germany, and the Benelux group would have to purchase subsidized and expensive French wheat instead of the Canadian crop which had long provided for the needs of EEC bakers and pasta and pastry makers. In short, there were 'special problems' for Ottawa relating to agricultural trade.[34]

As noted above, any move to link the two trading blocs was anathema for the Canadians; a linkage, however was the objective of British policy and Canadians could only assume that it would not help them. A British memorandum pointed up the disadvantages as the Canadians saw them. Ottawa worried that 'new artificial trade barriers will shut [Canadian] goods out of European markets ... The Canadians dislike the idea of a 'bridge' linking EFTA with the Six. Like the Americans, they fear that it can be built only at the expense of North America. Canadians have all the United States' fears of being shut out of Europe as a result of a preferential system, but they superimpose on them a suspicion that their own ... preferential arrangements in the United Kingdom will be impaired as a result.'[35]

Indeed, the Canadians raised with the British the possible extension of inverse preferences within the EFTA, which could further impair Anglo-Canadian trade. Norman Robertson, Canada's undersecretary of state for external affairs even dredged up to Sir Edgar Cohen the legal argument of Britain's Most-Favoured-Nation commitment to Canada under the Exchange of Letters of 1947.[36] The letters had freed Canada and the United Kingdom from bound margins of preference, a reflection of the new prevailing attitude that the International Trade Organization (ITO) and the GATT would free up global commerce. Robertson's telegram caused some scrambling in Whitehall to determine exactly what Ottawa was getting at. British legal opinion tended to interpret the Exchange of Letters as being supplementary to the GATT, 'which leaves countries free, within the no new preference rule, to discriminate in the application of preferential duties as between one preferred source of supply and another, and not as negating the GATT insofar as the GATT recognizes special exceptions for customs unions and free trade areas.' In short, the United Kingdom undertook via the Exchange of Letters to maintain existing preferential rates of duty and to give Canadian goods treatment not less favourable than goods from any other country. Still, as C.W. Sanders of the board of trade told H.A.F. Rumbold, the permanent secretary at the Commonwealth relations office, in reference to a conversation with James Grandy from Canada's finance department, 'I might have remarked that if the Canadians wanted these [potential] duties removed against them, they had our offer to form a free trade area with them.'[37]

As the British told the Commonwealth at Montreal, they were on guard for the organization's interests in the negotiations between the EEC and the EFTA, a reassurance which provided scant comfort to Canada. After all, London was negotiating a regional trading bloc. It became the mantra in Ottawa that regional developments in Europe were, by their very nature, a bad thing. Generally, Canadians took the line that 'all outward looking countries should unite their efforts to resist regional and divisive pressures.'[38] While Ottawa appreciated Britain's professed commitment to liberalism as opposed to the French penchant for protectionism, it was also agreed that, given the French attitude, some compromise would be necessary if a Six-Seven link were to be negotiated.[39] That compromise, it was feared, could only harm Commonwealth efforts to increase trade. However, concern was premature; negotiations between the two blocs broke down in November 1958. The French conception of the EEC prevailed, which left Britain to continue the attempt to establish the Seven as a separate free trade group. They did accomplish that goal and signed the EFTA treaty in November 1959.[40]

The British were bitter about the breakdown. In the Commonwealth economic consultative committee, the board of trade's Sir Frank Lee said that there was 'no specific issue upon which this occurred. In none of these cases ... did it seem to the United Kingdom that the gap – if one existed in all cases – would have been unbridgeable if all participants in the negotiations had wanted a Free Trade Area ... Fundamentally, the reason ... lay elsewhere.'[41] The British also were irritated about Canada's lack of support and claimed that the Canadian government had 'no positive policy [with respect to the EFTA and the EEC] at all and [did] not seem to take seriously enough the need to evolve one.' There was no sign 'of any positive contribution of practical significance from their side ... it is feared [that is] a poor prospect in the future.' The main Canadian players were 'parochial protectionists' (James Roberts, deputy minister of trade and commerce), 'doctrinaire ideologues' (Jake Warren, assistant deputy minister of trade and commerce and Louis Rasminsky, deputy governor of the Bank of Canada) 'hard-headed and unimaginative,' (minister of finance Donald Fleming) or 'cautious' (A.E. Ritchie, external affairs, and A.F.W. Plumptre, assistant deputy minister of finance).[42] Of course, Canada did have a policy but it did not recommend itself to London, opposed as it was to European solutions. The Canadians were 'cool towards EFTA and ... they actively disliked the EEC in its economic aspects.'[43] As one of those so-called protectionists, Jake Warren, noted, 'it was important that the rift in Europe should not be repaired at the expense of the countries outside Europe.'[44] As well, the Canadians thought that it was 'not at all clear that [UK] membership would bring great political benefit to the West.'[45]

While the formal negotiations for a bridge between the two European groups had failed, informal talks had continued to the dismay and opposition of the Canadians, who remained very sensitive to anything that could compromise their exports to the United Kingdom. But the British were not interested in buying more from Canada as things then stood, which made nonsense out of George Hees' remark as a new minister of trade and commerce that 'I'm willing to do anything that will increase Canadian exports. I'd stand on my head in Piccadilly Circus if I thought it'd do any good.'[46]

The Canadians wanted assurances from the British that were not forthcoming. Even their threats of retaliation against evolving British policy seemed hollow, as when Donald Fleming warned Whitehall in October 1960 that 'If there is going to be any tampering with the advantages now enjoyed by Canadian exports in the United Kingdom market, we would have to re-examine the terms of access of British goods to the Canadian market.'[47] That was to happen in the very near future without any British tampering, impelled by a worsening economic situation in Canada and an unemployment rate that hit 7.6 per cent in September 1960, the highest rate in the post-war period. Against that worry any attempt to disturb the status quo in trading arrangements as the British were suggesting was a non-starter, or so some in Ottawa thought. Hees estimated that British membership in any trading group would cost his country CAN$690 million in foregone sales. Canada would face not only the loss of preference in the British market, but also, in most cases, preferences that would favour European products over Canadian. Given the recession, the Conservative government was facing pressures from business for higher tariffs, many of which targeted the United Kingdom. The private sector prevailed in the terms of the 'baby budget,' introduced in Parliament on 20 December 1960. Tariffs were increased on a wide range of items and the government changed the 'Made in Canada ruling,' a move that was particularly punitive against British manufacturers. The practice had been to consider goods 'of a class or kind not made in Canada' if less than 10 per cent of a particular item was produced outside the country: 'When classified in this way, the good could enter Canada at a seven percent duty rather than the 22 percent protective tariff on goods produced in Canada. Under the new regulation, if the "know-how" existed in Canada, producers would be able to obtain protection even if the physical facilities were not available. In other words, if a Canadian manufacturer [could] show the government that it [was] capable of producing a good if it had a market, protection [would] be granted so that the company [could] acquire the machinery and capital necessary to produce it.'[48] The *Toronto Telegram* labeled this change 'the greatest single stride toward a higher protectionist policy since the Bennett tariffs of the 1930s,' while the *Globe and Mail*'s Bruce Macdonald told his readers that 'the whole trend [of government policy] has been toward higher protectionism.'[49] Fleming did not disagree, and in his budget speech on 20 June 1961 said that he had not been convinced 'that a sweeping elimination of our tariffs in relation to any existing trade grouping can be reconciled with a healthy secondary industry or the balanced growth of the Canadian economy.'[50]

With the EFTA-EEC connection a non-starter, the British opted for EEC membership in late July 1961. In Ottawa, Britain's inclusion was the moral equivalent of war with some ministers believing that British policy 'seemed to amount to facing [us] with the invidious choice of whether [we] wished to be halved or quartered.'[51] John Diefenbaker was particularly upset. Despite the fact that comparatively little of Canada's trade now went to the United Kingdom and that he had turned down cold the September 1957 proposal for an Anglo-Canadian free trade area, the prime minister did not appreciate the announcement. Some of his opposition lay in his fear of reduced trade if the United Kingdom joined a restrictive customs union: the price of British entry, so Ottawa thought, would be '(1) a common tariff with the Six; (2) a common agricultural policy; and (3) the disappearance of UK tariff preferences by the end of the transitional period.'[52]

The main Canadian complaint was the potential loss of custom that could result from any British move into Europe. A memorandum prepared in September 1960 by the Interdepartmental Committee on External Trade Policy (ICETP), a committee of senior officials in Ottawa, noted that Canada had 'indicated its sympathy for the broad objectives of the Rome Treaty [the instrument which established the Community] on the understanding that the EEC arrangement would not be restrictive of trade.'[53] That was not proving to be the case as average tariff rates went up in Canada's two primary markets in the Community, low-tariff Belgium and moderate-tariff West Germany.

The increase was allowed under the GATT, whose rules held that the average common external tariff of any customs union must not be higher or more restrictive than those prevailing, on average, prior to the formation of any union. As Sidney Dell has written, 'In arriving at the common tariff, the pre-existing national tariffs were averaged arithmetically without regard to the value of goods imported in each case: had allowance been made for the value of imports by each country under every tariff heading, the common tariff would have been significantly lower.'[54] Moreover, the low-tariff Benelux bloc was treated as a single unit in the averaging process, while France, Italy, and West Germany were treated as another bloc, which gave the high tariffs of France and Italy a disproportionately large weight in the final outcome.[55] And given the discussion taking place among the Six with respect to some sort of common agricultural policy which would advantage only Community members, Canada was certain that with British membership, a significant market for Canadian farm products would be compromised.

The British were certainly aware of Ottawa's unhappiness, but also believed that Canada's opposition was particularly self-interested: 'Canadians have all the United States' fears of being shut out of Europe as a result of a preferential system, but they superimpose on them a suspicion that their own ... preferential arrangements in the United Kingdom will be impaired as the price of getting a special arrangement.'[56] At a minimum, it was certain that Canada would lose its remaining preferences in the British market that had been in place since the 1932 Ottawa Agreements and reaffirmed in the Exchange of Letters in 1947. However, under the scheme being contemplated, reverse preference would be imposed in favour of European suppliers. In 1960, Canadian manufacturers had sold more than CAN$160 million worth of goods to the United Kingdom, exports that included chemicals, office machinery, mining machinery, and electrical apparatus. These sales had only been possible because of the preference system. As a result, a memorandum to the Canadian cabinet suggested that 'The primary objective ... should be to safeguard to the fullest possible extent Canadian access to the United Kingdom market.'[57] Commodities affected by these reverse preferences would include aluminum, semi-fabricated metals, most agricultural items, and the whole range of semi-manufactured and manufactured goods.

The case of aluminum was particularly problematic as far as Ottawa was concerned, and demonstrated how British EEC membership could affect many products. It was generally accepted that the EEC would establish a common tariff of at least 10 per cent on primary aluminum. That tariff would affect the almost 58,000 tons of aluminum that Canadians had sold to EEC countries in 1960, and the 55,000 tons which had gone to the United Kingdom. And this total was growing – consumption in the Community would, it was forecast, increase to about 1 million tons by 1965. Ottawa thought that a tariff would initiate a '"hot-house" growth of production facilities within the Community without regard to free world supply and demand.'[58] Imports from Canada and the United States would be diverted to newly constructed smelters in the EEC, as European (and North American) producers took advantage of new opportunities. Moreover, in the early 1960s, there was a surplus of aluminum in the world, which would be made worse by these anticipated new facilities. Accordingly, it was decided that Canada would encourage the Six to consider a reduction in the common market tariff from 9 to 5 per cent (they had wanted a nil tariff in the beginning) and try to secure an undertaking that the enlarged Community would be prepared to negotiate further reductions in the tariff in the GATT. That position, however, was a non-starter.

The situation with respect to agricultural exports was arguably worse. The United Kingdom was very important as a destination for Canadian agriculture – about 32 per cent overall, but higher for some important commodities including wheat and flour, oil seeds, apples, barley, cheese, and tobacco.[59] The Canadians went out of their way to emphasize that 'free entry into the United Kingdom was the foundation of Canada's agricultural exports, and for some of them the tariff preferences were essential.'[60] As well, the Canadian Wheat Board (CWB), the organization that sold Canada's wheat and barley abroad, had huge surpluses to contend with, built up during the 1950s. It was imperative to run these down before more poured into elevators, a difficult proposition if Britain, Canada's largest overseas market, discriminated against Canadian wheat because of British membership in the EEC. This issue resonated for both sides; as the British observed in a note written during their negotiations with the EEC over entry, 'The major problem is that of wheat.'[61]

The obvious question for Canadian trade was, if not the United Kingdom, then where? As events unfolded, the People's Republic of China and Communist Europe were to save Canadian wheat farmers with their huge purchases of wheat and barley during the 1960s.[62] Even given that happy development, it remained inconceivable that Ottawa, the CWB, or prairie farmers could be sanguine about disappearing sales in Britain and Europe. Clearly, the course of European integration would result in new discrimination in Europe.

The French, the driving force of so much EEC policy, were successfully placing their restrictionist imprint on the embryonic Community's development. Soon after the election of Charles de Gaulle as president in 1958, Paris had adopted a much more nationalist foreign economic policy. The British, in a characterization loaded with history, believed that de Gaulle was 'becoming more and more Napoleonic and self-centred,' sentiments with which the Canadians would have agreed.[63] Indeed, Dana Wilgress, then the Canadian representative on the council of the Organization for European Economic Cooperation, had earlier set the tone for Canadian perceptions when he had told a group of policy makers that 'General de Gaulle is not interested in the Common Market as a step towards political unity in Europe. His approach is nationalist. He is more interested in restoring the power and influence of France than in promoting the European idea.'[64] In French calculations, *la gloire de France* could be better achieved from within a strong and focused EEC. To that end, they were to propose that the first step toward a common tariff be taken on 1 July 1960, instead of 1 January 1962, the date negotiated in 1957. Paris wanted to speed up progress in order to 'intensify the existing split in Europe' to its benefit.[65] But all EEC countries 'felt that discrimination [against others] was essential to enable them to weld together as one economic unit.'[66] This direction could not augur well for Canada's exports.

Prime minister Diefenbaker continued to air his unhappiness with any British minister or official unlucky enough to be sent to Ottawa. He told Duncan Sandys, the secretary of state for Commonwealth relations, that the end of the preference system that had been developed and implemented via the Ottawa Agreements of 1932 would destroy the Commonwealth. When Sandys demurred, suggesting that 'most of the new Commonwealth countries did not regard preferences as the main basis of the Commonwealth,' Diefenbaker replied that if the old Commonwealth lost interest, then it would break up.[67] The logic of Britain's choice was clear; the EEC would become a powerful global political and economic entity whether or not the United Kingdom joined. If the country stayed out, its political and economic influence would be reduced 'with a consequent reduction in the strength of the Commonwealth.' If Britain were to join, its influence in Europe would increase, making 'it a more valuable partner in the Commonwealth.'[68]

Ottawa did not buy that, and went on the offensive soon after the July announcement. British trade with the EEC accounted for only 14 per cent of its total trade, they pointed out, as compared with the Commonwealth's 40 per cent and the other 46 per cent that went outside of both blocs. How could Britain square those figures with the fear that they would be left behind in the slipstream of history if they stayed outside the EEC? At the Commonwealth economic consultative council meeting of 20–1 September 1960, Gordon Churchill, then the minister of trade and commerce, had told the chancellor of the exchequer, Sir Reginald Maudling, and Edward Heath, the Lord Privy Seal and the government's point man on negotiations with Europe, that any move by Britain to join a restrictive trade bloc 'would damage important Canadian interests.'[69] The minister went on:

> Exports to the United Kingdom were important for Commonwealth producers because of the size of her market and the terms on which Commonwealth countries had access to it. In return, most Commonwealth countries gave reciprocal advantages to United Kingdom exporters. The advantages enjoyed by Commonwealth producers in the United Kingdom market were threatened in three ways by the proposal mentioned: there was the effect of free entry; the effect on preferences not only for foodstuffs but also for materials and manufactures; and, finally, over a range of goods of importance to Canada and affected by special contractual commitments, there was the threat of reverse preferences in favour of Europe against the Commonwealth ... Free entry into the United Kingdom was the foundation of Canada's agricultural exports, and for some of them the tariff preferences were essential ... It seemed out of the question to expect any accord to be reached between the United Kingdom and the EEC which did not deal with agriculture.

The British later described Churchill's statement as 'hostile.'[70]

If the United Kingdom joined, Canada would be left in an untenable situation, or so the government believed. In reality, only 10 per cent of Canada's already small and declining trade volume with Britain would be affected by British entry, a tiny proportion of the country's total imports and exports. Canadians themselves did not agree in large numbers with the Conservatives' approach, while many officials and business people also demonstrated unconcern over the possibility of Britain joining the Six.[71] Still, Canadian ministers believed that there was no substitute for the existing terms of access to the British market and that if Canadians lost economic advantages that had been paid for through reciprocal concessions in their market, then it was doubtful that Canada could continue to maintain advantages offered to the United Kingdom in Canada. Moreover, a widening gap between Canada and the United Kingdom could lead Canadians to look on an increasing scale to the U.S. market: 'Any weakening of the Commonwealth would ... reinforce the strong economic and political pulls to the South which already existed.' For a government that had pledged to reverse the Canadian fixation with the United States and restore some semblance of balance in its external trade relations, that was a difficult idea to acknowledge. However, the British discounted Canada's trade dilemmas; for them, the Diefenbaker government had been elected partly on a program of diverting purchases to Britain but it had done 'singularly little to help and a lot to hinder [trade].'[72]

The British put the hard Canadian line on their EEC application down to several factors that included tougher economic times in Canada, unhappiness with Canada's position in world trade, and an inability to see how old alliances would now fit. Canada viewed any United Kingdom-EEC discussions not as an isolated event, but as a first stage in a series of global trade negotiations which would exclude them. The idea of a British association with Western Europe combined with an obsession with the short-term economic disadvantages to Canada coloured the country's thinking.

Things went from bad to worse over the next months. In September 1961 in Accra, Ghana, for a gathering of the Commonwealth's economic consultative council, the minister of finance, Donald Fleming, and George Hees blasted the British for wanting to join the EEC.[73] Fleming's professional demeanor made him doggedly opposed to their membership and he did his best to make it difficult. Peter Newman has pointed out that Fleming defended the Canadian position 'with a savage fury that obliterated any admission of even the possibility of slightest error. 'Don Fleming doesn't just fight an issue ... He beats it to death. Then cuts its throat, slashes its wrists, throws acid in its face, and sets fire to it.''[74] The Canadian attack in Accra was so vicious that Harold Holt, the Australian treasurer, told Macmillan that Ottawa was 'out to smash [the] United Kingdom Government by foul means or fair.'[75]

A few days later in Washington, the minister accused the Americans of having 'given a blessing to UK membership in the Six.'[76] Of course, Diefenbaker's suspicions of U.S. motives was well-known: Washington wanted the British in so as to destroy the system of Commonwealth preference. The Americans were 'adamant against the continuance of Commonwealth preference, their view being that this was a form of discrimination in trade which should not exist.'[77] Even the British high commissioner in Ottawa told the Commonwealth relations office that the Canadian prime minister was suspicious of the Americans. Diefenbaker had said that he had it on good authority that the United States government was determined to 'push' Britain into Common Market and equally to 'push' Canada into agreeing. His experience 'did not lead him to believe that the Americans were as disinterested as they suggested and he did not forget that President [Kennedy] was above all a politician.'[78]

In November, George Drew, Canada's high commissioner in London, 'snubbed' the British when he did not attend an information session on United Kingdom-EEC negotiations, a 'new level of kindergarten diplomacy' according to the Canadian press.[79] And Diefenbaker himself was caustic in discussions with the British. During a meeting with Lord Amory, the secretary of state for Commonwealth relations, the prime minister complained that 'the Canadian government had been promised consultation and that there had been no consultation.'[80] Amory's response – that the British considered informing Canadian officials every second day of progress made to be 'consultation' – did not satisfy Diefenbaker, who refused to give up. Following some particularly difficult United Kingdom-EEC exchanges over agriculture, the secretary of state for external affairs, Howard Green, fired off a telegram to Britain insisting that 'the British government demand proposals which would safeguard Canadian interests.'

It was an amazing display of intemperate politics. When the United Kingdom's high commissioner gave Diefenbaker a message outlining progress, the Canadian prime minister remained 'in a grim mood' and 'not very constructive.' What sort of alternative plan, he wanted to know, did Macmillan have? None, was the answer, but then Diefenbaker could not offer anything either. Later, he skewered Macmillan and his Europe policy at a prime minister's meeting held in September 1962; his speech was 'very hostile'[81] and, as the London Sunday Observer noted, he was intent upon 'pulling [Macmillan's] recently-hoisted flag of Europe' down.'[82] In that summer's general election the Conservatives had lost 92 seats in Parliament, from 208 to 116, which had increased the already high level of paranoia in the government. The Liberals took 98 seats, Social Credit 30, and the New Democrats 19. London had hoped, given the magnitude of the loss, that Diefenbaker would demonstrate some caution, but 'his precarious political situation and his misjudgement of the Canadian public opinion'[83] did not change his attitude. Through an increasingly bitter quarrel, Diefenbaker was convinced that the United Kingdom was 'hustling' Canada.[84] 'British patience,' the London Sunday Times opined, 'with the Diefenbaker-Fleming administration is wearing thin.'[85]

Of much greater interest was the French veto over British entry into the EEC on 29 January 1963. Many Canadians expressed regret that the negotiations had broken down. The Winnipeg Free Press noted the following day that 'The outcome at Brussels [was] very discouraging to everyone who believes that Britain's entry into the Common Market would strengthen both parties and would lead some day to a freeing of trade ... and the establishment of an Atlantic economic community.'[86] And while Diefenbaker remained unrepentant, his government did believe that it should try to 'mend Commonwealth fences as quickly as possible' and to demonstrate that Canada had not been the cause of the refusal.[87] Indeed, the cabinet went on record as implying that Britain had refused to join the EEC because it could not secure terms that would protect essential Commonwealth interests. When this analysis was rejected outright by Edward Heath,

Diefenbaker had 'shown some hurt feelings ... his line being that he was only trying to be a good Commonwealth man and to rally the Commonwealth to [Britain's] support'[88] Surely the British heaved a sigh of relief when the Canadian Conservatives were defeated in the April 1963 federal election, taking only 95 seats against 129 for the Liberals, 24 for Social Credit, and 19 for the New Democratic Party. Lester Pearson, a man with some reputation and experience in foreign affairs, was now prime minister.

New Government – Same Trend

Following the encouraging statistics of the late 1950s, the next decade opened on a different note for Anglo-Canadian trade. In 1962, British exports to Canada were down from the previous year by 14 per cent, from CAN$618 million to CAN$563 million. In 1963, they fell further to CAN$528 million. British exporters were, according to senior officials at the Commonwealth relations office, 'disillusioned' because of increasing difficulties being experienced in the Canadian market.[89] At the best of times, Canada had not been an easy market. There was always strong competition from the United States now complicated by the aftermath of Canada's financial crisis of May and June 1962.[90] Part of the solution to that crisis had been the imposition of temporary surcharges on certain classes of imports, ranging from 15 per cent for less essential imports through 10 per cent on items like imported automobiles, to a 5 per cent surcharge on about CAN$2.5 billion worth of imports. Generally, the British thought, the Canadians were acting 'in a rather protectionist way.'

They also believed that they had suffered more than their competitors from these measures. Exports had fallen and they had taken a smaller share of the Canadian import market, 9 per cent in 1962, as compared with 11 per cent in 1960 and 1961. By 1963 that share was down to 8 per cent. Canada, which had consistently been Britain's third or fourth largest export market in the world, had dropped to seventh place by mid-1963. At the same time, U.S. exports to Canada had increased from CAN$3.864 billion in 1961, to CAN$4.309 billion in 1962.[91] The situation had soured so quickly from the British point of view that in January 1963 the president of the board of trade, now Edward Heath, wrote to Howard Green to draw attention to the serious lack of balance in Anglo-Canadian trade and the growing British trade deficit with Canada, which had reached CAN$291 million in 1961 and CAN$346 million a year later.[92] Indeed, warning lights over its size were beginning to flash all over Whitehall, and reached a particular intensity in 1964, following a large increase in imports stimulated by expansionary government policies.

The disagreement over possible British membership in the EEC that had dragged out over the years had certainly damaged Anglo-Canadian relations. The political relationship had soured, while the economic one continued in freefall. Canada's position was also outdated. Whether or not the United Kingdom joined the EEC was not much of an economic concern for Canada by 1963, but it was of tremendous importance to the United Kingdom. However, once British entry had been rejected, the country focused on its Commonwealth ties once again. As Mitchell Sharp remarked in his memoirs, 'the British government [now] attached a great deal of importance to trade with Commonwealth countries – much more than we did – partly because of the uncertainty about the future of trade with the European Community.'[93]

Prime Minister Pearson also took a dim view of the importance of the Commonwealth. It was Pearson's opinion that the old Empire/Commonwealth was 'in rapid dissolution by the emergence of the colonial entities into independent states and that this advent of African Commonwealth states doomed the Commonwealth system.'[94] The best that could be hoped for was that some sort of special relationship could continue among Canada and Australia, New Zealand, the United Kingdom, and perhaps India.

A new Labour government in Britain, elected in October 1964 and led by Harold Wilson, sought at least initially to reinvigorate Commonwealth. Ben Pimlott, in his biography of the British prime minister, writes that 'Wilson's personal preference was for a new emphasis on the Commonwealth, and an expansion of Commonwealth trade. [He] had an attachment to the old dominions which went back to his youth'[95] That was the message given to British trade departments in the months following the Labour win and given some shape during the 1965 Commonwealth prime ministers' meeting. At that meeting Wilson proposed a three-point plan for Commonwealth economic cooperation, but very little was actually accomplished; he was 'acutely disappointed ... [that] there was virtually no willingness to improve intra-Commonwealth trading arrangements.'[96]

Canada's disinterest stemmed from its connection with the United States, which dwarfed all others in importance. By 1965, Canadian exports to the United Kingdom had increased only slightly, from CAN$915 million in 1960 to CAN$1.174 billion. On the other hand, sales to the United States had gone from CAN$2.9 billion to CAN$5 billion, almost 60 per cent of the country's exports, and were going up at a rate of more than CAN$1 billion per year. British exports to Canada had stayed more or less static, at CAN$589 million in 1960, and CAN$619 five years later. By 1965 the United Kingdom held a mere 7 per cent of the Canadian market, down from 9.5 per cent in 1960. Britain's exporters were 'disillusioned' because of what they perceived to be the increasing difficulty of the Canadian market.[97] The Americans did not share that perception; from

1960 to 1965 their exports to Canada had held steady at roughly 70 per cent of total Canadian imports.

Britain Lack of Interest in Canada

It also appeared that much British business was increasingly uninterested in Canada. The dynamics had not been good during a March 1964 meeting between Mitchell Sharp, the minister of trade and commerce in the Liberal government, and members of the Federation of British Industries. While Sharp was there to learn about British problems, 'there [had been] no real discussion or exchange of views.'[98] The Canadian impression was 'that British businessmen were concerned to point out that Canada was only one market among many to which they exported and ... that they were reluctant to take special steps to get their products to meet the requirements of the Canadian market.' Sharp was particularly taken aback by the president of British Leyland who had emphasized that his company had no intention of undertaking the 'special modifications that were required if Leyland buses were to meet Canadian conditions.' Therein lay the crux of the matter. Canadian diplomats at Canada House believed the British to be most uncompetitive; their approach to economic problems appeared to completely ignore the built-in structure of restrictive practices that were based to a considerable extent on the country's class structure.

The Americans, in conversation with members of the Canadian embassy in Washington, spoke of 'fundamental and persistent economic weakness which has led to a growing inability of British industry to compete with European and North American industry, and this has resulted in the current serious gap between exports and imports.'[99] They were also pessimistic that the new Labour government would take steps to curtail internal demand or to institute the sort of fundamental change that was necessary to improve productivity and efficiency. A.F.W. Plumptre, an assistant deputy minister of finance, believed that the heart of the problem lay in machine tools on which the British depended so heavily for their industrial strength. There had recently been an increase in the importation of these tools, not because their order books were unduly long, but because British manufacturers seemed satisfied to go on producing standard models while foreign manufacturers were making increasingly sophisticated and complicated products.[100]

It was not surprising, given such attitudes, that Canadians assigned most of the blame for the sharp decline in trade on British exporters. Even some British officials questioned the commitment of manufacturing to ship more to Canada. Robert Samples from the board of trade wrote that 'we do seem to be particularly vulnerable to charges that our deliveries and our trading methods in North America leave something to be desired.'[101] He thought that the information effort that the British had undertaken to popularize their goods in Canada should be only gently pushed, if at all, because of numerous examples of British contractors falling down on major contracts. Canadians, he believed, would certainly not be receptive to promotions without products.

Similarly, British bankers were largely uninterested in investing in Canada by the 1960s, the result, thought Simon Reisman, the assistant deputy minister of finance, of British ignorance. Their reluctance 'stemmed from the fact that they had overestimated the ease with which large profits could be made during the Canadian boom of the Fifties; that they had invested in Canada when the boom was at its height and had got their fingers badly burnt during the recession at the end of the Fifties, at which better time better opportunities had opened up in Europe on which they were still concentrating ... they showed insufficient awareness of the Canadian recovery that had been going on for three years ... this was due partly to the fact that the recovery had been overshadowed by the 1962 crisis of confidence ... All of this created a bad impression of Canada and tended to make the bankers lose sight of Canada's real economic position.'[102]

Even given the attitudes of some industrialists and bankers, the British had their own list of legitimate complaints in dealing with Canada that they brought up at every possible opportunity. The president of the board of trade had written to Ottawa citing some of these, which included: 'devaluation; the temporary import surcharges; ... Canadian duty valuation practice and automatic antidumping duty; the shipbuilding subsidies; discrimination against Scotch whisky both in the Federal tariff and by Provincial liquor boards; the Ontario Trade Crusade; and the Ontario Special Place of Business Tax.'[103]

British automobile sales to Canada had also taken a pounding, falling to about 18,000 vehicles worth about £6.6 million in 1963, from 77,000 units valued at £38.5 million in 1960. Part of the drop was due to the availability of more desirable American cars, some of them made in Canada, but it was also a result of Canadian policy. Until 1960, there had been a special concession for British cars which had allowed them to be sold in Canada at the British list price less 30 per cent without attracting a dumping duty. This was modified to 22.5 per cent because of the Canadian recession in the late 1950s. As a Canadian discussion of this issue noted, 'In view of the [un]employment situation throughout Canada, it was not unreasonable to make this change.'[104] When the economic downturn had passed, Ottawa had refused to reinstate the previous favourable treatment. The British then tried another tack: to be allowed to give larger discounts to Canadian purchasers because of 'duplicated costs.'[105] The Canadians declined to allow this, citing the success of Volkswagen, which had prospered relative to British manufacturers in Canada despite the handicap of a 17.5 per cent preference in favour of Britain. The automobile issue, especially following the negotiation of the Auto Pact with the United States in 1965, was to continue to plague Anglo-Canadian economic relations.

When asked by Bruce MacDonald, the *Globe and Mail*'s London correspondent, what Canada could do to help British exporters, Kenneth MacGregor from the board of trade suggested a number of things: '1) Give what was refused at Montreal in 1958, that is, the restoration of certain preferences not involving breaches of the GATT, the binding of preferential margins and binding of preferential rates on items cut out of the British Montreal list; 2) amend Canada's anti-dumping legislation; 3) administer labeling and similar food and drugs regulations with less pedantry and more common sense applicable to the products of a civilized country; and 4) administer shipbuilding subsidies so as at least to encourage maximum use of British components.'[106]

The Valuation for Duty System

The British reserved their special concern for the Canadian system of valuation for duty, coupled with an anti-dumping duty that was automatically imposed. As a memorandum to the president of the board of trade noted, he might remind Mitchell Sharp at their meeting scheduled for 1 December 1964 'of the importance which we attach to changing certain aspects of the Canadian dumping legislation which bear unreasonably on our exports.'[107]

The Canadian system did work to the detriment of British exporters to a much greater extent than it did against most others, and especially the Americans. The Canadian formula for valuation was normally based upon the fair market value of like goods sold in the exporter's home market. In addition, Canadian law provided that when goods of a class or kind made in Canada were sold in the country below the fair market value, an anti-dumping duty must be imposed equal to the difference between the selling price and the fair market value.[108]

The valuation system meant that goods from Britain, when dutiable, were often liable for higher duties than similar products from countries such as the United States, where an advantageous home trade pattern had established a lower fair market value. The disadvantage to Britain stemmed from differences in the distribution systems of Canada and the United Kingdom. In a compact, densely populated market like the latter, there were relatively few links in the distributive chain. When exporting to Canada, the manufacturer sold to an agent, who in turn sold to regional distributors. Therein lay the problem. Exporters were prevented by the automatic dumping duty from reducing the price of their goods to take account of the overheads, which would have to be borne by the Canadian agents. This was advantageous for American manufacturers who usually had distribution systems in their home market similar to Canada's. Canada had recognized the 'psychological' barriers raised by these difficulties and had suggested that they would at least investigate their valuation system, but that had not happened.

A large part of the reason the valuation system had attained almost sacred status in Ottawa because it was viewed as 'essential as a protection against ... US [dumping] ... and [no Canadian] administration [was] prepared to abandon it.'[109] The fear of American dumping was well-founded. Reisman, for one, thought the Americans were 'ruthless price cutters, particularly where marginal production was involved [and] could quickly swamp the Canadian market with dumped goods.'[110] While the British did not disagree, they also thought that the rigidity of Canadian law meant that 'some British exporters find themselves severely penalized, not because they are damaging Canadian industry by dumping, but because of differences between British and Canadian trade patterns which bring them *technically* within the law's scope.'[111]

The large British trade deficit with Canada continued to grow. The obverse of the British deficit was a Canadian surplus which went part way toward canceling out Canada's CAN$1 billion trade deficit with the United States.[112] Britain's adverse balance of trade with Canada amounted to some CAN$581 million in 1964, almost one-third of its overall balance of payments deficit. Nor did it seem likely that it would go away. There was a good chance, the first secretary of state, George Brown, informed the new Labour cabinet, that the British deficit with all countries could very likely exceed the staggering figure of £1.2 billion.[113] Figuring prominently into the causes was a large and growing import bill that was not being offset by an equally large expansion in exports. The government had a few unpalatable choices; it could borrow to cover its current account deficit, it could restrict the flow of imports, or it could place a surcharge on imports. As had Canada in mid-1962, the United Kingdom resorted to the latter to redress its situation. Approximately 24 per cent of Canadian exports to the United Kingdom were affected, primarily paper, chemicals, non-electric machinery, and iron and steel. The chancellor of the exchequer, James Callaghan, told the nation of the government's intention in his budget speech of 15 April 1964. He was 'quite at ease' in reading it, likely because he kept 'spiking his glass of water liberally with scotch from a pocket flask.'[114]

Ottawa's own need to impose import surcharges in 1962 to address a similar problem should have given the Canadians more sensitivity and sympathy to the British policy. They were, however, intent only upon demanding special exemptions. The Canadian expectation was that the surcharges would be rapidly removed as improvement in Britain's balance of payments permitted.[115] Sharp declined to help when asked by the British if something could be done about the unfairness of Canada's import valuation policy in order to assist British exporters and, in the process, help to correct Britain's large trade deficit. Canadian action on dumping, the minister said, 'would mean legislation and Canada wished to keep this in reserve as a bargaining counter in the [GATT's] Kennedy Round.'[116] As the president of the Federation of British Industries mused, that was 'no more than a conditional offer of jam tomorrow.' However, the mention of the Kennedy round had Canadian officials on edge – they were very concerned about the effect that the implementation of the import surcharges might have on the tariff reduction exercise.

It did seem that Ottawa was determined not to change its legislation. Sharp believed that Canada's anti-dumping and valuation laws did not constitute a significant obstacle to British exports; other countries' exporters were, potentially, as badly affected as the United Kingdom, but they did much better. The main requirement 'was for British salesmen to show more drive and initiative and for British manufacturers to pay more attention to quality, delivery, and so on. It was these factors, rather than price, which were preventing British exports from expanding as much as they might.'[117] The British found that charge 'facile,' although they admitted among themselves that their 'deliveries and ... trading methods in North America leave something to be desired.'[118] In any event there was not too much hope that Ottawa would help British exporters. Norman Robertson, then chairman of a special committee to deal with Canadian preparations for the Kennedy round and recently, the under-secretary of state for external affairs, got it right when he apprised Lintott of the political realities in Canada. He felt 'very doubtful whether the present Government, with its minority position, its dependence on Ontario seats, and its other current difficulties, would be all that anxious to introduce the necessary legislation.'[119] It was an indication, as Tom Keating has written, of a government 'concerned about protecting its immediate narrow [economic] interest.'[120]

Several months later, Alex Currall of the British high commission in Ottawa reported that the Canadians were simply not moving. In a letter written to Douglas Carter of the board of trade that oozed exasperation, Currall rehashed all that he had done the previous week to make the Canadians pay attention. He had begun by telling Jake Warren that there were three areas that unfairly penalized their exporters: the general valuation and anti-dumping problem; the special case of motor vehicles; and Canadian government procurement policies.[121]

Not surprisingly, he was turned down flat on valuation. To make a good showing at the Kennedy round then underway meant reducing the country's tariffs or freeing up trade in some other way. To do that and to ask industry to accept any limitation on its other form of protection, the valuation and anti-dumping duties, would not be feasible. 'Ministers,' the official explained, 'were reluctant to face up to [the British proposal] which involve them "punching a large hole in the anti-dumping protection."' Currall did hold out hope for some action in the Canadian budget, to be introduced in the House of Commons in late April 1965 and action on dumping was then being considered by countries participating in the GATT tariff round.

With respect to procurement policies, Warren had also suggested that little could be done. He told Currall that by comparative international standards, Canadian procurement policies were not ungenerous to the external supplier and it was unrealistic to expect Canadian ministers to go further towards meeting the British. At the federal level, the general rule seemed to be that a price advantage of up to 10 per cent should be given to Canadian suppliers. However, in some areas, so the British believed, 10 per cent had become a minimum and premiums of as much as 50 per cent were given to Canadians manufacturers. That was simply a political reality in Canada, as C.M. Drury, the minister of industry in the second Pearson government, told Douglas Jay, the president of the board of trade: 'Preference for Canadian manufacturers [was] based on the need to give protection to Canadian industry.'[122] Similar margins applied to provincial and municipal purchases.

The British did not believe they had much negotiating room given the Canadian strategy in the Kennedy round. It had been the Canadian position in all post-war tariff negotiations to reduce Most-Favoured-Nation rates without correspondingly lower British Preferential rates, thereby reducing the margin of preference. Given the fact that the same policy would presumably be followed in the current round, and that the British had very little with which to bargain in a tariff negotiation with Canada, they correctly assumed that their negotiations were going to make the Anglo-Canadian trading problem worse and not better.

The Canadians did come through in the April budget and change their anti-dumping and valuation legislation to address some aspects that bore inequitably on British imports. If, on a report from the minister of national revenue, the department was satisfied that certain provisions discriminated against a class of goods imported from one country compared to the same goods imported from another, the government could, by Order in Council, reduce the value for duty. As a British comment on the proposed change noted with some perspicacity, 'Much will depend on how the provision is administered.'[123]

However much discretion it gave the government to determine cases, the legislation did seem to be an attempt to get to the heart of the major British complaint of the mid- and later-1960s – that the rules penalized U.S. exporters less than the British because the scale and level of American sales in the British and Canadian domestic markets were so similar. Walter Gordon, the minister of finance, emphasized in the House of Commons that the new powers would be used to remove discrimination against British goods. 'It is the hope of the government,' he ended this section of his budget speech, 'that this proposal will be taken by British exporters as a decisive response to their pleas that Canada give a clear signal that we welcome their goods.'[124]

However, by the end of 1965, despite the promising beginning, the British were irritated at how the legislation, section 37A of the Customs Act, had been interpreted. By December, of twenty applications for dispensation under the new rule, none had been disposed of. Moreover, according to British manufacturers, the department of national revenue was demanding a large amount of irrelevant information as well as adopting a very narrow view of the rule. The British believed that 'there seems to be no question of the Canadian Department accepting any statement made by a British firm in a 37A application at its face value.'[125]

Following the brief lull in the war that followed the passage of 37A, Lintott thought that the United Kingdom should 'return to the attack on improvement of terms of entry for British exports.'[126] An important part of the strategy was to involve trade ministers with less restrictive views, like Mitchell Sharp, in the application process; otherwise things got bogged down in the 'official machine which [was] geared to protectionist practices.' The department of national revenue was rightly singled out for criticism. It was, British officials believed, 'clearly very inbred [with] the Ministry of Finance and other Departments concerned with international trading relations often knowing little of what goes on in it and why.'[127]

There had also been some change in the Canadian political landscape which had not helped the British case. A federal election had been held on 8 November 1965, and the Liberals under Lester Pearson had been returned, albeit with an only slightly increased minority.[128] According to the high commissioner, this was the worst possible result. He believed that had Pearson been returned with a solid majority, the prime minister might have felt strong enough to take on some of the protectionist elements in his government and in the country at large. As events turned out, 'Pearson's position was weaker than before, and ... it would be more difficult to persuade Canadian Ministers to do anything effective.'[129]

Tellingly, no political party or candidate had made much specific mention of Anglo-Canadian trade problems and issues, or even trade more generally. It was all medicare, pensions, and improved educational and training facilities. Moreover, on 15 February 1965, a new, quintessentially Canadian flag had flown from the pole atop the Peace Tower on Parliament Hill – the old Red Ensign that incorporated the Union Jack in the upper left and Canada's coat of arms in the lower right was history. The new flag was a symbolic departure from a past in which the United Kingdom had figured prominently. As J.L. Granatstein has written, 'The flag marked a new direction for Canada, a step into independence that ranked with the Statute of Westminster and the later patriation of the constitution.'[130] More and more, Britain was a country *comme les autres.*

The Ending of an Era: An Estranged Relationship

By the end of 1965, the British were clearly at a loss in their trade position with Canada. In a strategy session convened in Whitehall, Sir Henry Lintott discussed with several officials options to exercise pressure on Ottawa. One possibility was to reduce purchases of Canadian wheat, but that threat would be limited since the Soviets and the Chinese were now buying millions of bushels of wheat from Canada, and would continue to do so. Moreover, the British noted that the strength of the Liberal party who was the real enemy in all this, they assumed, did not lie in the Prairies; indeed, western farmers were friends of Britain and were most sympathetic to the British cause. What was wanted instead was something that would hurt the growing Canadian trade with the United Kingdom in manufactured goods, and Canadian manufacturing was centred in Ontario, where Liberal Members of Parliament predominated. That went to the heart of the problem: industrialization in Canada during the 1950s and early 1960s had continually reduced the number of British industrial goods that received free entry into Canada, while at the same time increasing the value of Canada's preferences in Britain. About 96 per cent of Canada's exports to the United Kingdom were duty free, compared with only about 60 per cent of British exports to Canada.

The British thought the Auto Pact a good example of the collateral damage caused by Canadian industrialization. The agreement, approved in Canada as of 18 January 1965, provided for the free trade in automobiles in North America. It linked the Canadian and American auto manufacturing sectors in a way that would adversely impact on British attempts to cultivate a market in Canada. The British complained to Ottawa; indeed, Harold Wilson raised the point with Pearson in December 1964 and with the Americans in January 1965. Wilson raised in both Ottawa and Washington the issue of damage to British trade, but also the effect of the Auto Pact on the GATT. 'The whole idea,' he expostulated, 'was a complete breach of [the] MFN principle which is central to the GATT ... it was not the sort of thing which British Government would have contemplated doing itself.'[131] The agreement was also discussed in cabinet, where ministers agreed that 'the British position would be affected by the loss of the preferences vis-à-vis the United States and the disappearance of Commonwealth content from Canadian customs calculations.'[132]

However, to attempt to discriminate against Canadian industrial products was to run afoul of the GATT, the very thing that the British had condemned the North Americans for doing in the Auto Pact case. As well, it would be very difficult, if not impossible, to impose duties on Canadian manufacturers without also imposing them on similar goods imported from other Commonwealth countries. To do so would be to open up the whole question of Commonwealth free entry and to expose the British government to strong pressure from British manufacturers to put duties on cotton textiles imported from India and Hong Kong.

The only reasonable avenue open to the British was to seize any opportunity to impress upon the Canadians their concern about the state of their trade balance with Canada and the latter's unhelpfulness in efforts to correct it. While this strategy had been in place for many months, the British were determined to make their case even more strongly to Ottawa. They intended to focus on the April 1965 budget, and to advocate for their position: the budget was of little value unless it was reinforced by a determination to make its valuation policy effective in the spirit, as well as the letter, of the legislation. The British were appalled that in 1965, their total trade deficit with all other countries would be about equal to that with Canada. And while they had halved their deficit with the rest of the world during 1964, with Canada it had remained unchanged.[133]

Progress on Britain's 37A applications remained dismal by the end of 1966. None of the cases under consideration had advanced significantly during the previous three months. Moreover, 'Finance [was] pressing the department of national revenue to "clear outstanding cases" and faced with this sort of pressure, the DNR might react by refusing many of the cases under consideration.'[134] The British hope was that Canada's department of finance would involve itself in the process as it wanted a number of settlements 'so that [the British] would not rock the boat too violently before the Kennedy Round negotiations [ended].'

The Labour government, now with a more comfortable majority following the election of March 1966 (364 seats to the Conservative's 253), was battling on number of fronts. The increasingly serious balance of payments problem, would escalate into a crisis of confidence in sterling in 1966, partly fed by the constant trade deficits, and aggravated by the seamen's strike from May to July 1966. On 20 July the government announced a restrictive package comprising an interest rate increase, freezes on wages and prices, increased purchase tax, cuts in government expenditure, limits on foreign travel allowances, and tighter hire purchase regulations. None of these measures worked over the longer term as had been hoped, and by the autumn of 1967, a full-scale external crisis hit Britain. On 18 November the pound was devalued by approximately 14 per cent. To make matters worse, a paper prepared for cabinet by the eminent economist, Nicholas Kaldor, painted a depressing picture of British competitiveness: 'The relatively low rate of growth of the real GNP in the UK (2.9 percent for the decade 1955–1964 as against 4.6 percent for the average of the 18 member countries of the OECD [Organization for Economic Cooperation and Development]) is generally attributed to managerial inefficiency, bad industrial organization, restrictive labour practices, technological incompetence and insufficient domestic invest-ment.'[135] Finally, Harold Wilson's biographer Ben Pimlott describes a mood of constant intrigue and suspicion between Wilson and some of his more senior ministers, which set the tone for government.

A Possible British Move into Europe

The problems and issues enumerated in Kaldor's litany prompted the British to look once more to Europe for possible salvation. As then postmaster general, Anthony Wedgewood-Benn, has perceptively noted in his diaries,

> Defence, colour television, Concorde, rocket development – these are all issues rais-ing economic considerations that reveal this country's basic inability to stay in the big league. We just can't afford it. The real choice is, do we go with Europe or do we become an American satellite? Without a conscious decision being taken the latter course is being followed everywhere. For personal reasons, I would see much attrac-tion in an English-speaking federation, bringing in Canada, Australia, New Zealand and Britain to a greater United States. But this is a pipe dream and in reality the choice lies between Britain as an island and a US protectorate, or Britain as a full member of the Six, followed by a wider European federation. I was always against the Common Market but the reality of our isolation is being borne in on me all the time.[136]

The logic of British membership in the EEC was clear, and in May 1967 the Labour government made another formal application to join the Community. While their effort was again unsuccessful, the United Kingdom would finally enter the EEC on 1 January 1973. One repercussion of the act of applying was that Britain downgraded its interest in the Commonwealth. A good indication was the British response to letters received from the prime minister of Jamaica and the high commissioner of Trinidad and Tobago who had requested that a com-mittee be established to begin to explore the possibility of a free trade agreement between those nations and Britain. London's position was that any such initiative would 'now wait until there has been some definitive progress in the consultations in Europe.'[137] Commonwealth entanglements were to be avoided, at least those which might make the United Kingdom a less attractive EEC partner.

A renegotiation of the United Kingdom-New Zealand trade agreement in June 1966 was also done with an eye toward British membership in the Commu-nity.[138] The agricultural products that New Zealand was exporting to Britain were precisely those that were covered in the EEC by the Common Agricultural

Policy's import quotas and subsidies. By extending the agreement for three years, negotiations with Wellington would be made easier. The United Kingdom 'could hardly be expected to join the Community before the beginning of 1968 at the earliest, and 2½ years from then could be regarded as a minimum transitional period.'[139] The thinking was that as Britain eased seamlessly into EEC membership, the arrangement with New Zealand would expire.

The Canadian position on Britain's EEC application was clear. Ministers from the two countries met in April 1967 under the auspices of the UKCCC to discuss potential British entry, announced on 10 May. 'It would require,' so they thought, 'all of Mr. Wilson's skill and leadership to maintain control [of his cabinet] in the circumstances.'[140] However, the Canadians were very conscious of the mistakes committed by Ottawa in 1961 and 1962, and Paul Martin, the secretary of state for external affairs, made it clear that Canada 'could not be accused in any way of obstructing British entry.' Cabinet agreed 'to adopt a sympathetic attitude towards the British application, whatever difficulties it might entail in the short term for Canada with particular respect to agriculture.'[141]

The effect on Canada's trade with Britain would be substantial. Traditional free entry for wheat and other foodstuffs would be replaced by the variable levy under the EEC's Common Agricultural Policy. Many of the industrial materials that Canada exported to the United Kingdom free of duty would also be slapped with a tariff. For manufactured goods, the free entry and preferences that now characterized trade would be taxed. The only potential bright spot, or so officials thought, was that in the longer run, Canada 'could benefit if British membership ... resulted in a higher rate of growth in Britain ... and could also benefit to some extent from increased British sales to the EEC of products incorporating Canadian materials.'[142]

Of more concern to Ottawa than the potential loss of trade, it seemed, was the potential loss of the counterbalance that Britain had provided to American influence. In answer to the question 'Is British entry into the EEC likely to enhance or to weaken the effectiveness of this traditional counterweight?' Ottawa thought that 'In the short run both political and economic ties with Britain might be weakened without an offsetting strengthening of our ties with an enlarged Community. In the longer term, it may be that more varied and substantive economic, political and cultural relations with a more prosperous, larger EEC including Britain could be developed which would benefit Canada in terms of the effectiveness of the counterweight.'[143] That was stretching it, however, and the Canadians knew it.

Even given this Canada's concern, they were reluctant to discuss the issue of preferences and their maintenance when the British raised them. Britain had talked in a general way about their desire to keep their margins of preference to the extent that it was possible, consistent with the Kennedy round. Prior to the April ministers' meeting, the United Kingdom had given Ottawa a list of items where it was particularly anxious to maintain the margin. The Canadian delegation gave no ground on this point, agreeing to consult at the GATT in Geneva as, in fact, it was already committed to do.

That said, Martin and his colleagues fully expected that the British could not be expected to protect Commonwealth interests if they were to succeed in their efforts to join the EEC. And any attempt to assess the full impact of British membership could wait until the results of the Kennedy round were known but at most, Pearson observed, 'Canada could not be too enthusiastic about the British entry into the Common Market.' There was some talk about what might happen with the CAN$1.1 billion worth of exports that Canada had sent there in 1966, 95 per cent duty free, but no conclusions were reached. However, Canada also believed that British entry was not a foregone conclusion: de Gaulle remained opposed, Germany remained cool, and Italy supported a policy of preparing a detailed, unhurried study of the implications of British entry. As for the UKCCC meeting, the first to be held in more than four years, James Grandy, an assistant deputy minister of finance, told a American colleague that the 'meeting [was] not one that accomplished anything.'[144]

Increasingly, the EEC figured into British calculations, and the Commonwealth concomitantly less. Mitchell Sharp, now minister of finance, and C.M. Drury, the minister of industry, put a sharp point on this feeling in meetings they had with Douglas Jay, the secretary of state for Commonwealth relations. Both noted 'that working relations at senior official level seemed much closer in the early fifties when they were Deputy Ministers.'[145] Recent years, one critic noted in the late 1960s, had 'not been good ones for the Commonwealth ... In Ottawa, there was little enthusiasm for the once-powerful organization.'[146] Similarly, as John Holmes wrote in July 1966, 'Two countries closely associated for centuries, Britain and Canada, are drifting apart, and it is a pity ... What has gone wrong?'[147] As Charles Ritchie, Canada's high commissioner in London from 1967 until 1971 mused: 'We and the British were excellent friends who had known each other for a long time, but were no longer members of the same family. If our attitudes had changed, so had those of the British. With their loss of influence [in the world] had come some loss of interest ... There remained the bonds of the past, but our future was no longer any concern of theirs. If our preoccupations were with the United States, theirs were increasingly with Europe.'[148] Moreover, Ritchie knew that 'there [was] no interest in Canada in tightening relations with the United Kingdom or in reporting ... on British policies.'[149] In short, the British connection was 'far from popular' in Ottawa.[150]

In an attempt to begin the resuscitation process, the Canadians on the spot in

London had urged that Ottawa devote some attention to the poor state of the Anglo-Canadian relationship. That had prompted Marcel Cadieux, the undersecretary of state for external affairs, and his senior associates 'to concentrate their attention on the subject.'[151] Geoffrey Murray, the minister and second-in-command at Canada House in London, was then instructed to prepare a report on the subject. The comprehensive document began 'by examining the weakening of traditional ties since the Second World War. He then assessed various irritants apparent in the mid-sixties, according the greatest importance to economic issues such as the Canadian system of import valuations for customs duties on manufactured goods which the British considered to be prejudicial to their interests.' As well, the Canadian purchase of the French Mystère aircraft by Ottawa and the greater Canadian sympathy for the pending French withdrawal from NATO's integrated military command roiled the relationship.

External took the report seriously and to halt the slide of the relationship the Canadians proposed an annual gathering of senior ministers, along the same lines as that with their American counterparts.[152] The idea for the committee had come out of discussions exploring ways to increase Anglo-Canadian trade that Robert Winters, the minister of trade and commerce, had had with several British ministers, including Jay and Brown. Ironically, at the same time that Ottawa was exploring the possibility of regularized ministerial meetings, the UKCCC was quietly buried. That, too, was the fate of the ministerial committee; it met once on 19–20 April 1967 and was disbanded due to a lack of interest. Similar arrangements with the United States and Japan had had much longer lives, working effectively through the 1950s and 1960s.

Still, the agenda of the ministers' meeting and the approach the Canadians chose to take are suggestive of the new relationship. The Canadians expected the British to emphasize the importance of greater sales of their products to the Canadian government, and their interest in seeing more British firms in a position to compete for contracts let by Ottawa. The United Kingdom had earlier proposed an exchange of national treatment in public procurement, but it had been put aside by the Canadians. The latter did think, however, that there could be some movement in this area as Britain's post office, airlines, railways, and defence establishment did discriminate against foreign firms.

While it was not clear how far the British were prepared to go in such an exchange, the Canadians thought that it would, at a minimum, involve the removal of the application of the 10 per cent premium for Canadian content and some understanding regarding the circumstances in which Canadian contracts could be restricted to national sources. There were definite reservations on the Canadian side about any such proposal, given Canada's relations with its major trading partners, particularly for the country's defence production sharing

Table 5.1 British Applications under section 37A of the Canada Customs Act,
Aug. 1966–March 1967

Applications submitted under 37A by UK exporters	57
Extra discounts granted under 37A	10
Concessions granted under other sections of Customs Act	10
Applications refused by Canadian authorities	19
Applications withdrawn	7
Applications still under consideration (of which at least four will fail)	11

Source: PRO, BT 11, vol. 6525, F.P. Horne, Minute Sheet, 21 March 1967.

arrangements with the United States. It was a dicey proposition whether an agreement could be worked out, but even if one could, it was incumbent upon Ottawa to explore possibilities with the United States first. In the ministerial meeting, cabinet decided that it would be appropriate 'to indicate [to the British ministers] that [while] Canadian authorities are continuing to look into this matter, it is not possible to draw a conclusion at this stage on the practical possibilities of finding a basis for an exchange of 'national treatment' between Canada and Britain.'[153] Clearly, the relationship with the United States was much more important than any with Britain.

The Anglo-Canadian trade relationship continued in the doldrums, the result of, from the British point of view, the 'vexed question of valuation' as demonstrated by table 5.1.

Moreover, the dollar value of exports covered by the successful applications was depressingly low. The only possible solution seemed to lie in the negotiations on an international dumping code taking place as a part of the Kennedy round in Geneva. As a May 1967 British memorandum noted,

> Agreement on such a code has now been reached *ad referendum* and acceptance of the Code by the Canadians will mean radical amendment of Canadian legislation under which automaticity will be replaced by the introduction of material injury criterion. It is understood that the Canadians are thinking of making the legislative changes in their 1968 Budget and with the legislative changes the particular problem of valuation with which Section 37A aimed to deal could arise only if it could be established that dumped goods were causing or threatening material injury. The acceptance of a material injury criterion by Canada is a most welcome move. While we must see how the new arrangements – when introduced – will work in practice, the proposed change should go a long way to remove the anti-dumping problem created for United Kingdom exporters in the Canadian market.[154]

When Harold Wilson visited Ottawa in February 1968, he pushed the Canadians once again, raising 'the perennial question about the Canadian customs' handling and valuation of British exports.'[155] As he recalls, Pearson was embarrassed and covered it up by parodying a Whitehall brief: 'Yes,' he said, 'this is it. Canadian customs valuation. Defensive brief. The [Canadian] Prime Minister is advised not to raise this matter unless raised by the British Prime Minister. If it is raised, the Prime Minister is advised to say no more than ...' Wilson took the point; there was little to be said that had not been gone over many times since 1964. However, the British criticism of Canadian policy was finally met in the 1968 Canadian budget, tabled on 22 October 1968 with the revisions to take effect on 1 January 1969. The most significant change related to the provision that there be a formal inquiry into the impact of dumping on production in Canada. Prior to this, tariffs had been automatically imposed by the department of national revenue. It would now not be so easy to impose penalties on suspected wrongdoers.

The budget provision did nothing to slow the decline of the Anglo-Canadian economic and political relationships. While the British might suggest that problems with valuation were at the bottom of their problem, it went much deeper than that. Devaluation in November 1967, continuing crises of confidence in sterling and, even following devaluation, a growing balance of payments problem as imports increased all contribute to Britain's economic slide. During the first quarter of 1968, the total external monetary deficit of US$1.07 billion was slightly worse than that of the final quarter of 1967. As a Canadian report to the deputy minister of finance, R.B. Bryce, noted, 'The Europeans were very uneasy about the British situation and were very rough on the British [at the WP 3 meetings of the OECD], especially in connection with monetary policy.'[156]

By the turn of the decade, though, the Canadians were contemplating the effects of the EEC on their trade, and paid relatively little attention to the United Kingdom. Indeed, Britain and the Commonwealth received virtually no mention in Canada's White Paper, *Foreign Policy for Canadians*.[157] Anglo-Canadian trade figures had reached all-time lows, and by 1973 Japan was Canada's second largest trading partner. The share of Canadian imports from Britain in 1970 was 5 per cent or CAN$762 million and 4.5 per cent or CAN$832 in 1971. By comparison, imports from the United States for the same years comprised 66 per cent and 67 per cent respectively. On the export side, Britain's share of the Canadian market was 8 per cent in 1970 and 7 per cent in 1971, compared to the United States, which sold Canada 64 per cent and 67 per cent of its exports for those years. Canada's trade with Japan had increased steadily throughout the 1960s, from CAN$118 million in 1960 to CAN$2.8 billion by 1973. In 1967 alone Canadian exports to Japan had increased by a staggering 40 per cent.

When the British were invited to apply again for Community membership in 1970, Ottawa's official reaction was to regard it with faint interest. The government of Pierre Trudeau, elected in June 1968, did undertake several studies of its potential impact and an interdepartmental committee was established to coordinate studies on the effect of EEC enlargement on the country's trade policy. A.E. Ritchie, the under secretary of state for external affairs, suggested to a high-level group of senior officials that the committee might look at issues that could arise concerning Canada's contractual relations under the GATT and also its bilateral rights with various applicants.[158]

The undersecretary also thought the group should investigate where Canada would fit in a world dominated by two trading blocs, the EEC and the United States. The committee would develop papers on the effects and possible responses to the proliferation of EEC preference agreements, and assess how the Community's enlargement might affect Canada's dependence on the U.S. market. Potential British entry did not arouse the same sort of hysteria in 1970 that it had a decade earlier; Ottawa could contemplate 'the (further) loss of the British market' not unduly disturbed.[159]

Still, Canadian officials applauded when British negotiators requested special tariff arrangements for nine commodities of interest to Canada as their talks with the EEC continued. Among these were aluminum, newsprint, and plywood – not entirely critical to the functioning of the Canadian market. However, the nine commodities did account for about 20 per cent of total Canadian sales in the United Kingdom. When the EEC refused to countenance the British position, it was dropped and Ottawa filed no complaint.

The 1960s had not been kind to the development of Anglo-Canadian trade. Neither the so-called anglophile Diefenbaker Conservatives nor the Liberals who followed them ultimately demonstrated much concrete interest in encouraging trade. Clearly, the United States was the overwhelming interest of Canadian trade policy development in a way that had not been the case in the 1950s and earlier. Canada had become a truly North American nation even as Britain was becoming more European. It was bound to happen and the Anglo-Canadian relationship, after some initial hesitation, evolved accordingly and in response to the rhythms of international trade as overseen by the GATT.

Chapter 6

Canada, the GATT, and the European Economic Community

The European Conundrum

'If,' the leader of Her Majesty's Official Opposition, Lester Pearson, began in his reply to the Speech from the Throne on 22 January 1958, 'we do not wish to weaken the western coalition [ranged against the USSR]; and if, in Canada, we do not wish either to face the United States alone or become too economically dependent on it, then surely the best policy for us is to seek economic interdependence within the North Atlantic Community through freer trade.'[1] The notion of a North Atlantic Community, uniting North America and Western Europe, remained an attractive proposition for the generation of Canadians who had matured during the Great Depression. However, Pearson's intervention in the debate raises the question: was he serious or merely electioneering, sensing the Conservative government's vulnerability as its mandate slowly ran out?

More likely, it was a combination of the two. But it was undeniable that the Liberals before 10 June 1957 and again after 8 April 1963 and the Conservatives in between, had proved unable to nudge Canada's trade figures with Western Europe higher. Indeed, by the 1960s Canada's foreign economic policy with respect to Europe was replete with unrequited expectations. The dream of millions of bushels of wheat and other agricultural products, tons of steel, aluminum and copper, zinc and nickel, and shiploads of manufactured end products pouring across the North Atlantic to satisfy an enormous European demand did not materialize. In the post-Second World War era, it was probably never a realistic possibility, at least on the scale envisaged by Ottawa, despite Pearson's admonition.

In the years following 1945, it was inconceivable that Canada's economic diplomacy would neglect such a potentially fertile trading partner. Canada had strong ties of heritage and history and was overwhelmingly a 'European' nation, its orientation clearly facing east. Moreover, as the years passed there was a growing concern about the dominance of the United States in Canada's trade dossier, against which Europe would provide a useful counterweight. For all those reasons, the Canadian government continued to devote resources to the effort to develop significant trade linkages with the continent.

That progress might have been possible had the Cold War not settled over Europe, and had the Americans been less focused on a potential Soviet adversary. In short, considerations other than the purely economic increasingly informed U.S. policy making. Trade took a back seat to military and strategic calculations, designed to prevent Soviet expansionism. Even that most celebrated example of American aid, the European Recovery Program (ERP), popularly known as the Marshall Plan, and which ran from 1948–52, was arguably more important for Washington from a military perspective than it was as an economic rehabilitation program. Hunger, poverty and political and economic instability, or so the United States believed, prepared the ground for communism's message. And without a total American commitment to promote the multilateral and non-discriminatory trade agenda that had first been articulated by Cordell Hull, Franklin Roosevelt's secretary of state in the 1930s, there was much backsliding in terms of the trade liberalisation that was so important to Canada.[2]

The United States initially provided unquestioning support to measures designed to enhance Western European strength, such as the development of the European Economic Community (EEC), formally proclaimed on 1 January 1958. But as American policy unfolded over the next decade, it did not always sit well in Ottawa. Washington was 'obsessed with problems of security and [was] prepared to subordinate other problems to a strong unified Western Europe.'[3] Canadians generally believed that the U.S. attitude toward developing European economic integration was 'out of touch with reality.' As John Holmes has so cogently noted, Ottawa was 'less inclined to see [European unification] as a giant step towards world order, and more as a manifestation of ... blocism.'[4] The Americans placed too much reliance (the Canadians called them naïve) on the General Agreement on Tariffs and Trade (GATT) to sort out the trade challenges posed by European unification. And while Ottawa, too, would make its case against discrimination in the GATT, it was under no illusions as to the power of the agreement to mediate disputes and enforce decisions.

The European experiment had implications for Canada. The country was far more dependent than most on exports to support domestic prosperity, as a briefing paper laid out clearly; 'If some countries can create, to some degree at least, a viable economy within their own border, Canada cannot: the prosperity of our farms and industries are inextricably linked to the markets of the world.'[5] Indeed, by 1960 about 25 per cent of the country's gross national product was directly related to merchandise exports. Still feeling the aftershocks of the ten lost years of the Great Depression, Ottawa was focused on its agenda of multilateralism, non-discrimination, and exchange rate stability. Unfortunately, the global commercial system did not evolve after 1945 as Canada had hoped. For a variety of reasons, convertibility of European currencies was delayed until the later 1950s, and some trade discrimination against Canada and the United States lingered into the 1960s as the post-war transition period stretched out far longer than any had anticipated.[6]

While Canada prospered during the 1950s, supplying a growing American market with raw materials, it still exhorted Western Europe and the United Kingdom to reduce barriers to trade. However, the establishment of the EEC in March 1957 put Canadian trade policy at risk. Six European countries, the Benelux bloc, France, Italy, and West Germany, comprised the Community, which provided for both a customs union and a free trade area as exceptions to the principle of non-discrimination under article XXIV of the GATT. The British initiated discussions with six other countries, Austria, Denmark, Norway, Portugal, Sweden, and Switzerland, designed to lead to the European Free Trade Area (EFTA) in industrial goods.

Ottawa worried publicly that the creation of a powerful European trading group that imposed restrictions on outside competition would distort global trading patterns to Canada's disadvantage. Although the country's trade with Europe was relatively meagre, both Conservative and Liberal governments in the 1960s pushed the Europeans to declare their adherence to multilateralism and non-discrimination and open their markets to Canadian goods. Donald Fleming, the Conservative minister of finance from 1957 to 1962, later said that it would have been 'indefensible' not to have done so, especially as the area became more prosperous. Similarly, Louis Rasminsky, a deputy governor at the Bank of Canada, told an April 1960 meeting of the Commonwealth economic consultative council, 'The outstanding feature [of the global economy] was that of the changed position of Europe. One had long been accustomed to the situation in which the European economy had been the tail which was wagged by the American dog. But it was no longer clear that this was the case. Europe had an independent business cycle of her own and European economic trade and policies were now of great importance to the rest of the world.'[7]

The Canadian position was a mixture of principle and pragmatism. Since 1947 Ottawa had constructed its trade policy around the General Agreement that the developing EEC now seemed to threaten. That policy made good sense – as Fleming suggested, if Canada missed the opportunity that a rapidly developing Europe presented, it 'could [have been] very costly to us.'[8] Ottawa also pressed its concern on American governments, but to little effect. Accordingly, it perceived the revival of GATT tariff reduction rounds in the early-to-mid 1960s as perhaps a last chance to encourage the Europeans to negotiate in good faith with Canada and reduce impediments to the flow of Canadian goods to Europe. This chapter will discuss that process and Canadian activities designed to secure a freer trade regime with Western Europe in general, and the EEC in particular.

During the early 1960s, possible British membership in the EEC was *the* critical issue in terms of Canadian trade policy development toward Europe. Ottawa had generally been opposed to any British move into Europe, whether it was a bridge between the two trade blocs, or a British request to join the Six. As events transpired, Canadian concern over their place in the British market was premature; negotiations between London and the Community collapsed with a French veto on 29 January 1963. Lester Pearson later told Britain's Harold Macmillan, that French president Charles de Gaulle had confided to him that 'the United Kingdom was slowly learning to become European, but they must expect to and would suffer a few rebuffs in the process.'[9] And European they must be, or so Georg Lilienfeld, the minister at the German embassy in Washington, told a meeting of senior officials; for the present, de Gaulle saw Britain as 'the American Trojan Horse,' a grave sin given de Gaulle's anti-Anglo-Saxon mindset.[10]

The Europeans Stake Out Their Protectionist Position

While possible British membership in the EEC raised problems in Ottawa, the government was also very concerned about the effect developing Community policy might have on the GATT. Its primary interest was in improving access to European markets for raw materials and agricultural products, but restrictions were almost crippling in both areas. Trade barriers were particularly iniquitous with respect to agricultural commodities, at least according to Canada and the United States, who believed that EEC agricultural policies should be discussed, for what it was worth, in the GATT. Indeed, as early as 1958, Canada, in concert with Australia and the United States had been 'instrumental in the move by the contracting parties of the GATT to establish a panel of distinguished economists [led by Gottfried von Haberler] ... to report on trends in agricultural trade, with particular reference to the impact of protectionism on primary products.'[11] They focused on the system of agricultural support schemes as the principal culprit and recommended that countries refrain from using trade policy to achieve domestic agricultural stabilization. The panel also made two recommendations: that protection be separated from stabilization; and that governments refrain from using trade policy to achieve domestic stabilization. The Haberler report, published by the GATT as *Trends in International Trade*, was ahead of its time. No government wanted to tackle such a thorny issue, and the report was immediately shelved by affected contracting parties. Governments in Europe, in particular, but also the United States, were not ready to contemplate a reduction of subsidies.

The deafening silence in Europe that greeted the Haberler report was predictable. Certainly it informed the critical views of European agriculture held by Canada's minister of agriculture, Douglas Harkness. In a meeting of Canadians and Americans a few years later he suggested that 'In view of the policies which seemed to be emerging in Europe, Canada and the United States might find that there were more agricultural restrictions in the future than in the present, and that our prospects for increasing agricultural exports to the common market might not be very bright.'[12] Hector McKinnon, an official of enormous ability and experience who came out of retirement in mid-1960 to chair Canada's GATT delegation to the Dillon round of tariff reduction negotiations, offered an even more pessimistic interpretation: 'The utmost skill and caution would be needed to hold onto our present position [in the GATT].'[13]

Canadians continued to raise the issue of agricultural protectionism at the GATT as they had since their first proposal in 1957 that a special agricultural trade committee of the Organization for European Economic Cooperation (OEEC) be struck, and through their subsequent participation in a number of consultative meetings between the EEC and the major agricultural exporting nations to discuss the developing Common Agricultural Policy (CAP). They were helped in this by the GATT's Committee II, which dealt with the expansion of agricultural trade. It concluded that a moderation of agricultural protection in both importing and exporting countries was desirable, similar to the recommendations of the Harberler committee. Despite these discussions and recommendations, however, the Canadians' worst nightmares were becoming real as the CAP began to take more firm shape. If it was the case, and the Canadians felt it was, that the negotiations provided an indication of Community intentions with respect to the rest of the world, then it seemed clear that the EEC would not meet the multilateral and non-discriminatory test. The Canadian's fundamental point in all discussions with Europeans was to emphasize the principles which underlay the GATT.

This was the position that guided the ministerial delegation, headed by George Hees, the minister of trade and commerce, to the nineteenth session of the GATT in late November 1961. He was directed by cabinet to accomplish the impossible – convince the Europeans that agricultural protectionism was a serious problem, affecting not only the development of the international system of agricultural exchange, but trade more generally and the entire multilateral concept on which the GATT was based. As was well known in Ottawa, the trade rules of the GATT were being frustrated in the agricultural sector to a significant degree. Since Canada had a major stake in global agricultural trade, the Canadian delegation should cooperate in any GATT action to address that problem.

In what would surely be another herculean effort, Hees was also asked to 'encourage' his colleagues to work towards the expansion of international trade in agricultural products through the moderation of non-tariff measures that stimulated 'excessive production, inhibit[ed] consumption and adversely affect[ed] normal trade.'[14] Finally, and perhaps most importantly, the delegation was instructed to convince others that the expansion of trade should be negotiated in the multilateral and non-discriminatory GATT, and not in regional blocs like the EEC.

Not surprisingly, the Canadians made virtually no headway in Geneva, although Canada led the United States forward to initiate another GATT round with a wider mandate than the Dillon round of 1960–1. The results of the latter round were generally disappointing, despite initial forecasts by the Americans that it would be 'the broadest ever.'[15]

For the Canadians on the spot in Geneva, some disturbing rumours emanating from Ottawa could have serious implications for Canada's negotiating position in the Dillon round. For example, they had heard that cabinet might rebind certain agricultural items and possibly some others, which would affect the direction of the country's commercial policy. In a wide-ranging and very cogent letter written by the ranking official at the GATT round, J.H. Warren, to James Roberts, the deputy minister of trade and commerce, the delegation's position was made very clear. Any attempt to raise a bound Canadian tariff or withdraw a binding would be counterproductive. It 'would quickly put us in a position where we would face compensatory withdrawals by other countries – and of course this would mean that we would have little or no scope for direct participation in the new negotiations.'[16] If Canada followed such a path, Warren insisted, 'we will come out of this Conference with a good deal less favourable terms of access for our exports than we now have.' The United States would withdraw trade concessions, it would be difficult to maintain Canada's place in the British market, and the EEC would continue to slip away as a destination for Canadian exports.

As well, any attempt to increase protection afforded to Canadian farmers would be 'ill-advised,' it would certainly be badly timed from the point of view of Canada's interests as an exporter. Warren told Roberts that Canada had recently joined with its trading partners in an effort to do something about the frustration of trade in agricultural products by domestic protection. As he noted, 'As a major agricultural exporter, our interest in this exercise is obvious. The success of this initiative is by no means assured and our capacity to bring the work to a fruitful conclusion will of course be greatly inhibited if domestically we now move in the reverse direction.' The EEC and the United States would feel less constrained about increasing protection for their farmers if Canada took that step.

Warren's thoughts about the effect of heightened protectionism on Canadian agriculture and industry, also bear mentioning and provide some context to the debates raging in cabinet over the proper course of action:

If without being satisfied that a move to give increased protection to a particular industry or sector is in the national interest, the Government were to yield to pressures for greater protection, it seems to me that we would be starting down a long and dangerous road, with no end to the claims which would be pressed on Ministers. We are living in a [resources] buyer's market and in a world which promises to become more rather than less competitive. In these circumstances should we embark on a policy which promises to increase our costs and undermine the position of our exports relative to that of our competitors? There must be measures other than tariff protection which can be taken to keep our efficient and economic industries in a position to enjoy an appropriate share of the domestic market, and to compete in markets abroad. If we insulate our economy through higher tariffs, we will build in outdated patterns of production and lose the flexibility and dynamism which it is so necessary to maintain in our day and age if we are to keep up technologically and otherwise with other countries throughout the world.

At the same time that Warren was counselling Roberts about the evils of protectionism, the delegation was also very concerned about the EEC intention 'to maintain excessive protection for agriculture which would seriously restrict our access to the market and stimulate uneconomic production in Europe' and how that would play out in the GATT negotiations.[17] Earlier, the Canadians had raised this issue with President Eisenhower; they had emphasized their important trade interests in Europe and that in order to keep European markets as open as possible, 'sustained pressure will be required, particularly from the United States.'[18] Ottawa, the president was told, was particularly concerned at the arrangements the Six might work out with the CAP, and thought the 'closest cooperation' between the United States and Canada necessary if certain agricultural exports were not to be blocked. As well, the Canadians wanted to throw their lot in with the U.S. department of agriculture and not with the department of state; any backbone, they thought, was the result of the former's influence, while the latter, at least in this area of agricultural protectionism, was 'less firm.'[19]

In one worrisome example of how European protectionism was changing trade patterns, Ottawa instructed its embassies in Belgium, France, and West Germany to protest the excessive subsidization of EEC flour exports to what had been Canadian markets. As Community flour-milling capacity had grown, so too had its support of exports. Canadian subsidies, on the other hand, had been eliminated. In *aides-mémoire* submitted to Paris and Bonn, the Canadian government expressed its displeasure at the effect of the 'present [EEC] subsidization ... of flour exports on Canadian flour exports in our traditional markets; such export subsidies generate unfair competition vis-à-vis countries such as Canada where livelihood of wheat producers depends upon returns from commercial exports.'[20] This *démarche* had little effect on EEC behaviour, perhaps for reasons noted by the political scientist, Peyton Lyon, in a polemic written in 1962. He remarked that a Dutch official of the EEC Commission had told Clive Baxter, the assistant editor of the *Financial Post*, that 'Canada overrates its own importance these days. We want to trade with you, but you must understand that if necessary we can get on without you.' Another official pointed out that 'Canada isn't being very realistic right now. Your representatives complain a little too often to impress us ... There is the implication that if we don't oblige, Canada will pack up and go home. Let us suppose you do. Then what happens? You will be driven into even closer ties with the United States and your problems will get worse.'[21]

The proposed Common Market tariff on industrial items being discussed at the Dillon round was also of concern. These would mean higher tariff barriers for Canadian exports that had been going to relatively low tariff West Germany and the Benelux bloc. Reductions in the rates of duty that Canada would receive from high tariff France and Italy would not compensate for increases in rates from the others, since they had been Canada's biggest markets in the Six.

The GATT round's two largest participants, the EEC and the United States, reached agreement on only a fraction of the tariff negotiations between them, and the contentious areas of agriculture, chemicals, and steel were excluded from the discussions altogether. As John Evans has suggested, the lack of agreement was due in large part to 'the impotence of the American negotiators and the determination of the Community to keep its hands free to construct its common agricultural policy.'[22] That disappointment also extended to the Canada-United States relationship; the total of U.S. concessions to Canada was about US$65 million, less than 2 per cent of Canadian-American trade.[23] In part, that seemed to reflect a new and more self-interested American attitude buttressed by a very limited negotiating authority. While in previous negotiations, or so the United States believed, officials had discussed with U.S. industry what could be conceded to other countries, by the early 1960s they were examining the situation with these sectors with a view to determining what other countries could concede, and how impediments on U.S. exports could be removed. That shift reflected American concern over their deteriorating balance of payments situation – in 1958, they had suffered their first deficit but had had them ever since. Washington's ability to negotiate tariff reductions was limited by Congress to reductions of 20 per cent from existing U.S. rates subject to the limits of: '(i) the extent to which reciprocal concessions [could] be obtained in the tariffs of other countries, ... (ii) the peril-point procedures whereby no concessions can be made which would in the view of the U.S. Tariff Commission, cause or threaten serious injury to U.S. industry, and (iii) no authority to go free on any tariff items.'[24] Nor were the Canadians entirely free of protectionist impulses. As Ronald Anderson reported in the *Globe and Mail*, the 'meagreness of the concessions made by Canada [was] an indication that Ottawa had dug in its heels on trade liberalization.'[25] These changing attitudes toward trade led to a whole new dynamic in international negotiations.

The Canadians Move into Europe: The OECD

A generalized fear was emerging among some countries, and especially Canada, that the multilateral agenda was slipping away in the late 1950s and early 1960s as the GATT proved powerless to divert the EEC, and perhaps the Americans, from a protectionist path. The Europeans were focused on constructing their Community behind tariff walls that had resulted in a 28 per cent increase in trade among EEC members between 1959 and 1960. They now exuded strength and confidence.

That was a part of the motivation behind the U.S. administration's initiative, supported strongly by Ottawa, to reconfigure the OEEC into what would become the Organization for Economic Cooperation and Development (OECD) in 1961.[26] The former had been established as the continental body to disperse Marshall Plan assistance to European countries between 1948 and 1952. Canada and the United States had become associate members in 1951, and when the ERP had wound up its operations the following year, the OEEC had remained. Both countries now wanted to become full members with all the rights and privileges of membership and the ability to become more formally involved in European economic issues. Ottawa, at least, was anxious not to become more marginalized in the economic affairs of Europe than it believed it already was, especially as the EEC became a more cohesive and restrictive organization, with the apparent blessing of the GATT under article XXIV.

The Canadian embassy in Brussels, the EEC 'capital' explained this in a novel way: 'It is rumoured these days in Brussels that the battle hymn of [Walter] Hallstein, the president of the Common Market Commission, is "GATT mit uns." For the mathematical economists of the Department [of External Affairs] this can also be expressed in the equation OEEC – EEC = O.'[27] The 'O' was to be avoided at all costs, and from the Canadian perspective, there were important objectives to be achieved through a reconstituted OEEC. Ideally, it would help to keep Europe and the United States outward-looking and cooperative on a non-discriminatory basis, as well as provide a means of overcoming divisions within

Europe itself. Ottawa believed that the terms of access to European markets would determine the orientation of U.S. policies in the 1960s and pondered this in regular meetings early in the decade. Even though the United States had given full support to the political and economic objectives of the EEC, there was no assurance that support would be maintained once its impact was felt and various domestic pressures and interests became active. 'Would it not be disastrous,' a Canadian document asked, 'if Europe ... pursued inward-looking policies that led to a revival of protectionism in the United States with all the divisive effects that this would have on the free world?'[28] Surely Canada shared a common aim with Europe of resisting protectionism in the United States, and a new organization could provide additional opportunities for Canada to exert some influence, however modest, on the United States as well as on Europe.[29]

At the very least, it would provide another high-level forum where Canada could participate fully in deliberations, unlike the OEEC where associate member status had imposed limitations. In short, Canada considered it important that the new OECD should contribute to the expansion of trade and the realization of better trading relations among its members. And it would be tested soon; Canada wanted to bring the whole issue of sixes and sevens to the new OECD, where it 'could be discussed in the presence of the United States and Canada, thus enabling them to safeguard their interests and to impart to any settlement an outward looking orientation.'[30]

Canada's *Bête Noir*: The Common Agricultural Policy

The Six were moving ahead with their program. By 1962, they had passed the second stage of the Treaty of Rome and had adopted on 30 June what was to become the focus of so much Canadian hostility, the CAP.[31] The CAP was designed as an import levy system to eventually protect about 300 agricultural products, among them wheat, eggs, milk, poultry, and sugar, against competition from outside suppliers. These products comprised 90 per cent of EEC agricultural output. The EEC's Agricultural Guidance and Guarantee Fund would purchase a farmer's entire production that would then, given the great increase in farm productivity and the inability of the Community to use all of it, be stored, dumped, denatured, or given away to other markets. These practices not only potentially affected Canada's producers but high price supports without any production controls created massive food surpluses. The policy met the objectives of the French and Germans in particular, who both wanted to maintain protection for their farmers for as long as possible.[32] It was necessary, or so Walter Hallstein, now the president of the Commission of the EEC, suggested, to preserve rural Europe against more productive foreign competition. Agriculture, he had told the Americans, '[was] not so much a branch of production but a way of life.'[33]

While the CAP had been in development, Ottawa had pulled no punches in expressing its displeasure. In late 1959 the Canadian government had delivered an *aide-mémoire* to the Quai d'Orsay, the French foreign ministry, 'pour attirer l'attention du Gouvernement français sur les très importants intérêts commerciaux que présentent les marchés agricoles de la CEE pour le Canada.'[34] At that time, the common market countries had taken about CAN$400 million worth of total Canadian exports, about half agricultural products. Wheat was the single most important item, representing about 30 per cent of all Canada's exports to the Community. And the export of wheat, Emile Lacoste of the French embassy in Ottawa told his foreign minister, 'est pour le Canada une obsession continuelle. Economiquement, financièrement, socialement, politiquement, c'est un des problèmes majeurs auxquels l'Administration canadienne doit faire face.'[35]

Ottawa believed that the development of a common agricultural market would halt any progress toward reducing discrimination in agricultural products; moreover, the rapid and sustained economic growth then taking place in EEC countries presented an opportunity to eliminate discrimination. Such hopes flew in the face of developing policy among the Six. The government also made clear its concern over reports that the European Commission was considering the use of quantitative restrictions on agricultural imports such as wheat to encourage local production. This policy would work to the detriment of Canadian exports and could only have serious and adverse implications for international trade. There was, however, also a particularly Canadian agenda; the government wanted to control the growth of international grain surpluses and to support international grains prices, which would be more difficult to achieve if the EEC stimulated production.[36] Moreover, Canadian negotiators had been waging a rearguard action against an aggressive American agricultural surplus disposals program and their domestic price support policy for some time.[37] For Canada, it had turned out to be a war fought on many fronts.

The rather intense nature of some of the negotiations then taking place, especially those between the Six and the United Kingdom over the terms of the latter's admission, created a need for more personnel at the Canadian delegation in Brussels. The delegation had been established in 1961 as an offshoot of the Canadian embassy in the city but accredited to the EEC. Many believed that a separate mission should be established in the Belgian capital to deal directly with the European Commission when it seemed necessary, particularly if Ottawa thought that its interests should be included in any EEC-UK discussions. As the negotiations progressed, 'the views of the Six were becoming more firm, and consequently it was important for Canada to take steps to safeguard its interests before it was too late.'[38]

And safeguard it must, for the French were more often setting the tone in the EEC with consequent negative results for Britain, Canada, and the United States. Olivier Wormser, the director of economics and financial affairs at the Quai d'Orsay, had told the Canadians exactly what to expect in any negotiations with his government: France was a protectionist country, had always been a protectionist country, and probably would always be a protectionist country. And in agriculture, 'the French farmer wields great political influence and ... he is very vigilant.'[39] Paris, and in particular de Gaulle, had their own grievance to nurture against Canada. Ottawa's refusal to sell uranium to France for its nuclear power stations during the earlier 1960s without waiving its right of inspection was a tremendous irritant. The president was a formidable enemy; he was a larger-than-life figure and would have subscribed to Louis XIV's characterization, 'L'état – c'est moi.'[40]

Nor were the Germans, the other big power in the Community, prepared to temper French enthusiasm for protectionism. Chancellor Ludwig Erhard, during a visit to Ottawa in mid-1964, pointed out to Prime Minister Lester Pearson that he was strongly in favour of Atlantic cooperation, 'but was also very much a European and would try to maintain the special contacts between Germany and France which [former] Chancellor Adenauer and President de Gaulle had developed.'[41] Smug was a word that seemed to sum up the European attitude toward their accomplishments, at least according to Sydney Pierce, Canada's ambassador to Belgium.

What was the Canadian stake in EEC markets? There was much talk and beating of chests, but was it a case of more smoke and less fire? Certainly exports had increased slowly during the first half of the decade, and by the mid-1960s, they hovered around CAN$600 million out of Canada's total export trade of approximately CAN$8.7 billion. The country's most important market among the Six was West Germany, which took only about CAN$170 million worth of Canadian exports. The composition of those products had remained relatively constant since the Community's establishment in 1958 – 40 per cent comprised of agricultural products, primarily wheat, and 60 per cent ranged from primary materials to manufactured goods. Table 6.1 illustrates actual numbers from 1959 to 1966 of Canada's exports to, and imports from, the EEC.

As the figures amply demonstrate, the EEC was not, in absolute terms, of great importance to Canada's exporters, but Ottawa was not prepared to let the EEC slip comfortably behind its high tariff walls. In speeches, memoranda, and personal contacts, Canadian officials and politicians continued to press their case. The Pearson government sympathetically viewed Britain's wish to join the EEC,

Table 6.1
Canadian Exports and Imports with the EEC (CAN$million)

	1959	1960	1961	1962	1963	1964	1965	1966
Exports	430	450	485	452	451	500	587	633
Imports	237	293	308	312	309	372	480	529

but it also remained as opposed to protectionism as had its Conservative predecessor. Indeed, it was the Pearsonian position that Canada's best chance to cultivate markets outside of the United States was in Europe, and that every effort must be expended in developing these.[42]

It was this general philosophical context that animated ministers connected with the trade file. For example, the Liberal minister of trade and commerce, Mitchell Sharp, made a strong appeal for the freer movement of agricultural goods, telling the United States Association of Grain and Food Dealers in March 1964 that 'The central problem facing agricultural exporters ... is agricultural protectionism.' Sharp focused in particular on European protectionism, noting that unless exporting countries could at least maintain their terms of access to Community markets, they could be caught in the long-term logic of EEC policy, 'reduced to the position of residual suppliers, and of competing against EEC subsidized [agricultural] exports in world markets.'[43]

Sharp's pessimism was well-founded. The world largely unfolded as he had sketched in his address, due in large part to the French insistence that the CAP move ahead. Producer prices for wheat, the commodity of particular concern for Canadian farmers, were increased, which led to greater output while consumption in EEC countries dropped. By 1963, the Community was 100 per cent self-sufficient in wheat, and it had a surplus in 1964–5, compared with less than 90 per cent self-sufficiency when the EEC was established.[44]

However, there was some discord between France and its five EEC partners around the implementation of the CAP and the desirable path of EEC evolution. The French made no bones about their position 'that it should be more expensive to buy [agricultural] products from outside the Common Market that were available from within it.'[45] This insistence and the five's resistance resulted in the so-called French empty seat, where France physically vacated its place in the EEC Commission for six months, from 30 June 1965 until January of the following year, and brought the EEC machinery to a halt in bending the others to their will. The French returned following a 'compromise' arranged in Luxembourg.

A *London Times* editorial captured French policy and intent: 'This is not a tactical bluff but a clear statement that if France cannot get what she wants, she is not interested in going on. What she wants, essentially, is to have the advantage of the agricultural common market without the rest of the package. The rest want to force the rest of the package on her. The issue is whether the Six are to become a political community with supranational institutions.'[46] If the French view prevailed, which it did with the CAP, it would clearly make it difficult for Canada's agricultural exports to EEC countries, to say nothing of future EEC competition with Canadian wheat in third markets.

The French view was best articulated by de Gaulle. First and foremost was his insistence on the primacy of national sovereignty and French interests, which would also eventually inform Community policy. As Canada's embassy in Paris interpreted the general, 'He was prepared to tolerate the EEC only if was 'equitable' and 'reasonable'; by equitable, he meant the inclusion of agriculture in the [protectionist] Common Market; and by reasonable, he meant that the EEC should not be allowed to encroach too much on national sovereignty.'[47]

Why did the Germans acquiesce to French pace and policy, given Bonn's close military and political relationship with the United States? In large part the Community was in their interest as well, and the Community's evolution suited them. The foundation of the EEC's political contract was high agricultural prices for France in return for access for German manufactured goods to the French market. As a result, trade between France and West Germany had tripled between 1958 and 1962, and their scale of investment in each other had grown considerably.[48] There was also substantial growth in German exports to other Community countries; by the late 1960s, about one in four German jobs was export related. Similarly, in the harmonization of their fiscal and monetary policies, the two partners were closer together than they ever had been in the short history of the EEC. The relationship was more than a mere matter of economics; the Canadian embassy in Bonn later rightly observed that 'the most significant result of [1968] Paris meetings [between Erhard and de Gaulle] is that it has been made abundantly clear that the present German government will not contemplate progress on the European plane without France [mirroring former Chancellor Adenauer's policy]. Outside Germany, this could be regarded as German capitulation to France; in the view of German officials, it is the emanation of a realistic assessment on contemporary European attitudes.'[49]

The Kennedy Round

De Gaulle's stand had important implications for GATT's Kennedy round negotiations, which had begun on 4 May 1964, largely in response to an American re-examination of their trade policy.[50] This was the sixth tariff reduction exercise since 1947 sponsored by the agreement and it was viewed as crucially important by Ottawa. Some saw it as a last chance to maintain any forward movement in reducing barriers to trade given the developments of the past several years. The Canadians, though, believed the French to be largely uninterested in the GATT and its program, especially if they represented threats to the common external tariff and to the CAP, Canada's special interest. Sydney Pierce, head of Canada's Kennedy Round delegation, told officials in Ottawa at the end of February 1966 that the French priority was 'France, Europe, and lastly, K[ennedy] R[ound].'[51] In various preparatory meetings to set an agenda, the French proved to be most unhelpful: J.H. Warren, a member of Canada's GATT delegation, told Ottawa that 'The French position is ... negative.'[52] Earlier, Lester Pearson had had a conversation with President Johnson in which he described the Kennedy round negotiations as 'not going very well.' Part of that was attributed by him to the French, who were 'going to cause us a little more trouble than the Russians.'[53]

The Canadians had contemplated progress on the agricultural front, but the chances did not look good. As a document to cabinet had pointed out, 'What progress will in fact be made in the agricultural negotiations is not clear, particularly because the Six are still far from agreement among themselves on a number of basic policy decisions about their own agricultural arrangements.'[54] The complicating factor was that American negotiators had made it clear that real progress must be made toward reducing barriers to agricultural products. If noticeable progress was not achieved, the United States would be unable to reduce its industrial tariff. The whole Kennedy round could then be thrown into confusion since, as the Canadians believed, it was probably not realistic 'to suppose that barriers to trade in farm products [were] likely to be reduced significantly; indeed, it may be that all that can be achieved will be to secure more effective commitments about the continuation of present levels of trade.'

More than the French and agricultural products were under discussion at the GATT. In the complex formulas being developed for industrial tariff reductions in the Kennedy round, it was certain that the Europeans were now doing their best to insulate the common tariff from downward movement. As well, during and for some time after the French boycott, the EEC Commission was not able to obtain any negotiating leeway from the Council of Ministers. While sector discussions continued in steel, chemicals, pulp and paper, textiles, and aluminum, they did not make any significant progress. That served no one's purpose, particularly not the United States, which was focused on the increased trade with Community. In commercial and economic terms the United States saw improved access to the Common Market as a means of easing its balance of payments problem and helping it to improve economic growth. On the political front, the

Americans were very anxious to ease the split in Europe between EEC and non-EEC countries and to avoid a possible division in the North Atlantic community.

Washington realized that it was by no means certain that its delegation would succeed in getting a major negotiation off the ground, but they were determined to press it, even to the breaking point. They had not, Ottawa thought, developed fallback positions or alternatives in anticipation of possible failure. The Americans believed that in the final analysis, for political and economic reasons, the EEC would be brought to cooperate in a major trade negotiation.[55] The political and economic brinkmanship of the United States made the Canadians very uncomfortable.

The Six, pushed along by Paris, were not cooperating as the North Americans had hoped. In response to an EEC demand for special rules that would allow a smaller cut for low tariff items Warren noted that 'if low tariff items were dealt with as suggested by the Six, a very large volume of trade would escape any significant downward tariff adjustment.'[56] British import surcharges, levied in October 1964 as the Kennedy round was getting underway, also needed to be examined. These had poisoned the atmosphere to the extent that when they were discussed in the GATT council, the British delegation had been attacked by the EEC representative in a way that 'bordered on the vicious and constituted by far strongest statement in Council.'[57] Theodorus Hijzen of the EEC Commission, supported by the delegations from France, Italy, the Netherlands, and West Germany denounced the British import surcharges. 'He recognized UK difficulties but said sarcastically these were due to reasons he would prefer not to mention. He expressed gravest doubts that measures of protection would solve problem. In this connection, he pointed out that something must be wrong when measures are taken which will result in higher prices in circumstances where difficulties are partly due to poor export performance. He said that means should have been found to cure the problem and not the symptoms.' Taken altogether, it seemed that the Kennedy round was speeding toward disaster. *The Economist* had noted some months earlier that 'The Atlantic has rarely seemed broader, deeper or colder.'[58] The only bright spot from which Canadians could take any comfort was that the Americans and the Europeans had kept talking through all their disagreements. As long as that was the case, the round could not be counted out completely.

Canada had an additional incentive to keep going and to encourage the Americans and the EEC to settle their differences by having been granted a special position in the negotiations. The Americans had supported Canada, but the Europeans 'were reluctant to go along. After a rather intense session, "the Canadian view was finally accepted by the EEC, but with deep resentment over the way it had been pressed upon them [by the with the Americans]."'[59] Canada was not subject to the 50 per cent linear cut in tariffs that applied to most other countries. The linear cut was a new method of negotiating, which reflected the greater degree of complexity now facing the contracting parties in tariff discussions. Ottawa, however, could negotiate as it had in past rounds, on a product-by-product, principal supplier/principal purchaser basis which had greatly irritated the Europeans. As Mitchell Sharp explains, 'Because of the nature of our trade – the high proportion of foodstuffs and raw materials in our exports and manufactured goods in our imports – across-the-board percentage cuts in our tariffs gave exporters to Canada much more valuable access to the Canadian market for manufactured goods than we gained from an equal percentage cut in the already low tariffs on foodstuffs and raw materials in countries to which we exported. We insisted on equivalence of benefit, which meant that tariffs on our manufactured goods were not reduced as rapidly as those of the United States and Europe.'[60]

The Americans had expressed some reservations about the Canadian position in the days before negotiations began. Initially, they had been 'convinced that a linear reduction formula is the only appropriate basis for the new tariff negotiations.'[61] It might be possible, they thought, to exempt some Canadian industry under the exception provisions that would be an essential part of the formula, but most Canadian negotiations could not fit in this category. Canada could not have gone ahead to negotiate based on the 50 per cent cut. As the prime minister told Kennedy, the country had great difficulty with that process; he admitted 'ruefully that enunciation of principle when in opposition was wonderful, but application in practice was sometimes difficult.'[62]

The Americans 'appreciated' the sincerity of Ottawa's intent to give 'equivalent' benefits for their 50 per cent linear reduction, but had serious doubts that it could be done on a selective basis. Washington believed that to provide a special exemption for Canadian industry would undercut its efforts to include agriculture in the negotiations, without which neither of the North Americans could participate in the GATT round. This American hesitation had been communicated to Ottawa once the special case scenario had been realized; now it was doubly important for Canada that the negotiations proceed. It might not be possible, some thought, for Canada to be so favoured in a future negotiation were the Kennedy round to fail and the Canadians' first wish was certainly to be able to participate on the 50 per cent cut basis.

The GATT Falters

By January 1965, however, the Americans were not so sanguine. After some nine months of negotiation in Geneva, their analyses of the linear countries' excepted items showed that their offers to cut tariffs on all other items by 50 per cent would result in much broader and deeper tariff reductions than those offered by Canada. The U.S. offer was relatively twice as large in trade coverage and between two and three times as deep as the Canadian's.

Pearson had earlier telephoned Lyndon Johnson, ostensibly to congratulate him on his election victory in November 1964, but also to muse on the problems Canada was experiencing in the negotiations. The prime minister had observed to the president that 'Over in Geneva at these tariff trade negotiations ... they're not going very well.'[63] The Canadians were worried that they would have to put their list of tariff cuts on the table in late November, and they were feeling rushed. Pearson added, 'We're not going to put in our first list everything we would be willing to give if we were negotiating with you.' The prime minister rounded out the conversation with his explanation of why that strategy was necessary:

> Pearson: It would be politically very difficult for us to have made all these things known ... and then have the thing break down ... have leaks occur and we're on ... we're getting into an election here ... and we'd be accused of selling out and not getting anything.
>
> Johnson: Sure I understand.
>
> Pearson: But what we want you to know down there ... and we'll be talking to the State Department about this ... is that some of the things that we will be taking out of that list to avoid that danger we still will want to negotiate on when the time comes ... we'll have a period of negotiation ... so I don't want you to think in Washington that this is our final word, because, of course, it isn't. It's the kind of practical move ... and if you don't mind, we'll talk to Dean Rusk or somebody down there, George Ball, before we do ... but I didn't want to ...
>
> Johnson: I understand Lester.

Pearson's idea was to hold spring 1965 elections that would give the Liberals a majority. Then, he would improve the offer. However, the Americans were now not sure of the Canadian timeline; they thought that 'the recent scandal involving two Liberal cabinet ministers and the lack of legislative achievement in the last parliament now make it unlikely that the Prime Minister will want to call an election so soon.'[64]

Settlement with Canada would be very difficult on the terms that the country had offered. It would be impossible, so U.S. officials felt, 'to explain to the satisfaction of US industry.'[65] As well, any settlement with Canada on those terms would not be consistent with the requirements of the Trade Expansion Act (TEA). The United States was also forced to consider a Canadian exclusion from the negotiations, though a briefing note explained that exclusion could well endanger the Kennedy Round, in view of Canada's importance as a world trader. It could also be a retrograde step 'that might damage the present close relationship between the two countries.' The best solution, the Americans thought, would be a marked improvement in the Canadian offer, which was forthcoming later that year.

For the present, little progress was made, and Sydney Pierce spread the blame all around. Canada and the United States had both put too much emphasis on the successful conclusion of a suitable agricultural regime, which would not be achieved. Indeed, Pierce's commentary on American tactics is worth quoting:

> It seems foolhardy for the U.S. government to take the stand that the choice confronting us is all or nothing, total victory or total defeat and that trade negotiations come to an end for all time on July 1st, 1967. There is plenty of ground between these two extremes. What seems to be called for is a more flexible and realistic attitude on their part, fewer ultimatums, more reliance on the GATT executive and less on their own persuasiveness, more stress on the value of offers already tabled and on common achievement and less on the deficiencies of others. The aim should be at the same time to keep steady pressure on the negotiators, yet gradually to create a climate at home permitting the ultimate acceptance of a Kennedy round if the best is unattainable and creating an appetite for further rounds of negotiations, for carrying on work well begun which should never be completed, for maintaining the momentum of negotiations and the liberal tradition.[66]

The following two years of Kennedy round negotiations did not change things, other than to lay out the lines of disagreement more clearly. Robert Winters, then Canada's minister of trade and commerce, had emphasized the importance of the GATT session for global prosperity during talks with two French ministers, Michel Debré (finance) and Edgar Faure (agriculture). Debré and Faure had not disagreed, but then had pointed out a few of the problems they believed faced French compliance with the General Agreement, such as the weak structure of French industry when compared with that of the United States and West Germany, and the need to strengthen their industrial and scientific base. They also dropped the bombshell that they regarded the 30 June 1967 deadline for the termination of the GATT round as completely unrealistic. That date marked the expiry of the president's negotiating authority under the 1962 TEA, which had allowed the United States to support the launch of the Kennedy round in the first place, and was set in stone, as Winters emphasized to the ministers. No amount of persuasion could get them to even consider Winters' point; neither the French nor the other Europeans believed for a moment that the United States would not extend the TEA if circumstances warranted. Given the attitude of the French, Finn Gundelach, the deputy director of the GATT, was pessimistic about the chance of a successful conclusion to the round. It did indeed seem that the Kennedy round was 'up in the air.'[67]

The pace of negotiations was glacial at the beginning of 1967, only six months before the U.S. trade legislation ran out. The internal problems of the Six were complex, and the EEC's decision-making machinery was cumbersome and slow-moving. Indeed, the Canadians were certain that the preference of the Community's governments had been for no Kennedy round; they were 'at best, reluctant bargainers.'[68] A Canadian analysis pointed out that 'The Kennedy round [came] at too early a stage in European integration. The six countries, who are not yet one, are called to negotiate the most comprehensive trade deal of all time as if they *were* one.'[69] Lester Pearson told Cabinet in early May 1967 that 'there was a very difficult period ahead on the world economic front ... There was a danger of the failure of the Kennedy Round'[70]

That failure was too frightening to contemplate. Canada, more than most participants, had a major trade and economic interest in seeking further progress in the reduction of barriers to trade in a non-discriminatory manner and on as wide a multilateral basis as possible. A regional approach to trade was not appealing in the slightest. The thinking in Ottawa was that much would depend on the Kennedy round results, but also on European developments and the scope of the future negotiating authority of the United States. The attitude of the Americans was critical in all this, and it was disheartening to know that they, too, believed that the GATT discussions could fail. William Roth, the U.S. special representative for trade negotiations, told President Johnson just that.

While these pessimistic accounts suggested the round's failure, they may well have assured its success in the end as both sides stared into the abyss. Neither the EEC nor Washington wanted to go home empty-handed, and as the deadline loomed near they dug in for meaningful negotiations. Through many lengthy sessions, described variously in secret American papers as 'marathon,' 'crisis period,' 'log-jam,' and 'extremely difficult,' an agreement was reached close to zero-hour in late June.[71]

A Successful Conclusion?

The results negotiated between the EEC and the North Americans were not as good as had been hoped for in the heady days of May 1964, when the round had been officially launched. The Americans had caused some difficulty with their American Selling Price (ASP) valuation, which applied to four classes of imports: benzenoid chemicals, rubber-soled footwear, canned clams, and woollen knit gloves. Under ASP, the tariffs on these products were based on the wholesale price of a comparable item produced in the United States, as contrasted to the usual practice of basing tariffs on the wholesale price in the country of origin. Even the Americans called this system archaic, but were prevented from offering it up for sacrifice by congressional pressure.

Obviously, the range of imports affected by ASP was limited, and the classes involved not very important for American or European economic health. However, it was an emotional issue for both sides in Geneva, and it dominated the industrial negotiations. The Europeans, including the EEC, the British, and the Swiss, saw the ASP as a symbol of American protectionism.[72] They wanted the United States to eliminate ASP unilaterally, for which other countries would not be required to provide reciprocal concessions. The Americans refused. In a report to Washington, the delegation suggested that it was 'playing "chicken" with the Community on ... ASP,' and that was where matters stood as negotiations came to a head.[73] On 15 May 1967, the Americans blinked and the industrial tariff reduction talks were saved. This particular area lay in trade legislation, and while the U.S. delegation might propose, the constitution said that Congress would dispose, and it chose not to do so, at least during the 1960s. Still, this uncertainty in 1967 probably saved the Kennedy round; it was not possible to immediately abrogate the agreement without great cost once congressional intentions became more clear. The ASP finally died in 1970.

Negotiations around agriculture also proved to be difficult. The first tabling of agricultural offers had not taken place until November 1965, a year after industrial offers had been exchanged. The EEC had been paralysed by its internal difficulties including the French empty chair, and it was not until September 1966 that the Community was prepared to move. One of the main problems facing the Canadians in the EEC offer was the latter's insistence on what Brussels called a self-sufficiency ratio (SSR), which meant that the Community would provide no more than an agreed percentage of its wheat needs from its own production, leaving the remaining share to be supplied by other countries. At the outset, the EEC had offered an SSR that was above its actual degree of self-sufficiency at that time. For the Canadians, this was intellectually dishonest and they saw their markets in EEC countries disappearing, to say nothing of markets in third countries. Indeed, the concept of guaranteed access to the EEC market which had been negotiated at the time of the Dillon round had virtually disappeared in the Kennedy round. Table 6.2 demonstrates the effect of the CAP on a variety of agricultural commodities.

The Canadians were concerned about the wheat situation in the world market by the late 1960s, and that anxiety was quickly borne out in the aftermath of the Kennedy round. The new International Grains Arrangement (IGA), designed to set minimum and maximum prices for global wheat sales and negotiated during

Table 6.2
EEC Self-Sufficiency Ratio (average percentage)

	1968–70	1972–4
Wheat	90	104
Coarse Grains	81	83
All Dairy Products	96	103

Source: Nick Butler, *The International Grain Trade: Problems and Prospects* (New York: St Martin's Press, 1986), 32.

the GATT round to come into effect on 1 July 1968, collapsed in the face of worldwide overproduction. The growing European surplus stimulated by the CAP now competed vigorously with Canadian and American wheat in world markets. The result was a downward spiral as prices were slashed below the minimum price of US$1.73 to make sales, even though the IGA had stipulated that 'Each member country when exporting wheat ... [does] so at prices consistent with the price range.'[74] The United States always felt that the minimum price provisions permitted the exporter to price below the schedule in certain circumstances, a position completely rejected by the Canadians. And even the price denoted in the IGA was a significant compromise; Canada had originally demanded a minimum price of US$1.85 per bushel, but the important importing countries refused to budge above $1.73. As Donald Forster explains, 'Canada's wheat exports and share of the world market [in 1968] continued to decline ... The result was mounting [Canadian] surpluses and increasingly desperate calls for action by Western farmers.' In 1967–8, Canadian farmers had grossed CAN$1.216 billion; the following crop year they had received only CAN$836 million for their wheat. Prairie agriculture was staring at a disaster.[75]

An anti-dumping accord was also created as a sidebar of the negotiations. The separation of the anti-dumping measure from the main agreement was necessary as Gardner Patterson, the director of the trade policy division of the GATT, told Canadians A.R.A. Gherson and Rodney Grey, because of the possibility of non-ratification by U.S. Congress. If that happened and the measure was a part of the overall agreement, it would provide a pretext for the EEC to delay implementing the tariff cuts. Gherson and Grey strongly agreed. Patterson's analysis was prescient as the U.S. tariff board refused to abide by the terms of the anti-dumping code. Congress did not approve it as it operated on principles that legislators disliked. For example, anti-dumping investigations should only be initiated on the basis of a complaint from producers that represented a substantial proportion of domestic production of the product under review. As well, there should be a concurrent examination of dumping *and* injury, and 'industry for the purposes of measuring injury should be defined specifically in terms of product coverage and with rigid rules restricting regional subdivisions.'[76] The problem in the years ahead was that the United States completely rejected that position – it was necessary first to establish dumping, *then* injury.

For the present, agreement was reached in Geneva in the areas that counted for Canada. Ottawa was relieved in large part because it obtained a good result, not with the EEC, but with its North American neighbour. As John Evans points out, 'the Kennedy round made more important inroads into the barriers to trade across the border than had any previous negotiation.'[77] Canada had negotiated reductions in U.S. tariffs to the tune of CAN$2.5 billion, and had reduced its own tariffs by CAN$2 billion on imports from the United States. Ottawa's delegation could take the credit for that; as Francis Bator, President Johnson's deputy special assistant for national security affairs, told the president, it had been 'very hard bargaining' with the Canadians.[78]

Once the results were known, Robert Winters, the minister of trade and commerce, told cabinet that it was 'important to avoid the risk of disturbing the agreements through an official expression of elation.'[79] However, he did speak publicly about the success achieved by the contracting parties in Geneva, and especially about the good result with the United States that opened up enormous potential: 'Trade opportunities will become available for the first time to a very wide range of manufactured goods, many of which will be Canada's exports of tomorrow ... It may well be that the Kennedy round will be regarded in the future as a crucial turning point in the transformation of Canada from a resource-based economy to one of the most advanced industrial nations of the world.'[80]

But why had the United States continued to participate in this round, given the great difficulties it faced? In part, larger issues transcended the matter of tariff levels. Quite apart from President Johnson getting personally involved in the negotiations, and the fact that he considered a successful outcome a 'matter of greatest concern,' an American document noted that there were other reasons for reaching an acceptable conclusion: 'At stake in the Kennedy round was the maintenance of the set of rules governing international trade which had been painstakingly developed during the postwar years in the GATT framework. The failure of the Kennedy round might have brought on a spiralling of protectionism – and thus risked a return to the damaging nationalistic trading practices of the 1930s.'[81] There were particularly American reasons that made it imperative that some success was achieved. 'Its failure,' the document suggests, 'undoubtedly would have encouraged those forces within the EEC which were seeking to turn the Community inward, and would inevitably have taken on anti-U.S. overtones.

Failure would also have alienated the less developed countries. Thus the negotiations had significant foreign policy implications, and particularly for US policy in Europe.' Indeed, soon after the conclusion of the negotiations, the secretary of state told his opposite number in Canada, Paul Martin, that he was 'concerned over the drift in Western Europe toward isolation, a circumstance which he thought could have its effect in the United States.'[82]

Given the U.S. position, it was ironic that protectionist forces in the United States reasserted themselves after 1968. A continuing decline in the U.S. balance of payments, a perceived weakening of the U.S. economy, and a widespread feeling that protectionist pressures in the EEC and Japan contributed to American problems were cited as the causes.[83] The 1968 TEA, proposed by the Johnson administration to allow the United States to continue to participate in further trade negotiations, was never put to a vote because of the administration's fear of failure. A similar fate met Richard Nixon's attempts to obtain congressional approval for trade negotiation authority. Not until 1975 did Congress vote the necessary instrument even as the Tokyo round of 1973–8 was well underway.

The Canadians, on the other hand, were pleased with the results of the negotiations. As the ink was drying on the GATT result, they met with Americans to discuss the immediate future. Among the points raised was importance of maintaining momentum in trade liberalization, and the necessity that the two countries share a common view as to the major trade issues in the post-Kennedy round period. And while problems remained such as the trade in agricultural products, East-West trade, low cost imports, and trade with less developed countries, they would be the focus of continuing negotiations. For the present it was time to celebrate.

Canada also participated in a ministerial session of the GATT that launched a new program for the expansion of international trade designed to identify the remaining barriers to trade and establish a mutually acceptable basis for further trade liberalization. The approaches then being considered included further tariff cuts, the liberalization of non-tariff barriers to trade (NTBs), and a proposal put forward by Ottawa for the multilateral freeing of trade by sectors of industry. In the case of agriculture, discussions focused on examining the problem of bringing domestic production and support policies under international discipline.

The Kennedy round provided a catapult effect to the liberalization of world trade but there was much talk in its aftermath of maintaining the way forward. The American secretary of commerce, Maurice Stans, called for the early negotiation of NTBs, a move seconded by Jean Rey, the president of the EEC commission. The new director general of the GATT, Olivier Long, had gone public with his objective to bring the work of the agreement's committees on industrial and agricultural products to a point where negotiations could be launched at the 1970 GATT session. In short, while there were dark clouds beginning to form on the horizon, for the most part the skies seemed clear.

An Expanding EEC and the Third Option

When the United Kingdom again applied for EEC membership in 1970, official Canada expressed some apprehension. As described in chapter 5, a study of the impact for Canadian trade was initiated by Ottawa, and at a meeting on 3 December 1972, Pierre Trudeau pointed out to British prime minister Edward Heath that 'undoubtedly Canadian trade would suffer substantially.'[84] The Trudeau government also saw increased ties with the EEC as a useful counterweight to the influence of the United States in Canada. In an earlier policy statement issued in the run-up to the June 1968 election, the government had laid out its view: 'Canada continues to have a very large stake in Europe, perhaps not so much in the military sense of two decades ago but in political, commercial and cultural terms ... It seems axiomatic that ... Canada should seek to strengthen its ties with the European nations ... We should seek to join with them in new forms of partnership and cooperation in order to strengthen international security, to promote economic stability on both sides of the Atlantic and in other regions of the world, to balance our own relations in the Western Hemisphere.'[85]

As well, there was a more general apprehension about the intensification of protectionist pressures south of the border, especially with Washington's implementation of the New Economic Policy on 15 August 1971, more popularly known as the Nixon Shock, which included U.S. imports from Canada and other countries among its targets.[86] This unsettling development had the potential to destabilize the country's economy, which depended to a significant degree on exports to the United States. As matters then stood, the new policy surcharge applied to about CAN$2.5 billion worth of exports. Moreover, there was much speculation that the so-called special relationship that had existed between Canada and the United States since the war was over. What that would mean to Ottawa was as yet unknown.

The increasingly chilly climate led finance minister Edgar Benson to tell the House of Commons on 7 September 1971 'that Canada might have to reconsider its whole industrial and commercial policies in light of events of the past few weeks.'[87] A month later, that 'might' had become 'will'; Mitchell Sharp, now the secretary of state for external affairs, informed a television interviewer that 'the government was undertaking a fundamental review of economic policies.'[88]

By mid-1972, cabinet authorized the establishment of a team of senior officials 'to explore with officials of the EEC Commission and member states of the enlarged Community possible ways of strengthening relations between Canada and the Community, including ... the possible scope for negotiating a bilateral trade agreement.'[89] Imminent British membership in the EEC provided an even greater impetus to pursue this policy. This new interest was given shape as 'Canada-U.S. Relations: Options for the Future,' which laid out three options open to the government, and was published in *International Perspectives* under Sharp's name. Sharp's third option, to 'pursue a comprehensive, long-term strategy to develop and strengthen the Canadian economy ... and reduce the present Canadian vulnerability' fulfilled an oft-expressed demand that the government take steps to confront American influence in Canada.[90] Indeed, a resurgent Canadian nationalism was a factor that governments ignored at their peril. At the same time, a memorandum to cabinet submitted by a trio of heavyweight ministers, those for external affairs, finance, and industry, trade and commerce, recommended that an exploratory mission of senior officials be authorized to hold discussions with the EEC Commission. These talks, set in the framework of Canada's European policy as published in the Trudeau government's *Foreign Policy for Canadians*, were to cover 'the development of trade and economic relations between Canada and the EEC and prospects for future multilateral negotiations; and ways of strengthening the relationship between Canada and the enlarged Community, including the establishment of arrangements for periodic consultations and possible negotiation of a Canada/EEC trade agreement.'[91]

The intended target of Canadian policy, the EEC, was not overly interested in their *démarche*. In Ottawa to meet with senior officials following the late September announcement, Theodore Hijzen, the director general for external trade of the EEC commission, told a meeting of Community ambassadors that 'politically ... [Canada] has no decisive [global] influence' which made the country less appealing as a possible partner.[92] However, both the Germans and the British were reluctant to reject Canadian overtures outright. Hans Freiherr von Stein, the economic counsellor at the German embassy in London, told H.T.A. Overton of the Foreign and Commonwealth Office, that a position paper on Canada being developed in Bonn was directed toward 'helping Canada, and not do anything which would push her back into the arms of the U.S., especially now that Canada is losing her exclusive relationship with the UK.'[93] Still, as the rationale of the third option did not recommend itself to the EEC Canada would not be dictating the terms of the connection. As Hijzen told the ambassadors when he had pressed James Grandy, the deputy minister of industry, trade and commerce and his opposite number in Ottawa, on what the Canadians wanted from any linkage with the Community, three items were of importance:

1 A desire to obtain a greater measure of freedom of movement v.a.v. the US;
2 The development of trade between Canada and Great Britain, especially after
   January 1, 1973, as a result of the UK entering into the common market;
3 The internal deterioration of the position of the balance of payments and trade,
   the large unemployment, etc.[94]

Clearly, Hijzen believed, the Canadians 'wanted diversification for reasons of pure ... Canadian self-interest.' Finally, the EEC could not accommodate Canada without taking a similar position towards the United States, and there would be very slow forward movement from Brussels on that file.

Following more than three years of negotiation, the EEC and Ottawa signed a Framework Agreement for Commercial and Economic Cooperation, by which time the world had changed considerably. The 1973 oil crisis had put the stagflation cat among the capitalist economy pigeons, and economic dislocation was widespread. In Canada, wage and price controls occupied official attention, while the election of the separatist Parti Québécois government in 1976 focused Trudeau's attention on the threat to domestic unity. In light of such developments, interest in the third option proved ephemeral and its results were negligible; it had 'a sad history.'[95] Indeed, the government should have known, given the very recent past, that large-scale trade with Europe was a non-starter. The Canadian corporate community had, for the most part, written off Europe 'as either a 'closed shop' or as one that was so difficult to crack that it was not worth the effort.'[96] The policy was declared officially dead in 1982.

The 1960s were crucial in terms of fixing Canada's trade relations into a North American pattern, as much as governments might lament that. More and more, Canadian prosperity was ensured by access to American markets, discussions and negotiations in the GATT and with the EEC notwithstanding. While that displeased the chattering classes, it was a fact of life. The electorate seemed not to mind; as a young Jack Granatstein wrote in 1971, 'a sneaking suspicion [exists] that Canadians preferred a prosperous existence – even as a satellite – to a poor but pure nationalism.'[97] Twenty-five years of seeking access to European markets had not paid off, nor would it in the future. For want of a better option, Canada was now thoroughly North American.

Conclusion

Clearly, Canada had benefited enormously in terms of economic development from its favoured connection with the United States during the late 1950s and 1960s. The policy of exemptionalism practiced by various administrations over that period, the negotiation of the Auto Pact in 1965, and a relatively benign U.S. attitude towards Canada on economic matters, all helped the country to achieve a prosperity that was the envy of much of the world. Those critics of government policy who complained about Canada's obsession with things American were correct in pointing out that those measures *enhanced* the extent of continental integration between the two. It might also have constrained Canada's freedom of action in terms of foreign policy development, although that is a more debatable proposition.

As a western nation firmly ensconced on that side during the Cold War, it is arguable that Ottawa adopted many of its foreign policy positions out of self-interest. The case could be made that a number of other U.S. allies, including Australia, Britain, New Zealand, and West Germany, did likewise. Given U.S.-USSR hostility in the decades following 1945, no ally of either had much latitude for experimentation. Sweden and Switzerland, alone among the important countries of the West, were 'neutral,' although their orientation was certainly westward-looking. They also both spent much more than Canada did on defence and neither lay in America's strategic foreground. If they had, neutrality would not have been an option for them either.

In other areas, Ottawa did operate in a relatively independent fashion. During the long and tortuous Law of the Sea Conference (LOS), for example, Canadians were very active in opposing the American position, even to the point of making common cause with the Soviets or Third World countries whose interests were similar to Canada's. For example, at the first LOS meeting in 1958, the U.S. delegation could write to the state department of 'the completely selfish attitude of Canada.'[1] In the 1970s, the Canadians actively opposed the voyage of the USS *Manhattan* through what Canada perceived as its Northwest Passage. The United States did have an undeniable influence on Canadian foreign policy development, but when Washington's national security antennae were not tingling, Ottawa or, for that matter, other allied capitals, did have some room to act.[2] This suggests that U.S. domination of Canada's economy did not necessarily lead to its domination of other aspects of the country's existence. Moreover, the standard of living which Canada achieved during the 1960s allowed it to become much more involved in international affairs than had been the case in the past.

The critics are correct in their assertion that Ottawa focused on developing markets in the United States for Canadian exporters. As trade percentages rose, so too did the economic nationalists' temperature. To what extent, then, was it possible for Canada to press for the diversification of markets keeping in mind that in order to be prosperous, the country had to export, and that it was by far the smallest of the world's major economies.[3] By the early 1970s, approximately 25 per cent of Canada's gross national product (GNP) came from exports. Even if the federal government had been capable of directing the private sector, which it was not in the Canadian system, it would have been very difficult to achieve a satisfactory result. The British knew this following John Diefenbaker's 15 per cent diversion proposal; they allowed that a shift in trade from the United States to the United Kingdom was an impossibility. As well, Britain continued to suffer an economic decline throughout the period under investigation, compounded by inadequate leadership, outdated industry, and a class system that stifled innovation. In short, all attempts to increase trade in that quarter failed and as the decade wore on Britain's orientation was increasingly toward Europe and less toward the Commonwealth.

The European Economic Community (EEC) was no more promising. The Europeans, to a large extent, had an economic agenda that did not include Canada. Try as it might, Ottawa could not force its way into their considerations. Like the Japanese, the EEC wanted raw materials but very little by way of value-added content. Moreover, the suspicion exists that the French and the Germans, had they had the capability to exploit Canada and its resources, would have been much more self-interested than the Americans. As the EEC developed into a more thorough-going institution, it also increasingly discriminated against Canadian products, even those like wheat, where Canada's producers had long had a presence. Given its structure, the General Agreement on Tariff and Trade (GATT) did not materially help Ottawa blast a way into those markets but ironically, it assisted in the further development of the North American market. Finally, other parts of the world were not terribly keen to develop trade relations with Canada, aside from wheat sales to the People's Republic of

China and the Soviet Union. In spite of some effort in that area, the results remained meagre.

Canadians, despite their dependent relationship with the United States, did not complain; they liked the jobs the economy produced, the optimism that this wealth generated, and the comfortable lives the great majority lived. Similarly, as Penny Bryden has pointed out, Canada's welfare state was given shape during the decade: 'The Pearson administration social programs were devised as part of a broad policy of social betterment'[4] made possible by the 'relative economic security of the 1950s and 1960s.'[5] The domestic economic improvement that underlay those developments would not have been possible without the great surge in Canada's GNP experienced in the 1960s. That anti-Americanism became a fixture of Canada's political and cultural landscape did not detract from any of that. Many might have disliked the United States in an institutional sense, but welcomed its companies and its people into their own communities.

Ottawa also had greater latitude for independent political and economic action than has been conceded by critics. Indeed, in many cases American officials were left scratching their heads, wondering how Canadians had manage to achieve a given objective in spite of Washington's disagreement. Moreover, governments proceeded to do what they believed to be in Canada's own interest. For example, the Diefenbaker Conservatives demanded of Washington that oil be regarded as a continental resource and that is what transpired, despite an abundant U.S. supply and American reluctance to take this step. When shortages became endemic by the early 1970s, the Trudeau government simply reduced the supply of that commodity to the United States against intense American protest. These were not the actions of a country cowed into submission or in lockstep with its larger neighbour.

The period between 1957 and 1973 witnessed the flowering of Canada into one of the richest countries in the world and, ironically, the near-total domination of its economy by American business. It had emerged strengthened from the Second World War and had gathered steam throughout the 1950s. Canada's growth was based at least partly on U.S. investment and markets that, in the context then prevailing, seemed to represent the only option for politicians who were mesmerized by the siren call of prosperity and the re-election it seemed to promise. The strength of the relationship was brought home via the third option policy of 1972; despite some effort on the part of the government to diversify Canada's economic linkages away from the United States it failed miserably and by 1982 was declared officially dead.

Efforts since then to reduce Canada's dependence on the United States have also gone nowhere. The last Trudeau government began the process of exploring the possibilities of sectoral free trade with the United States along the lines of the

Auto Pact. With the defeat of the Liberals in 1984, the Mulroney Conservatives chose what was euphemistically called free trade with the United States as their option. What this brief list seems to demonstrate is that no matter the political party in office or the temper of the prime minister, all foreign economic policy development eventually comes back to the United States. That is the reality that Canadians have lived with since 1945.

Notes

Abbreviations

BCA	Bank of Canada Archives, Ottawa
BCR	Bank of Canada Records, BCA
BT	Board of Trade Records, PRO
CAB	Cabinet Records, PRO
CRO	Commonwealth Relations Office, PRO
DDEL	Dwight D. Eisenhower Library, Abilene, KS
DEA-R	Department of External Affairs Records, LAC
Debates	Canada, *House of Commons Debates*
DFR	Department of Finance Records, LAC
DO	Dominions Office Records, PRO
DSR	Department of State Records, USNA
DTC	Department of Trade and Commerce Records, LAC
FRUS	*Foreign Relations of the United States*
GPO	U.S. Government Publishing Office, Washington, DC
HCUK	High Commissioner, United Kingdom
JFKL	John F. Kennedy Library, Boston, MA
LAC	Library and Archives Canada, Ottawa
LJPL	Lyndon Johnston Presidential Library, Austin, TX
NSC	National Security Council, LBJL
NSF	National Security Files, USNA, LBJL
PCO	Privy Council Office Records, Ottawa
POF	President's Office Files, USNA, JFKL
PREM	Prime Minister's Office Records, PRO
PRO	Public Records Office, London, England
T	Treasury Records, USNA, PRO

UKNA   National Archives of the United Kingdom, Richmond, Surrey
USNA   United States National Archives, Washington, DC

Introduction

1 For an account of the period 1945–57, see B.W. Muirhead, *The Development of Canada's Foreign Economic Policy: The Failure of the Anglo-European Option* (Montreal and Kingston: McGill-Queen's University Press, 1992).
2 Ibid., 15.
3 Kari Levitt, *Silent Surrender: The Multinational Corporation in Canada* (Toronto: Macmillan, 1970), 61–2.
4 LAC, Basil Robinson Papers, MG31E 83, vol. 1, file: Aug. 28, 1957, John Holmes, 'Report of the US Ambassador on Mr. Dulles' Visit,' 31 July 1957.
5 Al Purdy, ed., *The New Romans: Candid Canadian Opinions of the US* (Edmonton: M.C. Hurtig, 1968). Margaret Atwood later suggested that Canadians focus more on the development of their own civilization and society. In *Survival*, published in 1972, she paraphrases Northrop Frye as saying that in Canada, 'the answer to the question "Who am I?" is at least partly the same as the answer to another question: "Where is here?" "Who am I" is a question appropriate in countries where the environment, the 'here' is already well-defined, so well-defined in fact that it may threaten to overwhelm the individual ... "Where is here?" is a different kind of question,' one more suited to the Canadian context. Margaret Atwood, *Survival: A Thematic Guide to Canadian Literature* (Toronto: Anansi, 1972), 17.
6 Margaret Atwood, 'Backdrop Addresses Cowboy,' in Purdy, ed., *The New Romans*, 10–11.
7 Louis Dudek, 'O Canada,' in ibid., 82.
8 Farley Mowat, 'Letter to My Son,' in ibid., 1.
9 Donald Creighton, *The Forked Road: Canada, 1939–1957* (Toronto: McClelland and Stewart, 1976).
10 George Grant, *Lament for a Nation: The Defeat of Canadian Nationalism* (Toronto: McClelland and Stewart, 1970).
11 See *Canada 1970* (Toronto: McClelland and Stewart, 1969). This publication was a snapshot of Canadian attitudes compiled by a group of senior editors and writers of the *Toronto Telegram*. In the section dealing with the United States, 81 per cent of those polled rejected any suggestion that Canada join the United States. When asked if such a union was inevitable, 72 per cent said no. If, as John Porter was to write in 1975, 'Radicalism has retreated at our universities, and elsewhere in North America, at a rate which has surprised ... those who viewed it with panic and as a permanent feature of academic life,' it certainly made its presence felt during the previous decade. John Porter, 'Foreword,' in Wallace Clement, *The Canadian Corporate Elite: An Analysis of Economic* Power (Toronto: McClelland and Stewart, 1975), xi.

12 See for example, Abraham Rotstein, ed., *The Prospect of Change* (Toronto: McGraw-Hill, 1965), published under the auspices of the University League for Social Reform (ULSR); Peter Russell, ed., *Nationalism in Canada* (Toronto: McGraw-Hill, 1966). This volume was also published under the auspices of the USLR and included contributors who were to make their marks in Canadian academe in the 1970s and later, among them, historians Carl Berger, Craig Brown, Michel Brunet, and Kenneth McNaught, and political scientists such as Stephen Clarkson and Melville Watkins, as well as Rotstein and Russell; Abraham Rotstein, *The Precarious Homestead* (Toronto: New Press, 1973); Viv Nelles and Abraham Rotstein, eds., *Nationalism or Local Control* (Toronto: New Press, 1973); Abraham Rotstein and Gary Lax, eds., *Independence: The Canadian Challenge* (Toronto: The Committee for an Independent Canada, 1972); Abraham Rotstein and Gary Lax, eds., *Getting It Back: A Program for Canadian Independence* (Toronto: Clarke, Irwin, 1974); Dave Godfrey and Mel Watkins, eds., *Gordon to Watkins to You: Documentary – The Battle for Control of Our Economy* (Toronto: New Press, 1970); James Laxer, *The Liberal Idea of Canada: Pierre Trudeau and the Question of Canada's Survival* (Toronto: James Lorimer, 1977); Wallace Clement, *The Canadian Corporate Elite: An Analysis of Economic Power* (Toronto: McClelland and Stewart, 1975); Wallace Clement, *Continental Corporate Power: Economic Elite Linkages between Canada and the United States* (Toronto: McClelland and Stewart, 1977); Walter Gordon, *Troubled Canada: The Need for New Domestic Policies* (Toronto: McClelland and Stewart, 1961), and Gordon, *Storm Signals: New Economic Policies for Canada* (Toronto: McClelland and Stewart, 1975). Many of these names would also appear in books and conference proceedings published by the Committee for an Independent Canada and in the pages of *Canadian Forum* and *Canadian Dimension*.

13 Peyton Lyon and Brian Tomlin, *Canada as an International Actor* (Toronto: Macmillan 1979), 108.

14 Nixon's comment reflected sentiments expressed by Christian Herter, a secretary of state in the Eisenhower administration, who had remarked to one of his officials in early April 1958 that 'the overall United States policy objective toward Canada is to maintain the most intimate and harmonious relationship ... that is possible with a foreign power ... We do not take our relations with Canada for granted. They demand, and receive, a great deal of individual attention ... Essentially I would say that [we have a] unique relationship.' USNA, DSR, RG59, file: 611.42/3-2158, Herter to Gray, 2 April 1958.

Chapter 1

1 USNA, DSR RG59, file 742.00/3-1357, Embassy Ottawa to State, 13 March 1957.

2 USNA, DSR 842.00/2-1557, Robert Redington to Department of State, 15 February 1957.

3 Royal Commission on Canada's Economic Prospects, *Final Report* (Ottawa: Queen's Printer, 1957). The final report was made public in April 1958.

4 USNA, DSR, file 842.00/2-1257, Embassy Ottawa to Department of State, 12 February 1957. The head of the Royal Commission, Walter Gordon, attempted to legislate some of these ideas after he had been made minister of finance in Lester Pearson's first government, established in April 1963. The Americans had a similar characterization at that time.

5 LAC, Basil Robinson Papers, MG31E 83, vol. 1, file: Aug. 28, 1957, John Holmes, 'Report of the U.S. Ambassador on Mr Dulles' Visit,' 31 July 1957.

6 BCA, Louis Rasminsky Papers, LR 76, Misc, 'Memorandum of Meeting with Mr. Heeney, n.d.

7 LAC, Basil Robinson Papers, MG31E83, Holmes, 'Report ... Mr Dulles' Visit.'

8 *Globe and Mail*, 6 March 1955, 5.

9 BCA, BCR, RD 5C-100, R.G.C. Smith, 'Trends in United States Foreign Economic Policy,' 14 August 1957. It was renewed with a large majority in Congress.

10 BCA, Rasminsky Papers, LR76-358-1, Joint US-Canada Committee on Trade and Economic Affairs, 16–17 February 1960.

11 John Diefenbaker, 'Address Delivered at the Annual Dinner of the Toronto Board of Trade,' 4 February 1957.

12 See Bruce Muirhead, *Against the Odds: The Public Life and Times of Louis Rasminsky* (Toronto: University of Toronto Press, 1999), 251–60 for a discussion of the effects of the IET.

13 USNA, DSR, file: 842.05111/7-1857, Merchant to Dillon, 18 July 1957.

14 DDEL, CFEP Records 1953–4 (Randall Commission), Benet's Charts and Tables, Box 45, file: Drafts of Reports, Staff Report 2, Bloomfield, A.P. Toner to Goodpaster, 13 September 1957.

15 John Diefenbaker, *One Canada: Memoirs of the Right Honourable John G. Diefenbaker: Years of Achievement, 1957–1962* (Toronto: Macmillan, 1976), 73. C.D. Howe, the minister of trade and commerce in various Liberal governments, had gone several times to the United States to complain about U.S. investment policies. See, for example, 'Allow Canadians Share in Branch Operations Howe Asks U.S. Firms,' *Globe and Mail*, 16 October 1956, 22. He demanded that Canadians be permitted to invest more freely in U.S. subsidiaries located in Canada, as well as to be appointed to senior managerial ranks.

16 For an account of his life and death, see Roger W. Bowen, ed., *E.H. Bowen: His Life and Scholarship* (Toronto: University of Toronto Press, 1984), 46–71.

17 See John English, *The Worldly Years: The Life of Lester Pearson*, vol. 2, *1949–1972* (Toronto: Lester A. Knopf, 1992) 191–3.

18 USNA, DSR, file 742.00/1-1658, Ottawa to Secretary of State, 16 January 1958.

19 For an account of this, see Bruce Muirhead, 'From Dreams to Reality: The Evolution

of Anglo-Canadian Trade during the Diefenbaker Era,' *Journal of the Canadian Historical Association* New Series, 9 (1998), 244–5.

20 English, *Worldly Years*, 2: 209.

21 DDEL, U.S. Council on Foreign Economic Policy, Office of the Chairman: Records, 1954–61, Randall Series, Subject Subseries, Box 2, file: Canada (5), Dulles to Randall, 25 July 1957. Later, Dulles spoke with Randall about his reply. His letter 'had been partly 'for the record' in case [Randall's] letter became public. I said to him, however, that I felt that particularly after my talks in Ottawa it would not be timely to have any debate about this matter at this time which might become public. I mentioned to him the strongly nationalistic motivation of the present Government and its desire to develop economic cooperation with the UK rather than with the US.' See DDEL, Dulles Papers, General Correspondance, Memo Series, Box 1, file: Memoranda of Conversations General, N – R (1), 'Memorandum of Conversation with Mr. Clarence B. Randall,' 8 August 1957. See also BCA, BCR, 3C-300, Canadian Embassy Washington to USSEA, 27 November 1959. Senator Mike Mansfield also suggested exploratory talks leading to the establishment of a free trade area of the Americas. His suggestion was discouraged by the State Department. 'Senator Mansfield will be told privately that a United States Government proposal for a hemispheric Common Market would be unlikely to receive a favourable reception from Canada and the Latin American republics. This initiative would have to come from them in order to avoid this proposal carrying the stigma of American imperialism that might soon be placed upon it.'

22 BCA, Rasminsky Papers LR76-357, 'Note to the United States Government Protesting Restriction of Imports of Canadian Oil,' 15 January 1958. See also *Economist*, 12 September 1959, 837–41.

23 NSC, 5822/1, 'Certain Aspects of US Relations with Canada,' 30 December 1958, in *FRUS 1958–1960*, vol. 7, pt. 1, *Western European Integration and Security; Canada* (Washington, DC: GPO, 1993), 730.

24 See for example, John N. McDougall, *Fuels and the National Policy* (Toronto: Butterworths, 1982), 92–3.

25 LAC, Robinson Papers, vol. 1, file: July 1958, 'Meeting of Canadian Ministers and United States Secretary of State,' 9 July 1958.

26 NSC, 5822/1, 30 December 1958 in *FRUS 1958–1960*, vol, 7, p. 1, 730. See also James Laxer, *Canada's Energy Crisis* (Toronto: James Lewis and Samuel, 1974), 16–19 for a brief history of U.S.-Canada relations in this area.

27 BCA, Rasminsky Papers, LR76-358-1, 'Canada-US Trade.'

28 *Debates*, 30 April 1959, 3179.

29 USNA, DSR, file 742.00(W)/4-1158, Embassy Ottawa to Department of State, 11 April 1958.

30 H. Basil Robinson, *Diefenbaker's World: A Populist in Foreign Affairs* (Toronto: University of Toronto Press, 1989), 44.

31 USNA, DSR, 842.00/4-2958, Merchant to Secretary of State, 29 April 1958.

32 See 'Memorandum of Discussion at the 376th Meeting of the National Security Council,' 14 August 1958, *FRUS 1958–1960*, vol. 7, pt. 1, 725.

33 Ibid., 726.

34 USNA, Special Trade and Economic Program File 1947–1963, Bureau of International Commerce, Office of Regional Economics, European Division/Canada Section, Memorandum of Conversation, 'Canadian Proposal of Fixed Minimum Values for Duty Purposes,' 7 May 1958.

35 Ibid.

36 For a fuller discussion of this, see Frank Stone, *Canada, the GATT and the International Trade System* (Montreal: Institute for Research on Public Policy, 1984), 33.

37 BCA, Rasminsky Papers LR76-357, 'Canadian Import Controls on Turkeys,' 2 January 1959.

38 Memorandum from Secretary Dulles to President Eisenhower, 3 July 1958, in *FRUS 1958–1960*, vol. 7, pt. 1, 686–7.

39 BCA, BCR, 5C-112, Rasminsky to Bryce, 4 July 1958.

40 DDEL, Papers as President of the United States, 1953–1961, Ann Whitman File, International Series, Box 6, Canada (5), Dulles to Eisenhower, 21 September 1958.

41 Ibid., Diefenbaker to Eisenhower, 28 October 1958. The Americans had considered placing import controls on lead and zinc earlier, but had not done so because of the possible 'very damaging effect on our relations with Canada.' even if they were to do so, 'there [was] an important question of timing involved. To avoid embarrassment for the Canadian government no public announcement regarding the possibility of increases should be made prior to the election on June 10.' See *FRUS 1955–1957*, vol. 9, *Foreign Economic Policy; Foreign Information Program* (Washington, DC: GPO, 1991), 230.

42 BCA, BCR, 5C-100, R.G.C. Smith, 'Trends in United States Foreign Economic Policy,' 14 August 1957.

43 BCA, Rasminsky Papers, LR76-428, Commonwealth Trade and Economic Conference, 1958: Report by Officials, 21 June 1958.

44 BCA, LR76-613, Diefenbaker to Eisenhower, 28 October 1958.

45 BCA, Rasminsky Papers, LR76-357, 'Lead and Zinc,' 23 December 1958.

46 LAC, DFR, RG19, vol. 4226, file 8800-04-3, vol. 2, 'Briefing and Instructions to the Canadian Delegation to the United Nations Lead and Zinc Conference,' 16 April 1959.

47 Joint United States-Canadian Committee on Trade and Economic Affairs, February 16–17, 1960 in *FRUS 1958–1960*, vol. 7, pt. 1, 784–5.

48 LAC, DFR, vol. 4181, file 8522/U575-1 (59), UKCCC (59) 2nd Meeting, 2 July 1959.

49 USNA, DSR, 611.42/12-2453, Ottawa to Secretary of State, 24 December 1958.

50 Tammy Nemeth, 'Consolidating the Continental Drift: American Influence on Dief-

enbaker's National Oil Policy,' Paper presented at the Canadian Historical Association Conference, Toronto, 29 May 2002, 21.

51 Ibid., 21.

52 Memo of Discussion at the 446th Meeting of the NSC, 31 May 1960, in *FRUS 1958–1960*, vol. 7, pt. 1, 799.

53 Arnold Heeney, *The Things That Are Caesar's: Memoirs of a Canadian Public Servant* (Toronto: University of Toronto Press, 1972), 158.

54 'Memorandum of Telephone Conversation between President Eisenhower and Secretary of State Herter,' 8 April 1960, *FRUS 1958–1960*, vol. 7, pt 1, 788.

55 Heeney, *Things That Are Caesar's*, 159.

56 Memorandum of Conversation, 20 September 1960, in *FRUS 1958-1960*, vol. 7, pt. 1, 809. See also Heeney, *Things That Are Caesar's*, 166–7.

57 Memorandum of Conversation, 20 September 1960, in *FRUS 1958–1960*, vol. 7, pt. 7, 810–11.

58 George Freeman interview, 25 January 1995.

59 'Memorandum of Discussion at the 376th Meeting of the National Security Council,' 14 August 1958, in *FRUS 1960*, vol. 7, pt. 1, 728.

60 Joint United States-Canadian Committee on Trade and Economic Affairs,' 16–17 February 1960 in *FRUS 1960*, vol. 7, pt. 1, 776.

61 Mel Watkins, 'Canada Can't Wish Away Legal Imperialism,' in Dave Godfrey with Mel Watkins, eds., *Gordon to Watkins to You: Documentary – The Battle for Control of Our Economy* (Toronto: New Press, 1970), 207.

62 LAC, Robinson Papers, vol. 1, file: July 1958, 'Meeting of Canadian Ministers and the United States Secretary of State,' 9 July 1958.

63 BCA, Rasminsky Papers, LR76-357, 'Examples of Foreign Assets Control Influence over Canadian Trade,' n.d.

64 LAC Robinson Papers, vol. 4, Feb. 1961, 'Conversations between the President ... and the Prime Minister, February 20, 1961.

65 BCA, Rasminsky Papers, LR76-357, 'United States Foreign Assets Control,' n.d. At least one critic of FAC, however, thought the issue was overdone. As Peyton Lyon wrote, 'There seems to be virtually no basis for this complaint. The impact of foreign investment upon Canada's political independence has been wildly exaggerated. A few cases involving the Foreign Assets Control Regulations of the United States have been given publicity out of all proportion to the substance involved.' Peyton Lyon, *The Policy Question: A Critical Appraisal of Canada's Role in World Affairs* (Toronto: McClelland and Stewart, 1963), 25.

66 'US-Canadian Joint Committee on Trade and Economic Affairs,' 2 January 1959, in *FRUS 1958–1960*, vol. 7, pt. 1, 745.

67 'Memo of Discussion at the 446th Meeting of the NSC,' 31 May 1960, *FRUS 1958–1960*, vol. 7, part 1, 797–8.

68 BCA, Rasminsky Papers, LR76-358-1, Joint US-Canada Committee on Trade and

Economic Affairs, 'International Economic Policies and Prospects,' 16 February 1960.

69 Ibid.

70 'U.S.-Canadian Joint Committee,' 2 January 1959.

71 DDEL, White House Office, Office of the Staff Secretary: Records, 1952–61, L. Arthur Minnich Series, Cabinet and Legislative Meetings, Index B–CE, Box 18, Cabinet Meeting, 16 January 1959.

72 See BCA, BCR, 4B-200, 'Some Comments on the Economic Outlook,' August 1960. Unemployment went up as employment opportunities grew because of a number of factors. These included: substantial productivity increases in certain areas; a relative shift from employment in mining, construction, and manufacturing toward the service and trade industries; an accompanying increase in female workers and relative stability in the number of male employees; a sharp increase in the labour force; and growing rates of participation in the labour force by married women.

73 LAC, Robinson Papers, vol. 3, Nov.–Dec. 1960, N.A. Robertson, 'President-Elect Kennedy,' 10 November 1960. Of some interest, however, Prime Minister Diefenbaker believed that 'with Kennedy in control ... we were closer to war than we had been before. When [Robinson] expressed surprise at this statement ... [Diefenbaker said that] he pictured Kennedy as "courageously rash" and that he had pushed himself to the top against all odds, had spoken of bringing world leadership back to Washington, and had given every indication of intending to pursue an active policy which the Prime Minister feared might prove dangerous ... In domestic matters, the Prime Minister said, without elaborating at all, that although he ... was a left-wing conservative, further to the left than many right-wing liberals, there were many things in Kennedy's platform that he could not have accepted. The Prime Minister made some references in this context to the tendency toward government intervention which he thought would be much more pronounced under Kennedy.' See LAC, Robinson Papers, vol. 3, Nov.–Dec. 1960, 'Results of US Elections,' 9 November 1960.

74 LAC, Robinson Papers, vol. 4, Feb. 1961, 'Conversations between the President ... and the Prime Minister,' February 20, 1961.

75 Memorandum of Conversation, 8 March 1961 in FRUS 1961–1963, vol. 13, West Europe and Canada (Washington, DC: GPO, 1994), 1150.

76 Heeney, 174. Things That Are Caesar's, Basil Robinson, probably as close to Diefenbaker as anyone, notes in his autobiography that 'My diary entry on 18 January [1961] records that Diefenbaker 'has formed an irrational prejudice against Kennedy ... which could be a serious portent." Robinson, Diefenbaker's World, 168.

77 LAC, Robinson Papers, vol. 3, file: Nov–Dec 1960, 'Exchange of Messages with Senator Kennedy,' 22 November 1960. See also PRO, PREM11, vol. 3229, Ottawa to CRO, 22 February 1961.

78 Embassy Ottawa to Department of State, 27 November 1961, *FRUS 1961–1963*, vol. 13 1165–66.

79 USNA, DSR, POF, Box 113, 4, Memorandum for the President, 'Prime Minister Diefenbaker's Visit, February 20, 1961,' 17 February 1961.

80 Ibid.

81 Quai d'Orsay Archives, Paris, France, Archives Diplomatiques, B – Amérique 1952–1963, Canada, vol. 75, Série 8, Carton 2, Lacoste to Couve, 12 December 1960. A public opinion poll taken in early January 1961 showed that 42 per cent of Canadians answered in the affirmative to the question 'Should Canada become a neutral nation like the Swiss?' Blair Fraser, the editor of *Maclean's* wrote in the *Times* (London) that 'The growth of neutralism is one consequence of the decline of our confidence in the leadership of the US.' The Canadian author and professor, Hugh MacLennan, wrote 'Pour le moment, nous devons considerer les E-U comme une plus grande menace que la Russie.' The French official who read this communication from Ottawa underlined this sentence in thick orange pencil and placed two slashes and an exclamation mark beside it. See Quai d'Orsay Archives, Série 8, Carton 6, Dossier 1, Canada – Affaires Intérieure, vol. 47, Lacoste to Couve, 11 January 1961.

82 Embassy Ottawa to Department of State, 27 November 1961 in *FRUS 1961–1963*, vol. 13, 1164.

83 USNA, DSR, NSF Box 18, Canada, General, Rostow, Memorandum 5/16/61 and Related Materials, 5/61–5/63, State to Amembassy Ottawa, May 1961.

84 See Diefenbaker, *One Canada*, 180. See also Knowlton Nash, *Kennedy and Diefenbaker: Fear and Loathing across the Undefended Border* (Toronto: McClelland and Stewart, 1990), 132–3. Nash suggests that this telephone conversation, 'so vividly told by Diefenbaker to his intimates was rooted more in his enriching, creative imagination ... than in reality. He occasionally changed the locale of the conversation from the telephone to the President's office in February, four months before the incident actually occurred, and said the president had 'thumped' the table. He once told Southam columnist Charles Lynch that Kennedy may have called him a son of a bitch. Diefenbaker's telling off the president was more likely what he wished had happened, but it didn't.'

85 Diefenbaker, *One Canada*, 180.

86 Nash, *Kennedy and Diefenbaker*, 12.

87 Oral, History, Robert Kennedy, 27 February 1965.

88 Ibid.

89 Donald Fleming, *So Very Near: The Political Memoirs of the Hon. Donald M. Fleming* (Toronto: McClelland and Stewart, 1985), 441–2.

90 Robinson, *Diefenbaker's World*, 276.

91 LAC, Robinson Papers, vol. 3, file: Nov.–Dec. 1960, Heeney to External, 2 February 1961.

92 LAC, Robinson Papers, vol. 4, February 1961, Robert Bryce, 'Memorandum for the Prime Minister,' 18 February 1961.

93 LAC, Robinson Papers, vol. 4, file: Feb 1961, Memorandum for the President, 'Prime Minister Diefenbaker's Visit, February 20, 1961,' 17 February 1961.

94 BCA, Rasminsky Papers, LR76-359, Heeney to External, 7 March 1961.

95 BCA, Rasminsky Papers LR76-515-4, 'Unemployment and the Budget,' 16 February 1961.

96 Ibid.

97 Bank of England Archives, Bank of England Records, OV58/7 71, cp=6, 'Some Impressions from My Visit to the Bank of Canada,' 9 February 1961.

98 BCA, BCR, 4B-200, 'Some Comments on the Economic Outlook,' August 1960.

99 Bank of England Records, OV58/7 71 cp=6, 'Some Impressions ...,' 9 February 1961.

100 Robert Bothwell, Ian Drummond and John English, *Canada since 1945: Power, Politics and Provincialism* (Toronto: University of Toronto Press, 1981), 184. See also Kari Levitt, *Silent Surrender: The Multinational Corporation in Canada* (Toronto: Macmillan, 1970), 9 for her account of this.

101 *Debates*, 21 March 1960, 2671–2.

102 Ibid., 2279. That brought Coyne's rebuttal in a speech in Hamilton on 12 May: 'I shall probably not make myself popular by remarking that all is not gold that glitters.'

103 'Visit of Canadian Prime Minister Diefenbaker,' 20 February 1961 in *FRUS 1961–1963*, vol. 13, *West Europe and Canada* (Washington, DC: United States GPO, 1994), 1143.

104 Bank of England Archives, Bank of England Records, OV58/771, cp=6, 'Some Impressions,' 1961.

105 *Globe and Mail*, 21 December 1960, 1.

106 For an account of the firing, see Muirhead, *Against the Odds*, 167–82.

107 USNA, DSR, POF Box 113, file 11, 'President's Trip to Ottawa, Bilateral Economic Issues,' 4 May 1961. Emphasis added.

108 'Canada's Defence Perplexities,' *Economist*, 28 March 1958, 1187.

109 'The Avro Nettle Patch,' *Economist*, 28 February 1959, 790.

110 USNA, DSR, POF Box 113, file 4, Memorandum for the President, 'Prime Minister Diefenbaker's Visit,' 17 February 1961.

111 Ibid.

112 PRO, T299, vol. 182, M.H. Parsons to Sir Denis Rickett, 11 December 1962.

113 For a discussion of the exchange crisis, see Muirhead, *Against the Odds*, 193–205.

114 Tom Keating, *Canada and World Order: The Multilateralist Tradition in Canadian Foreign Policy* (Toronto: McClelland and Stewart, 1993), 139.

115 Ball to Dillon, 5 July 1962 in *FRUS 1961–1963*, vol. 13, 1184.

116 LAC, Rasminsky Papers LR76-375-1, 'Notes on Discussions with Treasury and Federal Reserve Officials,' 23 July 1962.

117 Jock Finlayson and Stefano Bertasi, 'The Evolution of Canadian Postwar Interna-

tional Trade Policy,' in A. Claire Cutler and Mark W. Zacher, eds., *Canadian Foreign Policy and International Economic Regimes* (Vancouver: UBC Press, 1992), 22.

118 See Ronald Anderson, 'Fears High European Entry Fee,' *Globe and Mail*, 30 March 1962. Anderson emphasized the protectionist mentality of Canadian business. The government was prepared to do what it could with tariffs and quotas. See also Peyton Lyon, *Canada in World Affairs, 1961–63* (Toronto: Oxford University Press, 1968), 346. He had a different (and dated) interpretation, remarking on the damage done 'to Canada's ability to promote the multilateral trading environment' and to Canadians' reputation as 'the most consistent and emphatic advocates of multilateral trade.'

119 *Debates*, 20 June 1961, 6650.

120 USNA, T, PDF, Box 89A, Departments and Agencies, Treasury, 7/16/62–7/31/62, Memorandum for the President, 'Understanding with Canada on Emergency Financial Program,' 17 July 1962.

121 LAC, Rasminsky Papers, LR76-545-4, 'Measures to Increase Canadian Production and Sales and to Improve the Competitive Position of Canadian Industry,' 29 June 1962.

122 Bank of Canada, *Annual Report of the Governor to the Minister of Finance for the Year 1962*, 33 (emphasis mine).

123 Newman, *Renegade in Power*, 213

124 Fleming, *So Very Near*, 386.

125 Newman, *Renegade in Power*, 124.

126 By September 1962, however, Diefenbaker had changed his mind and was in support of the program.

127 JFKL, POF, Box 89A, file: Treas 7/16/62–7/31/62, Memorandum to President from Ball and Dillon, 17 July 1962.

128 See Glen Williams, *Not for Export: The International Competitiveness of Canadian Manufacturing* (Toronto: McClelland and Stewart, 1994), 152.

129 LAC, Rasminsky Papers, LR76-545-4, 'Measures to Increase Canadian Production and Sales and to Improve the Competitive Position of Canadian Industry,' 29 June 1962.

130 Embassy Ottawa to State, 17 July 1962 in *FRUS 1961–1963*, vol. 13, 1189.

131 Nash, 173.

132 *Debates* 25 January 1963, 3126–37.

133 Memorandum from the assistant secretary of state for European affairs to Ball, 29 January 1963 in *FRUS 1961–1963*, vol. 13, 1193. Knowlton Nash has a delightful section in his book dealing with this crisis. See Nash, 222–72.

134 Charles Ritchie, *Storm Signals: More Undiplomatic Diaries, 1962–1971* (Toronto: Macmillan, 1983), 33.

135 Butterworth to Ball, 15 April 1963 in *FRUS 1961–1963*, vol. 13, 1200. For another interpretation, see Ritchie, 34. He confided to his diary 'While I disapprove entirely

of the manufactured anti-Americanism of the government, yet deep down I feel satisfaction at hearing the Canadian government finally lash out at the omniscience and
unconscious arrogance of Washington, and I am not immune to that fever of irritation with the United States government which at home could become a national
rage – could, but I do not think it will.'

136 USNA, DSR, Box 3426, file 10, Foreign Exchange – Canada, U.S. Embassy Ottawa
to State, 8 February 1963.

137 Ritchie, *Storm Signals*, 47.

138 Nash, *Kennedy and Diefenbaker*, 301.

139 For an interesting analysis of the last months of the Diefenbaker government in its
relations with the Kennedy administration, see Peyton Lyon, 'Canadian–United
States Relations during the Final Months of the Diefenbaker Regime,' in R.H.
Wagenberg, ed., *Canada and the United States in the World of the Seventies* (Windsor,
ON: University of Windsor Press, 1970), 17–24.

140 George Grant, *Lament for a Nation: The Defeat of Canadian Nationalism* (Toronto:
McClelland and Stewart, 1970), 13.

Chapter 2

1 USNA, RG273, NSC, NSAM 234, 18 April 1963.

2 John Hilliker and Donald Barry, *Canada's Department of External Affairs*, vol. 2 *Coming of Age, 1946–1968* (Montreal and Kingston: McGill-Queen's University Press,
1995), 263.

3 Charles Ritchie, *Storm Signals: More Undiplomatic Diaries, 1962–1971* (Toronto:
Macmillan, 1983), 48. The Americans had described Ritchie in the following way:
'Earlier in his career, in Ottawa, one United States official reported he believed Ritchie
tended to favour the United Kingdom both through background and inclination.
Other United States officials have since claimed that Ritchie's Oxford education
extended only to his British accent and somewhat "old world" manner. The estimate
now is that he is a regular Canadian, no more disposed to the United Kingdom than to
the United States.' See USNA, POF, Box 113, file 5, 'Mr. Charles Stewart Almon
Ritchie,' n.d.

4 JFKL, Oral History, William R. Tyler, Assistant Secretary of State for European
Affairs, 1962–1965.

5 John English, *The Worldly Years: The Life of Lester Pearson*, vol. 2, *1949–1972*
(Toronto: Alfred A. Knopf, 1992), 269.

6 Kari Levitt, *Silent Surrender: The Multinational Corporation in Canada* (Toronto:
Macmillan, 1970), 5–6.

7 USNA, NSF, Box 19, file: Canada, Subject: Pearson Visit 5/63, 'Meeting with the
President on Canada,' 9 May 1963.

8 USNA, NSF, Box 19, file: Canada, Subject: Pearson visit, 5/63, 'Canadian Oil Exports,' 10 May 1963.

9 LAC, DEA-R, vol. 6057, file 50316-8-40, pt. 1.2, Joint Studies – Oil, 6 September 1963.

10 USNA, NSF, Box 19, file: Canada, General, 7/12/63–7/30/63, 'Trade Matters,' 10 May 1963.

11 Stephen Azzi, *Walter Gordon and the Creation of Canadian Nationalism* (Montreal: McGill-Queen's University Press, 1999), 114.

12 English, *Worldly Years*, 2: 270.

13 *Economist*, 29 June 1963, 237.

14 Richard Gwyn, *The 49th Paradox: Canada in North America* (Toronto: Totem, 1985), 67.

15 Pearson was uneasy with the budget. For an account of his acceptance of the budget and why he later disowned it, see Stephen Azzi, '"It Was Walter's View": Lester Pearson, the Liberal Party and Economic Nationalism,' in Norman Hillmer, ed., *Pearson: The Unlikely Gladiator* (Montreal and Kingston: McGill-Queen's University Press, 1999), 104–11.

16 Louis Rasminsky, the governor of the Bank of Canada, was one of those. See Bruce Muirhead, *Against the Odds: The Public Life and Times of Louis Rasminsky* (Toronto: University of Toronto Press, 1999), 210–11 for a discussion of this.

17 BCA, Louis Rasminsky Papers, LR76-541-6, A.W.F. Plumptre, 'U.S. Preliminary Comments on Canadian 1963 Budget,' 15 June 1963.

18 Ibid.

19 LJPL, NSF, Box 165, Canada Cables, vol. 1, Butterworth to Rusk, 8 February 1964.

20 Peter Stursberg, *Lester Pearson and the Dream of Unity* (Toronto: Doubleday, 1978), 125.

21 Eric Kierans with Walter Stewart, *Remembering* (Toronto: Stoddart, 2001), 74. For an account of the budget controversy between the two, see also John N. McDougall, *The Politics and Economics of Eric Kierans: A Man for All Canadas* (Montreal and Kingston: McGill-Queen's University Press, 1993), 43–7.

22 McDougall, *Politics and Economics*, 44.

23 As events transpired, most close to the government thought the budget a mistake. For example, the secretary of state for external affairs, Paul Martin, recalls his reaction: 'Cabinet should have realized that, given Gordon's well-known economic views, any proposal he made regarding foreign investment should have been put forward with the utmost care, and Washington should have been consulted about them in advance.' Paul Martin, *A Very Public Life*, vol. 2, *So Many Worlds* (Toronto: Deneau, 1985), 388.

24 USNA, DSR, RG59, Box 3427, file: Finance Canada, 'Canadian Budget Resolutions,' 21 June 1963.

25 USNA, NSF, Box 19, file: Canada, General, 7/12/63–7/30/63, 'Discriminatory Tax Measures in the Canadian Budget,' 28 June 1963.

26 Ritchie, *Storm Signals*, 52.

27 USNA, NSF, Box 19, file: Canada, General, 7/12/63–7/30/63, Memorandum to McGeorge Bundy, 16 July 1963.

28 See JFKL, POF, Box 90, file: Departments and Agencies, Treasury, 1/63, Memorandum for the President, 30 January 1963.

29 See JFKL, POF, Box 90, file: Departments and Agencies, Treasury, 1/63, Memorandum for the President, 'Preliminary Breakdown of 1962 Payments Deficit,' 25 January 1963.

30 Ritchie, *Storm Signals*, 52.

31 For an example of U.S. thinking on this issue, see JFKL, POF, Box 88A, Departments and Agencies, Department of State, 9/63, 'A Plan and Scenario for Bringing Our Balance of Payments under Control,' 24 September 1963.

32 JFKL, POF, Box 90, Departments and Agencies, Treasury, 4/17/63, Douglas Dillon, 'Action Program for Balance of Payments,' 17 April 1963.

33 Ibid.

34 Rasminsky interview with Peter Stursberg, 1 June 1978.

35 USNA, DSR, 1964–1966, Econ Finance Box 841, file 12, Balance of Payments Can-U.S. 1/1/64, Livingston Merchant, 'Memorandum for this file,' 9 October 1964.

36 USNA, NSF, Box 19, Canada, General, 7/12/63/–7/30/63, 'Canadian Reaction to Proposed US Balance of Payments Measures,' 19 July 1963.

37 JFKL, POF, Box 90, Departments and Agencies, Treasury, 4/17/63, Douglas Dillon, 'Overall Recommendations on Balance of Payments,' 17 April 1963.

38 JFKL, Oral History, James Reed, Assistant Secretary of the Treasury, 1961–1965.

39 BCA, Rasminsky Papers, LR76–365–15(a), *aide-mémoire*, 20 August 1963. ·
    See also ibid., LR76–360–5, 'The Canadian Balance of Payments and Related Problems,' 10 September 1963 for an excellent account of the negative effects of foreign ownership. The so-called Canadian nationalist school could not have made a better case against it.

40 LAC, DEA-R, vol. 6057, file 50316-8-40, 'Discussions between Mr. Walter Gordon and Mr. George Ball on Canada-U.S. Economic Relationships,' 2 August 1963.

41 USNA, NSF, Box 19, file: Canada, General, 11/9/63–12/2/63, Ottawa to SecState, 15 November 1963.

42 LBJL, NSF, Box 165, Canada Cables, vol. 1, Butterworth to Rusk, 8 February 1964.

43 USNA, DSR, RG56, Memoranda to the Secretary, Jan-Fe1964, B. 22C-ES, John Bullitt to the Secretary, 13 February 1964.

44 LBJL, NSF, Box 165, Canada Cables, vol. 1, Butterworth to Rusk, 8 February 1964.

45 USNA, NSF, Box 19, Canada, General, 11/9/63–12/2/63, Ottawa to SecState, 15 November 1963.

46 BCA, Rasminsky Papers, LR76-368-17, Bryce to Sharp, 'Quebec's Proposals Concerning Information,' 15 November 1965.

47 Ibid.

48 Ritchie, *Storm Signals*, 60.

49 BCA, Rasminsky Papers, LR76-365-31, 'Conversation with Secretary Dillon,' 10 December 1964.

50 Levitt, *Silent Surrender*, 11.

51 Hilliker and Barry, *Canada's Department of External Affairs*, 2: 362.

52 LAC, DEA-R, vol. 6057, file 50316-8-401, pt. 1.2, Embassy Washington to External, 12 September 1963.

53 BCA, Rasminsky Papers, LR76-366-4, 'Notes on Interdepartmental Meeting re: U.S.-Canada Proposed Statement of Economic Principles,' 12 February 1964.

54 See Hilliker and Barry, *Canada Department of External Affairs*, 2: 364.

55 John English, 'Serving the Public: Paul Martin, Minister,' in Ryan Touhey, ed., *Paul Martin and Canadian Diplomacy* (Waterloo, ON: Centre on Foreign Policy and Federalism) 33. For Heeney's reaction, see Arnold Heeney, *The Things That Are Caesar's: Memoirs of a Canadian Public Servant* (Toronto: University of Toronto Press, 1972), 194–7.

56 LBJL, Francis Bator Papers, Box 16, file B/D – Canada, Dillon to the President, 8 February 1965.

57 BCA, Rasminsky Papers, LR76–361, 'The U.S.A Trade Balance of Payments Guidelines,' February 1966.

58 Ibid.

59 BCA, Rasminsky Papers, LR76–361, 'The U.S.A Balance of Payments Guidelines' February 1965.

60 See Levitt, *Silent Surrender*, 10.

61 PCO, 'Canada-U.S. Ministerial Meeting,' 7 March 1966.

62 BCA, Rasminsky Papers, LR76-362, Joint Canada–United States Ministerial Committee on Trade and Economic Affairs, 'Foreign Investment in Canada,' June 1967.

63 John D. Harbron, 'Business and Industry,' in John Saywell, ed., *Canadian Annual Review for 1960* (Toronto: University of Toronto Press, 1961), 213.

64 See Donald Forster, 'The National Economy,' in John Saywell, ed., *Canadian Annual Review for 1961* (Toronto: University of Toronto Press, 1962), 243.

65 Robert Bothwell, Ian Drummond, and John English, *Canada since 1945: Power, Politics and Provincialism* (Toronto: University of Toronto Press, 1989), 197.

66 DEA-R, vol. 6057, file 50316-8-40, pt. 1.1, Washington DC to External, 12 August 1963.

67 LAC, DFR, RG19 (DFR), vol. 3943, file 8522-U-585 (64), A.F.W. Plumptre, 'Canadian Policy Regarding International Current Account,' 27 April 1964.

68 United States International Trade Commission Report on the United States-Canadian Automotive Agreement, 'Canadian Automotive Agreement,' January 1976, 111.

69 LAC, DFR, vol. 3943, file 8522-U-585 (64), Joint United States–Canadian Committee on Trade and Economic Affairs, 'Trade Policies and Problems,' April 1964.

70 Knowlton Nash, *Kennedy and Diefenbaker: Fear and Loathing across the Undefended Border* (Toronto: McClelland and Stewart, 1990), 316.

71 USNA, NSF, Box 19, file: Canada, General, 11/9/63–12/2/63, Rusk to Ball, 14 November 1963.

72 USNA, DSR, Classified White House 1963 (2), B. 13C-ES, Bundy to Dillon, 11 November 1963. In reply, Dillon wanted to make it clear 'that the Treasury Department, which has the legal obligation under the law to impose countervailing duties on imports which enjoy a grant or bounty, still is of the opinion that the provisions of the law are mandatory.' Ibid., Dillon to Bundy, 15 November 1963. He did, however, 'quite agree with the ... [rest of the] note.'

73 USNA, NSF, Box 19, file: Canada, General, 11/9/63–12/2/63, Rusk to Ball, 14 November 1963. It had been reported in the Canadian press that the government intended to extend this plan to office machinery.

74 USNA, NSF, Box 19, file: Canada, General, 11/9/63–12/2/63, Butterworth to Secretary of State, 15 November 1963.

75 See USNA, NSF, Box 19, file: Canada, General, 11/9/63–12/2/63, Douglas Dillon, 'Memorandum for Mr. McGeorge Bundy,' 15 November 1963. Dillon writes 'I want to make it clear that the Treasury Department, which has the legal obligation under the law to impose countervailing duties on imports which enjoy a grant or bounty, still is of the opinion that the provisions of the law are mandatory. We have seen no opinion that the legal aspects of the matter are not open and shut ... In the past the law has been applied with some flexibility in cases where evidently domestic pressure was not too severe or did not last. In this case, too, I think we have some flexibility in timing and, if domestic interest should disappear, we might wish to reconsider in the light of past practice. This is unlikely, however, and is quite different from our assuming that there is doubt about the applicability of the law.' For the Canadian position see LAC, DFR, vol. 3943, file 8522-U-585 (64), Reisman to R.B. Bryce and Walter Gordon, 28 April 1964. In this memorandum, Reisman lays out his position as to why there was some discretion in the law.

76 USNA, NSF, Box 19, file: Canada, General, 11/9/63–12/2/63, Brubeck to the President, 19 November 1963.

77 Nash, *Kennedy and Diefenbaker*, 315.

78 Ritchie, *Storm Signals*, 70. See also Martin, *A Very Public Life*, 2: 394–7.

79 Memorandum of Conversation, 'Meeting of the President and Canadian Prime Minister Pearson,' 25 November 1963, in *FRUS 1961–1963*, vol. 13, *West Europe and Canada* (Washington, DC: GPO, 1994), 1215.

80 English, *Worldly Years*, 2: 362.

81 Ibid., 357. The reassessment was partly because of the new president's admission that he knew 'nothing about Canada.'

82 Memorandum from Secretary of State Rusk to President Johnson, 12 December 1963 in *FRUS 1961–1963*, vol. 13, 1217.

83 Ritchie, *Storm Signals*, 79.

84 LBJL, NSF, Box 167, file: Canada: Pearson Visit 1/22/64, Auto Parts 23, 'Canada Sub-Cabinet Committee Meeting,' 7 January 1964.

85 LBJL, NSF, Box 167, file: Canada: Pearson Visit 1/22/64, Auto Parts 23, Memorandum of Conversation, 'Auto Parts,' 22 January 1964. The Studebaker decision, according to Pearson, had 'astonished' the president. See Lester Pearson with John A. Munro and Alex Inglis, *Mike: The Memoirs of the Right Honourable Lester B. Pearson*, vol. 3, *1957–1968* (Toronto: University of Toronto Press, 1975), 123.

86 PCO, 'Prime Minister's Visit to Washington,' 23 January 1964.

87 LBJL, NSF, Box 167, file: Canada: Pearson Visit 1/22/64, Auto Parts #23, Memorandum of Conversation, 'Auto Parts,' 22 January 1964.

88 USNA, DSR, Memoranda to the Secretary, Jan–Feb 1964, B. 22C-ES, Memorandum for the President, 13 February 1964.

89 PCO, 'Prime Minister's Visit to Washington,' 24 January 1964.

90 English, *Worldly Years*, 2: 366. See also Pearson, *Mike*, 3: 125–8 for his account of his meeting with President Johnson on the occasion of the signing of the Auto Pact agreement. His recollections certainly reinforce English's conclusions.

91 USNA, DSR, Box 16C-ES, Memorandum to the Undersecretary 1963, James A. Reid, 'Possible imposition of countervailing duty against Canadian automotive parts,' 30 October 1963.

92 DFR, vol. 3943, file: 8522-U-585 (64), Joint United States–Canada Committee on Trade and Economic Affairs, 'Trade Policies and Problems,' April 1964.

93 See Greg Donaghy, 'A Continental Philosophy: Canada, the United States, and the Negotiation of the Autopact, 1963–65,' *International Journal* 53 (summer 1998), 453.

94 LBJL, Box 165, Country File – Canada Memos, Memorandum for the President, 'Report on meeting of Joint U.S.-Canadian Committee on Trade and Economic Affairs,' 1 May 1964.

95 LBJL, George Ball Papers, Box 1, file: Canada I, Telcon, Ball to Dillon, 13 May 1964.

96 LBJL, Box 165, Country File – Canada Memos, Memorandum for the President, 'Report on the Joint US-Canadian Committee on Trade and Economic Affairs,' 1 May 1964.

97 James F. Keeley, 'Cast in Concrete for All Time? The Negotiation of the Auto Pact,' *Canadian Journal of Political Science* 16 (1983), 287.

98 USNA, DSR, Memoranda to the Secretary, May–June 1964, B. 22C-ES, Belin to the Secretary, 31 August 1964.

99 LBJL, George Ball Papers, Box 1, file: Canada I, Telcon, Ball to Dillon, 29 May 1964. See also USNA, RG56, Memo of Conversation 1964, B. 24C-ES, Gordon and Dillon, 17 June 1964. During this meeting with the secretary of the treasury, Gordon asked again 'whether the [treasury countervailing] reference could be modified to restrict it to Modine. He said that he understood that this type of broad reference had only been made in one previous case, in a German situation sometime in the 1930s.' Dillon replied that it was not possible to modify anything.

100 The Columbia River project, designed to dam the river for hydroelectric generation, had a U.S. as well as federal-provincial dimension since the river meandered through British Columbia before crossing into the United States and flowing into the Pacific Ocean. The Americans had wanted to construct generating facilities in Washington state, using water that had been stored in BC. Hence the involvement of Ottawa, Victoria, and Washington. The project had run aground in Canada over federal-provincial relations, with the BC government of W.A.C. Bennett taking issue with the federal administrations of John Diefenbaker and Lester Pearson over his ideas about developing the river for BC's own hydroelectric needs. As time passed, the Americans became increasingly irritated. Through many twists and turns, it finally came to a resolution in September 1964 with Ottawa and Washington signing the Columbia River Treaty.

101 USNA, DSR, Memorandum to the Secretary May–June 1964, B. 22C-ES, G. d'Andelot Belin to the Secretary, 31 August 1964.

102 USNA, DSR, Memoranda to the Secretary, Jan.–Feb. 1964, B. 22C-ES, Memorandum for the President, 'Canadian Automobile Export Incentive Plan,' 13 February 1964.

103 Ibid.

104 Azzi, Walter Gordon, 125. The Canadian ambassador in Washington had presented a paper to the department of state outlining Ottawa's concern with the evolving American intention to impose countervailing duties against automotive parts. 'Such a development,' it noted, 'would be widely regarded in Canada as a major set-back in trade and economic relations with the United States.' See USNA, DSR, Memoranda to the Secretary, May–June 1964, B226-ES, Canadian Paper, 12 June 1964.

105 Peter Stursberg, Lester Pearson and the American Dilemma (Toronto: Doubleday, 1980), 229.

106 Keeley, 'Cast in Concrete,' 289.

107 USNA, DSR, Memoranda to the Secretary July–September 1964, B. 22C-ES, Butterworth to Rusk, 25 August 1964.

108 LBJL, NSF, Box 165, Country File – Canada Memos, vol. 2, Henry Ford to the President, 22 September 1964.

109 LBJL, NSF, Box 165, Country File – Canada Memos, vol. 2, McGeorge Bundy to the President, 27 November 1964.

110 LBJL, George Ball Papers, Box 1, file: Canada I, Telephone Conversation, Ball to Dillon, 2 November 1964. In any event, the Modine decision was never announced.

111 LBJL, White House Aides – H.H. Wilson, Box 1, file: Wilson – Canada, Memorandum for the President, 'Canadian-American Free Trade in Automobiles and Parts,' 25 November 1964.

112 LBJL, George Ball Papers, Box 1, file: Canada I, Telcon, Ball to Katzenbach, 9 December 1964.

113 John Holmes, *Life with Uncle: The Canadian-American Relationship* (Toronto: University of Toronto Press, 1981), 55. See also Pearson *Mike*, 3 134–5. Pearson notes that Canadian troops were on Cyprus within twenty-four hours. 'President Johnson was amazed and filled with admiration at our ability to act so quickly, and I think this may have changed his attitude toward Canada ... Having praised us for our action, he concluded: 'Now what can I do for you?' I replied: "Nothing at the moment, Mr. President." But I had some credit in the bank.'

114 LBJL, NSF, Box 165, Country File – Canada Memos, vol. 2, McGeorge Bundy to the President, 27 November 1964.

115 For a further discussion of this, see PCO, 102/65, Memorandum to the Cabinet, 'Instructions for Canadian Delegation to the Twenty-Second Session of GATT,' 3 March 1965.

116 PCO, 'Canada-U.S.A Negotiations: Automotive Industry,' 21 December 1964. See also Donaghy, 'Continental Philosophy,' 463.

117 PCO, 'Canada-U.S.A Negotiations: Automotive Industry,' 21 December 1964. See also PCO, 'Prime Minister's Visit with the President of the United States: Automotive Agreement,' 13 January 1965.

118 BCA, Rasminsky Papers, LR76–367–17, the Johnson Guidelines, 19 February 1965.

119 LBJL, NSF, Box 166, Country File – Canada Memos vol. 3, Memorandum for the President, 'U.S.-Canadian Automotive Products Agreement – Proposed Legislation and Message,' 25 March 1965.

120 BCA, Rasminsky Papers, LR76–361, Joint Canada–United States Ministerial Committee Meeting, 'Canada–United States Automotive Agreement,' March 1966.

121 Pearson, *Mike*, 3: 128.

122 BCA, Rasminsky Papers, LR76-361, Joint Canada–United States Ministerial Committee Meeting, 'Canada–United States Automotive Agreement,' March 1966.

123 LBJL, Fowler Papers, Box 38, file: Canadian Auto Parts Agreement, Barr to Secretary of the Treasury, 26 October 1965.

124 J.L. Granatstein, *Canada, 1957–1967: The Years of Uncertainty and Innovation* (Toronto: McClelland and Stewart, 1986), 207.

125 Bank of Canada, *Annual Report of the Governor to the Minister of Finance for the Year 1969* (Ottawa: Bank of Canada, 1970), 67.

126 United States International Trade Commission Report on the United States–Canadian Automotive Agreements, 'Canadian Automobile Agreement,' January 1976.

127 Muirhead, *Against the Odds*, 270.

128 BCA, Rasminsky Papers, LR76-525-6, Pearson to Johnson, 22 January 1968.

129 LBJL, NSF, Box 166, Country File – Canada, vol. 5, 'Canadian Dollar Crisis,' 7 March 1968. For a complete account of the 1968 Canadian dollar crisis, see Muirhead, 269–80.

130 For a longer account of this, see Richard Nixon Library, CF, FG 6-20, [CIEP] 1971 [1971–4] CIEP Study Memoranda List, 8 June 1972.

131 Donald Forster, 'The National Economy,' in John Saywell, *Canadian Annual Review for 1969* (Toronto: University of Toronto Press, 1970), 347.

132 BCA, Rasminsky Papers, LR76-363, Joint Canada–United States Ministerial Committee on Trade and Economic Affairs, 'Canada/United States Automotive Products Agreement,' 19 June 1969.

133 Carl E. Beigie, *The Canada-U.S. Automotive Agreement: An Evaluation* (Montreal and Washington, DC: Private Planning Association of Canada and National Planning Association, 1970), 111n7.

134 BCA, Rasminsky Papers, LR76-363, Joint Canada–United States Minsterial Committee on Trade and Economic Affairs, 'Canada/United States Automotive Products Agreement,' 19 June 1969. For an account of this, see Beigie, 49–50.

135 Ibid.

136 USNA, DSR, Box 595, file E-1-CAN-UK, Butterworth to Secretary of State, 15 August 1968.

137 BCA, Rasminsky Papers, LR76-365, Washington to External, 17 April 1964.

138 LBJL, NSF, Box 166, Country File – Canada, vol. 5, Butterworth to Department of State, 4 September 1968.

139 Martin, *A Very Public Life*, 2: 403.

140 USNA, DSR, Box 594, file E 2-2 CAN, Butterworth to Secretary of State, January 1968.

141 Ibid.

142 USNA, DSR, Box 1941, file POL 15-1 CAN, 1-1-68, Butterworth to Secretary of State, 25 April 1968. In this interesting interview, Butterworth also commented on Sharp's assessment of who would have been the best man to take over from Pearson: 'He explained to me why he thought it was desirable, if he could not win, to enhance Trudeau's candidacy by throwing to him his delegates on the eve of the convention. He said he telephoned Trudeau and said that he thought he, Sharp, would make the best prime minister but since he did not think he would get it, he favored Trudeau as the best substitute. He expressed confidence in Trudeau's mental capacity and his ability to communicate ... and the importance of his pragmatic attitude "aided by good advice."'

143 LBJL, White House Central Files, 1963–1969, John Macy to the President, 24 August 1966.

Chapter 3

1 Bank of Canada, *Annual Report of the Governor of the Bank of Canada to the Minister of Finance for the Year 1968* (Ottawa: Bank of Canada, 1969) 5.
2 Louis Rasminsky, *A Very Personal Piece* (unpublished), 82.
3 USNA, DSR, Box 1941, file POL 15-1 CAN, 7/1/67, Butterworth to Department of State, 25 September 1967.
4 Bank of Canada, *Annual Report 1968*, 6.
5 Bruce Muirhead, *Against the Odds: The Public Life and Times of Louis Rasminsky* (Toronto: University of Toronto Press, 1999), 226–7.
6 Ibid., 228.
7 George Ball, *The Discipline of Power: Essentials of a Modern World Structure* (Boston: Little, Brown, 1968), 113. The publication of the book featured prominently in Canadian newspapers. Representative of the commentary were the stories in the *Globe and Mail*, two denouncing it and explaining why Ball had gotten it so wrong, and an editorial doing likewise. See *Globe and Mail*, 3 May 1968, 1 and 4 May 1968, 6.
8 USNA, DSR, Box 592, file E-4/1/68, Butterworth to State, 4 May 1968.
9 George Bain, 'A Conversation with the Prime Minister II,' *Globe and Mail*, 23 May 1968, 6.
10 USNA, DSR, B. 1938, file POL 7 CAN, 3/1/69, Embassy Ottawa to Secretary of State, 5 March 1969.
11 Donald Forster, 'The National Economy,' in John Saywell, ed. *Canadian Annual Review for 1968* (Toronto: University of Toronto Press, 1969) 330. See also Robert Bothwell, Ian Drummond, and John English, *Canada since 1945: Power, Politics, and Provincialism* (Toronto: University of Toronto Press, 1989), 345 and Peter Stursberg, *Lester Pearson and the American Dilemma* (Toronto: Doubleday, 1980), 243–9. For Gordon's recollections of the process, see Walter L. Gordon, *A Political Memoir* (Toronto: McClelland and Stewart, 1977), 253–5, 310–12.
12 Forster, 'National Economy,' 330.
13 *Globe and Mail*, 4 March 1969, B-3.
14 Ibid., 27 May 1968, 1.
15 J.L. Granatstein, 'External Affairs and Defence,' in John Saywell, ed., *Canadian Annual Review for 1969* (Toronto: University of Toronto Press, 1970), 210.
16 See Stephen Clarkson, ed., *An Independent Foreign Policy for Canada?* (Toronto: McClelland and Stewart, 1968) and Kari Levitt, *Silent Surrender: The Multinational Corporation in Canada* (Toronto: Macmillan, 1970). For a brief analysis of Levitt's influence on the political debate, see Stephen Azzi, *Walter Gordon and the Rise of*

Canadian Nationalism (Montreal and Kingston: McGill-Queen's University Press, 1999), 168–9. Other critics, such as James Laxer, Abraham Rotstein, and even Michael Bliss (for a while), joined the initial group. Another issue that gained attention during this period was U.S. draft dodgers or deserters claiming refugee status in Canada. During Trudeau's Washington National Press Club address in March 1969 following his meeting with President Nixon, he floated a trial balloon to test administration attitudes. Up to this point, Ottawa had been reluctant to allow military deserters, as opposed to draft dodgers, into the country. In his speech, Trudeau noted that 'Canadian policy has been a little less free with deserters than with draft evaders.' CBC Radio, *Sunday Morning*, 14 September 2004. When he received no response from Washington, Canadian policy changed and deserters were as welcome as draft dodgers. This decision met with universal approbation in Canada.

17 USNA, DSR, Box 1938, file POL & CAN, 3/1/69, American Embassy Ottawa to Secretary of State, 5 March 1969.

18 USNA, DSR, Box 1398, file POL 7 CAN, 3/1/69, Memorandum for the President, 'Trudeau Visit: Scope and Objectives,' 20 March 1969. A few months later, the minister of energy, mines and resources, J.J. Greene, told a Washington press conference that a continental energy policy would best suit both countries.

19 Paul Daniel and Richard Shaffner, 'Lessons from Bilateral Trade in Energy Resources,' in Carl Beigie and Alfred O. Hero, eds., *Natural Resources in U.S.-Canadian Relations* vol. 1, *The Evolution of Policies and Issues* (Boulder, CO: Westview Press, 1980), 308. For a general review of the Canada-U.S. oil situation, see J. Alex Murray, ed., *North American Energy in Perspective*, Proceedings of the Canadian-American Seminar, University of Windsor, November 14–15, 1974, (Windsor, ON: University of Windsor, 1975).

20 USNA, Nixon [TA] Trade Agreements, 5 of 16, Mar–May 1971, Peter Flanigan to the President, 18 May 1971. Canadian petroleum exports increased steadily from 1960 to 1971. Following the change of Canadian policy, exports did not reach the 1971 level until 1988. Some sample years of petroleum exports in millions of metric tons include: 1958 – 4.2; 1961 – 8.8; 1965 – 14.5; 1968 – 22.5; 1971 – 35. Exports then fell off dramatically, to 14 million metric tons in 1977 and 8 million in 1982, whereupon they again began to climb.

21 *Debates*, 11 January 1973, 168. See also Murray, ed., *North American Energy*, i.

22 See USNA, RG273, NSSM 237, NSC, National Security Study Memorandum 237, 'US International Energy Policy,' 5 February 1976. For the Americans, the situation had become critical after the 1973 oil shock which saw prices spiral upward. Committees were struck to investigate measures to ensure a reliable supply of required energy imports at reasonable prices over the next five years. And that supply, by and large, meant imports from Canada. Later the search for assured supplies of oil became much more vigorous.

23 Judith Maxwell, 'North American Energy: Facts, Fiction and Perspectives,' in Murray, ed., *North American Energy*, 12. For a brief history of Canadian oil since 1960, see John N. McDougall, 'Canada and the World Petroleum Market,' in Norman Hillmer and Garth Stevenson, eds., *A Foremost Nation: Canadian Foreign Policy and a Changing World* (Toronto: McClelland and Stewart, 1977), 85–109.

24 USNA, Nixon [TA] Trade Agreements, Box 67, F 11 of 16, January 1973, Jim Akins to Peter Flanigan, 'Canada,' 15 January 1973.

25 USNA, Nixon [TA] Trade Agreements, Box 67, F 12 of 16, Feb.–May 1973, Flanigan to Bill Simon, 'Agreement with Canadians on Oil,' 22 March 1973.

26 BCA, Louis Rasminsky Papers, LR76-363, Joint Canada–United States Ministerial Committee on Trade and Economic Affairs, 'Post Kennedy Round Trade Problems and Liberalization,' 19 June 1969.

27 See *Debates*, 4 June 1969, 9728.

28 BCA, BCR, 1E-750, External to Washington, 4 June 1969.

29 Ibid.

30 With respect to restrictions on financial institutions, see Muirhead, *Against the Odds*, 213–16. The magazine issue centred around so-called Canadian editions of *Time* and *Reader's Digest*, both of which received favourable treatment from Canadian tax laws.

31 BCA, Rasminsky Papers, LR76-363-4, Joint Canada-U.S. Ministerial Committee on Trade and Economic Affairs, 'General Notes,' 20 June 1969.

32 See the statement sponsored by the Canadian-American Committee, 'Toward a More Realistic Appraisal of the Automotive Agreement' (1970), 7–8.

33 See 'Johnson Says Autopact Has Proved Its Importance,' *Globe and Mail*, 23 March 1967, B-1. Gore and Hartke aside, there was little support in Congress to repeal the legislation.

34 USNA, RG 273, file NSC NSSM 49, Henry Kissinger, 'US Trade Policy during the 1970's,' 24 April 1969.

35 *Canada 1970* (Toronto: McClelland and Stewart, 1969), 49.

36 Abraham Rotstein, *The Precarious Homestead: Essays on Economics, Technology and Nationalism* (Toronto: New Press, 1973), 22.

37 See USNA, DSR, Box 1948, file: POL 7/1/69, American Embassy Ottawa to State, 30 July 1969.

38 Peyton Lyon, 'Canada–United States Relations' in H. Edward English, ed., *Proceedings of the Academy of Political Science* 32, no. 2 (1976), 18.

39 J.L. Granatstein, 'External Affairs and Defence,' in John Saywell, ed., *Canadian Annual Review for 1968* (Toronto: University of Toronto Press, 1969), 217.

40 Bruce Thordarson, *Trudeau and Foreign Policy: A Study in Decision-Making* (Toronto: Oxford University Press, 1972), 4.

41 J.L. Granatstein, 'Foreign Affairs and Defence,' in John Saywell, ed., *Canadian Annual Review for 1970* (Toronto: University of Toronto Press, 1971), 314.

42 *Foreign Policy for Canadians* (Ottawa: Department of External Affairs, 1970), 15–16.

43 Ibid., 25.

44 See for example, J.L. Granatstein and Robert Bothwell, *Pirouette: Pierre Trudeau and Canadian Foreign Policy* (Toronto: University of Toronto Press, 1990), 33–4. See also Denis Stairs, 'Reviewing Foreign Policy, 1968–70,' in Don Munton and John Kirton, eds., *Canadian Foreign Policy: Selected Cases* (Toronto: Prentice-Hall, 1992), 200.

45 USNA, DSR, Box 730, file E-1-CAN-US, 1/1/70, Memorandum for the President, 'US-Canada Joint Cabinet Meeting,' 24 November 1970.

46 USNA, DSR, Box 730, file E-1-1 CAN-US, 1/1/70, Schmidt to Secretary of State, 18 November 1970.

47 BCA, Rasminsky Papers, LR76-522-251, R.W. Lawson, 'Reactions of Dr. Arthur Burns to Canada's Recent Exchange Rate Decision,' 11 June 1970.

48 USNA, Nixon CF, BE – Bus/Econ (1971–1974), Peter Peterson to the President, 12 July 1971.

49 The following discussion comes largely from USNA, Nixon CF, BE – Bus/Econ, (1971–1974), Peter Peterson to the President, 12 July 1971.

50 John S. Odell, 'The U.S. and the Emergence of Flexible Exchange Rates: An Analysis of Foreign Policy Change,' *International Organization* 33 (1979), 67. See also Lyon, 'Canada–United States Relations,' 18.

51 Odell, 'US and the Emergence of Flexible Exchange Rates,' 69.

52 Theodore H. Cohn, *Global Political Economy: Theory and Practice* (Toronto: Longman, 2000), 149.

53 BCA, Rasminsky Papers, LR76-373-3, Washington DC to External, 15 August 1971.

54 See Odell, 'US and the Emergence of Flexible Exchange Rates,' 74. For a personal account of the process leading up to Camp David and its aftermath, see Robert Solomon, *The International Monetary System, 1945–1976: An Insider's View* (New York: Harper and Row, 1977), 176–215.

55 *FRUS*, vol. 3, *Foreign Economic Policy; International Monetary Policy, 1969–1972* (Washington, DC: GPO, 2001), 454.

56 Granatstein and Bothwell, *Pirouette*, 65.

57 BCA, Rasminsky Papers, LR76-374-1, Prime Minister's Meeting with the President of the United States, December 6, 1971, 'John B. Connally–Secretary of the Treasury,' n.d.

58 For a discussion of the new economic program, see Muirhead, 284–94.

59 Peter Dobell, 'Reducing Vulnerability: The Third Option, 1970s,' in Munton and John Kirton, eds., *Canadian Foreign Policy*, 237.

60 *Globe and Mail*, 16 August 1971, 2.

61 United States Information Service, John Connally, 'Press Conference,' 16 August 1971.

62 Michael Tucker, *Canadian Foreign Policy: Contemporary Issues and Themes* (Toronto: McGraw-Hill Ryerson, 1980), 80–3.

63 *Globe and Mail*, 16 August 1971, 2. See also 'Transcript of the Press Conference Given by the Honourable Mitchell Sharp, Acting Prime Minister, August 16, 1971.'

64 BCA, Rasminsky Papers, LR76 374–1, Prime Minister's Meeting with the President of the United States, 'Temporary Import Surcharge,' 2 December 1971.

65 Muirhead, *Against the Odds*, 287.

66 BCA, Rasminsky Papers, LR76-299-19, 'Notes of a Conversation between Mr. Benson and Secretary Connally,' September 1971.

67 BCA, Rasminsky Papers, LR76-373-12, Treasury Secretary Connally on the *Today* show, NBC-TV. See also Dobell, 'Reducing Vulnerability,' 244. In more colloquial language, Dobell records that Connally told Pepin that 'he had decided to shake the world. And that, brother, includes you!'

68 BCA, Rasminsky Papers, LR76-373-3, Washington to External, 16 August 1971.

69 Ibid.

70 BCA, Rasminsky Papers, LR76-374-1, Prime Minister's Meeting with the President of the United States, 'Trade Discussions,' 2 December 1971.

71 Ibid.

72 BCA, Rasminsky Papers, LR76-373-14, Washington to External, 26 August 1971.

73 Ibid.

74 BCA, Rasminsky Papers, LR76 374-1, PMs Meeting with the President of the United States, 2 December 1971.

75 Dobell, 'Reducing Vulnerability,' 237.

76 BCA, Rasminsky Papers, LR76-299-20, D.J. Orchard to Reisman, 20 September 1971. President Nixon said something similar: 'We have too long acted as Uncle Sugar and now we've got to be Uncle Sam.' Granatstein and Bothwell, *Pirouette,* 61. See also John Holmes, *Life with Uncle: The Canadian-American Relationship* (Toronto: University of Toronto Press, 1981), 59. 'Americans [were] now more inclined to see themselves as victims of their own generosity to other countries and Canada as a rich hoarder of resources and industrial competition rather than a junior partner deserving particular consideration in the mutual interest.'

77 BCA, Rasminsky Papers, LR76-299-19, 'Notes of a Conversation between Mr. Benson and Secretary Connally,' September 1971.

78 BCA, Rasminsky Papers, LR76-299-26, Geneva to Rome (Delegation to G-10), Pepin's Talks re: U.S. Surcharges, 27 November 1971.

79 BCA, Rasminsky Papers, LR76-299-19, 'Notes of a Conversation.

80 Ibid.

81 *Globe and Mail*, 16 October 1971, 6.

82 UKNA, FCO82, vol. 24, 'Record of a Conversation between the Foreign and Commonwealth Secretary and the Canadian Minister of External Affairs,' 2 June 1971.

83 'Polar Explorers,' *Economist*, 23 October 1971, 45. See also Granatstein and Bothwell, *Pirouette*, 195. The authors record that during his visit to Moscow in May 1971, Trudeau told the Russians that 'Canada has increasingly found it important to diversify its channels of communication because of the overpowering presence of the United States of America and that is reflected in a growing consciousness amongst Canadians of the danger to our national identity from a cultural, economic and perhaps even military point of view.' See also *Globe and Mail*, 19 October 1971, 14; *Globe and Mail*, 20 October 1971, 1. Here the headline read 'Kosygin Criticizes US Policy, Says It Is Killing Jobs in Canada.' For an insider's account, see Ivan L. Head and Pierre Trudeau, *The Canadian Way: Shaping Canada's Foreign Policy, 1968–1984* (Toronto: McClelland and Stewart, 1995), 249–52.

84 Granatstein and Bothwell, *Pirouette*, 196. Still, this perceived thaw in Soviet-Canada relations could be misconstrued. The Canadians refused the visa applications for a number of official Russians who wanted to attend a session of the Soviet-Canadian commission in Ottawa in early December 1973. Apparently, they were spies. See UKNA, FCO 82, vol. 234, NHRA Broomfield, British Embassy Moscow to BJP Fall, Eastern European and Soviet Department, Foreign and Commonwealth Office, 12 December 1973.

85 UKNA, FCO 82, vol. 19, John Dunrossil to Julien Bullard, 15 September 1971. From this thaw in relations came the vaunted Canada-USSR eight-game hockey series of August and September 1972, which Canada won by one point. The author attended the games in Montreal and Toronto.

86 USNA, DSR, Box 726, file E-2 CAN 1/1/70, US Mission OECD to Secretary of State, 15 October 1971. The U.S. delegation, on the other hand, thought the Canadians too pessimistic and suggested that their 'pall of doom' was wildly overstated.

87 USNA, DSR, Box 730, file E-1-CAN-US, American Embassy Ottawa to Secretary of State, 6 November 1971.

88 94th Congress, 1st Session, 9th Annual Report of the President to the Congress on the Operation of the Automotive Products Trade Act of 1965, Will E. Leonard, chair, International Trade Commission, to Russell Long, chair, Senate Committee on Finance, 22 January 1976.

89 USNA, DSR, Box 730, file E-1-CAN-US, 1/1/70, American Embassy Ottawa to Secretary of State, 17 November 1971.

90 USNA, DSR, Box 730, file E-1-CAN-US, 1/1/70, 'U.S. Economic Policies toward Canada: Request for Embassy Contributions to CIEP Study,' 11 November 1971.

91 USNA, DSR, Box 730, file E-1-CAN-US, 1/1/70, American Embassy Ottawa to Department of State, 24 December 1971.

92 USNA, DSR, Box 730, file E-1-CAN-US, 1/1/70, Embassy Ottawa to Secretary of State, 6 November 1971.

93 BCA, Rasminsky Papers, LR76-299-31, JRB, 'Canada's Short Run Need for Greater Exchange Rate Flexibility than Other G-10 Countries,' 3 December 1971.

94 BCA, Rasminsky Papers, LR76-374-2, Prime Minister's Meeting with the President of the United States, 6 December 1971.

95 Granatstein and Bothwell, *Pirouette*, 70.

96 BCA, Rasminsky Papers, LR76-299-35, G-10, Washington, 17 December 1971. For a full account of Rasminsky's role and the Canadian position at the Smithsonian talks, see Muirhead, 289–93.

97 Odell, 'US and the Emergence of Flexible Exchange Rates,' 74–5. As Odell writes, 'Until this time Kissinger had not participated at all in this issue. He admitted that he was not interested in economic matters, but he became concerned that this conflict could interfere with other diplomatic efforts. Kissinger and Nixon were arranging a series of summit meetings with key allied governments preparatory to Nixon's 1972 trips to Peking and Moscow, when Britain's Prime Minister Edward Heath refused to meet Nixon until the United States took steps to end the monetary crisis. One close observer has hypothesized that Kissinger suggested this tactic to the British in order to provide himself with the tool he needed for pulling Nixon away from Connally ... The effort succeeded ... by influencing the President, for whom military-political issues were most salient.' See also 'Foreign Economic Policy Lights Up,' *Economist*, 7 October 1972, 53 for an analysis of Kissinger and his new role.

98 Robert Bothwell, 'Canada–United States Relations,' *International Journal* 57 (Winter 2002–3), 79.

99 BCA, Rasminsky Papers, LR76-575, 'Canada-US Relations: Some General Perspectives,' 30 November 1971.

100 USNA, DSR, Box 730, file E-1-CAN-US, 1/1/70, US Embassy Ottawa to Secretary of State, 28 October 1971.

101 Bank of Canada, *Annual Report of the Governor to the Minister of Finance and Statement of Accounts for the Year 1971* (Ottawa: Bank of Canada, 1972), 5.

102 USNA, DSR, Box 730, file E-1-CAN-US, 1/1/70, American Embassy Ottawa to Department of State, 24 December 1971.

103 See R.B. Byers, 'External Affairs and Defence,' in John Saywell, ed., *Canadian Annual Review for 1971* (Toronto: University of Toronto Press, 1972), 259.

104 USNA, DSR, Box 730, file E-1-CAN-US, 1/1/70, American Embassy Ottawa to Secretary of State, 17 November 1971.

105 *Globe and Mail*, 4 February 1972, B-3.

106 BCA, Rasminsky Papers, LR76-373-25-2, Paul A. Volcker, 'Canada and the US: The New Crunch,' 16 February 1972. See also *Economist*, 11 December 1971, 55.

107 Harald B. Malmgren, 'The Evolving Trading System,' in English, ed., 125.

108 USNA, Nixon, NSC, County File – Europe, Box 671, file: Canada, vol. 3, Sonnenfeldt and Hormats to Kissinger, 4 February 1972. British observers of this stalemate

remarked that 'the Canadians showed a surprising degree of resilience and refused to make the concessions the Americans were looking for.' See UKNA, FCO 82, file 115, 'Visit of the Prime Minister of Canada to the United Kingdom,' 30 November 1972.

109 USNA, Nixon, NSC Files, Country File – Europe, Box 671, file: Canada, vol. 3, Sonnenfeldt to Kissinger, 'Canadian Ambassador Anxious to See You,' 7 February 1972.

110 USNA, Nixon, NSC Files, Country Files – Europe, Box 671, file: Canada, vol. 3, Robert Hormats to Kissinger, 25 April 1972.

111 'Making Amends to Canada,' *Economist*, 22 April 1972, 53. The Canadians were being asked to rewrite the Auto Pact in a way that dropped three safeguards inserted to protect the Canadian share of the motor industry, to increase the duty-free allowance for Canadian residents who shop in the United States, and to give up some preferences reserved to Canadian producers in the shared defence production program.

112 USNA, Nixon [CF] F1 9 – Monetary Systems [1971–74], William Eberle to Peter Flanigan, 28 February 1972.

113 Ross Munro, 'Slump in U.S. Relations Likely,' *Globe and Mail*, 11 February 1972, 1.

114 Part of this conundrum was represented by the Foreign Trade and Investment Act, commonly known as the Hartke-Burke Bill, which would impose quotas on most imports to the United States.

115 *Debates*, 14 April 1972, 1327.

116 Holmes, 4. See also Head and Trudeau, *Canadian Way*, 189–90. The two authors note that content of Nixon's speech was suggested before he gave it. They wanted, or so they claim, the end 'of the old "special" economic relationship between the two countries that was so endearing to some Canadian ministers and to some of the most senior public servants.' Head 'had suggested in a lengthy letter to Kissinger in March that Nixon's speech should be employed by the president as an opportunity to fix a clear milestone in relations between the countries ... Head expressed the hope that the president would declare that Canadian independence clearly extended to its own determination of its economic policies, free from US interference.'

117 Alexandra Gill, 'Nixon's Bushy-Haired "Bastard" Bites Back,' *Globe and Mail*, 23 March 2002, 1. This *Globe* story is in reference to the release of some of Nixon's White House tapes in early 2002.

118 Unattributed source, Briefing Papers for Schultz Dinner, 28 September 1972, Jean Luc Pepin, 'Notes on My Conversation with Secretary Schultz,' 27 July 1972.

119 USNA, DSR, Box 730, file E-1-1 CAN-US, 1/1/71, American Embassy Ottawa to Secretary of State, 1 September 1972.

120 Peyton V. Lyon and Brian W. Tomlin, *Canada as an International Actor* (Toronto: Macmillan, 1979), 108.

121 R.B. Byers, 'External Affairs and Defence,' in John Saywell, ed., *Canadian Annual Review for 1972* (Toronto: University of Toronto Press, 1973) 260.

122 Claude Julien, *Canada: Europe's Last Chance*, trans. Penny Williams (Toronto: Macmillan, 1968), 6.

123 Granatstein and Bothwell, *Pirouette*, 161.

124 R.B. Byers, 'External Affairs and Defence,' in John Saywell, ed., *Canadian Annual Review for 1973* (Toronto: University of Toronto Press, 1974), 222.

125 J. Alex Murray and Lawrence Leduc, *A Cross-Sectional Analysis of Canadian Public Attitudes toward U.S. Equity Investment in Canada* Working Paper No. 2/75, June 1975, 27. Almost 5,000 Canadians were polled.

126 For an account of the rationale of the third option, see Byers, 'External Affairs and Defence' (1974), 221–4. For an account of its failure, see, for example, Granatstein and Bothwell, *Pirouette*, 175–7, 379; Roy Rempel, *Counterweights: The Failure of Canada's German and European Policy, 1955–1995* (Montreal and Kingston: McGill-Queen's University Press, 1996), 81–8; Thomas Axworthy, 'A Singular Voice: The Foreign Policy of Pierre Elliott Trudeau,' in C. David Crenna, ed., *Lifting the Shadow of War* (Edmonton: Hurtig, 1987).

127 Jim Cutt, 'The National Economy,' in John Saywell, ed., *Canadian Annual Review for 1972* (Toronto: University of Toronto Press, 1973), 365.

128 See Barbara Jenkins, *The Paradox of Continental Production: National Investment Policies in North America* (Ithaca, NY: Cornell University Press, 1992), 113–4. As she writes, 'The Gray Report of 1972 [argued] that the large number of branch plants in Canada had led to the "truncation" of the Canadian economy. The authors argued that since these branch plants were only part of the integrated operations of multinational enterprises, they were often bereft of critical parts of the production process, such as R & D, and were left only with assembly and sales operations. For this reason the Gray Report recommended the establishment of a screening process that would monitor the process of foreign corporations in the Canadian economy and pressure them to increase the benefits they provided to the economy.' See also 'One Card Fewer,' *Economist*, 11 December 1971, 55. The periodical asked the question in an editorial, 'Why so angry?' It speculated that 'the irritation arose *just because* the proposed measures were so modest. The reasoning ... is that Canada and America are now engaged in a protracted poker game. Cards are Canada's hard line on gas exports to America, and American refusal to agree that Canada is being unfairly penalized by the Nixon measures. On this reasoning, one of Canada's bargaining points is the threat of stringent controls over American-owned subsidiaries. But this card, it now seems, is only a weak one' (emphasis added). Still, as Robert Bothwell, Ian Drummond, and John English note in *Canada since 1945*, the Gray Report 'was much more hostile and interventionist than the Watkins Report' (345).

129 John Holmes, *Canada: A Middle-Aged Power* (Toronto: McClelland and Stewart, 1976), 253.

130 See John Herd Thompson and Stephen Randall, *Canada and the United States: Ambivalent Allies* (Montreal and Kingston: McGill-Queen's University Press, 1994), 255–6.

131 Bank of Canada, *Annual Report of the Governor to the Minister of Finance for the Year 1973* (Ottawa: Bank of Canada, 1974), 9.

Chapter 4

1 Nick Butler, *The International Grain Trade: Problems and Prospects* (New York: St Martin's Press, 1986), 4.

2 Jon McLin, 'Surrogate International Organization and the Case of World Food Security, 1949–1969,' *International Organization* 33 (1979), 35.

3 Theodore Cohn with Inge Bailey, 'Canadian-American Relations and Agricultural Trade Surpluses: The Case of Barter,' in Irene Sage Knell and John English, eds., *Canadian Agriculture in a Global Context: Opportunities and Obligations* (Waterloo, ON: University of Waterloo Press, 1986), 179. The following table demonstrates the magnitude of the increase in exports from Canada and the United States between 1957 and 1973:

Exports of Wheat (millions of metric tons)

	Canada	US		Canada	US
1957	6.3	11.3	1965	12.0	17.7
1958	7.4	9.0	1966	14.6	22.5
1959	7.2	9.7	1967	9.5	17.5
1960	6.6	13.7	1968	9.3	16.1
1961	10.7	17.4	1969	6.7	12.0
1962	8.0	14.0	1970	10.7	17.4
1963	10.7	17.4	1971	12.9	16.2
1964	13.6	20.6	1972	14.0	21.3
			1973	12.3	37.4

Source: B.R. Mitchell, *International Historical Statistics: The Americas, 1750–1988.* New York: Stockton, 1993, 275.

4 Luther Tweeten, *Foundations of US Farm Policy* (Omaha: University of Nebraska Press, 1979), 34.

5 LAC, DFR, RG 19 (DFR), vol. 4226, file 8800-04-2 vol. 2, 'Background Paper for Meeting of Ministers on 'Food for Peace' Proposals,' n.d.

6 See B.W. Muirhead, *The Development of Postwar Canadian Trade Policy: The Failure of*

the Anglo-European Option (Montreal and Kingston: McGill-Queen's University Press, 1992), 143–58 for a discussion of the decision to award the United States a waiver for its GATT obligations.

7 LAC, DEA-R, vol. 3479, file 9-C-1964-1, 'Disposal of Commodity Surpluses,' 4 March 1955.

8 Patrick Kyba, *Alvin: A Biography of the Honourable Alvin Hamilton, P.C.* (Regina: Canadian Plains Research Center, 1989), 105.

9 USNA, DSR, file 611.42/7-1557, 'Meeting of the Canadian Ambassador with the Secretary,' 15 July 1957. See also W.E. Hamilton and W.M. Drummond, *Wheat Surpluses and Their Impact on Canada–United States Relations* (Canadian-American Committee, 1959), 1. As the authors write, 'The disposal of surplus [wheat] has become a very real problem in United States-Canadian relations.'

10 *Debates*, 10 August 1960, 7891.

11 Embassy Ottawa to Department of State, 12 October 1955, *FRUS 1955–1957,* vol. IX, *Foreign Economic Policy; Foreign Information Program* (Washington DC: GPO, 1987), 155

12 See McLin, 'Surrogate International Organization,' 46. The value of all commodities shipped under PL 480 between 1955 and 1969 totaled about US$204 billion. This was more than the Canadians felt was necessary.

13 Hamilton and Drummond, *Wheat Surpluses*, 2.

14 H. Basil Robinson, *Diefenbaker's World: A Populist in Foreign Affairs* (Toronto: University of Toronto Press, 1989), 16.

15 LAC, Basil Robinson Papers, MG31 E83, J.W. Holmes, 'Report of US Ambassador on Mr. Dulles' Visit,' 31 July 1957. The U.S. practice of liquidating surpluses under PL 480 remained, as did the negotiation of tied wheat sales, where a certain proportion of the deal went as aid with the rest being purchased by the recipient country. However, as a result of these talks, they were relaxed somewhat. See Theodore Cohn, *The International Politics of Agricultural Trade: Canadian-American Relations in a Global Agricultural Context* (Vancouver: UBC Press, 1990), 95.

16 However, Canada did join with the United States in establishing an aid consortium for India in 1958. The North Americans were joined by France, Japan, the United Kingdom, and West Germany in a group that was designed to disburse World Bank assistance to the subcontinent. India, the world's largest democracy and the foil to the example presented by another Asian power, the People's Republic of China, was a special prize.

17 Hamilton and Drummond, *Wheat Surpluses*, 4.

18 DDEL, CFEP Records 1953–54, (Randall Commission) Bennet's Charts and Tables, Box 45, file: Drafts of Report, Staff Report 2, A.P. Toner to General Goodpaster, 13 September 1957.

19 BCA, Louis Rasminsky Papers, LR76-357, 'U.S. Surplus Disposal,' 30 December 1958.

20 DDEL, US Council on Foreign Economic Policy, Office of the Chairman, Records 1954–61, Randall Series, Subject Subseries Box 2, f C(5), 'US-Canadian Economic Relations,' 30 April 1957.

21 USNA, DSR, file 611.42/3-2158, Dillon to Gray, 16 June 1958.

22 BCA, Rasminsky Papers, LR76-452, Misc 'Memorandum of a Meeting with Mr. Heeney,' n.d.

23 *Debates*, 9 August 1956, 7303.

24 *Globe and Mail*, 17 October 1956, 25.

25 'Canadian Reaction to U.S. Foreign Economic Policy,' *FRUS 1955–1957*, vol. 9, 218.

26 DDEL, US Council on Foreign Economic Policy, Office of the Chairman, Records, 1954–61, Randall Series, Subject Subseries, Box 2, f. C(5), Isaiah Frank to Edward Galbreath, 11 January 1957. The Americans reported Isbister's point of view.

27 The newspaper accounts are from USNA, DSR, Foreign Service Dispatch, file 742.00/ 3-1356, Embassy Ottawa to State, 30 November 1956. The embassy in Ottawa had collected these and forwarded them to Washington.

28 USNA, DSR, file 842.00/7-1 757, Ottawa to Department of State, 12 July 1957.

29 LAC, DFR, vol. 4226, file 8800-04-2, vol. 2, 'General Policy of Protection for Agriculture in respect to Imports,' 16 October 1957.

30 LAC, DFR, vol. 4226, file 8800-04-2, vol. 2, 'Report on General Policy of Protection for Agriculture,' 22 November 1957.

31 For a brief discussion of the act, see LAC, DEA-R, vol. 6753, file 428–40 pt. 3.2, 'Briefing Material for the Prime Minister's Commonwealth Tour,' n.d. 'For nine key commodities, the Act requires that a support price of 80 per cent of the base price be maintained at all times. (The base price is the average price of the products during the preceding ten years). These nine commodities represent approximately 65 per cent of the farm cash income apart from western cereal grains. Price support levels for 1958 (expressed as a percentage of the base price) are: steers – 80 percent; hogs – 84 percent; lambs – 80 percent; butter – 107 percent; cheddar cheese – 110 percent; eggs – 85 percent; wheat, oats and barley outside the Canadian Wheat Board area – 80 percent. In addition to these, support prices were also established for eleven other commodities.'

32 LAC, DFR, vol. 4207, file 8718-03-15, A.F.W. Plumptre to Fleming, 'Instructions for the Fifteenth Session of GATT,' 14 October 1959.

33 LAC, DEA-R, vol. 6753, file 11270-40, pt. 2, N.A. Robertson, Washington to External, 13 March 1958.

34 J.L. Granatstein, *Canada, 1957–1967: The Years of Uncertainty and Innovation* (Toronto: McClelland and Stewart, 1986), 38.

35 LAC, DEA-R, vol. 4304, file 11270-40 pt. 3, Washington to External, 31 December 1958.

36 Ibid.

37 Memorandum of Conversation, 'President's Visit to Canada,' 9 July 1958 in *FRUS 1958–1960*, vol. 7, pt. 1, 704.

38 DDEL, CFEP Records 1953–54 (Randall Commission) Bennet's Charts and Tables, Box 45, file: Drafts of Report, Staff Report 2, Toner to Goodpaster, 13 September 1957.

39 'US ... Policies Upheld by Eisenhower,' *Globe and Mail*, 10 July 1958 1.

40 See *Debates*, 9 July 1958, 2084.

41 DDEL, White House Office, Office of the Staff Secretary and Records, 1952–61, L. Arthur Minnich Series, Cabinet Meetings, Index–B–CE, Box 18, Cabinet Meeting 16 January 1959.

42 This practice, where the United States bartered wheat in exchange for minerals for American national security stockpiles, had earlier caused some difficulty for Canada. Ottawa argued that it competed unfairly with commercial exports of wheat and of many of the mineral commodities. And when the United States stopped stockpiling, as it inevitably did, the price of mineral exports collapsed. See McLin, 'Surrogate International Organization,' 56.

43 BCA, Rasminsky Papers, LR76-357, 'Note to the US Government,' 24 November 1958.

44 BCA, Rasminsky Papers, LR76-357, 'US Surplus Disposal,' 30 December 1958.

45 BCA, Rasminsky Papers, LR76-357, Washington to External, 31 December 1958.

46 Ibid.

47 LAC, DFR, vol. 4226, file 8800-04-3, vol. 2, ICETP Doc. 202, 16 April 1959. There was also much speculation that Eisenhower's announcement was to counteract the efforts of Democratic senator Hubert Humphrey from Minnesota, to modify PL 480 and make it more sensitive to the economic needs of developing nations. See Peter A. Toma, *The Politics of Food for Peace: Executive-Legislative Interaction* (Tucson: University of Arizona Press, 1967), 43.

48 LAC, DFR, vol. 4181, file 8522/U575-1 (59), UKCCC (59) 2nd Meeting, 2 July 1959.

49 LAC, DEA-R, vol. 2445, file 50-EO-AG-1-40, vol. 5, Committee on Commodity Problems, Consultative Sub-committee on Surplus Disposal, 27 March 1961.

50 Cohn, *International Politics*, 95.

51 USNA, GATT Box 1398, Memorandum of Conversation, 'GATT Issues,' 29 October 1959.

52 USNA, GATT Box 1399, Memorandum of Conversation, 'GATT Issues,' 3 December 1959.

53 LAC, DEA-R, vol. 6753, file 428-B-40, 'Meeting of Canadian and U.S. Officials on Wheat Problems' 17 September 1959.

54 LAC, Robinson Papers, vol. 3, file: June 1960, Memorandum for the Prime Minister, 2 June 1960.

55 *Debates*, 6 June 1960 4530. He also said that he and the president had spoken 'frankly

about the concern that Canadians [felt] over recent United States wheat surplus disposal policies which damage Canadian wheat export markets.'

56 LAC, Robinson Papers, vol. 3, file: June 1960, 'Notes on Discussion in President Eisenhower's Office,' 3 June 1960.

57 See, for example, Joint United States–Canadian Committee on Trade and Economic Affairs, Washington, 16–17 February 1960, *FRUS 1958–1960*, vol 7, *Western European Integration and Security; Canada* (Washington DC: GPO, 1993), 782.

58 Cohn and Bailey, 'Canadian-American Relations,' 192.

59 BCA, Rasminsky Papers, LR76-358-1, 'Canada-United States Committee on Trade and Economic Affairs,' February 16–17, 1960.

60 BCA, Rasminsky Papers, LR76 358-2, Memo to Cabinet, Canada-United States Committee on Trade and Economic Affairs, 11 February 1960. For the communiqué, see *Debates*, 18 February 1960, 1228–9.

61 LAC, Robinson Papers, vol. 3, June 1960, 'Notes on the Discussion in President Eisenhower's Office, June 3rd 1960,' 17 June 1960.

62 *Debates*, 6 June 1960, 4529.

63 LAC, Robinson Papers, vol. 3, Nov.–Dec. 1960, Memorandum for the Prime Minister, 'President-elect Kennedy,' 10 November 1960.

64 BCA, Rasminsky Papers, LR76-359, Item III(b) (2) United States Import Restrictions – Agriculture, 8 March 1961.

65 Ibid.

66 BCA, Rasminsky Papers, LR76-359, Washington to External, 7 March 1961.

67 C. Ford Runge, 'The United States: Domestic and International Interactions,' in Grace Skogstad and Andrew Fenton Cooper, eds., *Agricultural Trade: Domestic Pressures and International Tensions* (Halifax, NS: Institute for Research on Public Policy, 1990), 61.

68 Peter C. Newman, *Renegade in Power: The Diefenbaker Years* (Toronto: McClelland and Stewart, 1973), 142.

69 Ibid. 142.

70 UKNA, DO 196, vol. 175, 'Record of a Conversation between the Foreign Secretary and Mr. Dean Rusk,' 11 December 1962.

71 LAC, DFR, file 8522/U585-4 (63), Joint Canada–United States Committee on Trade and Economic Affairs, 15 September 1963.

72 JFKL, POF, Box 113A, Canada, Person Visit, S/63, 'Visit of Prime Minister Pearson on May 10–11, 1963,' 9 May 1963.

73 JFKL, POF, Box 91, Departments and Agencies, Treasury, 10/63–11/63, Memorandum for the President, 'US Grain Sales Abroad,' 25 October 1963.

74 USNA, DSR, Classified White House 1963 (2), B. 13C-ES, Bullitt to the Secretary, 17 October 1963.

75 JFKL, POF, Box 91, Departments and Agencies, Treasury 10/63–11/63, Memo to the President, 'US Grain Sales Abroad,' 25 October 1963.

76 Kyba, *Alvin*, 165.

77 LAC, DEA-R, vol. 4304, file 11270-40, pt. 3, Washington to External, 9 October 1963.

78 PCO, Cabinet Conclusions, 'Prime Minister's visit to President Johnson,' 11 December 1963.

79 LAC, DEA-R, vol. 4304, file 11270-40, pt. 3, Washington to External, 10 October 1963.

80 Ibid.

81 Ibid.

82 LAC, DEA-R, vol. 4304, file 11270-40, pt. 3, Washington to External, 9 October 1963.

83 Ibid.

84 PCO, 'International Meeting on Cereals in GATT,' 25 June 1963.

85 GATT Reports Under Waivers, 'United States–Import Restrictions on Agricultural Products,' Report of Working Party adopted on 6 April 1966, vol. 23, 195.

86 Ibid.

87 PCO, Memorandum to the Cabinet, 'Canada-United Kingdom Ministerial Committee on Trade and Economic Affairs,' 11 April 1967.

88 BCA, Rasminsky Papers, LR76-362, Post-Kennedy Round Prospects, Appendix III, Agriculture, June 1967.

89 BCA, Rasminsky Papers, LR76-362, Appendix III, Agriculture, June 1967.

90 Ibid.

91 Cohn, 69.

92 BCA, Rasminsky Papers, LR76-363, Joint Canada-U.S. Ministerial Committee on Trade and Economic Affairs, 'International Grains Arrangement,' 19 June 1969.

93 Andrew Cooper, *In Between Countries: Australia, Canada, and the Search for Order in Agricultural Trade* (Montreal and Kingston: McGill-Queen's University Press, 1997), 33.

94 Donald Forster, 'The National Economy,' in John Saywell, ed., *Canadian Annual Review for 1969* (Toronto: University of Toronto Press, 1970), 357.

95 USNA, DSR, Box 1939, file POL 7 CAN, 1/1/69, Embassy Ottawa to Secretary of State, 20 February 1969.

96 USNA, DSR, Box 591, file E-CAN, 'Deputy Minister's Views on Economy,' 31 July 1969.

97 Cooper, *In Between Countries*, 71. See also Murray Goldblatt, 'Grow Less Wheat PM Tells Western Farmers,' *Globe and Mail*, 15 July 1969, 1 and David Crane, 'World Wheat Price Cut,' *Globe and Mail*, 15 July 1969 1.

98 BCA, Rasminsky Papers, LR76-363, Joint Canada-United States Ministerial Committee on Trade and Economic Affairs, 'International Grains Agreement,' 19 June 1969.

99 Ibid.

100 Cooper, *In Between Countries*, 85.

101 Donald Forster, 'The National Economy,' in John Saywell, ed., *Canadian Annual Review for 1970* (Toronto: University of Toronto Press, 1971), 424–5. See also *Debates*, 5 May 1970, 6569. For an outline of the program, see *Debates*, 27 February 1970, 4159–61.

Chapter 5

1 All trade percentages and numbers are to be found in F.H. Leacy, ed. *Historical Statistics of Canada* (Ottawa: Statistics Canada, 1983), G381–85 to G408–14.

2 See P.J. Madgwick, D. Steeds, and L.J. Williams, *Britain since 1945* (London: Hutchison, 1982), 95. Growth rates of real national income from 1950–64 and from 1955–64 (in parentheses) among a number of countries are as follows: Germany, 7.1 (5.6); Italy 5.6 (5.4); France, 4.9 (5.0); United States, 3.5 (3.1); United Kingdom, 2.6 (2.8)

3 While the North American economic relationship was denounced by the chattering classes resulting in a deluge of books and newspaper and magazine articles condemning it, the electorate ultimately seemed not to mind. Jack Granatstein caught that mood in a 1971 piece written for the *Canadian Annual Review*: 'A sneaking suspicion [exists] that Canadians preferred a prosperous existence – even as a satellite – to a poor but pure nationalism.' See J.L. Granatstein, 'Continentalism and the New Nationalism,' in John Saywell, ed., *Canadian Annual Review, 1970* (Toronto: University of Toronto Press, 1971), 349.

4 USNA, DSR, RG59, Box 76, file 742.00/3-1357, Embassy Ottawa to State Department, 13 March 1957.

5 See B.W. Muirhead, *The Development of Postwar Canadian Trade Policy: The Failure of the Anglo-European Option* (Montreal and Kingston: McGill-Queen's University Press, 1992).

6 H. Basil Robinson, *Diefenbaker's World: A Populist in Foreign Affairs* (Toronto: University of Toronto Press, 1989), 4.

7 BCA, BCR, 3B-305, Douglas LePan to Louis Rasminsky, 12 October 1956.

8 PRO, T236, vol. 5235, HCUK to CRO, 10 September 1957.

9 For a fuller account, see *Debates*, 23 October 1957, 308. In order to increase trade with Britain, the Conservative government sent a 50-person trade mission led by Gordon Churchill to the United Kingdom to explore opportunities. It left on 21 November and returned one month later.

10 PRO, T236, vol. 5235, HCUK to CRO, 10 September 1957.

11 See PRO, DO35, vol. 8731, Minute Sheet, H.J.B. Lintott to Sir G. Laithwaite, 31 October 1957.

12 John Diefenbaker, *One Canada: The Memoirs of the Right Honourable John G. Diefen-baker: The Years of Achievement, 1957–1962* (Toronto: Macmillan, 1976), 74.

13 PRO, DO35, vol. 8381, Visit by the President of the Board of Trade to Canada, 25–27 January 1960.

14 Ibid.

15 *Debates*, 15 November 1957, 1198–9.

16 PRO, T236, vol. 5235, 'Discussion between United Kingdom and Canadian Ministers, 3rd October 1957,' 7 October 1957.

17 PRO, T236, vol. 5235, HCUK to CRO, 10 September 1957.

18 LAC, DFR, vol. 4226, file 8800-04-2, Memorandum for Discussion by Commonwealth Finance Ministers, 9 August 1957.

19 For an analysis of this trend, see BCA, Rasminsky Papers, LR76-665-8, Rasminsky, 'Canada's Trade and Payments with the Sterling Area,' 5 June 1958.

20 BCA, Rasminsky Papers, LR76-667, 'Highlights of UK Trade and Payments with Canada,' 8 July 1959.

21 LAC, DFR, vol. 4181, file 8522/U575-1(58), UKCCC (58), 2nd Meeting, 20 June 1958.

22 BCA, BCR, 5D-400, 'Proposed Opening Statement on Agenda Item III of Mont Tremblant Conference,' 20 September 1957.

23 BCA, BCR, 5D-450, file: Canada-UK Trade Talks, 'Meeting of Commonwealth Finance Ministers,' F.M. 57, 1st Meeting, 28 September 1957.

24 PRO, T236, vol. 4062, Record of an Informal Meeting with Canadian Officials, 30 July 1958.

25 BCA, Rasminsky Papers, LR76-428, Commonwealth Trade and Economic Conference, 1958: Report by Officials, 21 June 1958.

26 LAC, DEA-R, vol. 3445, file 1-1958-2, Brief for Montreal Conference, Progress Towards the Common Objective of Freer Trade and Payments, June 1958. See also Fleming's comments in *Debates*, 17 February 1958, 1239.

27 PRO, CAB 128, vol. 32, C.C. 70 (58).

28 LAC, DEA-R, vol. 3444, file 1-1957-3, Canadian Views on the Trading Arrangements, 26 May 1958. With the Stockholm Convention of November 1959 establishing the EFTA, an effort was made to arrange tariff reductions by the two groups so that discrimination between them was kept to a minimum. For a record of Canadian strategy discussions, see LAC, DFR, vol. 4140, file 8625-01 pt. 2, ICETP, 23 June 1960. See also BCA, Rasminsky Papers, LR76-432, UKCCC, 28–29 June 1960, Brussels to External 17 May 1960. The telegram quoted the EEC's declaration of intention concerning foreign relations between the Community and the EFTA: 'In this framework, the [tariff] negotiations to be undertaken with the members of EFTA ... should preferably be directed towards the maintenance of the traditional trade between the EEC and the countries of the EFTA ... The search for a cooperation of this kind with

a view to a reciprocal reduction in trade barriers must be included ... It is on this basis ... that cooperation can be sought, particularly in the tariff sphere. The EEC recalls its decision made on Nov 24/59 in which it proposed the creation of a contact committee which would enable a watch to be kept on the development of trade flows.'

29 BCA, BCR, SD-400, 'Proposed Opening Statement.'

30 BCA, Rasminsky Papers, LR76-431, 'Canadian Interest in the UK Market,' July 1959.

31 BCA, Rasminsky Papers, LR76-429, C.T.E.C. (58) 3rd Meeting, 16 September 1958.

32 John Hilliker and Donald Barry, *Canada's Department of External Affairs*, vol. 2, *Coming of Age, 1946–1968* (Montreal and Kingston: McGill-Queen's University Press, 1995), 322.

33 LAC, DFR, vol. 4178, file 8522/U575-1 (57), Memorandum for the Prime Minister on Common Market, 26 February 1957. See also Muirhead, 162–77.

34 BCA, Rasminsky Papers, LR76-429, C.T.E.C. (58) 3rd Meeting, 16 September 1958

35 PRO, DO35, vol. 8381, Kenneth McGregor to H.A.F. Rumbold, 31 December 1959.

36 See, for example, PRO, BT11, vol. 5603, E.W. Donahoe, 22 October 1959. See also PRO, BT11, vol. 5603, R.W. Gray, Most Favoured Nation Treatment in the 1947 Exchange of Letters with Canada, 9 July 1959.

37 PRO, BT11, vol. 5730, Sanders to Rumbold, 26 June 1959. See also PRO, DO35, vol. 8381, UKCCC (60) 23 June 1960. A form of inverse preferences was established. For example, Britain eliminated duties on bacon and certain other products from its EFTA partners without extending those concessions to imports from other GATT contracting parties. Canada was also critical of the British attitude in claiming that a member of a free trade area has the right to remove restrictions on imports from fellow members on balance of payments grounds faster than it removes such restrictions from imports of other GATT CPs, and to exempt imports from fellow members from fresh restrictions that might be imposed in a balance of payments crisis.

38 BCA, Rasminsky Papers, LR76-431, C.T.E.C. (58) 3rd Meeting, 16 September 1958.

39 Ibid.

40 BCA, Rasminsky Papers, LR76-434, C.E. (O) (59), 3rd Meeting, 6 May 1959.

41 PRO, DO35, vol. 8381, Frank Lee, Discussions with Mr. Norman Robertson, 2 November 1959.

42 PRO, DO35, vol. 8381, Visit by the President of the Board of Trade to Canada, January 1960. Despite this British condemnation, Roberts noted that 'it was difficult to have firm opinions as to what the Canadian attitude to the Six and Seven problem should be. The position in Europe was changing almost daily.' LAC, DFR, vol. 4190, file 8625-01, pt. 2, ICETP, 23 June 1960.

43 PRO, DO35, vol. 8731, Minute Sheet, H.J.B. Lintott to Sir G. Laithwaite, 31 October 1957.

44 Diefenbaker, *One Canada*, 74.

45 PRO, DO35, vol. 8381, Visit by the President of the Board of Trade to Canada, 25–27 January 1960.
46 Peter C. Newman, *Renegade in Power: The Diefenbaker Years* (Toronto: McClelland and Stewart, 1973), 156.
47 Robert Spencer, 'External Affairs and Defence,' in John Saywell, ed., *Canadian Annual Review for 1960* (Toronto: University of Toronto Press, 1961), 135.
48 Douglas Hartle, 'The Economy,' in ibid., 182.
49 *Globe and Mail,* 12 December 1961, B1.
50 *Debates* 20 June 1961, 6640.
51 PRO, DO35, vol. 8682, UKCCC 28–9 June 1960.
52 LAC, DEA-R, vol. 3448, file 1-1962-1, 'British/EEC Negotiations: Specific Trade Objectives,' 31 August 1962. For an account of the advice given to Diefenbaker by the Canadian high commissioner in London, see J.L. Granatstein, *A Man of Influence: Norman A. Robertson and Canadian Statecraft, 1929–1968* (Toronto: Deneau, 1981), 335.
53 LAC, DFR, vol. 4226, file 8800-04-3, vol. 2, ICETP Document 208, 'European Trade Problems,' 8 September 1960.
54 Sidney Dell, *Trade Blocs and Common Market* (London: Constable, 1963), 86.
55 Muirhead, *Development of Postwar Canadian Trade Policy,* 171–2.

Increases in West Germany's Tariff (per cent)

	West German Tariff in 1960	Proposed Common External Tariff of the EEC
Automobiles	13–16	27–29
Motorcycles	11–14	24–26
Bicycles	9	21
Cameras	4	18
Machinery	0–9	4–17
Linoleum	4	20
Carpets	14–16	22–40

Source: *International Financial News Survey,* 6 May 1960.

56 PRO, DO35, vol. 8381, McGregor to H.A.F. Rumbold, 31 December 1959. See also LAC, DFR, vol. 4190, file 8625-01, pt. 2, ICETP, 22 July 1961 for a Canadian analysis of the effects on Canada of British membership in the EEC.
57 LAC, DEA-R, vol. 3448, file 1-2-1961-1, Memorandum to Cabinet, 'Possible United Kingdom Association with the Six: Further Consultations with the United Kingdom,' 22 August 1961.
58 BCA, Rasminsky Papers, LR76-422, 'Regional Trading Arrangements in Europe and

the Aluminum Industry in Canada and the United States,' n.d. Canadian exports to the EEC increased from 46,500 short tons in 1958 to 112,700 short tons in 1960, a rise of 240 per cent. During the same period, U.S. exports rose from 2,450 short tons to approximately 107,000, a more than 4,000 per cent increase. Such a situation had already occurred with synthetic rubber in what had become a very important market for Canada. In early 1958, the French, who had been taking about 25 per cent of Canadian production, had stopped buying. This had outraged the Canadians, and Mitchell Sharp, then deputy minister of trade and commerce, had telephoned the French trade commissioner in Ottawa, Emile Lacoste, to make that point and to emphasize that this decision ran contrary to the GATT. The reason Sharp was given to explain the situation was that France had built its own factories. See Quai d'Orsay Archives, Paris, série: Amérique, 1952–1963, sous-série: Canada, vol. 59, file: 8 janvier 1958–3 décembre 1959, Sharp à Lacoste, 21 mars 1958.

59 Bank of England Archives, London, England, Bank of England Records (BER), OV47/46 78 cp=17, 'Economic Implications for Canada of the United Kingdom Joining the Common Market,' 26 August 1961. The percentages for these products were: wheat – 34 per cent; flour – 36 per cent; oil seeds – 38 per cent; apples – 41 per cent; barley – 56 per cent; tobacco – 86 per cent; cheese – 90 per cent.

60 BCA, Rasminsky Papers, LR76-438, Commonwealth Economic Consultative Committee, 20–1 September 1960, 31.

61 PRO, T299, vol. 187, 'The UK's Observations on Cereals,' 23 March 1962. See also LAC, DEA-R, vol. 3448, file 1-1962-1, London to External, for an account of the Canadian reaction to the negotiations in this area.

62 For a good account of the sale to China, see Patrick Kyba, *Alvin: A Biography of the Honourable Alvin Hamilton, P.C.* (Regina: Canadian Plains Research Center, 1989), 163–71. For an account of the sales to Communist Europe, see John Saywell, ed., *Canadian Annual Review for 1962(–1969)* (Toronto: University of Toronto Press, 1963[–1970]. Kyba also deals with the growing unhappiness in Western Canada among prairie farmers with the Conservative government of John Diefenbaker. With one of 'their own' in power, they expected better, but, constrained by financial difficulties and a deteriorating economic situation, the government did not come through in the way farmers had hoped. Michael Barkway, in a *Toronto Star* article written in August 1960, commented on the 'general disillusionment with the Diefenbaker government [that] is evident throughout the Western provinces.' Quoted in Kyba, *Alvin*, 162. See also Karen Minden, 'Politics and Business: The Canada-China Wheat Trade, 1960–84,' in Irene Knell and John English, eds., *Canadian Agriculture in a Global Context: Opportunities and Obligations* (Waterloo, ON: University of Waterloo Press, 1986), 103–22.

63 PRO, PREM 11/3559, Macmillan to Lord Privy Seal, 29 July 1961.

64 LAC, DEA-R, vol. 3479, file 9-C-1964/1, L.D. Wilgress, 'The Free Trade Area in

Europe,' n.d. See also 'European Economic and Political Developments,' 26 November 1963 in *FRU.S, 1961–1963*, vol. 13, 237. The Germans had the same idea. During a meeting in Washington between Chancellor Erhard and some senior American officials, the former noted that 'When de Gaulle speaks of Europe, he has in mind a power bloc that would be independent of the United States. His order of priorities is (1) a strong France, (2) a solid French-German relationship, (3) a powerful Europe, and lastly, (4) trans-Atlantic ties.'

65 BCA, Rasminsky Papers, LR76-358-2, 'Canada-U.S. Committee on Trade and Economic Affairs, Washington, 16–17 February 1960.'

66 BCA, Rasminsky Papers, LR76-436, Commonwealth Economic Consultative Council, C.E. (O) (61), 3rd meeting, 27 April 1960.

67 PRO, T299, vol. 184, Ottawa to CRO, 14 August 1962. For the Canadian position, see LAC, DFR, vol. 4226, file 8800-04-2, R.B. Bryce, 'Possible United Kingdom Association with the EEC,' Memorandum to Cabinet, 28 June 1961.

68 BCA, Rasminsky Papers, LR76-440, Meeting of Canadian Ministers with the Right Honourable Duncan Sandys, 13 July 1961. See also PRO, T236, vol. 6549, 'Political Aspects of United Kingdom Membership of the EEC,' June 1961. This document noted that the 'long-term political advantages of membership of the EEC are so strong that they outweigh ... the disadvantages involved.' See also PRO, PREM11, vol. 3558, Sandys to Macmillan, 15 July 1961.

69 BCA, Rasminsky Papers, LR76-438, C.E.C.C., 20–1 September 1960, 31.

70 PRO, T236, vol. 6549, 'The Problem of the Six and Seven,' 6 February 1961.

71 For and account of business attitudes following the French rejection of Britain's application, see *Globe and Mail*, 30 January 1963, 17. In an article headlined 'Some Sad, Some Glad that European Common Market Snubs UK,' the reporter suggested that Canadian business leaders appear to be disappointed by the failure of Britain to gain membership in the European Common Market.' For example, Victor Oland, the president of the Canadian Chamber of Commerce, was quoted as saying 'Britain's exclusion from the EEC is most unfortunate ... Canadian trade might have been hurt a little in the short term ... In the long run, her entry would have been of benefit to Canada.'

72 PRO, T236, vol. 6549, Ottawa to CRO, 5 June 1961.

73 For Fleming's account of this, see Donald Fleming, *So Very Near: The Political Memoirs of the Honourable Donald M. Fleming*, vol. 2, *The Summit Years* (Toronto: University of Toronto Press, 1985), 389–96. He offers a different version of reality. Rather than hindering Britain's application, he claims that 'it is possible that the stand I took at Accra assisted Britain to obtain better terms from the Six and these made it politically possible for her to enter the Common Market without disrupting the Commonwealth.' He suggests that newspaper accounts of him having 'led' the ganging up on Britain at Accra were nothing more than a Liberal-orchestrated distortion of the truth.

74 Newman, *Renegade in Power*, 124.

75 Harold Macmillan, *At the End of the Day, 1961–1963* (London: Macmillan, 1973), 29.

76 LAC, DFR, vol. 4227, file 8800-04-4, pt. 1, Canadian Embassy Vienna to External, 19 September 1961.

77 LAC, Robinson Papers, MG31E 83, vol. 5, file: March 1962-5-19, 'Prime Minister's Conversations with Lord Amory,' 15 March 1962.

78 PRO, T236, vol. 6549, HCUK to CRO, 12 June 1961. See also Robinson, *Diefenbaker's World*, 203.

79 J.L. Granatstein, *Canada, 1957–1967: The Years of Uncertainty and Innovation* (Toronto: McClelland and Stewart, 1986), 53.

80 LAC, Robinson Papers, vol. 5, file: March 1962-5-19, 'Prime Minister's Conversations with Lord Amory,' 21 March 1962.

81 PRO, T299, vol. 186, Commonwealth Conference, 11 September 1962.

82 Granatstein, *Canada, 1957–1967*, 54.

83 PRO, T299, vol. 184, Ottawa to CRO, 21 August 1962.

84 PRO, T299, vol. 183, Ottawa to CRO, 15 March 1962.

85 Robert Spencer, 'Foreign Affairs and Defence,' in John Saywell, ed., *The Canadian Annual Review for 1961* (Toronto: University of Toronto Press, 1962), 166.

86 Donald Forster, 'The National Economy,' in John Saywell, ed., *Canadian Annual Review for 1963* (Toronto: University of Toronto Press, 1964), 213.

87 PRO, PREM/11, vol. 4121, Brief for Mr. Diefenbaker's Visit, February 1963.

88 John Campbell, *Edward Heath: A Biography* (London: Jonathan Cape, 1993), 125.

89 PRO, BT11, vol. 6056, Canada's Trade with Britain, 1964.

90 For an account of this, see Bruce Muirhead, *Against the Odds: The Public Life and Times of Louis Rasminsky* (Toronto: University of Toronto Press, 1999).

91 PRO, BT11, vol. 6056, Brief for the Minister's State Visit to Canada,' n.d.

92 In 1963, Canada's trade surplus with the United Kingdom was CAN$480 million, in 1964, CAN$600 million, and in 1965, CAN$451 million.

93 Mitchell Sharp, *Which Reminds Me: A Memoir* (Toronto: University of Toronto Press, 1994), 117.

94 USNA, NSF, Box 18, file: Canada – General, 5/4/63 – 5/31/63, Memorandum of Conversation, 'Canadian Internal, Trade and Defense Affairs,' 23 May 1963.

95 Ben Pimlott, *Harold Wilson* (London: HarperCollins, 1993), 433.

96 Harold Wilson, *The Labour Government, 1964–1970: A Personal Record* (London: Weidenfeld and Nicholson and Michael Joseph, 1971), 117.

97 PRO, BT11, vol. 6056, Brief for Minister of State's Visit to Canada – June 1963, 29 May 1963. See also BCA, Rasminsky Papers LR76-443-5, Canada's Trade with Britain, 1964.

98 PRO, BT11, vol. 6057, Note for the Record, 11 March 1964.

99 BCA, BCR, 4D-101, Washington, DC to External, 23 October 1964.

100 BCA, Rasminsky Papers, LR76-444-22, A.F.W. Plumptre, 'Notes on Conversations in London,' 4 November 1964.

101 PRO, BT11, vol. 6056, R. McC. Samples, 'Tactics on the Economic Front,' 14 May 1963. However, when Lionel Chevrier, Canada's newly appointed high commissioner in London, visited the president of the board of trade, Douglas Jay, the latter spoke with some vehemence of Britain's export drive and also complained of Canadian blockages to U.K. exports. See PRO, BCR, 4D-101, London to External, 13 November 1964.

102 PRO, BT11, vol. 6056, Brief for Minister of State's Visit to Canada.

103 Ibid.

104 LAC, DFR, vol. 4190, file 8625-01, pt. 2, ICETP, 23 June 1960.

105 See PRO, BT11, vol. 6269, UKCCC (64) A.7, 'Motor Cars,' June 1964. Car manufacturers in the United Kingdom argued that the minimum Canadian price of list less 22.5 per cent that was based on the British list price less trade discounts should be adjusted to allow for the fact that the Canadian importer did not get as much for his money as the home distributor in the United Kingdom. The latter received with the vehicle certain facilities, the cost of which has been included by the manufacturer in arriving at the selling price. The facilities, including sales and service assistance from the factory and warranty claims administration, had to be provided in Canada by the importer, and an allowance should be made for their duplication, since they were charged for by the factory in the selling price on the British home market – that is, the price on which the Canadian 'fair market value' was assessed.

106 PRO, BT11, vol. 6056, Kenneth MacGregor to Bill, 27 February 1963.

107 PRO, BT11, vol. 6414, Mr. Mitchell Sharp's courtesy call on the President, 1st December, 1964.

108 PRO, BT11, vol. 6056, The Canadian Method of Valuation for Duty and Their Automatic Anti-Dumping Duty, 25 June 1963.

109 PRO, BT11, vol. 6056, Lionel Lightman, Confidential Minute, 19 April 1963.

110 PRO, BT11, vol. 6056, Lightman to Mervyn Trenaman, 29 April 1963.

111 PRO, BT11, vol. 6353, Note for a Meeting Between the President and the Hon. Lionel Chevrier, High Commissioner for Canada, Friday 13th November 1964. Emphasis added.

112 The current account deficit, of which a good portion was comprised of the country's overall trade deficit, had been the subject of study during 1965. The then minister of finance, Walter Gordon, had initiated a study 'to examine the character and cause of the current account deficit and consider what steps can be taken to correct it.' See for example, BCA, BCR, 4B-300, 'Projection of the Canadian Balance of Payments to 1970,' 30 December 1965.

113 PRO, CAB 128/39, 'Economic Situation.' See also PRO, PREM 13, vol. 851, UKCCC (65), 19 May 1965.

114 BCA, BCR, 4D-101, London to External, 15 April 1964.

115 BCA, BCR, 4D-101, External to London, 31 October 1964. See also Oslo to External, 30 October 1964. The Norwegians, bitterly opposed to the surcharges, told Canadian embassy staffers in Oslo that they had been very pleased to find in their files British comment on the similar Canadian action in 1962, 'and that they had been able to use some of these comments almost verbatim in present situation.'

116 PRO, BT11, vol. 6414, Note of a Meeting with Mr. Mitchell Sharp, 2 December 1964. The Kennedy round, 1963–7, was the first of the modern GATT rounds to reduce tariffs. It was deemed to have been very successful, and the primary benefit to Canada was because of its negotiations with the United States.

117 See PRO, BT11 vol. 6310, Charles de Hoghton, Committee for Exports to Canada, 'Notes on a Visit to Canada,' December 1964. In an extended essay, de Hoghton records his impressions following a trip to Canada. 'The celebrated complaints about bad British deliveries may often be as fairly attributed to poor forward planning on the Canadian side as to sluggishness or maladministration on the British ... Essentially extraneous factors apart (the anti-dumping legislation), the toughness of the Canadian market could be significantly mitigated by greater understanding of what I have called the strategic questions, by greater use by smaller British firms of co-operative export efforts and marketing services offered by specialist firms and by a strengthening of our representation on the ground.'

118 PRO, BT11, vol. 6056, R. Samples, Memorandum, 14 May 1963.

119 PRO, BT11, vol. 6058, 'Note of a Conversation with Mr. Norman Robertson, 15th October, 1964.'

120 Tom Keating, *Canada and World Order: The Multilateral Tradition in Canadian Foreign Policy* (Toronto: McClelland and Stewart, 1993), 142.

121 PRO, BT11 vol. 6058, Currall to Carter, 25 February 1965.

122 PRO, BT11, vol. 6761, 'Canada: Visit of the President of the Board of Trade from 25–27 May 1966,' 9 June 1966.

123 PRO, BT11, vol. 6058, UKCCC (65) Brief no. 9, May 1965.

124 *Debates*, 26 April 1965, 438–9.

125 PRO, BT11, vol. 6523, 'Meeting with Mr. L Chapin, Minister/Counsellor (Economic) Canadian High Commission London,' 23 November 1965.

126 PRO, BT11, vol. 6058, Lintott to Secretary of State for Commonwealth Relations, 16 November 1965.

127 PRO, BT11, vol. 6525, C.W. Sanders, 'Visit to Canada, September 1966,' 23 September 1966.

128 The final result in 1965 and (1963) were Liberal – 131 (129); Conservative – 97 (95); New Democrats – 21 (17); Créditiste – 9; Social Credit – 5 (24).

129 PRO, BT11, vol. 6523, Minute Sheet, W. Hughes, 15 November 1965.

130 Granatstein, *Canada, 1957–1967*, 205.

131 LJPL, NSF, Box 165, Country File – Canada Memos, vol. 2, D.K. to McGeorge Bundy, 19 January 1965.

132 PCO, 'Canada-U.S.A Negotiations: Automotive Industry,' 21 December 1964.

133 Nor would the Canadians go even part way, at least so the British thought. An excellent opportunity for Ottawa to demonstrate goodwill was to purchase the HS-125, a British military aircraft. Instead, the government bought the French-made Mystère Falcon despite the lower cost of the HS-125 and the roughly equal technical performance of the two aircraft. The Canadian purchase was the subject of a prime minister to prime minister letter. The British thought that the HS-125 'provided a good opportunity for the Canadian government to give a practical demonstration of its readiness to lessen the trade gap and seize an opportunity of influencing official procurement policy which they usually declare themselves ready to do in suitable cases.' See PRO, BT11, vol. 6760, Ottawa to CRO, 16 May 1966.

134 PRO, BT11, vol. 6525, 'Section 37A,' 14 November 1966.

135 PRO, PREM 13, vol. 852, Nicholas Kaldor, 'Causes of Low Rate of Economic Growth in the United Kingdom,' 12 April 1966.

136 Tony Benn, *The Benn Diaries*, Ruth Winstone, ed. (London: Hutchison, 1995), 121.

137 PRO, BT241, vol. 767, letters to R.C. Lightbourne and W. Andrew Rose, June 1966.

138 This agreement covered the duty-free entry into Britain of specified percentages of New Zealand dairy products, meat, apples, pears, and butter in return for Wellington's guaranteed margins of preference for certain British products.

139 PRO, BT241, vol. 767, Foreign Office to Bonn, 23 June 1966. However, given New Zealand's special relationship with Britain, it was also unanimously agreed by EEC governments that it would be given some sort of exceptional treatment following Britain's adhesion to the Treaty of Rome.

140 PCO, 'Canada–United Kingdom Ministerial Committee on Trade and Economic Affairs,' 2 May 1967.

141 PCO, 'Canada–United Kingdom Ministerial Committee,' 13 April 1967.

142 BCA, Rasminsky Papers, LR76-362, Joint Canada–United States Ministerial Committee on Trade and Economic Affairs, 'Britain and the EEC,' June 1967.

143 Ibid.

144 USNA, DSR, RG 56, Box 595, file E-1-CAN-US, American Embassy Ottawa to State, 4 May 1967.

145 PRO, BT11, vol. 6761, 'The High Commissioner's Dinner Party for Mr. Douglas Jay,' 27 May 1966.

146 J.L. Granatstein, 'External Affairs and Defence,' in John Saywell, ed., *Canadian Annual Review for 1968* (Toronto: University of Toronto Press, 1969), 257.

147 John W. Holmes, *The Better Part of Valour: Essays on Canadian Diplomacy* (Toronto: McClelland and Stewart, 1970), 103. See also John Holmes, *Canada: A Middle-Aged Power* (Toronto: McClelland and Stewart, 1976), 147–60.

148 Charles Ritchie, *Storm Signals: More Undiplomatic Diaries, 1962–1971* (Toronto: Macmillan, 1983), 90. See also Paul Martin, *A Very Public Life*, vol. 2, *So Many Worlds* (Toronto: Deneau, 1985), 419–20. As Martin remembered, when he gave up External Affairs he did so 'at the close of an era,' when 'the new Britain tended to be more orientated towards Europe, and Pierre Trudeau, certainly, was less conscious of our links to the United Kingdom.'

149 Ritchie, *Storm Signals*, 129.

150 Ibid., 114.

151 Hilliker and Barry, *Canada: Department of External Affairs*, 2: 323.

152 For an account of this, see ibid., 322–6.

153 PCO, Memorandum to the Cabinet, 'Canada–United Kingdom Ministerial Committee on Trade and Economic Affairs,' 11 April 1967.

154 PRO, BT11, vol. 6758, Minute Sheet, C.W. Sanders, 9 May 1967.

155 Wilson, *Labour Government*, 503.

156 BCA, Rasminsky Papers, LR76-446-22-1, A.B. Hockin to R.B. Bryce, 17 June 1968.

157 For another point of view, See John Holmes, 'Shadow and Substance: Diplomatic Relations between Britain and Canada,' in Holmes, *Canada: A Middle-Aged Power*, 147–60. Holmes argues that despite a changing international context, Britain and Canada had much in common and should re-evaluate their relationship. The article, written in 1971, is clearly dated.

158 BCA, Rasminsky Papers, LR76-543-33, Ritchie to Rasminsky, 30 October 1970.

159 For an account of Britain, the Commonwealth, and Canada, see Margaret Doxey, 'Canada and the Commonwealth,' in John English and Norman Hillmer, eds., *Making a Difference? Canada's Foreign Policy in a Changing World Order* (Toronto: Lester, 1992), 34–53. See also, Doxey, 'Canada and the Commonwealth,' in Paul Painchaud, ed., *From Mackenzie King to Pierre Trudeau: Forty Years of Canadian Diplomacy* (Quebec: Presses de l'Université Laval, 1989). For the opinions of Trudeau and Sharp, see PRO, OD 27, vol. 17, 'The United Kingdom and the European Communities,' 15 July 1971.

Chapter 6

1 *Debates*, 22 January 1962, 44. For a discussion of the idea of a North Atlantic Community, see, for example, John Holmes, 'Odd Man Out in the Atlantic Community,' in John Holmes, *Canada: A Middle-Aged Power* (Toronto: McClelland and Stewart, 1976), 126–37; Kim Richard Nossel, 'A European Nation? The Life and Times of Atlanticism in Canada,' in John English and Norman Hillmer, eds., *Making a Difference? Canada's Foreign Policy in a Changing World* (Toronto: Lester, 1992), 79–102; Michael Tucker, *Canadian Foreign Policy: Contemporary Issues and Themes* (Toronto: McGraw-Hill Ryerson, 1980), 126–8. For the Pearsonian view of the North Atlantic

Community, see 'At the Atlantic Award Dinner, 11 June 1966,' in Lester B. Pearson, *Words and Occasions* (Toronto: University of Toronto Press, 1970), 254–59.

2 For an account of U.S. backsliding, see B.W. Muirhead *The Development of Postwar Canadian Trade Policy: The Failure of the Anglo-European Option* (Montreal and Kingston: McGill-Queen's University Press, 1992), 146–58. Canada was not above ignoring its GATT commitments when pressed. For example, in the summer of 1962, the government imposed a surcharge on CAN$3 billion worth of imports without prior consultation with the General Agreement, which was required under GATT rules. Peyton Lyon argued that 'the damage done to the Canadian reputation as the most consistent and emphatic advocates of multilateral trade' was great. Canadians could no longer adopt a holier-than-thou attitude toward the Europeans. But, of course, they continued to do so. See Tom Keating, *Canada and World Order: The Multilateralist Tradition in Canadian Foreign Policy* (Toronto: McClelland and Stewart, 1993), 137.

3 LAC, DFR, vol. 4226, file 8800-04-2, ICETP, 9 June 1961. For a clear statement of U.S. views, see LAC, DFR, vol. 4227, file 8800-04-4, pt. 1, Canadian Embassy Washington to External, 28 September 1961.

4 Holmes, 'Odd Man Out,' 130. See also BCA, Louis Rasminsky Papers, LR76-436, Commonwealth Economic Consultative Council, C.E. (O) (60) 4th meeting, 27 April 1960. J.H. Warren, the assistant deputy minister of trade and commerce, told the council that 'Reference has been made to the burgeoning economic strength of Europe and there was always a danger that Europe, instead of giving liberal world leadership in commercial policy matters, would tend to become a narrow regional *bloc* and, therefore, other countries could not be committed to support the long-term aim of a wider free trade area at this stage.'

5 BCA, Rasminsky Papers, LR 76-363, Joint Canada–United States Ministerial Committee on Trade and Economic Affairs, 'Post Kennedy Round Trade Problems and Liberalization,' 19 June 1969.

6 For an account of this, see Muirhead, *Development of Postwar Canadian Trade Policy*.

7 BCA, Rasminsky Papers, LR76-436, Commonwealth Economic Consultative Council, C.E. (O) (60) 1st meeting, 26 April 1960.

8 Donald Fleming, *So Very Near: The Political Memoirs of the Honourable Donald M. Fleming*, vol. 2, *The Summit Years* (Toronto: McClelland and Stewart, 1985), 138.

9 PRO, PREM11, vol. 4665, 'Extract of Record of Talk Between Prime Minister and Mr. Pearson,' 10 February 1964.

10 'European Economic and Political Developments,' 26 November 1963 in *FRUS 1961–1963* (Washington, DC: GPO, 1994), 237. A reason for French hostility toward the United Kingdom, and perhaps as background for the 'Trojan horse' comment, lay in a rebuff that de Gaulle had suffered at the hands of British prime minister Harold Macmillan. According to *Le Monde*, 27 November 1963, 'The Nassau Accords [of 19 December 1962] appear to have played a decisive role in De Gaulle's attitude

toward the British candidacy [for the EEC]. In the course of Macmillan's visit to Rambouillet a few days before Nassau, the General made the suggestion to him, which the Prime Minister left unanswered, concerning the joint production of strategic missiles; instead, Macmillan hastened to negotiate with Kennedy with the exclusion of France the replacement of Skybolt missiles ... by the Polaris.' The French believed that the United Kingdom would rely on the United States for defence and would limit its ties to Europe to purely economic concerns. See Bela Balassa, *Trade Liberalization among Industrial Countries* (New York: McGraw-Hill, 1967), 28.

11 Andrew Cooper, *In Between Countries: Australia, Canada and the Search for Order in Agricultural Trade* (Montreal and Kingston: McGill-Queen's University Press, 1997), 35. For a brief account of the Haberler Report, see Fred H. Sanderson, 'Agriculture and Multilateralism,' in Orin Kirshner, ed., *The Bretton Woods-GATT System: Retrospect and Prospect After Fifty Years* (Armonk, NY: M.E. Sharpe, 1996), 262.

12 BCA, Rasminsky Papers, LR76 358-2, 'Canada-U.S. Committee on Trade and Economic Affairs, Washington, February 16–17, 1960.' An American congressman, Frank Chelf, representing a tobacco-growing district in Kentucky, used more colourful language in a letter he wrote on his constituents' behalf to Secretary of State Christian Herter as the Six moved to impose a 30 per cent tariff on the import of Kentucky's Burley tobacco: 'The American people – my good people if you please – after World War II helped to put food in the mouths, clothes on the backs, rattling money in the pockets, roofs over the heads, and smiles on the faces of these very same people who today unwittingly are seeking to nail my little tobacco farmers to the cross of financial ruin. This is not 'biting the hand that feeds' – it is literally chewing both arms off clear up to the shoulder.' See Quai d'Orsay Archives, DE-CE, vol. 655, Chelf to Herter, 4 April 1960.

13 LAC, DFR, vol. 4226, file 8800-0402, ICETP, 10 May 1960.

14 LAC, DTC, vol. 463, file: GATT 19–Session, 'Instructions for the Canadian Delegation to the Nineteenth Session of the Contracting Parties,' 8 November 1961. See also Quai d'Orsay Archives, DE-CE, vol. 31, GATT A-10-13, Dossier-Général juin–décembre 1960. Hector McKinnon, the chair of Canada's GATT delegation, in the run-up to the tariff negotiations, noted in his opening address that 'les travaux qui nous retiendront avant la nouvelle année et plus particulièrement la renégociation des concessions tarifaires de la Communauté économique européenne, sont d'une importance vitale ... Nous avons de interêts commerciaux considerables en Europe et en dehors de l'Europe: nous sommes ici pour proteger et pour défendre ces interêts.' See also DE-CE, vol. 31, M. Wormser, 'Instructions Pour la Délégation Francaise à la XVIIIème Session du GATT,' 31 octobre–18 novembre 1960. Point VIII–CEE for the French point of view. This denunciation of agricultural protectionism was also an old Canadian song. For example, while the CAP was an as yet unnamed policy in 1959, Jake Warren had told a meeting with Americans that Canada was concerned that the

Six 'might maintain [quantitative import restrictions] on a discriminatory basis in the agricultural field.' When the Americans said that they did not see this as an issue, Warren pointed out that 'the problem already exists.' USNA, GATT Box 1398, file 394.41/10-2959, Department of State, Memorandum of Conversation, 'GATT Issues,' 29 October 1959.

15 BCA, Rasminsky Papers LR76-358-1, Joint Canada-U.S. Committee on Trade and Economic Affairs, 17 February 1960. See also BCA, Rasminsky Papers LR76-359, Joint Canada-U.S. Committee on Trade and Economic Affairs, 'GATT Negotiations,' 8 March 1961. Even a year later, progress in the Dillon round had been 'disappointingly slow.'

16 LAC, DEA-R, vol. 6753, file 428-40, pt.3.2, Warren to Roberts, 15 September 1960.

17 BCA, Rasminsky Papers, LR 76-359, Joint Canada-U.S. Committee on Trade and Economic Affairs, Item III(d) – GATT Negotiations, 8 March 1961.

18 LAC, Basil Robinson Papers, vol. 3, June 1960, 'Conversation with President Eisenhower,' 2 June 1960.

19 However, the department of agriculture was also very interested in protecting U.S. farmers from foreign competition in the domestic market.

20 LAC, DEA-R, vol. 4304, file 11270-40, pt. 3, External to Paris, Bonn, Brussels, Washington DC, 25 May 1962.

21 Peyton Lyon, *The Policy Question: A Critical Appraisal of Canada's Role in World Affairs* (Toronto: McClelland and Stewart, 1963), 104.

22 John Evans, *The Kennedy Round in American Trade Policy: The Twilight of the GATT?* (Cambridge: Harvard University Press, 1971), 161. By 'impotence,' Evans means that the U.S. delegation was constrained by legislation as to how large a percentage reduction in any given item it could negotiate.

23 See USNA, Special Trade and Economic Program, file: 1947–1963, Bureau of International Commerce, Office of International Regional Economics, European Division/Canadian Section, 'Conversations with Canadian Embassy re: GATT Tariff Negotiations,' 26 July 1960. Prior to the negotiations, the Canadians had been more hopeful. For example, Thomas Burns, Canada's commercial counsellor in Washington, had been instructed to tell members of the U.S. trade agreements committee, then developing request lists for the U.S. tariff discussions, that if the Americans '[laid] a good-sized offer on the table at Geneva ... you will find that we will make a serious effort to match it.'

24 BCA, Rasminsky Papers, LR76-440, CECC Ministerial Meeting, Accra, September 7, 1961, 'Tariff Negotiations and Future Plans.'

25 Ronald Anderson, 'Fears High European Entry Fee,' *Globe and Mail*, 30 March 1962, B-1.

26 Donald Fleming suggests in his memoirs that he played an indispensable role in the birth of the OECD, that he gave the crucial speech at the right time, enabling twenty

squabbling nations to proceed. See Fleming, 138–44. He was also elected by the twenty countries comprising its membership as the organization's first chairman. See also LAC, Robinson Papers, vol. 4, file: Feb 1961, Norman Robertson, Memorandum for the Prime Minister, 'Your Meeting with President Kennedy,' 17 February 1961. In the memo, Robertson writes that 'There have been clear indications in recent weeks that the new United States Administration intends to give strong support and impetus to the OECD and that it looks to the new Organization to provide an effective forum for developing economic and financial policies both in Europe and in North America ... [however] opposition to approval of the OECD Convention [has] developed in Congress. Criticism of the OECD appears to be rather more vigorous and organized than anticipated. Protectionist interests in the United States have consistently opposed United States membership in any international organization with responsibilities in the trade field.' See also BCA, BCR, 3C-300, Washington to External, 15 May 1961.

27 LAC, DFR, vol. 4203, file 8710-01, Canadian Embassy Brussels to External, 3 August 1959. The 'GATT mit uns' comment is a play on words. With the exchange of one letter, GATT becomes Gott, and 'Gott mit uns' was the phrase on the belt buckles of soldiers in Imperial Germany. Clearly, God (and GATT) were with Hallstein and the EEC.

28 LAC, DFR, vol. 4225, file 8800-04-1, 'The Political Implications of a United Kingdom Move into Europe,' 9 June 1961.

29 BCA, Rasminsky Papers, LR76-358-2, 'Canada-U.S. Committee 16–17 February 1960.' The Canadians believed that American protectionism was on the rise, and that the OECD could help to moderate it. By early 1961, President Kennedy had announced a program for improving the U.S. balance of payments situation. As a Canadian document noted, 'The success of this program will depend to a considerable degree on the extent to which the major Western European countries pursue compatible policies. The OECD recognizes this interdependence of national economies. It will provide a forum for regular and continuing consultation and review of the economic and financial policies pursued by member governments.'

30 BCA, Rasminsky Papers, LR76-359, Joint Canada-US Committee on Trade and Economic Affairs, 'EFTA, EEC and Related Problems,' March 1961.

31 For a good discussion of the CAP, see Alex Cairncross, et al., *Economic Policy for the European Community: The Way Forward* (London: Macmillan, 1974), 90–115.

32 LAC, DEA-R, vol. 3479, file 9-C-1964/1, 'The Implications for Canadian Export Trade of the Measures Taken by the EEC Countries toward Their Full Integration,' n.d.

33 'Common Agricultural Policy of the EEC,' 17 May 1961 in *FRUS 1961–1963*, vol. 13, 15. There was a huge drop in U.S. exports to the EEC in protected commodities. For example, in 1965–6, before the variable levy was imposed, American exports of rice and grains to the Community totalled U.S.$708 million. In 1968–9, they totalled

US$327 million. See Joan Edelman Spero, *The Politics of International Economic Relations* (New York: St Martin's Press, 1981), 86.

34 Quai d'Orsay Archives, DE-CE, vol. 655, file A-30-6, Marché Commun nov 1959–déc 1960, 'Aide-mémoire,' 17 novembre 1959. See also ibid., 'Aide-mémoire du Gouvernement américaine concernant la discussion éventuelle de la politique agricole commune au GATT,' 8 octobre 1960. The Americans had told the French that the CAP was of such importance to the United States that it should be submitted for discussion to the GATT. Their *aide-mémoire* ended: 'The failure of the EEC representative at the 17th session of the GATT to indicate that the EEC is prepared to discuss the common agricultural policy in GATT could only be interpreted by the United States as a significant indication that the EEC proposes to follow restrictive agricultural policies which would be damaging to United States interests. Subsequent US comments and actions would have to reflect this new appraisal.'

35 Quai d'Orsay Archives, Série: Amérique, sous-série: Canada, vol. 59, file: 8 janvier 1958–3 décembre 1959, Lacoste à Couve de Murville, 30 mars 1959.

36 Cooper, *In Between Countries*, 31.

37 LAC, Robinson Papers, vol. 1, August 28, 1957, John Holmes to Robinson, 31 July 1957. The Conservatives had not been in power very long when, in a meeting with the U.S. secretary of state, John Foster Dulles, Donald Fleming, Canada's minister of finance, complained loudly about the wheat surplus disposals program of the United States. In response, Dulles said that 'he wished Canadian Ministers to understand the purposes of this action. He said that they recognized the difficulties caused some of their friends. However, these policies had been pursued for general international purposes with which he was sure the Canadian Government would be in agreement. If, as he expected, the US would cease disposing of agricultural goods in this way, Canada would find itself with still greater problems connected with such surpluses. The US had been using this policy for the most part to help countries like India and Pakistan which were in desperate need and which would be in a very serious position if they did not receive such assistance ... In reply to Mr. Fleming's statement that Canadians particularly objected to the fact that these disposal agreements negotiated with the US tied the market of the recipient countries to the American purchase in the future, Mr Merchant [the US ambassador in Canada] said that he told Mr. Fleming that this was true in only a very few cases, that out of a hundred or more such agreements, he knew of only about four in which there was such provision. Mr. Fleming said that he had not understood this to be the case.' However, this was the case and Canadians returned to this theme regularly.

38 LAC, DFR, vol. 4226, file 8800-04-2, ICETP 10, 12 February 1962.

39 Fleming, *So Very Near*, 2: 415.

40 See Thomas Hockin, 'De Gaulle and l'Affaire Québec,' in John Saywell, ed., *Canadian Annual Review for 1967* (Toronto: University of Toronto Press, 1968), 235. In this

article, Hockin alludes to de Gaulle's tremendous irritation over Canadian policy, writing that 'General de Gaulle, so conjecture went, only got interested in the French Canadians when he thought that he might use their resentments as a lever to pry a cheap, long-term uranium contract out of Ottawa.'

41 PCO, 'Visit of Chancellor Erhard,' 11 June 1964.

42 Tucker, *Canadian Foreign Policy*, 37. The articulation by Sharp of the Third Option policy in late 1972 in a paper published in *International Perspectives* (Autumn 1972), can be seen as a reflection of this. It should also be noted that the cabinet was not entirely united on this point. Mitchell Sharp represented the freer trade side, while Walter Gordon had the protectionists behind him. In a speech before the Vancouver Board of Trade in January 1964, Sharp suggest that there was 'a growing recognition that an inward-looking protectionist policy for Canada leads nowhere.' Gordon was reported by the *Montreal Gazette* as saying that the government would take a hard line in Geneva and that 'There must be a reasonable balance between concessions obtained and those we grant.' See Donald Forster, 'The National Economy,' in John Saywell, ed., *Canadian Annual Review for 1964* (Toronto: University of Toronto Press, 1965), 288–9.

43 LAC, DEA-R, vol. 3479, file 9-C-1964/1, 'The Implications for Canadian Export Trade ...' n.d. In the media of the day, as well as in *Hansard*, there are numerous references to ministers and officials making the case for lower tariffs in all areas. However, cabinet was not solidly in favour of freer trade; Walter Gordon, the minister of finance, for one, was opposed to further liberalization as he believed that Canada should take steps to protect its own economy.

44 Lawrence B. Krause, *European Economic Integration and the United States* (Washington, DC: The Brookings Institution, 1968), 97.

45 BCA, BCR, 4D-101, 'Visit to London of the French Prime Minister and Foreign Minister,' 6–8 July 1966. Despite French policy at the time of the Kennedy round, the EEC had a substantial trade deficit with the United States in agricultural products. In 1962, the year that the Trade Extension Act was passed by Congress, the deficit was about US$2 billion and in 1966, it was US$1.925 billion. With respect to the French position, a document prepared for the Canada-U.S. ministerial committee on trade and economic affairs noted that even following the Luxembourg compromise and the return of the EEC to the Kennedy round, there was 'no guarantee that the EEC will participate effectively ... France attaches the highest priority to the solution of outstanding internal Community problems ... France does not appear attracted by the prospect of extensive multilateral tariff reductions.' See BCA, Rasminsky Papers, LR76-361, Joint Canada-U.S. ministerial committee on trade and economic affairs, 'European Trade Developments,' March 1966.

46 *Times* (London), 7 July 1965, 12.

47 BCA, BCR, 4E-260, EmbParis to External, 17 September 1965.

48 Robert Spencer, 'The Community and the Original Six: West Germany and the
    Commuity, 1957–1982,' in Nils Orvik and Charles Pentland, eds., *The European
    Community at the Crossroads: The First Twenty-Five Years* (Kingston ON: Centre for
    International Relations, 1983), 16. Spencer goes on to note that 'One may conclude ...
    that the European community remains more important for the Federal Republic than
    its partners. Bonn still has more to lose economically and politically from [its] stale-
    mate or collapse ... than do the other participants.' See also BCA, Rasminsky Papers
    LR76-359, Joint Canada-U.S. Committee on Trade and Economic Affairs, 'EFTA,
    EEC and Related Problems,' March 1961. Early on in the EEC's evolution, the per-
    centage of trade among its members increased substantially. For example, between
    1959 and 1960, it rose by 28 per cent.

49 BCA, BCR, 4E-260, Bonn to External, 26 February 1968. See also BCA, Rasminsky
    Papers, LR76-362, U.S.-Canada Joint Committee meeting, 20–22 June 1967. This
    meeting of North Americans had decided that Germany was particularly cautious and
    was now cool to British entry into the Community. Bonn wanted better relations with
    France.

50 LBJL, Administrative History of Special Representative for Trade Negotiations vol. 1,
    Narrative History, 1963–1969. As a result of this trade policy review, the U.S. admin-
    istration concluded that 'a bold and far-reaching attack on barriers to trade was needed
    in order to help build the economic foundations for a stronger Atlantic partnership.'
    The U.S. legislation passed by Congress, the Trade Expansion Act, authorized the
    president for a period of five years to reduce tariffs by as much as 50 per cent of the
    rates existing on 1 July 1962. In tariff agreements with the EEC, he was empowered to
    eliminate duties completely on products in which the United States and the Commu-
    nity together accounted for more than 80 per cent of the world market. Joan Spero
    suggests that the Kennedy round was to (unsuccessfully) ensure 'that European inte-
    gration would remain open and non-discriminatory.' Spero, 85.

51 BCA, Rasminsky Papers, LR76-371, 'Notes for Use by Sydney Pierce ... in reporting
    on February 28 1967 to Canadian officials.'

52 LAC, DFR, vol. 3942, file 8522-4575-2 (63), 'Kennedy Round and Other Matters –
    J.H. Warren's Notes on European Visit,' 7 October 1963.

53 LBJL, NSF, Box 165, Country File – Canada, vol. 2, Telephone Notes, Pearson to
    Johnson, 8 November 1964.

54 BCA, Rasminsky Papers, LR76-360, United States–Canada Joint Committee, 'GATT
    Trade Negotiations: Situation Report and Prospects,' 13 September 1963.

55 Ibid.

56 LAC, DFR, vol. 3942, file 8522-4575-2 (63), 'Kennedy Round and Other Matters.'

57 BCA, BCR, 4E-260, Geneva to External, 30 October 1964.

58 *Economist*, 4 May 1963, 429.

59 See also Keating, *Canada and World Order*, 141.

60 Mitchell Sharp, *Which Reminds Me: A Memoir* (Toronto: University of Toronto Press, 1994), 118. See also BCA, Rasminsky Papers, LR76-371, 'Notes Used by Sydney Pierce ... in reporting on February 28 to Canadian officials on the Kennedy Round,' As Tom Keating points out, 'Canadian tariff rates were almost uniformly higher thatn those of its principal trading partner, the United States. As a result an equal percentage cut in Canadian tariff rates would lead to a much more substantial reduction in Canadian rates vis-à-vis those of the United States.' Keating, 141.

61 USNA, NSF, Box 19, file: Canada, Subject: Pearson Visit 5/63, Briefing Book, 'Trade Expansion Act: Linear Tariff Reductions,' 3 May 1963.

62 USNA, NSF, Box 19, file: Canada, Subject: Pearson Visit 5/63, Briefing Book, 'Trade Matters,' 10 May 1963.

63 LBJL, NSF, Box 165, file Country File – Canada Cables, vol. 2, Telephone Notes, Prime Minister of Canada to the President, 8 November 1964.

64 LBJL, NSF, Box 167, file: Canada – Pearson Visit Briefing 1965, 'Canadian Participation in the Kennedy Round,' January 1965. The two scandals centred around Guy Favreau, a newly appointed minister of justice and Pearson's Quebec lieutenant.

65 Ibid.

66 BCA, Rasminsky Papers, LR76-371, 'Notes Used by Sydney Pierce ... in reporting on February 28 to Canadian officials on the Kennedy Round,' n.d.

67 BCA, Rasminsky Papers, LR76-371, EmbParis to External, 15 February 1966. See also BCA, BCR, 4E-250, London to External, 8 February 1963.

68 LAC, DFR, vol. 3942, file 8522-4575-2 (63), 'GATT Trade Negotiations: Situation Report and Prospects,' 13 September 1963.

69 BCA, Rasminsky Papers, LR76-371, 'Notes Used by Sydney Pierce ... in reporting on February 28, 1967 to Canadian officials on the Kennedy Round.'

70 PCO, 'Canada-United Kingdom Ministerial Committee on Trade and Economic Affairs,' 2 May 1967. As well, Pearson went on, 'international liquidity planning was progressing very slowly; and the United States were becoming very deeply and irretrievably involved in Vietnam.'

71 LBJL, NSC-Security Council History, Box 52, Kennedy Round Crisis, Book I, Ap-Ju 1967, 1(a).

72 Ibid. See also Memorandum from the acting special representative for trade negotiations (Roth) to President Johnson, 15 February 1967, in *FRUS 1964–1968*, vol. 8, *International Monetary and Trade Policy* (Washington, DC: GPO, 1998), 881. Roth writes that 'The ASP issue is not only critical to the successful conclusion of the Kennedy Round, it is also the trickiest political issue we face in the negotiations.'

73 'Memorandum from the President's Deputy Special Assistant for National Security Affairs to President Johnson,' 10 May 1967, in *FRUS 1964–1968*, vol. 8, 920.

74 See GATT Library, vol. 24, 'Memorandum of Agreement on Basic Elements for the Negotiation of a World Grains Arrangement,' 24th Session, April 1968 20.

75 Donald Forster, 'Trade Policy,' in John Saywell, ed., *Canadian Annual Review for 1969* (Toronto: University of Toronto Press, 1970), 333. For an account of a cabinet discussion over wheat at Geneva, see PCO, Records, 'Kennedy Round Tariff Negotiations,' 9 May 1967.

76 LAC, DFR, vol. 4682, file 8776-06-01, vol. 2, Tariff Delegation Geneva to External, 18 October 1966.

77 Evans, *Kennedy Round*, 288. See also J.L. Granatstein, *A Man of Influence: Norman A. Robertson and Canadian Statecraft, 1929–68* (Toronto: Deneau, 1981), 371.

78 'Memorandum from the President's Deputy Special Assistant for National Security Affairs to President Johnson, 1 May 1967,' in *FRUS 1964–1968*, vol. 8, 909.

79 PCO, 'The Kennedy Round,' 25 May 1967. Canada also implemented the results of the Kennedy round early. Instead of 1972, when all the tariff reductions were to be in effect, Ottawa had them all in place by mid–1969. See also 'Memorandum from the Under Secretary of State for Political Affairs' Special Assistant to Secretary of State Rusk,' 16 May 1967, in *FRUS 1964–1968*, vol. 8, 937. Despite the Canadian characterization of their success, Thomas Enders told Dean Rusk that the American agreement with Canada was 'a very significant – in some ways brilliant – deal.' Obviously, Enders thought that the United States had also won.

80 Donald Forster, 'Trade Policy,' in John Saywell, ed., *Canadian Annual Review for 1967* (University of Toronto Press, 1968), 333.

81 LJPL, NSC-Security Council History, Box 52, Kennedy Round Crisis, Book I, Ap-Ju 1967, 1(a).

82 USNA, DSR, B.6, Memorandum of Conversation 1967, The Secretary and Paul Martin, 7 September 1967.

83 For a discussion of the balance of payments issue in the context of its relations with Canada, see Bruce Muirhead, *Against the Odds: The Public Life and Times of Louis Rasminsky* (Toronto: University of Toronto Press, 1999), 251–95. John Connally, the U.S. secretary of treasury, was adamant in conversation with Edgar Benson, Canada's minister of finance, that the Europeans and Japanese must change the way they did business: 'The Common Agricultural Policy is an unconscionable evil. Japan does unbelievable things to keep our goods out.' See BCA, Rasminsky Papers, LR76-299-19, 'Notes of a Conversation between Mr. Benson and Secretary Connally,' September 1971. By mid-1969, there were more than 400 bills relating to tariff and trade matters before Congress, over half of which were quota proposals. And while they would probably not be reported out of the Ways and Means Committee, they clearly demonstrated the will of the legislative branch. See also Stephen D. Krasner, 'US Commercial and Monetary Policy,' *International Organization* 31 (1977), 635–72. Krasner offers a number of reasons the United States was becoming more protectionist during the latter half of the 1960s and 1970s.

84 UKNA, FCO 82, file 115, 'Record of a conversation between the prime minister and

Mr. Pierre Trudeau at Chequers,' 3 December 1972.

85 Tucker, *Canadian Foreign Policy*, 127.

86 See Muirhead, *Against the Odds*, 285. Some other items in Nixon's pronouncement were: the removal of the 7 per cent excise tax on cars; the introduction of a 10 per cent tax credit for investment in new, American-produced machinery and equipment; a cut in federal spending of U.S.$4.7 billion; the suspension of the convertibility of the dollar into gold; and renewed proposals for the introduction of the domestic international sales corporation export incentive.

87 *Debates*, 7 September 1971, 7582.

88 LAC, DEA-R, vol. 3172, file 36-FB-1972/1, Memorandum to Cabinet, 'Canada/EEC Relations,' 2 May 1972.

89 R.B. Byers, 'The Economic Crisis,' in John Saywell, ed., *Canadian Annual Review 1971* (Toronto: University of Toronto Press, 1972), 245.

90 See for example, Dave Godfrey with Mel Watkins, *Gordon to Watkins to You: The Battle for Control of Our Economy* (Toronto: New Press, 1970); Kari Levitt, *Silent Surrender: The Multinational Corporation in Canada* (Toronto: Macmillan, 1970); James Laxer, *The Liberal Idea of Canada: Pierre Trudeau and the Question of Canada's Survival* (Toronto: Lorimer, 1977); Abraham Rotstein, *The Precarious Homestead: Essays on Economics, Technology and Nationalism* (Toronto: New Press, 1973). Even Walter Gordon, Canada's erstwhile minister of finance, got in on the act, writing, among others, *A Choice for Canada: Independence or Colonial Status* (Toronto: Macmillan, 1966).

91 LAC, DEA-R, vol. 3172, file 36-FB-1972/1, Memorandum to Cabinet, 'Canada/EEC Negotiations,' 2 May 1972.

92 UKNA, FCO 82, file 115, 'Report by Mr. Th. Hijzen ... to the Ambassadors of member and applicant countries on his discussions with Canadian government authorities,' 8 December 1972.

93 UKNA, FCO 82, file 115, Overton to British High Commission Ottawa, 9 October 1972.

94 UKNA, FCO92, file 115, 'Report by Mr. Hijzen.'

95 Nossel, 92.

96 Cooper, *In Between Countries*, 108.

97 J.L. Granatstein, 'Continentalism vs. the New Nationalism,' in John Saywell, ed., *Canadian Annual Review for 1970* (Toronto: University of Toronto Press, 1971), 349. But the numbers were close, at least according to polling data collected in October and November 1974. In response to the question 'Would Canadians be willing to accept a lower standard of living in exchange for more controls over their economy by reducing or abolishing US investments,' Canadians indicated No – 47.7 per cent, Yes – 43.8 per cent, No Opinion – 8.6 per cent. See Murray and Leduc, 35.

Conclusion

1 Edelgard Mahant and Graeme S. Mount, *Invisible and Inaudible in Washington: American Policies Toward Canada* (Vancouver: UBC Press, 1999), 89.
2 As the proponents of free trade in the later 1980s pointed out *ad nauseum*, Canada was the only G-7 country that did not have a domestic market of at least 100 million consumers.
3 P.E. Bryden, *Planners and Politicians: Liberal Politics and Social Policy, 1957–1968* (Montreal and Kingston: McGill-Queen's University Press, 1997), xv.
4 Ibid., 167.

Illustration Credits

Index

Africa, 157
Agricultural Adjustment Act (U.S.), 141, 171
Agricultural Guidance and Guarantee Fund (EEC), 224
Agricultural Stabilization Act, 149, 278n31
agricultural trade, 122; barriers to Europe, 218–22, 224–5, 294n12, 294n14, 296n33, 298n45, 299nn48–9; Canada-U.S. policy, 147, 160–1, 171; Canadian farm income statistics, 161; European protectionism, 224–8; farm machinery, 145; fruit and vegetable growers, 19–21; GATT waiver, 146–7, 149–50; relations with EEC, 187; statistics on Canada-UK, 192, 286n59; subsidies, 139; support prices for, 149, 278n31; tariff negotiations, 235–9. *See also* General Agreement on Tariffs and Trade (GATT); wheat sales
Agricultural Trade Development and Assistance Act. *See* PL 480 (Agricultural Trade Development and Assistance Act)
airplanes: embargo on used, 124
Alcan metal, 28

Alliance for Progress, 34
aluminum, 192, 285–6n58
Aluminum Company of Canada, 28
American government: addressing Canadian anti-Americanism, 18–19; view of Liberals, 14
American Mandatory Oil Import Program, 54
American Selling Price, 234–5, 300n72
Amory, Lord, 179, 196
Anderson, Robert, 31; wheat sale discussions, 152–3
anti-Americanism: in 1961, 40; and April 1963 elections, 49; of Canadian ministers, 18–19, 26; in election rhetoric, 27; and FAC, 91; at the government level, 109, 257n135; and June 1963 budget, 57; of NDP, 138; polls indicating, 5; rise of, 7–8, 99–100, 267–8n16; since Confederation, 10–11; statistics on, 108; Trudeau talks with Nixon, 126
anti-dumping, 120, 200–6, 212–13, 236–7
Armstrong, Willis, 48, 55
Atomic Energy Commission (U.S.), 120, 129
Atwood, Margaret, 5, 248n5

Austin, Jack, 102
Australia, 157–8, 173
automotive industry (Canada): barriers
   to trade for, 71–3, 77–9; and British
   imports, 200–1, 289n105; embargo on
   used cars, 124; integration with U.S.,
   79; North American market discussions, 81–3; statistics on, 70–1, 78t,
   107; Studebaker plant, 76, 78; threats
   of countervailing duties, 73, 81–2,
   262n72, 262n75, 264n99, 264n104;
   U.S. complaints on, 80, 118. See also
   Auto Pact
Automotive Service Industry Association
   (U.S.), 85
Auto Pact: and balance of payments problem, 107; benefits to Canada, 7; British
   trade and, 201, 206; countervailing
   duties and, 83–4; criticism of, 52; institutional barriers to, 89–90; in New
   Economic Policy negotiations, 117–19;
   origins of, 47, 50, 70–7; passing of, 85–
   6; removal of safeguards, 124–5, 132–
   3; safeguards for Canadian industry,
   89–90, 129; statistics on, 86–7, 89;
   U.S. difficulties with, 135, 274n111
Avro Arrow, 41

baby-boomers, 8
Bain, George, 98
balance of payments: Auto Pact and,
   87–9, 132; Canada-U.S. disagreements
   over, 106–7; Canadian problems with,
   56–9; and decision to float Canadian
   dollar, 111–12; foreign aid and, 46,
   60–1, 143–4; U.S. pressures Europe
   about, 120–1, 224, 296n29; U.S. pressures trading partners about, 129; U.S.
   problems with, 30–2, 42, 67–8, 92, 95,
   222; U.S. solution to, 114–15; U.S.

statistics on, 60; U.S. surplus, 130–1;
   wheat sales and, 7, 165, 168, 172. See
   also Interest Equalization Tax (IET)
Balance of Payments Committee, 111
Ball, George: on automotive industry,
   76–7, 80; on countervailing duties, 83;
   on Diefenbaker government, 44; The
   Discipline of Power, 97–8, 267n7; on
   IET, 62; on origins of Auto Pact, 73; on
   trade relations with Canada, 49, 65
Bank of Canada: Annual Report 1973,
   138; April 1963 elections, 49; on the
   Auto Pact, 87; decision to float dollar,
   111; foreign ownership and, 40; on
   inflation, 96–7. See also Canadian econ-
   omy; Rasminsky, Louis
Barr, Joseph, 86
Barrow, B.G., 73
Bator, Francis, 85
Bell Canada, 124
Bennett, R.B., 184, 186
Benson, Edgar, 99, 116, 121–2, 239
Benson, Ezra, 150, 158–9
Big Three American automobile manufac-
   turers, 80–1, 83–5, 90, 116
bilateral air transport relations, 53
Bladen, Vincent, 70
Bliss, Michael, 267–8n16
Borden, Henry, 15
Borg-Warner, 77–8
Bothwell, Robert, 39, 127
Bourassa, Robert, 133
branch plants. See U.S. subsidiaries oper-
   ating in Canada
Britain. See United Kingdom
British Columbia: farm exports from,
   20–1
British Empire, 10
British Leyland, 199
Britnell, G.E., 143

Brown, George, 202
Brubeck, William, 72, 74
Bryce, R.B., 173
Bryden, Penny, 244
budgets (Canadian): anti-inflation
    November 1967, 96; April 1965, 204,
    207; December 1960, 190; Gordon's
    1963, 8; June 1961 speech, 44, 190;
    June 1963, 54–9, 63–4, 69, 259n15,
    259n23; March 1960, 40; October
    1968, 213
Bullitt, John, 163
Bundy, McGeorge, 51, 55, 72–3, 83
bunker C oil, 5
Burns, Arthur, 111, 113
Butterworth, Walton: on automobile mar-
    ket, 82; on Auto Pact, 73–4, 90; Can-
    ada-U.S. defence negotiations, 48–9,
    53; on Canadian inflation, 96; on con-
    tinentalization of resources, 91; on IET,
    63–4; on nationalist budget, 56, 58; on
    Pearson government, 92–4; on
    Trudeau, 266n142
Buy American Act, 41, 123
Byers, Roderick, 137

Cadieux, Marcel, 211
Callaghan, James, 202
Canada: Europe's Last Chance, 137
Canada and the United States: Principles for
    Partnership, 65–6
Canada Development Corporation
    (CDC), 54, 138
Canada-U.S. ministerial meetings, 69,
    105–6, 135, 150, 211–12. See also joint
    Canada-U.S. Committee on Trade and
    Economic Affairs
Canada-U.S. relations: Canadian victories
    in, 7–8; in context of British EEC
    membership, 195; crisis in, 131–3,
273n108, 274n111; quarterly wheat
    meetings, 155; as unusually close, 8,
    249n14; U.S. commentary on, 74,
    97–8; U.S. extraterritoriality, 27–8;
    U.S. study regarding economic policy,
    125. See also anti-Americanism; trade
    relations with U.S.; individual U.S. and
    Canadian governments
Canadian-American Committee, 107
Canadian Annual Review, 138
Canadian coastal zone, 53
Canadian dollar: and balance of payments,
    92; devaluation of, 38, 45–6, 56; ex-
    change rate of, 43–6, 92, 127; floating
    of, 111, 116, 119, 152; increase in,
    119, 127; shortages of, 179; as strong,
    3, 19, 145
Canadian economy: 1962 exchange crisis,
    43–6, 197, 202; business response to
    1963 budget, 56–7, 64; Canadianiza-
    tion of, 55–6, 62, 241, 302n97; capital
    shortage, 12–13; current account defi-
    cit, 65, 126, 202, 289n112; current
    account surplus, 181–2; development
    through wheat, 139–40; federal-provin-
    cial divide, 64–5; GNP statistics, 101,
    128; inflation, 96–7; international lia-
    bilities of, 60–1; New Economic Policy
    and, 123–4; recovery of, 95; stagflation,
    241; statistics on exports, 243; trade
    with UK, 190; U.S. domination of, 40,
    52, 127, 136–7, 177, 282n3. See also
    budgets (Canadian)
Canadian Exporter's Association, 129
Canadian flag, 205–6
Canadian Horticultural Council, 20
Canadian identity. See Canadian national-
    ism
Canadian Manufacturers Association, 44
Canadian nationalism: Atwood on,

248n5; in context of EEC, 240; economic, 55–6, 138; and FAC, 91; or prosperity, 241, 302n97; rise of, 5–6, 17–19, 100–1, 248n11; U.S. awareness of, 14–15, 30, 110–11, 248n11, 250n15

Canadian sovereignty, 8–9. *See also* foreign investment in Canada

Canadian Wheat Board (CWB), 151; global trade, 142; price of wheat, 172–3; production and demand relationship, 175–6; sales to China, 3, 28; sales to Japan, 163; trade restrictions with Britain, 192–3; U.S. argument with, 164–5. *See also* wheat sales

Cargill, 28

Chicago Tribune, 129

China. *See* People's Republic of China (PRC)

Chrysler Canada, 28, 79. *See also* Big Three American automobile manufacturers

Churchill, Gordon, 39–40, 47, 158–9, 194

citizenship of company directors, 29

Clarkson, Stephen, 100

Cold War, 11, 28–30, 216, 242. *See also* communism

Collins, Ralph, 109

Colombo Plan, 186

Columbia River Treaty, 53, 80, 264n100

Combines Act, 47

Common Agricultural Policy (Europe): Canada's disagreement with, 219, 224–5, 301n83; Canada seeks U.S. as ally against, 221; European self-sufficiency, 227, 235–6, 236t; general protectionist attitudes and, 156–7; importance to U.S., 297n34; surpluses, 168–9, 172; trade with Japan, 122. *See also* European Economic Community (EEC);

General Agreement on Tariffs and Trade (GATT)

Common Market tariff, 222

Common Market Treaty, 149

Commonwealth (British): Auto Pact and, 206; British membership in EEC, 193–5, 198, 208–9, 287n73; Canadian preferences, 17, 45; economic conferences of, 22, 183–7; export-import figures among, 182; trade amongst, 181–3. *See also* United Kingdom

communism, 14, 32–3, 161, 255n81. *See also* Cold War; USSR

Connally, John: on Canada-U.S. relations, 126, 129, 131; G-10 meeting, 126–7; on import surcharge, 117, 120–2; on New Economic Policy (U.S.), 113–15; relations with Nixon, 127, 273n97

Connor, John, 86

continental economic integration, 4–5, 10–11, 178, 183, 242. *See also* foreign investment in Canada

Cooper, Andrew, 175

Co-operative Commonwealth Federation, 4, 17. *See also* New Democratic Party (NDP)

copper, 91

Council on Foreign Economic Policy (CFEP), 15, 27–8

Council on International Economic Policy, 125

Coyne, James, 27, 38–41, 256n102

Creighton, Donald, 6, 10, 178

Cromer, Earl, 42

Currall, Alex, 203–4

Customs Act, section 37A, 205, 207, 212t

Cyprus, 83, 265n113

dairy products, 41, 171, 192, 236t, 286n59

d'Andelot Belin, G., 80

Davis, William, 133

defence: production sharing, 124, 129, 132–3, 136; trade and, 37, 48–9; U.S. and burden sharing, 121, 271n76; U.S.-Canada disagreement over, 33–4, 255n81; U.S. concern for continental, 26; U.S. control of Canadian policy, 42

Defence Production Sharing Agreement (DPSA), 34, 41–2, 53, 118, 129–30, 135

de Gaulle, Charles: agricultural protectionism, 228; British entry to EEC, 210, 218; British relations, 293n10; on Europe, 286–7n64; foreign economic policy, 193; uranium sales, 226, 297–8n40. *See also* France

Dell, Sydney, 191

development policy (Canada): assistance from Britain, 186; reliance on U.S. investment, 11; tax credit for jobs, 114–15; through wheat, 139–40; U.S. contribution to Canadian, 4

Diefenbaker, John: defeat of, 6, 49–50; early position on U.S. investment, 13–14; election of, 10, 17; on nuclear weapons, 48–9; in opposition, 52, 55, 57; relationship with Eisenhower, 22, 25, 29–30, 150, 152, 159; relationship with Kennedy, 33–7, 254n73, 254n76, 255n84, 257n135; U.S. domination of economy, 11–12; visit to U.S., 25

Diefenbaker government: automotive industry, 70; on British EEC membership, 189–97; British trade, 178–83, 243; Commonwealth relations, 184, 186; foreign policy development, 178; import surcharges, 43–4; June 1957 elections, 178; oil trade, 15–16, 23–5, 244; protectionism, 21–2, 50, 190;

relationship with prairie farmers, 286n62; trade policy of, 148–50; U.S. trade relations, 15; wheat sales under, 142–8, 157–8

Dillon, Douglas: on agricultural protectionism, 220; on automotive trade, 79, 86; balance of payments, 60–2; Canada-U.S. relations, 29–31, 35, 144; on countervailing duties, 81, 83, 262n72, 262n75, 264n99; on IET, 61–5; June 1963 budget, 58–9; on wheat sales, 153, 162–3

direct investment. *See* foreign investment in Canada

Dobell, Peter, 114, 120

Domestic International Sales Corporation (DISC), 114–16, 119, 122–3, 132

Dominion Bureau of Statistics, 6

Drabble, Bernard, 124

draft dodgers (U.S.), 267–8n16

Drew, George, 195–6

Drummond, Ian, 39

Drury, Charles M. (Bud), 79, 84, 88, 204, 210

Dudek, Louis, 5

Dulles, John Foster: Canada-U.S. relations, 22, 251n21; on Canada-U.S. economic integration, 14–15; on foreign investment in Canada, 4, 11–12; on U.S. subsidies, 28; on wheat disposals, 142–3, 150–1, 297n37

Dunbar-Kattle Company of Batavia, Illinois, 34

Eccles, David, 180

Economic Development Review Committee, 91

Economist, 42

Eisenhower administration: agricultural trade with Europe, 221; background to

president, 35; Canadian anti-Americanism, 18–19; Food for Peace, 155;
relationship with Diefenbaker, 22, 25,
29–30, 150, 152, 159; visit to Canada,
22, 25; wheat sales, 140, 157–8
election promises, 19
elections (Canada): of 1976, 137; April
1963, 49, 161, 197; June 1957, 147–8,
178; June 1961, 43; June 1968, 90–1,
98; March 1958, 184; November 1965,
205; October 1972, 103, 138; summer
1962, 196
elections (U.S.): November 1960, 159–60
Ellender, Allen, 150
employment, 70. See also unemployment
English, John, 14, 39, 52, 66, 75
Erhard, Ludwig, 226
Essex Wire company, 78
European Economic Community (EEC):
agricultural protectionism, 219–22,
224–5, 296n33; and British Commonwealth, 185, 187, 291n139; British
membership in, 47, 177, 190–1, 198,
208–14, 226–7, 239–40, 287n68,
287n71, 292n148; Canada relationship
with, 226–7, 227t, 240–1, 243, 285–
6n58; Canadian view of, 187, 217–18,
284n42; challenge to Canada's exports,
148–9, 191–7; issue of wheat sales,
169, 173–5; under Kennedy-Diefenbaker regimes, 35; and Kennedy round
negotiations, 228–9, 237–8, 299n50;
preferential trade system, 119; U.S.
attitude towards, 113, 216, 219, 224,
230, 294n12; U.S. tariff negotiations
with, 222–3; U.S. trade with, 103, 122;
wheat sales, 142, 156, 175. See also
Common Agricultural Policy (Europe)
European Free Trade Area (EFTA), 185,
187–90, 283n28, 284n37

European Recovery Program, 216
Evans, John, 222, 237
Exchange of Letters (1947), 188, 191
Eximbank, 30–1
Expo 67, 5
export financing, 30–1. See also balance of
payments
Export-Import Bank, 43, 144–5
exports (Canada): early Diefenbaker government, 12; exemptions to surcharges,
116–17, 129, 202; international subsidies, 174; relations with Europe, 216–
17; statistics on surcharges, 114; statistics to Europe, 148, 226, 227t; statistics
to U.S., 36, 159; to U.S., 3, 38. See also
foreign policy (Canada); oil
extraterritoriality (U.S.), 5, 27

farm machinery, 145. See also agricultural
trade
Federation of British Industries, 199,
203
Financial Post, 147
Flanigan, Peter, 102–3, 131
Fleming, Donald: on 15 per cent, 179–80;
on Commonwealth meeting, 184; on
EEC, 189, 195, 217, 287n73; on for-
eign investment, 27, 39–40; June 1961
budget speech, 190; origins of OECD,
295–6n26; on trade discrimination,
185–6; on Trade Expansion Act, 44–6;
on U.S. trade restrictions, 11–12; on
wheat surplus disposals, 143
Florida grapefruit, 12
flour milling, 221–2
Food and Agricultural Organization
(UN), 145, 165–6
Food for Peace, 155–6, 159–60
Ford, Henry, 82
Ford Motor Company, 5, 79. See also Big

Three American automobile manufacturers

foreign aid: and balance of payments, 46, 60, 143–4; to counter dumping, 120; as disposal of surplus, 168, 277n15; to promote economic development, 159, 166; reduced demand for, 175; tied to sales, 146, 151, 154, 277n16; U.S. to influence Canada on, 34. *See also* PL 480 (Agricultural Trade Development and Assistance Act)

foreign assets control (FAC) regulations, 27–9, 91, 253n65

foreign investment in Canada: differing perceptions of, 106; dominated by U.S., 8–9, 11, 13, 54, 244; dual message to U.S. about, 27; from European sources, 99; federal and provincial differences, 64; ownership after 1945, 4; public opinion of, 138; restrictions on, 39–42, 55–9, 275n128; statistics of U.S., 41; statistics on, 69, 106; taxes supporting, 63; voluntary guidelines on (U.S.), 67–8. *See also* continental economic integration

foreign investment in U.S., 95

Foreign Investment Review Agency, 138

foreign ownership in Canada. *See* foreign investment in Canada

foreign policy (Canada): defence, 42; development of, 109–10, 123, 128, 178; economic, 123–4, 127–9, 133, 272n83, 274n114, 274n116; 15 per cent trade with Britain, 22, 179–83, 243, 282n9; multilateralism, 3, 12, 23–4, 44, 147, 152, 160, 217; trade with Europe, 215 (*see also* European Economic Community [EEC]); trade with U.S., 102–3, 122, 243–5, 268n20, 268n22. *See also* exports

(Canada); Interdepartmental Committee on External Trade Policy (ICETP)

Foreign Policy for Canadians, 110, 116, 123, 213, 240

Foreign Trade and Investment Act, 274n114

Forked Road, The, 6

Foster, Donald, 236

Fowler, Henry, 67–9

Framework Agreement for Commercial and Economic Cooperation, 241

France: agricultural protectionism, 226, 228; devaluation of franc, 183; nationalist foreign policy of, 193, 286–7n64; Paris Canadian high commission, 186; in tariff negotiations, 233; wheat sales, 169, 173. *See also* de Gaulle, Charles

Freeman, George, 27

Freeman, Orville, 162, 164

free trade: with Britain, 14, 179–80, 183; discussions with U.S. on, 135, 245, 303n2; study for North American, 15, 251n21

fruit and vegetable growers, 19–21. *See also* agricultural trade

Fulford, Robert, 5

G-10, 120–2, 126–8

Galbraith, John Kenneth, 75

General Agreement on Tariffs and Trade (GATT): agricultural committee, 174; agricultural protectionism, 157, 218–22, 294n14; agricultural waiver, 141, 146–7, 149, 160, 166; Auto Pact and, 84, 206; continentalism, 6, 178; countervailing duties, 81; in EEC context, 222–3, 295n23; on EEC tariffs, 191, 285n55; EFTA conflicts with, 284n37; Geneva 1956, 146; global trade, 188; Group on Cereals, 166; import surcharges, 43–6, 293n2; Japan, October 1959, 150; under Kennedy-Diefenbaker regimes, 35; and New Economic Policy (U.S.), 114; North American trade relations, 243; steel exports, 104–5; tariff negotiations, 47–8, 217–18; Tokyo round of, 135; tourist duties, 132; uranium embargo, 130; U.S. metal quotas, 24; U.S. reminds Canada of obligations under, 20–2; waiver of obligations under, 21; wheat exports, 143–5. *See also* Common Agricultural Policy (Europe); Kennedy round tariff reductions

General Motors, 79. *See also* Big Three American automobile manufacturers

Germany (West), 7, 112, 226, 228, 242, 299nn48–9

global economy, 95, 142

Globe and Mail, 12, 123, 190

GNP (Canada), 3, 38, 101, 128

GNP (U.S.), 95

gold, 59–61, 112, 121, 183–4, 302n86

Gonick, Cy, 5

Gordon, Walter: on automotive industry, 71, 79–81; on Auto Pact, 7, 84; on CDC, 54; on foreign ownership, 64–5, 67; on IET, 62–4; nationalism of, 14; resigns from cabinet, 99; on trade with Britain, 204–5, 289n112. *See also* budgets (Canadian)

Gore, Albert, 107

Goyer, Jean-Pierre, 109

grain sales. *See* wheat sales

Granatstein, J.L., 109, 126, 150, 241, 282n3

Grandy, James, 129–30, 186, 188

Grant, George, 6, 50

Gray, Gordon, 144

Gray, Herb, 138, 275n128

Great Lakes Water Quality Agreement, 133

Green, Howard, 26–7, 29, 48–9, 196–7

gross national product (Canada). *See* GNP (Canada)

Gwyn, Richard, 54–5

Haberler, Gottfried, 171, 218–19

Haldeman, H.R., 134

Hall, Sir Robert, 186

Hallstein, Walter, 223

Hamilton, Alvin, 161, 163–4

hardboard exports, 12

Harkness, Douglas, 151, 219

Hartke, Vance, 77–8, 107

Hartke-Burke Bill, 274n114

Heath, Edward, 194, 196–7

Heeney, Arnold, 11, 26, 36–7, 66, 160

Hees, George, 189–90, 195, 219–20

Herter, Christian, 19, 25–7, 249n14

Hijzen, Theodorus, 230, 240–1

Hockin, Thomas, 146

Hodges, Luther, 77, 82

Hodgins, C.D., 124

Holmes, John, 83, 134, 210, 216, 292n157, 293n4

Holt, Harold, 195

Hong Kong, 28

Hormats, Robert, 131

Howe, C.D., 145, 250n15

Hull, Cordell, 216

Imperial Oil, 29

import duties: in automotive industry, 70–1, 81–2; on British trade, 190; reduction by Canadians of, 105; into U.S. on agricultural products, 141. *See also* General Agreement on Tariffs and Trade (GATT); New Economic Policy (U.S.)

Inco, 28

India, 34, 143, 157, 277n16

Interdepartmental Committee on External
Trade Policy (ICETP), 148–9, 155,
191

Interest Equalization Tax (IET): Canadian
exemptions from, 57, 66–8, 106, 161,
163–4; Canadian response to, 61–5;
origins of, 60; withdrawal of, 132

International Grains Arrangement (IGA),
166, 172–4, 235–6

International Monetary Fund (IMF), 46,
55, 71, 111, 128t

International Trade Commission, 125

International Trade Organization (ITO),
188

International Wheat Arrangements,
139–40, 154

International Wheat Council, 166

Ioanes, Raymond, 164

Isbister, Claude, 146

Jaenke, Hans, 164

Japan: as compared to U.S., 112; exports
to U.S., 92, 114; G-10, 120–2, 126–8;
response to New Economic Policy
(U.S.), 116–17; statistics of trade with,
213; steel exports to U.S., 103–4; trade
agreements with, 4; trade barriers of,
119; U.S. extraterritoriality, 28; wheat
sales to, 161–2, 164–5

job development investment tax credit
(JDITC), 114–15

Johnson, Griffith, 55–9, 65–8, 71

Johnson administration: on automobile
market, 82; on the Auto Pact, 52, 87;
on countervailing duties, 83–4,
262n72, 262n75, 264n99, 264n104;
European tariff negotiations, 232; on
relations with Canada, 75–6, 83, 232,

263n81, 263n85, 265n113; tariff negotiations with EEC, 237

joint Canada-U.S. Committee on Trade
and Economic Affairs: Canadian
import restrictions, 22; Canadian protection of automotive industry, 77;
on EEC, 299n49; on IET, 62; under
Kennedy-Diefenbaker regimes, 35;
meeting in March 1961, 37; U.S. mandate at 1959 meeting, 29–30; U.S.
restrictions on metal imports, 24; on
wheat sales, 144, 152–3, 158

Julien, Claude, 137

Kaldor, Nicholas, 207–8

Kalijarvi, Thorsten, 144, 147–8

Katz, Julius, 117

Keeley, James, 82

Kennedy, John: Canadian April 1963
elections, 49; Canadian automotive
industry, 72; Canadian wheat sales to
PRC, 29; Diefenbaker and, 32–6, 41,
254n73, 254n76, 255n84, 257n135;
GATT negotiations, 47–8; on IET, 62;
November 1960 elections, 159–60;
Pearson and, 51–5, 161–2

Kennedy, Robert, 35

Kennedy administration: on EEC, 35;
response to June 1963 budget, 55–9;
trade restrictions with Canada, 45–6;
on wheat sales, 160

Kennedy round tariff reductions: anti-
dumping code, 120, 203, 212; bargaining with Britain, 203; Canada's strategy in, 170–1; EEC attitude toward,
234; implementation of, 105, 119;
importance to Canada, 168–9, 231,
290n116; results of, 237–9, 301n79;
role of France in, 228–9; threats to, 88;
U.S.-EEC-Canada negotiations, 228–

31; U.S. strategy in, 232–4, 237–8. *See also* General Agreement on Tariffs and Trade (GATT)
Kierans, Eric, 56
Kimura, Kiyoaki, 122
Kissinger, Henry, 113, 127, 131, 273n97
Kosygin, Alexi, 123–4
Kriebel, Wesley, 10, 17, 178
Kyba, Patrick, 164

Lament for a Nation, 6
Lang, Otto, 175
Laos and Vietnam, 34
Latin America, 157
Latin American Free Trade Area partners, 167
Law of the Sea Conference, 242–3
Lawson, William, 111–12
Laxer, James, 7, 267–8n16
lead, 12, 23–4, 32, 41, 252n41. *See also* metals
Lee, Sir Frank, 189
Leonard, David, 164
Levitt, Kari, 6, 52, 68
Lewis, David, 103
Liberal Party of Canada: accused of selling out, 6; April 1963 elections, 49, 197; June 1961 elections, 43; June 1968 elections, 98; nationalism, 40–1; November 1965 elections, 205; October 1972 elections, 138; summer 1962 elections, 196
Linder, 101
Lintott, Sir Henry, 205–6
London Commonwealth conference, 178
London Sunday Observer, 196
Long, Olivier, 238
Louis Dreyfus, 28
Lower Inventories for Tomorrow (LIFT), 173, 176

Lynch, Charles, 66
Lyon, Peyton, 7, 109, 136, 222, 253n65

Macdonald, Donald, 102
MacGregor, Kenneth, 201
Mackenzie King, William Lyon, 10
Macmillan, Harold, 196, 218, 293n10
Made in Canada, 190
Mansholt, Sicco, 173
manufacturing industry (Canada): British trade and, 201–7, 290n117; competitiveness, 47–8; import surcharges, 44–5, 115, 123, 129, 257n118; market in USSR, 124, 272n83; negotiated tariff reductions, 237; preference given to, 204; productivity of, 95–6; statistics of sales to UK, 191; trade with Britain, 206, 291n133. *See also* foreign investment in Canada
Maritime farmers, 20–1
Markley, Robert, 86
Marshall, Charles, 109
Marshall Plan, 216
Martin, Paul: on automotive industry, 76–7, 80–1; on British free trade, 180; British membership in EEC, 209–10, 292n148; on foreign investment, 259n23
Massey-Harris, 115
Mathews, Robin, 5
Maudling, Sir Reginald, 194
Maxwell, Judith, 103
Mays-Smith, R.M., 38–40
McElroy, Neil, 19, 27
McGregor, Kenneth, 186
McKinnon, Hector, 219
media: on agricultural trade, 147, 164–5, 227–8; on anti-Americanism, 100; on Canada-U.S. relations, 123–4, 248n11, 267n7, 267–8n16; leaks to, 180; on

'Made in Canada' ruling, 190; on trade with Britain, 179, 196; on trade with EEC, 230; on trade with U.S., 223, 241, 282n3

Merchant, Livingston, 12–14, 17–18, 32–4, 60–1, 66, 94

Merchant-Heeney report, 65–6

Messina Declaration, 148

metals: export statistics, 23; exports to China, 28; quotas on, 12, 23–4, 252n41; steel, 103–4

Michelin Tire, 118, 124

Mills, Wilbur, 84

Modine Manufacturing Company (Wisconsin), 80, 83, 264n99

Mond, 28

monetary system, post-war instability, 31

Montreal Commonwealth meeting, 184–7. *See also* Commonwealth (British)

Montreal Gazette, 147

Montreal Stock Exchange, 56

Mont Tremblant meeting (Commonwealth), 183–4. *See also* Commonwealth (British)

Mowat, Farley, 5

multilateralism, 3, 12, 23–4, 44, 147, 152, 160, 217

multinational corporations, 106

Munro, Ross, 133

Murray, Geoffrey, 211

National Energy Board (Canada), 102–3

National Policy (Canada), 139

National Security Council (NSC) U.S., 18, 27, 30, 108

neutralism, 33

New Democratic Party (NDP): April 1963 elections, 197; on foreign ownership, 4; June 1961 elections, 43; June 1968 elections, 98; October 1972 elections, 103, 138; summer 1962 elections, 196

New Economic Policy (U.S.): changes in trade, 128*t*; details of, 113–20, 302n86; effect on Canada, 8, 239; G-8 talks, 120–2; internal criticism of, 127; manufacturing industry (Canada), 120

Newman, Peter, 5, 45, 195

New Romans, The, 5

New York stock market, 42, 58, 61–2, 64–5

New Zealand, 182, 198, 208–9, 242, 291n138–291n139

Nitze, Paul, 53

Nixon, Richard: internal government relations, 127, 273n97; on relations with Canada, 8, 101–2, 126, 133–4, 172, 249n14, 274n116; on Trudeau, 93; U.S. trade policy, 271n76

Nixon administration: on the Auto Pact, 88–9; personnel changes of, 113; rise of anti-Americanism, 7–8, 108. *See also* New Economic Policy (U.S.)

Nixon Shock. *See* New Economic Policy (U.S.)

non-tariff barriers to trade (NTBs), 238. *See also* General Agreement on Tariffs and Trade (GATT)

Norman, Herbert, 14

Norstad, Lauris, 48

North American Air Defence Command (NORAD), 26

Norway, 290n115

nuclear weapons, 11, 33–4, 41–2, 48

oil: 1973 crisis, 241; Canada a source for, 126; a continental resource, 244; disposition of Canadian, 104*t*; exports tied to defence, 53–4; exports to U.S., 32, 101–5, 268n22; price increases, 138;

statistics on exports of, 268n20; trade
relations under Diefenbaker, 15–16,
23–5; virtual free trade, 91
O'Keefe, Bryan, 89
Organization for Economic Cooperation
and Development (OECD): Canadian
current account deficit, 71; guidelines for multinationals, 106; under
Kennedy-Diefenbaker regimes, 35;
New Economic Policy (U.S.), 124; origins of, 223–4, 295–6n26, 296n27;
predicted trade changes, 128t; steel
exports, 104–5
Organization of American States (OAS),
34, 53
Organization of Petroleum Exporting
Countries (OPEC), 102
Ottawa Agreements, 184, 186, 191, 193

Paarlberg, Donald, 140
Pakistan, 143
Parti Québécois, 137. See also Quebec
Patterson, Gardner, 236–7
Pearson, Lester: on economic independence, 8, 41; meetings with Kennedy,
51–5, 161–2; on Nationalist Budget,
259n15; in opposition, 215; relationship with Johnson, 77, 232, 263n90;
relationship with Kennedy, 75; on trade
with Britain, 213; U.S. view of, 14; visit
with German chancellor, 226. See also
Liberal Party of Canada
Pearson government: 1963 elections, 34;
automotive industry, 81–2; on Auto
Pact, 73–5, 85–6; on British membership in EEC, 210, 226–7; Butterworth
commentary on, 92–4; European tariff
negotiations, 232–4; lessons for IET,
62–5; nationalist budget, 54–5;
November 1965 elections, 205; on

nuclear weapons, 48; Pearson trip to
UK, 186; popular perceptions of, 52–3;
social programs of, 244; vote of confidence on budget, 59; on wheat sales,
164–5
People's Republic of China (PRC):
Quemoy and Matsu, 28; recognition
of, 11; trade with, 3; U.S. attitude to,
26, 32; U.S. interference of shipments
to, 34–5; wheat sales to, 160–1, 163,
192–3, 243–4, 277n16
Pepin, Jean-Luc, 90, 116, 129, 133–6,
172
Peterson, Peter, 112
Petro-Canada, 103, 138
Pierce, Sydney, 229, 233
Pillsbury, 28
Pimlot, Ben, 198
PL 480 (Agricultural Trade Development
and Assistance Act): amendments to,
150; Canadian negotiations over,
151–3; revisions to, 153; on surplus
disposal, 168; U.S. wheat disposals
under, 140–3, 277n12, 277n15,
279n47; wheat surplus disposal, 166
Plumptre, A.F.W., 19, 55, 71, 189, 199
potatoes, 20–1. See also agricultural trade
Preliminary Report of the Royal Commission on Canada's Economic Prospects
(January 1957), 11
Prices Review Committee, 174
Principles of Surplus Disposal and Guiding
Lines, 166
Progressive Conservative Party: April 1963
elections, 49, 161, 197; election of
minority (1957), 10; June 1957 elections, 147–8; June 1961 elections, 43;
June 1968 elections, 98; March 1958
elections, 184; summer 1962 elections,
196. See also individual governments

protectionism, agricultural (Europe), 218–23, 226–8, 298n45. *See also* European Economic Community (EEC)

protectionism (Canada): under Diefenbaker, 21–2, 50, 190; disagreements over, 226–7, 298nn42–3; import surcharges, 43–6, 257n118; U.S. discomfort with growing, 22–5. *See also* General Agreement on Tariffs and Trade (GATT)

protectionism (U.S.), 12, 224, 235, 238, 296n29, 301n83. *See also* General Agreement on Tariffs and Trade (GATT)

public opinion: on anti-Americanism, 100–1, 108, 267–8n16; on Auto Pact negotiations, 133; on Canadian economic nationalism, 138; on trade with Europe, 137. *See also* media

public relations, 19–20, 22, 25, 28. *See also* Canada-U.S. relations

pulp exports, 28

Purdy, Al, 5

Quaker Oats, 28

Quebec, 58, 64–5, 110, 137

Quemoy and Matsu, 28

quotas: Canadian demands, 21, 274n114; global wheat, 153; on metals, 12, 23–4, 252n41; on oil, 16, 102–3; on softwood, 46; on turkeys, 21

Radio Club (Ottawa), 8

Randall, Clarence, 15, 144

Range Grain, 28

Rasminsky, Louis: on borrowing from New York market, 64–5; on Canadian dollar, 43; Commonwealth meeting, 186; on EEC, 189; G-10 meeting, 126–7; on IET, 60, 62, 260n39; on June 1963 budget, 56–7; on trade with Europe, 217; on trade with U.S., 22, 44. *See also* Bank of Canada

raw materials, 13

Reciprocal Trade Agreements Act (RTAA), 12

Reed, James, 62

Regan, Gerald, 137

Regina Leader-Post, 147

regional trading blocs, 188

Reisman, Simon, 73, 81, 118–19, 124, 200, 202

Report of the Royal Commission on the Automotive Industry, 70

Rest of the Sterling Area, 181–2

Rey, Jean, 238

Richler, Mordecai, 5

Ritchie, A.E. (Ed), 91, 103, 124, 189

Ritchie, Charles, 49; on British membership in EEC, 210; June 1963 budget, 59; on LBJ, 75; on relationship with Britain, 51–2, 258n3; response to IET, 61

Roberts, James, 189

Robertson, Norman, 32–3, 51, 142–3, 145–6, 160, 188, 203

Robin Hood, 28

Robinson, Basil, 17, 33, 35–6, 55, 57–9, 254n76

Rogers, William, 110

Rome Treaty, 191

Roosa, Robert, 44, 61

Rossiter, Fred, 19–20

Rostow, Walter, 34

Rotstein, Abraham, 7, 100, 108, 267–8n16

Royal Commission on Canada's Economic Prospects, 179

Royal Commission on Energy Policy (1957), 15

Ruether, Walter, 85

Rumbold, H.A.F., 188

Rusk, Dean: on automotive industry, 80, 82; on Canada's trade with China, 161; on IET, 63–4; origins of Auto Pact, 73–4; on relations with Canada, 75–6, 263n81; on U.S. subsidiaries, 69; on wheat sales, 163

SAGE-Bomarc system, 41–2. *See also* nuclear weapons

Samples, Robert, 199–200

Sanders, C.W., 188

Sandys, Duncan, 193

Saywell, John, 138

Schlesinger, Arthur, 35

Schmidt, Adolph, 110–11, 126

Schultz, George, 134–6

Schwarzmann, Maurice, 57–9, 172

Scott, Harold, 131

Sharp, Mitchell: on agricultural trade, 227; on Auto Pact, 81, 84–5; on British trade, 199, 201–3, 210; 'Canada-U.S. Relations: Options for the Future,' 240; on Canada-U.S. relations, 130; on Canadian economy, 123, 128; Canadian inflation, 96; on election, 91; on French trade, 285–6n58; on New Economic Policy (U.S.), 113–14, 116; on tariff negotiations with EEC, 231; the Third Option, 137, 240–1, 298n42; on Trudeau, 266n142; U.S. commentary on, 93–4; on U.S. subsidiaries, 69

shipbuilding, 200–1

Silent Surrender, 6, 68

Six-Seven link. *See* European Economic Community (EEC)

Smith, Adam, 139

Smith, R.G.C., 12

Smith, Sydney, 25

Social Credit: April 1963 elections, 197; June 1961 elections, 43; October 1972 elections, 138; summer 1962 elections, 196

softwood exports (Canada), 46, 53, 90–1

Sonnenfeldt, Helmut, 131

Soviet Union. *See* USSR

Standard Oil of New Jersey, 29

Stans, Maurice, 238

steel, 103–4. *See also* metals

Steele, James, 5

Stein, Hans Freiherr von, 240

Stevenson, Adlai, 33

St Laurent, Louis, 14, 52, 178, 187

Studebaker, 76, 78, 263n85

student population, statistics of, 8

Stursberg, Peter, 56

Suez, 183

Sunday Times (London), 196

Symington, Stewart, 78

Tariff Act of 1930 (U.S.), 72

Tariff Commission (U.S.), 25, 85, 120, 223

Task Force on the Structure of Canadian Industry, 105–6

taxes, 55–7, 102, 105, 114. *See also* Interest Equalization Tax (IET)

Taylor, Ken, 43, 186

Third Option, 4, 8, 137, 240–1, 244, 298n42

Thorneycroft, Peter, 180, 183–4

Times (London), 165, 227–8

Tomlin, Brian, 7, 136

Toronto Board of Trade, 12

Toronto Star, 100

Toronto Telegram, 190

tourist allowances, 43, 124, 129, 132–3, 136

Towe, Peter, 113, 117

Trade Agreements Act (U.S.), 31, 45
trade deficit (Canada): and auto parts,
165; restrictions on imports to U.S.,
41; role of automotive industry, 70–1;
statistics of, 13; with U.S. and surplus
with Britain, 202, 289n112. *See also*
foreign investment in Canada
trade deficit (U.S.), 113
Trade Expansion Act (U.S.), 45–6, 169,
232–3, 238, 299n50
trade fairs, 47
trade relations with Britain: 15 per cent,
22, 179–83, 243, 282n9; Canadian discrimination, 206–8; complaints about
Canadian practices, 200–1; in context
of EEC, 188–97, 209–14, 284n42,
292n148; in decline, 187, 292n157;
discriminatory practices, 185–6; statistics of trade, 197–8, 213; system of valuation for duty, 201–6, 212
trade relations with U.S.: automotive
industry, 81; as central to Canada, 241;
deterioration of, 15; influence on foreign policy, 243; objections to restrictions, 73, 78; statistics of, 78*t*, 198–9,
213; system of valuation for duty,
201–2; tied to nuclear weapons, 48–9;
as too concentrated, 183; U.S. protests
of restrictions, 12. *See also* agricultural
trade; Canada-U.S. relations
trade wars, 122
Treaty of Rome, 150, 191, 224
Trends in International Trade (the Haberler Report), 171, 218
Trezise, Philip, 80, 124–5; uranium
embargo, 130
Trudeau, Pierre Elliott: dealing with inflation, 96–7; on economic independence,
98–9; election of, 90–1; foreign policy
review, 109–10; meetings with Nixon,
101–2, 126, 133–4, 172; relations with
Nixon, 93, 134, 274n116; on relations
with U.S., 7; Sharp commentary on,
266n142; U.S. commentary on, 93; on
U.S. draft dodgers, 267–8n16; on
wheat production, 176
Trudeau government: British trade relations, 214, 239; economic policy of,
123–4, 127–9, 133, 272nn83–5,
274n114, 274n116; on oil trade with
U.S., 244; response to New Economic
Policy, 114–20; Third Option, 137; on
wheat sales, 172–3
turkeys, 12, 21. *See also* agricultural trade
Turner, John, 138
Tyler, William, 52

unemployment: Canadian rising, 138;
Canadian statistics on, 123; down in
Canada, 95; employment, 70; high
Canadian, 127; relationship with trade,
36; U.S. statistics on, 32, 37, 254n72;
in U.S. automotive industry, 77–8
unions, international, 5
United Auto Workers, 70
United Kingdom: 15 per cent of Canada's
trade, 22, 179–83, 243, 282n9; bilateral agreement on cereals, 169–70;
Canadian high commission, 186; discriminatory practice, 185–6; disinterest in Canadian market, 199–201,
289n101; economy, 183–4, 207–8;
EEC membership, 177, 190–7, 209–
10, 226–7, 292n148; free trade agreement with Canada, 14, 179–80; March
1966 elections, 207; trade statistics,
182, 197–8; trade with Canada, 187,
202–8, 212–14, 284n42, 289n112,
290n115, 290n117, 291n133,
292n148, 292n157; trade with New

Zealand, 291n138; U.S. extraterritoriality, 27–8; U.S. relations, 7; wheat sales, 175, 286n59. *See also* Commonwealth (British); European Economic Community (EEC)

United Nations: U.S. metal quotas, 24

United States: Canadian high commission, 186; Cold War, 11, 28–30, 216, 242; regional influences on government of, 11; statistics on GNP, 95

universities, 5, 8

uranium sales: to France, 226, 297–8n40; to U.S., 33–4, 120, 129–30

U.S. anti-trust laws, 27

U.S. economy, 112–13, 117

U.S. investment in Canada. *See under* foreign investment in Canada

U.S. public relations campaign, 19–20, 22, 25

U.S. recession, 32, 37–8

U.S. subsidiaries operating in Canada: American control of, 26–32; Canadian percentage ownership, 59; complaints by U.S. businesses of, 78; control by parent companies, 47; limitations on, 68–9, 275n128

U.S. trade agreements, 36, 136. *See also* General Agreement on Tariffs and Trade (GATT)

U.S. Trade Agreements Act, 37

U.S. Treasury, 28

USS *Manhattan,* 243

USSR: Canadian and U.S. differences over, 26; issue of wheat sales to, 161; Trudeau relations with, 123–4, 126, 272nn83–5; U.S. allies against, 215–16, 242; wheat sales, 155, 175, 192–3, 243–4. *See also* communism

Victoria Daily Times, 147

Vietnam war, 5, 34, 92, 100, 108, 112

Volcker, Paul, 119, 130–1

Volkswagen, 200

Warren, J.H. (Jake), 25, 168, 180, 189, 203–4, 220–1, 229–30

Watkins, Melville, 7, 27, 99–100, 275n128

Wedgewood-Benn, Anthony, 208

Weeks, Sinclair, 19

welfare state (Canada), 244

wheat sales: 1957 crop, 142; with Britain, 192, 206, 209, 286n59; Canada's balance of payments and, 7; Canada-U.S. negotiations, 151–3; Canadian criticism of U.S., 145–6; Canadian global share of, 140*t*; Canadian stores of, 19; on credit, 163; declining, 175; to Europe, 225, 227, 236*t*, 243; foreign aid, 277n16; fuel for ships for, 29; grain uploaders, 34–5; importance to Canada, 139–40; increased competition, 171–4; interference by U.S., 34–5, 41; international agreements, 170–1; to Japan, 162–5; to PRC, 28–9, 160–1; prices, 140, 174; statistics of prices, 172, 236; statistics on, 140*t*, 165, 167*t*, 276n3; statistics on U.S. disposal of, 144; U.S. practice of tied sales, 144–6, 148, 153–4, 279n42; U.S. surplus disposal, 15, 142–4, 146, 153–60, 166–7, 225, 277n9, 277n12, 277n15, 279n55, 297n37. *See also* PL 480 (Agricultural Trade Development and Assistance Act)

Wheat Utilizing Committee, 159

Whittaker Cable Corporation (Missouri), 78

Wigglesworth, Richard, 25

Wilgress, Dana, 193
Williams, Glen, 47
Wilson, Harold, 198, 206, 213
Winnipeg Free Press, 124, 147, 196
Winters, Robert, 93, 233, 237
Wormser, Olivier, 226

Wyndham White, Eric, 157

zinc, 12, 23–4, 32, 41, 91, 252n41. *See also* metals
Zolf, Larry, 5